LEGAL ETHICS

Legal Ethics

A Comparative Study

GEOFFREY C. HAZARD JR.

ANGELO DONDI

STANFORD UNIVERSITY PRESS

Stanford, California, 2004

Stanford University Press
Stanford, California
© 2004 by the Board of Trustees of the
Leland Stanford Junior University
Printed in the United States of America

Library of Congress Cataloging-in-Publication Data

Hazard, Geoffrey C.
  Legal ethics : a comparative study / Geoffrey C. Hazard Jr. and Angelo Dondi.
    p. cm.
  Includes bibliographical references and index.
  ISBN 0-8047-4882-9 (cloth : alk. paper)
  1. Legal ethics. 2. Lawyers. 3. Practice of law—Moral and ethical aspects. I. Dondi, Angelo. II. Title.
K123.H39   2004
174'.3—dc22   2004008458

This book is printed on acid-free, archival-quality paper

Original printing 2004

Last figure below indicates year of this printing:
13 12 11 10 09 08 07 06 05 04

Designed and typeset at Stanford University Press in 10/14.5 Minion

Contents

ACKNOWLEDGMENTS   *vii*

Introduction   *1*
The Rule of Law and the Legal Profession, 1.   The Social Functions of Modern Law, 5.   Can a Lawyer Be Ethical? 8.   The Law Governing Lawyers, 9.   The Relevance of Classical Philosophy, 10

1   A Historical Sketch of the Legal Professions   *15*
"Judges" and "Lawyers," 15.   The Roman Heritage, 18.   Officials Specialized in Law, 21.   Professional Knowledge and the Nature of "Law," 26.   Upper- and Lower-Level Lawyers, 30.   The Legal Profession from the Sixteenth to the Twentieth Century: Classic Law Practice, 37.   Modern Law Practice, 45.   Careers in Law in the "Legalized State," 54.   Persistent Grievances, Early Regulation, 60

2   The Roles of Judge and Lawyer   *63*
Differences in Roles, 63.   Office Lawyering, 69.   Role Conflict, 75.   Judicial Corruption, 82.   Ethical Justification of Advocacy, 87.   Social Justice and Legal Aid, 94.   Access to Justice for Ordinary Citizens, 105

3   The Professional "Virtues": Competence   *109*
Basic Professional Virtues, 109.   Competence More Fully Considered, 119.   The Continental European Model, 124.   The English Model, 128.   The American Model, 130.   Practical Competence, 134.   Finding a Good Lawyer, 139

4   Independence   *146*
Professional Independence, 146.   "Self-Government" of the Profession, 150.   Other Clients and the Lawyer's Own Interests, 155.   Independence from the Client, 158.   Legal Ambiguity and Ethical Ideals, 166

| 5 | Loyalty | *170* |

Loyalty to Client: The Basic Concepts, 170.   Who Is in Charge?, 176.
Concurrent Multiple Representation, 179.   Adversity of Interest, 186.
Consent to Conflict, 189.   Conflict of Interest in Successive
Representation, 191.   Commencement and Termination of
Representation, 195

| 6 | Confidentiality | *204* |

Confidentiality and the Attorney-Client Privilege, 204.   Disclosure of
Client Confidences, 209.   Corporation versus Corporate Official, 218.
The Boundary of Legality, 228

| 7 | Responsibility | *233* |

Multiple Responsibilities, 233.   Candor with the Court, 234.
Good Citizenship, 241.   Relationships with Other Lawyers, 242.
Relationships within Law Firms, 244.   Legal Aid: An Obligation? 247.
Self-Government through the Bar Association, 251

| 8 | Fees and Other Issues of Legal Economics | *258* |

Regulation of Fees, 258.   Contingent Fees, 264.   Fee Disputes, 267.
The Economics of Justice, 268.   Recent Regulatory Controversies: MDP
and MJP, 274

| 9 | Concluding Reflections | *280* |

The "New Model" Lawyer, 280.   Pretension and Practice in Ethics, 287.
Rules and Roles, 292.   Human Rights and Business Interests, 293

NOTES *299*

BIBLIOGRAPHY *339*

INDEX *343*

Acknowledgments

Colleagues: Professor Neil H. Andrews, Clare College, Cambridge, England; George Fox, Brisbane, Australia; Professor Antonio Gidi, Philadelphia, Pennsylvania; James G. Hazard, Paris, France; Lic. Ramon Mullerat, Barcelona, Spain; Justice Aida R. Kemelmajer de Carlucci, Mendoza, Argentina; Professor Michele Taruffo, University of Pavia, Italy; Dr. Vincenzo Ansanelli, University of Urbino. Special thanks also to Edwin J. Greenlee, Reference Librarian, Law School, University of Pennsylvania, and to Dr. Elena Lucertini, University of Genoa.

Students: Justice Bae, Renaud de Blegiers, Kathleen Craven, Matthew Hare Duncan, Andrew Edelstein, Kristin Fisher, Nicholas Gao, Rani Karnik Timothy Kemper, Karsie Kish, Alexandra Levin Kramer, Sonja Patrick, Horacio Segundo Pinto, Susan Pologruto, Eduardo Rivas, Tarana Sawhney, Michael Stamp, Arina Shulga, Thea Rozman, Aimee Torres, Hiroyuki Uranishi, Melinda Wang, David Weinberg, Johanna Wilson.

We gratefully acknowledge the splendid help of Teri Y. Broadnax in keeping control of the manuscript.

LEGAL ETHICS

Introduction

The Rule of Law and the Legal Profession

The rule of law has come to be appreciated as an essential element of a reasonably just society. In broad terms, the "rule of law" corresponds to constitutional government—that is, government in which the actions of officials are systematically controlled by established legal constraints. A corollary of this principle is that a constitutional regime must have an independent judiciary. An independent judiciary provides authoritative and disinterested application of the established legal constraints.

Perhaps less readily recognized is a further corollary, that a constitutional regime must have a legal profession sufficiently autonomous to be able to invoke the authority of the independent judiciary. This corollary translates as the right to assistance of an advocate in a court proceeding. A further corollary, functionally highly important and probably indispensable, is the right of people to consult a lawyer, in confidence, about situations with legal implications before they reach the attention of the judges. This translates as the right to consult a legal counselor.

The exercise of these rights, cumulatively over time and across life's eventualities, is therefore an essential institution of constitutional government. These rights are exercised by consultation with lawyers. A noted economist, William Baumol, has said, "there is no occupation whose total economic product is greater than that of lawyers; and none whose marginal contribution is smaller."[1] We hope in this analysis to indicate how the "total economic product" of lawyers is useful. We understand that the "marginal contribution" by lawyers consists of the value they add to specific transactions. Such a contribution is often invisible, sometimes exiguous, and indeed sometimes negative. (As businesspeople often say, "Keep the lawyers out of it.") And yet having the lawyers "in it," directly or indirectly, is a concrete manifestation of the rule of law. An explanation of this paradox is that the rule of law in real life is an interactive social process comparable to negotiation (which is itself an important activity of lawyers). Once a negotiation has concluded, what appears important is the resulting deal, whereas the haggling and posturing that preceded the conclusion seems to have been wasted effort. Nevertheless, some posturing and pretense is essential to closing the gap between the parties' positions. The same is true of much of lawyers' professional activity.

In any event, if the rule of law requires lawyers, lawyers also require rules for their governance. Conventionally, these regulations are called "professional ethics." It is a problem of long standing whether professional ethics is "law" or a normative scheme of a different kind. Whichever it may be, the rules of professional ethics constitute the normative regime to which judges and lawyers look in assessing the character of a lawyer's participation in the rule of law.

This study is an analysis and comparison of the ethical rules and conventions of lawyers in modern practice. It addresses law practice in the regimes of Europe, including England; in those based on the European civil law system, including Japan and now China; and in the countries with common law systems derived from England's, including Australia, Canada, and the United States. It is thus centered on law practice in Western constitutional legal systems and is pertinent to law practice in the westernized sectors of Islamic countries such as Egypt and Indonesia.[2]

The role of a lawyer is derived from that of the legal system in which the lawyer practices. Every legal system has a distinct cultural character, and there is much variance in legal systems even among the Western regimes.[3] Account must be taken not only of the formally stated ethical rules but also their practical significance for lawyers. The authors have access to the compiled rules of ethics in various countries, familiarity with practice in Italy and the United States, and secondhand acquaintance with practice in other countries. We have benefited from review of drafts of this study by lawyer colleagues in other countries and from research and accounts of younger associates and students in our advanced classes in the law faculties of several universities. Our focus has been on practice as experienced by lawyers, rather than what might be called an external or sociological analysis of the role of the bar. Many of the statements we make about practice and the practical significance of the rules of ethics cannot be documented, for the sources are oral and usually scattered, and many of our interpretations are derived from personal observation. Nevertheless, we are generally confident (although not complacent) about their accuracy.

The totality of lawyers' professional experience indeed can be interpreted as a distinct legal system shadowing the official version expressed in the written system of law. John Baker, the distinguished English legal historian, has referred to this relationship in his studies of law in England in the post-medieval centuries.[4] Baker refers to lawyers' practice as a second body of law and comments on its complex relationship with the law as pronounced by Parliament and the courts. The essence of lawyers' practice, according to Baker, was how lawyers got things done, as distinct from how legal rules said things should be done. We believe the same relationship continues today in England, as well as in other regimes.

"Legal ethics" includes not only ethical conventions of the legal profession but also legal regulations prescribed by the authority of the state ("government" as it is called in most common law systems). These regulations include statutes (particularly the codes in civil law systems patterned on the French *Code Napoléon*), some constitutional provisions (such as a constitutional right to assistance of counsel), and (particularly in common law systems) judicial decisions. Legal regulations are to be distinguished from formalized professional conventions and usages and also from moral or ethical conceptions apart from law.

Legal ethics, according to our viewpoint, is an amalgam of all these normative sources—law, social convention, and morality. We repeatedly refer to conventions and usages in practice—how lawyers "actually behave" so far as we can discern. We are also very mindful of ethical and moral concerns that prevail in the "background" culture of a social system and advert to them from time to time.

Salient in a lawyer's consciousness is continuing engagement with concrete realities, including ordinary experience in the modern capitalist political-economic order. The key term here is "concrete realities," meaning specific circumstances of place, time, participants, viewpoint, and course of events. The opposite concept is a "universal." A concrete event is an actual four-dimensional happening (in physical space, occurring over time), whereas a universal is a set of words signifying some aspect of an event, such as a "crime" or a "contract" in legal terminology, or "beautiful" in reference to a sunset. A concrete event is perceived at a specific time and from a specific location "in the trenches," and is not a pronouncement made from a detached or Olympian perspective. A perception from the trenches is necessarily incomplete and often inaccurate—the opposite of transparent. And, in a course of events, perception and possible ensuing action involve participation by actors who come with specific cultural, normative, and situational preconceptions.

These characteristics of real life were recognized by many thinkers in the nineteenth century—Herder, Hegel, Marx,[5] and the American "pragmatists," including Charles Peirce, William James, and Oliver Wendell Holmes Jr.[6] Of these, Karl Marx obviously had the greatest influence internationally. Marxist, Marxian, and post-Marxist thought had enormous influence in the twentieth century, remains the ostensible basis of the regimes in China and Cuba, and is embraced in some academic and political circles. A few words about our view of Marxism are appropriate.

As an observer and social critic of his time, Marx had extraordinary insight. As a social psychologist he was astute and emphatic in recognizing the influence of social conditions (emerging market capitalism in particular) on human perceptions, interpretations, and intellectual frameworks. As a moralist he summoned deep indignation at the condition of the poor. However, as an economic theorist he was primitive and fundamentally wrong, particularly in his "labor theory of value." As a political analyst he failed to discern the continuing force of religious affiliation, the emerging forces of nationalism[7] and ethnic identity,[8] and the possibilities of popular political action short of all-out violence. He was oblivious of the destructive political effect of violent language. Perhaps most important, Marx was a utopian. He posited a magical world-to-be in which there would be no classes and therefore no conflict, and portrayed that future as being a scientifically inexorable event. As applied, Marxism has been a verbal facade in regimes that pretend to have no social conflict while using authoritarian means to suppress conflict.[9] The world continues to function with various nonutopian conflict-ridden improvisations, chief among which are more or less democratic government and more or less competitive capitalism. Many of these nonutopian improvisations consist of legal institutions, rules, and procedures.

The Social Functions of Modern Law

Law and legal institutions are nonutopian social constructions for controlling social conflict within modern societies. Thus:

- Inasmuch as capitalist enterprise involves antagonisms among market participants, the law can impose controls and boundaries on those conflicts.
- Inasmuch as capitalist production involves innovation and speculation, the uncertainty and risk involved in those dynamics can be reduced or redistributed by legal arrangements. Capitalism also involves both confluence and conflict of interest between workers and entrepreneurs, which can be regulated by law, including contract law.
- Inasmuch as capitalism generates new wealth, that wealth is a source of tax revenue on which regimes depend to maintain their military forces and other social services. Legal rules can define the terms and administration of tax regulations, in contrast, for example, to the old weakly controlled "tax farming."
- The center of power in modern bureaucratic government regimes is the bureaucratic government itself.[10] Law is a mechanism for control of bureaucratic authority.
- The economically weak members of any society are at continual risk of exploitation by the powerful members, but law can impose restraints on the exploiters.
- Governments are constantly threatened by private adventurers wishing to exploit the government's own powers. Legal controls, such as the separation of powers and judicial review, can control or at least inhibit these tendencies.

The modern world may well have come to exaggerate the effectiveness of legal controls,[11] and war and other forms of violence retain their place as ordering mechanisms. Nevertheless, law is the final public arbiter in a functioning constitutional regime. Giving effect to constitutional and legal controls requires legal techniques. The techniques include, first, the specification of rights and obligations in statutes, regulations, bylaws, contracts, and other documents; second, the interpretation of these documents in accordance with evolving shared conventions; and, third and occasionally, the resort to courts, tribunals, and other officials for resolution of disputes over the meaning and application of the rules. These legal techniques are exercised on behalf of a clientele that includes central governments (the state or "the Crown"); provincial governments and municipalities; business enterprises; nongovernmental organizations (NGO's) such as churches, universities, unions, and charities; and individuals, particularly individuals charged with crimes and those with wealth to protect. "Lawyers" are the technicians regularly engaged in employing legal specification, interpretation, and adjudication. The regular employment becomes a calling. The calling is itself regulated by norms including statutes, directives from the courts, and local intramural conventions. The members of the calling have become a profession.

The basic function of these legal techniques is to control conflict within a large, diverse community. The product of these techniques is often referred to as "justice." Legal disputes by definition arise in the context of specific regimes that enunciate particular legal rules and supply concrete enforcement mechanisms. "Legal" issues are not universal or philosophical normative concepts, but particular legal rules derived from specific historical origins and applied in real-world contexts. Methods of effecting justice are universally understood to preclude wanton killing, unprovoked assault, and theft. However, justice in ordinary civilized life has no universal definition, but is necessarily "local" and hence "contextual."

An aspect of context—that is, of concrete reality—is time. One characteristic of time is that it cannot be repeated for subsequent observation, for example by reviewing the videotape of an event. The administration of the law is constrained by this reality in trying to determine truth. Consequently, the law must depend on inexact and often hotly disputed reconstructions of past events as bases for decision. This characteristic is captured in the traditional figure of justice, who is blindfolded.

A related temporal constraint is that legal processes cannot take an infinite amount of time to arrive at their verdicts. While a legal dispute is being framed in court and eventually adjudicated, events in the outside world continue, threatening the possibility that the law's decisional process will be irrelevant to practical affairs as they have evolved. In a broader perspective, the law itself is continuously obsolescent. Legal rules are pronounced at a first historical interval, are heeded (or disregarded) at a second historical interval, and are interpreted and applied at a third moment. The figure of the Roman god Janus, whose two faces look both backward and forward, captures this characteristic.

As we discuss later in this chapter, whereas ethical philosophy aims to be universal in content and transcendent in viewpoint (from which all things can be seen and are therefore transparent), the issues in real-world justice and law practice are concrete and specific. So also are the processes of law rigidly constrained by limitations on law's access to truth. Ethical analysis predicated on transparency—on hypothetical stipulations of what a normatively problematic situation "is"—therefore is necessarily incomplete and often misleading. In any event, in addressing problems of legal ethics we find the traditional distinction between deontological ethics and consequentialist ethics to be not very illuminating. We are encouraged in suggesting this conclusion by the interesting endeavor of Donald Nicolson and Julian Webb to apply that kind of analysis to modern legal ethics.[12]

Nevertheless, ethical philosophy properly employed has a place in professional ethics. The ideal of "justice" is real even if in practice it may be unattainable. The ideal of "truth" is real, at least for us, even if in practice its realization very often is incomplete, or indeed wholly frustrated. But approximating true justice and questing for actual truth are nonetheless worthy goals, indeed noble ones, notwithstanding that they are often unattained. The most serious ethical failing of the legal profession, judges as well as lawyers, would be in declining to make the attempt.

In pursuing truth and justice, the modern legal systems of the developed countries have important resemblances to each other—constitutional government, individual rights, private property, and broad freedom of contract, among others. These legal institutions define normative context and thus mediate between general ethical norms and actual ethical problems. As this study will explain, there are significant differences among modern legal systems. One salient example is the fact that common law judges usually are drawn from the ranks of practicing lawyers, whereas most civil law judges pursue a lifetime judicial vocation that begins in early adulthood. Another difference is the typical scale of the practitioner's office—solo and small firms have predominated in most countries, larger firms have emerged in many others. Thus legal ethics perforce is perhaps not a single subject but a cluster of related subjects.

Can a Lawyer Be Ethical?

In common parlance about lawyers—and sometimes in discourse within the legal profession—"legal ethics" is often referred to as an oxymoron, on the premise that lawyers are inherently unethical. Some lawyers are indeed unethical, a few of them egregiously so. Many lawyers occasionally are oblivious of ethical obligations, or deliberately disregard them. Most lawyers frequently encounter difficult legal or ethical problems concerning their own conduct, and sometimes resolve those problems improperly. But these patterns of behavior, far from indicating that "legal ethics" is an empty concept, demonstrate that it is a serious subject. We believe that most lawyers prefer to "do the right thing" when ethically significant decisions are theirs to make for themselves.

However, ethically significant dilemmas that lawyers confront usually must take account of the interests and preferences of others, including clients. That circumstantial fact introduces an unavoidable element of partisanship into the lawyer's deliberations—that is, lawyers must give preference to the interests of one set of people (clients) over the interests of another set (people who are not clients). The vocation of law necessarily involves partisanship on behalf of clients. One can imagine law without lawyers but not, in a real world, lawyers without clients.

Loyalty to the self-centered interests of a client is a kind of loyalty that many people are not comfortable with or find obnoxious. We think that the partisanship involved in law practice is indeed unattractive in many respects. However, in our view, the legitimacy of partisanship derives from the simple fact that human beings chronically have conflicts—conflicts of interest, to use a legal phrase. As summarized by Martin Redish: "Liberal democratic adversary theory recognizes the empirical reality that because individuals are

... worthy of dignity and respect ... their interests will differ [and] ... conflict is inevitable, whether on ideological, economic or personal grounds."[13]

Of course, everyone often wishes that all of humankind could "lie down in green pastures ... beside the still waters," as the peaceful kingdom is described in Psalm 23. But Psalm 23 is speaking of the work of God, not mortal governance. Experience with the problems of ordering human relationships leads most analysts to a less optimistic perspective.

Specifically, we believe conflict is endemic in all societies, primitive as well as modern, and that in modern societies law is an essential mechanism of controlling conflict. As a corollary of these propositions, the administration of law entails decisions and judgments by judges and other officials. As a further corollary, in making these judgments judges and other officials can make serious mistakes. There is no font of "justice" pure or simple. The service that lawyers provide is the close observation of and participation in the law's decision processes. Lawyers' services are therefore often very helpful to people at risk of entanglement with the law. The partisanship involved in law practice accordingly seems to us to be on the same plane, of necessity and legitimacy, as the partisanship in parliamentary and electoral politics of constitutional regimes, the partisanship exhibited in freedom of the press, and the partisanship in competition among enterprises in the economic sphere.

The Law Governing Lawyers

The significance of "law" in regulating the practice of lawyers is almost self-evident. In the modern world virtually all human activities are governed by legal regulations. In the European tradition, the practice of law has been governed by networks of regulation since the thirteenth century, if not before. These regulations include prohibitions and restraints, such as the rules prohibiting representation of clients who have opposing interests and rules requiring lawyers to maintain their clients' confidences.

Equally significant, the law has given lawyers two important empowering rights. One is the legal right of an advocate to speak to judges (and other officials) regarding pending adjudications and other official decisions. This is called the "right of audience"—that is, a lawyer's right to be heard in an argument on behalf of a client. Judges exercise an important form of political authority, and advocacy can influence how judges exercise that authority. Accordingly, the advocate's right of audience is an important form of political power.

The other legal right enjoyed by lawyers is the right to maintain the confidentiality of communications with their clients. The significance of this power is obvious in the legal representation of persons accused of a crime. Persons accused of crime usually can speak freely to their lawyers in terms that might well be incriminating if those messages were conveyed to prosecuting authorities. That relationship of professional confidentiality goes hand in hand with the right of the accused, in all modern legal systems, to refuse to give testimony against himself.

Yet the lawyer's right and duty to maintain client confidences—in shorthand, "client confidentiality"—has significance far beyond criminal cases. This book focuses on lawyers engaged in civil practice.[14] In civil practice, the affairs that clients bring to their lawyers generally can be sheltered from observation by curious eyes and ears, whether those of authorities of the state or of other private actors.

Problems of legal ethics arise from the convergence of the special legal powers conferred on lawyers and the special legal responsibilities imposed on exercising those powers. Thus the right of audience before courts is constrained by duties to the tribunal and to opposing parties and their counsel. Similarly, the right to maintain a client's confidences is burdened by duties to refrain from using secrecy as a cover for committing crime or fraud against others. The proper balance between empowerment and burden is the fundamental problem of professional ethics.

The Relevance of Classical Philosophy

In this analysis we have not made much reference to classical ethical theory as expounded, for example, in the writings of Aristotle, Hume, Kant, and such modern political philosophers as Jürgen Habermas and John Rawls. We understand and appreciate the views of these philosophers; we are also aware that, for many people, religious teaching is immediately relevant and often determinative in resolving the ethical dilemmas of everyday life. However, we have found these sources to be of limited value in our analysis.

Concerning ethical principles derived from religious belief, we observe that very different secular standards are derived in each of the major religious traditions—for example, concerning the position of women, the scope of the duty of candor, and the priority to be accorded to family relationship. Moreover, we are mystified by efforts to relate the teachings in our own religious tradition, Christianity, to the problems confronted in law practice.

The relevance of traditional ethical analysis to legal ethics is limited *not* because lawyers do not face ethical problems or because they have no ethics. All lawyers have ethical problems, in that they continually confront situations in which they must make decisions involving right and wrong. All lawyers also "have" ethics, in that no one can practice law without some underlying sense of direction in making these decisions. Instead, in our opinion the limited relevance of classical ethics to the present inquiries stems from the special outlook from which classical ethical analysis traditionally has proceeded.[15]

This classical outlook involves two basic elements: universality and transparency. By universality we mean ethical analysis undertaking to address all ethical problems, regardless of context. Analysis on this plane is often called "meta-ethics." By transparency we mean ethical analysis proceeding from a premise that the actor has access to the facts of the situation being confronted.

Concerning universality, until modern times the ethical philosophers were thinking about male actors and generally disregarded not only women and children but also slaves, "barbarians," nonbelievers, and others. But within this set of limitations, the classic ethical philosophers sought to state propositions that would hold for all ethically problematic decisions. For example, this is the scope of Immanuel Kant's concept of a "categorical imperative," defined as an ethical proposition that unqualifiedly applies to all situations within its terms.[16] The idea of universality has a corollary in the concept of human equality—that all persons of whom the actor must take account are entitled to equal attention and regard.[17] A related idea concerns the moral autonomy of an actor or "free will." The concept is that the actor has unconstrained freedom of choice in courses of action. There are complex connections between these concepts and the modern ethos of democracy.

By transparency, we refer to the assumption that the circumstances in which an actor must act are evident to the actor. On this premise, an actor does not view a problematic scene through a haze of uncertainty, or act on the basis of information provided by someone else, or confront confused or contradictory accounts about what has happened or what appears to be imminent. The main themes of classical ethics have addressed what an actor should do when he knew what he was doing.

The elements of universality and transparency are the essence of two ethical theories that have been salient in ethical philosophy since the early nineteenth century and that remain dominant at the beginning of the twenty-first century. These are the ethical philosophies of Immanuel Kant and Jeremy Bentham. As noted earlier, Kant's basic ethical concept was the "categorical imperative": an act can be justified only if it conforms with a universally applicable norm. In the terminology of ethical philosophy, this approach is deontological; that is, courses of action are properly determined by principles of duty, regardless of the consequences that a particular course of action might engender. In contrast, Bentham's concept was utilitarianism—that acts could be justified by their consequences, and that the consequences were to be assessed in terms of "the greatest good for the greatest number." In the terminology of ethical philosophy, Bentham's approach is consequentialist: a course of action is properly assessed by the consequences that would ensue. The ethical concepts of Kant and Bentham were and are very different in origin, logic, expression, and implications. Nevertheless, they are similar in important respects, particularly in relation to the ethics of any vocation involving interpersonal relationships.

The ethical systems of Kant and Bentham are similar, first and most importantly, in their universalist application: that a valid normative principle should be applicable to every act and all circumstances. They are also similar in their assumption of transparency: that the actor could know the circumstances in which he is to act. In these respects both the categorical imperative and utilitarianism seem to us serenely optimistic and indifferent to the crude and often cruel and intractable aspects of experience. A third similarity is their "transcendent" viewpoint: they view the human condition from an Olympian viewpoint that disregards the messy uncertainty of life As historians of philosophy, both Kant and Bentham can be considered inheritors of the Enlightenment. Enlightenment thinkers tended to interpret human experience as one of rationality in social intercourse, equality among the participants, and continuous improvement in the human condition.

In contrast to Kant and Bentham, in our opinion greater insight into problems of legal ethics emanates from earlier philosophers such as Hobbes and Hume (who were English), Bodin, Descartes, and Montesquieu (French), Grotius and Spinoza (Dutch), Machiavelli and Vico (Italian), and James Madison and John Adams (American). Perhaps most important are the insights of Alexis de Tocqueville, who came a little later.

These philosophers, in various ways and in different terms, responded to the problems of community life with acute real-world awareness, as the European regimes were transformed from the authoritarian systems of the medieval and Renaissance periods into societies of bourgeois ascendancy. In the Middle Ages and the Renaissance, government power and authority rested in the hands of kings, princes, bishops, and other magnates. The ideal in political behavior was service or subservience to the regime—service to "the prince," to borrow the title of Machiavelli's famous work. A systematic and sympathetic exposition of this ideal was expounded by Baldesar Castiglione in *Il Cortegiano*, a work that achieved broad recognition in the sixteenth century. Ideal political behavior in this viewpoint was service dedicated to the support and aggrandizement of the regime and the ruler.[18]

The more "worldly" political philosophers ranged from radical pessimists, such as Hobbes, to sober "constitutionalists" such as Locke, Montesquieu, and Madison, to legalists such as Grotius and troubled optimists such as Vico. However, they were all trying to fathom the new political and economic systems evolving in Western Europe. These new systems were penetrating or submerging the system of monarchy and papacy in France, Germany, Italy, England, and the Netherlands, and were increasingly based on capitalist production and bureaucratic governance systems. A concomitant evolution was the idea of constitutional limitation on the authority of government—that is, "the rule of law," including such related ideas as "rights of property," "freedom of contract," and "loyal opposition." The serious embrace of these concepts marks the end of the Middle Ages. As Ortega y Gasset said: "The political doctrine which has represented the loftiest endeavor towards common life is liberal democracy. Liberalism is that principle of political rights, according to which the public authority, in spite of being all powerful, limits itself and attempts, even at its own expense, to leave room in the State for those to live who neither think nor feel as the majority."[19]

The new constitutional concepts often were expounded as universal truths, as they were in the American Declaration of Independence.[20] However, they also were specific political claims given expression and implemented by a new class of legal specialists. These specialists were the "lawyers," serving as intermediaries between the central government regimes and regional magnates and among sectors of the bourgeoisie.

The viewpoint of these operatives was given official expression in a famous dictum by Lord Coke, chief judge of the King's Bench. Coke began with the proposition that the king was bound by the law, which was nothing new and indeed justified the claim that subjects should render obedience to kings. However, Coke's definition of "law" was unorthodox. Coke asserted that law emanated from a special form of "artificial reason" uniquely expounded by the judges. In answering King James's argument that the king could discern the law equally as well as judges, Coke said: "God had endowed his Majesty with excellent Science . . . but his Majesty was not learned in the Laws . . . and Causes which concern the Life, the Inheritance, or Goods, or Fortunes of his Subjects, are not to be decided by natural Reason but by the artificial Reason and Judgment of Law . . . which requires long Study and Experience, before that a Man can attain to the Cognizance of it."[21] In a modern sardonic rephrasing of that idea, the law is "what the judges say it is." On that basis, lawyers are endowed with a unique comprehension of law.

1

A Historical Sketch of the Legal Professions

"Judges" and "Lawyers"

The history of legal ethics is derived from the history of the legal profession. The history of the legal profession is long, obscure in many respects, and, because most histories have been written by lawyers, shrouded in self-congratulatory myth.[1]

Before beginning an analysis of legal ethics, it is important to define the concept of "lawyer" and the related concept of "judge." In concept and certainly in modern context, both lawyers and judges are members of the legal profession. This definition is itself derived from law: in modern regimes, a judge is constituted not by custom or religious tradition but by a legal procedure of appointment, usually a constitutional procedure. Similarly, in modern regimes lawyers are persons with an exclusive, legally conferred license to call themselves by that name, based upon legally prescribed educational qualifications. In the absence of such a legal definition, it is difficult to distinguish a "lawyer" from someone who acts as an intermediary in a dispute between private persons and government officials or in a dispute between private persons. Similarly, it is difficult to distinguish a "judge" from other kinds of government officials who make decisions guided by legal rules.

In this analysis we focus on the Western legal tradition, derived primarily from Roman law. At various points we refer to other traditions, notably those of China and the Islamic countries. The Chinese tradition is founded on the concept of harmonious deference to authority, in contrast to the internal disharmony that the Western legal system presupposes and undertakes

---

The text of this chapter was first published in *Zeitschrift für Zivilprozess International* 6 (2001); reprinted with permission.

to moderate. The Islamic tradition is founded on the unity of legal and religious authority, in contrast to the separation of these spheres that is typical in the West. The modern regimes in developing countries have adopted, and adapted, the Western approach, at least in the law governing commercial transactions. That approach includes not only separation of the legal from religious domains but also the principle of judicial independence and the right of representation by legal counsel. The interactive relationship between judges and lawyers is a major theme in our exposition.

The difficulties of definition are illustrated in the procedure for resolving legal disputes in classical Greece. Ancient Greece had a legal process but no developed substantive law, and a highly developed technique of advocacy but no "lawyers" recognized as such. The audience for the technique of advocacy was the *polis*—a city's adult, male, nonslave population sitting as a committee of the whole. The *polis* as a judicial forum determined the legal standards according to which judgment would be given, and also determined the relevant facts, and in this framework then gave judgment.[2] Advocacy consisted of orations given for and against the accused.[3] The technique in advocacy was called rhetoric, a term that comes down to us as describing all forms of partisan speech, including that presented in political and parliamentary debate.

Advocacy in Greek legal disputes apparently was like the closing arguments of advocates in modern judicial procedure: it included summations of evidence, invocation of the norms of proper decision-making, and sometimes appeals to civil responsibility. Because the Greek tribunal was constituted of ordinary citizens, the arguments resembled those made to juries in American procedure, resting on popular conceptions of right and wrong rather than precise legal definitions. It is evident that some speakers in ancient Greek proceedings, although not professionals in the modern sense, were more effective and more practiced than others. Apparently payment for services provided by such volunteers was prohibited, but it seems not improbable that the volunteers were permitted to accept gifts. Functionally, therefore, these orators can be identified as "lawyers" although they were not formally identified as such. Similar functional specialization no doubt emerged in other ancient societies.

A very different tradition evolved in China, now the world's most populous country and an emerging industrial giant. In Confucian China the lawyers were either assistants to central government officials administering the law (the "mandarins") or assistants to local officials interacting with representatives of the central authority. Since the Confucian philosophy emphasized social harmony based on hierarchical relations, "law" was a mechanism to effectuate that objective and not one for articulating claims or rights. This philosophical ambience enabled a very small intelligentsia to maintain effective authority over a large and sprawling peasant population through a system of administration that was, however, also pervaded with corruption. The few "lawyers," such as they may have been, were regarded as "rascally fellows [who] entrap people for the sake of profit."[4]

A political system with those cultural roots must undergo a large transformation to institutionalize a real legal system.[5] Some distance had been covered in China in the period from the modernist revolution in 1911 to the collapse of the Nationalists in 1949.[6] The example of Hong Kong demonstrates that such change is possible: Hong Kong for over a century has had a legal system genuinely replicating the English model (including the distinction between barristers and solicitors), with a strength that may survive the merger of the former colony with the People's Republic.[7] But the national tradition has been otherwise. As Stanley Lubman states: "Legal professionals did not develop the use of law on behalf of individuals, and any tendency for legal specialists to act as intermediaries between the individual and the state was actively discouraged."[8] A major undertaking not only of legal reform but in cultural reorientation is therefore involved in China's recent efforts to modernize.[9]

Russia also has a non-Western tradition. The regime was virtually "pre-legal" until the eighteenth century. Only then did Russia absorb some influence of Roman law, an absorption that was "third-hand through . . . a tenth-century Bulgarian code . . . a code of canon law of the Orthodox Church . . . and . . . a twelfth or early thirteenth century code."[10] There is no evidence of a legal profession before 1700.[11] A curriculum in law was established only in 1755. The Russian judiciary became formally independent from the state only in 1864, partly as a result of the influence of the new cohorts of university graduates with legal training.[12] After the Russian Revolution in 1918, the legal system, the judiciary, and the emergent legal profession become subordinate to the Soviet system of government and the interconnected dominance of the Communist Party. The reforms since 1980 have sought to overcome those influences and to reestablish the Russian legal order on the Western model.[13]

The Islamic legal tradition is yet another force in the modern world. That tradition has been described in scholarly works and has several distinct modern variations.[14] The central themes in the Islamic tradition are the close interconnection between law and religious belief (similar to Judaism in this respect), the concurrent offices of judge and priest, and the underlying social objective of promoting harmony through obedience to divine authority. The Islamic communities have complex social systems that function on different normative premises from those undergirding Western capitalism, and governmental systems based on different political postulates than those of parliamentary democracy. Modernized Islamic countries have retained the traditional *Sharia* as the basis of family law (covering marriage, divorce, and succession of property upon death); for commercial transactions it has adopted variations of Western law, usually from civil law systems. (The same dual system exists in Israel, where religious law is administered by a separate set of courts.) A major task in the currently emerging "globalization" is to calibrate the Islamic ethos with that of the West. Our analysis does not address that set of problems.

The Roman Heritage

The history of the legal profession in the Western tradition, therefore, conventionally begins with Rome.[15] In the Roman republican period, it came to be recognized that parties to legal disputes could engage knowledgeable helpers in dealing with the distress and complexities of legal controversy. Litigants accordingly could have representatives appear on their behalf, for example, standing in for a litigant who was abroad. They could also have advisers at their side during the hearing of a dispute. There was a conceptual difficulty and practical apprehension regarding both third-party appearances for a litigant and use of a legal adviser. The conceptual difficulty was that litigation is designed to conclude and determine personal rights, yet how could an assistant or agent do that for someone else? The practical apprehension was that allowing the use of advisers could confer unfair advantage on litigants who could afford such assistance. These issues concerning the authority and responsibilities of an attorney recur in the subsequent history of the legal profession.

Despite these unresolved questions, as Arthur Engelmann states, "Representation of parties to actions had already grown into a regular business, in the republican period." Acting as a representative was subject to various regulations: "None could appear as advocate unless he had studied law and obtained from a public official permission to exercise the calling. The advocates licensed to practice before a given court formed a corporation and were under the disciplinary power of the presiding judge." Professional advocates were permitted to charge honoraria, the equivalent of fees.[16] The professional corporation whose members were Roman advocates is a progenitor of the modern bar association, and the disciplinary authority of the courts is a mechanism still universally employed in modern legal systems.

It may be noted that the Roman term for forensic representative was "advocate," signifying one who made demands. Cicero, the most famous advocate of the Republican era, personified the role. The term "lawyer," obviously derived from "law," evolved later.

Another function of law-trained specialists in Roman practice was that of legal counselor or "jurisconsult." Some scholars suggest that this position was much more important than that of an advocate, in that provision of legal advice by jurisconsults was afforded through holders of political office and hence connected with political influence.[17] (A similar symbiotic relationship between legal advice and political influence will be familiar to observers in some localities in the United States and elsewhere.) In any event, no later than the founding of the Roman Empire in approximately 30 BCE, there was a distinct legal culture with formal legal rules and recognized legal practitioners. There certainly were persons especially conversant with the law and its procedures who could be consulted in connection with, and no doubt also in anticipation of, legal disputes.[18]

However, conducting a historical analysis of the Roman period is a complex undertaking. Some of the complexity results from the fact that we are required to discern the earlier Roman period through the lens of later Roman legal development, particularly the compilation of laws usually referred to as the Justinian Code. The Justinian Code, promulgated in the late Roman

Empire about the year 500 CE, had been commissioned by the emperor to eliminate contradictions and ambiguities in versions of the law coming down from earlier times. The fact that it was felt necessary to eliminate contradictions and ambiguities in Roman law signifies that there had been a long previous legal tradition in which the contradictions and ambiguities had arisen.

Criminal procedure in Roman law bore some resemblance to modern criminal procedure—that is, formal accusation followed by procedure of proofs—although the Greek procedure of decision-making by a committee of the whole persisted in some kinds of proceedings, exemplified by the performances of the rhetorician Cicero.[19] Procedural law in ordinary criminal cases took on distinct patterns called *formulae*. The formulae were the original form and core of the early Roman legal culture's concept of law. They consisted of a standardized format for defining the issues in controversy and specifying the means by which those issues were to be determined.[20]

Nevertheless, these fragments of information leave unexplained precisely how trials were conducted—whether the parties ordinarily had the assistance of legal advisers, and, if so, how the advisers interacted with the tribunal.[21] Through study of the formulae we know a great deal about the rhetorical or technical formulation of the law, and infer that the procedure was complicated. We also know that there was a category of practitioner with specialized legal knowledge to whom legal disputes were referred, the so-called *patronus*, who engaged in an adjudicative or legal counseling function of some kind.[22] However, we do not know the precise functions performed by Roman legal advisers, particularly in civil cases. For that reason we cannot know whether there were rules or conventions of ethics.[23]

A further problem with the Roman legal system, which we do know something about, was the diversity of legal regimes within the empire. In general, the Roman imperial policy was to support the local governance regimes of the remote provinces of the empire. Roman citizenship was a prized privilege that entailed the special right to be adjudged according to Roman law, while persons not Roman citizens were subject to provincial authority in various forms. Accordingly, in a famous example, at the hearing before Pontius Pilate concerning Jesus, the Roman governor is reported to have remanded the accused for trial before the provincial Jewish authorities.[24] By traditional account, the accused was unrepresented by counsel.

Officials Specialized in Law

Because of the paucity of detail about the function of participants in legal procedure under the Roman Empire, the earliest point in Western history at which there is detailed information about judges and lawyers is the late Middle Ages, the twelfth and thirteenth centuries. The emergence of a vocational class identifiable as lawyers coincides with the emergence of a body of officials identifiable as judges.[25] There continues to be a definitional problem, however.

The primary definitional problem in the regimes of the Middle Ages is to distinguish "judges" from other kinds of governmental and administrative functionaries. All judges exercised authority derived from some other source of political authority, for example, an executive agency of the government. A judge had to be constituted or recognized as such by an appointive authority who in turn was recognized by the relevant community as having authority to confer adjudicative authority. However, the judge had to be distinguished from other functionaries in a regime—officials such as sagacious adviser, "right-hand man of the king," or cabinet officer. Therefore, while all judges exercised delegated authority, not all officials who exercised delegated authority can properly be called judges.

In the modern context, a "judge" is an official given authority by the regime, through a regularized procedure, to hear and determine controversies that are framed as claims of legal right and is obliged to determine the controversy according to substantive legal standards and rules of procedure specified by law. A judge exercises authority not as a matter of discretionary dispensation, as would a king exercising the royal prerogative; instead a judge is "bound by" the law.[26] The judge personally accepts, and is expected by others to accept, the discipline that his decisions are to be governed by legal rules and not merely by considerations of expediency, kinship, or "reasons of state" in the Machiavellian sense.[27] Modern judges are selected through specified legal procedures, are usually required by law to have special qualifications (particularly a legal education), and are constituted in office by legal forms of appointment.

All lawyers are engaged in assisting people involved in controversies or questions about rights and duties, but not all people providing such assistance can properly be called lawyers. In modern business organizations, all kinds of functionaries in the course of their responsibilities apply various kinds of legal knowledge and technique—among them lending officers in banks, insurance company staff, and personnel officers supervising company compliance with employment law. Modern lawyers achieve distinct professional identity through specified legal procedures (for example, successfully passing a qualifying examination), are required by law to have special qualifications (a legal education), and are constituted in office by legal forms of appointment (being admitted to the bar). These elaborate modern legal formalities are the product of a long evolution.

In many modern regimes, there are distinctions internal to the category of "lawyer." Thus in England the function of barrister or advocate is distinguished from legal counselor ("solicitor" in English terminology). In civil law systems such as those of France, Germany, and Spain, there is a distinct category of *notaire*. A *notaire* is a legally trained public official, but one compensated by the parties to a transaction. A *notaire* documents and solemnizes standard transactions (particularly those affecting title to real property, such as deeds, leases, and wills); and authentication by a *notaire* is required to make such transactions legally effective. In many modern legal systems there are distinct branches of law, and corresponding branches of the legal profession, in admiralty and military law.[28] Several legal systems have jurisconsults, people who are legally trained but whose functions are restricted. For example, France at one time and the State of New York have authorized foreign lawyers to practice locally, but only concerning matters involving the law of their country of origin.[29] In Russia the title of jurisconsult refers to law-trained people employed in government agencies and corporations to give legal advice to the employer—essentially "house counsel" in American terminology.[30] In Sweden, no legal restriction prohibits anyone from functioning as a lawyer, but a person may not identify himself as an "advocate" unless he has been formally admitted to practice before the courts.[31] In Japan, the number of licensed lawyers, *bengoshi*, is very small, but a large number of legally trained officials are employed in public and private bureaucracies, performing transactional and advisory functions.

In China and many other developing countries at present, there are not enough law-trained people to staff the existing judicial systems. Accordingly, the formal standards are relaxed, and practical experience and general literacy are treated as sufficient qualifications.[32] As a result of these variations, the modern definition of "lawyer" is necessarily somewhat ambiguous.[33]

At approximately the beginning of the twelfth century, originating in Italy and thereafter evolving in other parts of Europe, there occurred what is retrospectively known as a "legal renaissance." This development was linked to the burgeoning city-states and to the rise in influence of a merchant class side by side with the more ancient military class.[34] At different stages in various parts of Europe, a body of functionaries emerged who could be called lawyers, or at least proto-lawyers. These functionaries performed two basic tasks. One was assisting people who had disputes with the governing regime, or disputes with neighbors in which one of the disputing parties petitioned the regime to impose a resolution or to mediate the dispute. This function corresponds to the function of the modern advocate. The other task was to advise people who were involved in such disputes, or who were concerned that they might in the future become involved in disputes, about how to mitigate the dispute or improve their position if the dispute devolved into litigation. Assistance of this kind could be pursued with even greater foresight where the aim was to avoid a dispute altogether. Providing such assistance corresponds to the function of the modern legal counselor.

Lawyers in all eras have had special legal knowledge and special access to the courts. The special legal knowledge can be called "technique." Technique in the classical Greek sense includes formally acquired knowledge derived from the study of texts and attendance at lectures, as in the legal curriculum at a university, and also includes specific professional arts or skills. A primary professional art for lawyers is skill in rhetoric—the art of persuasion. The art of persuasion is a complex interpersonal procedure, learned chiefly by experience. Lawyers employ the technique of persuasion as advocates in addressing judges and in negotiation when addressing other parties or lawyers representing other parties. Another professional art is gauging the opportunities and risks in resolving human conflicts, whether through litigation, negotiation, or other means. That art is often called the exercise of professional legal judgment, and it too is learned chiefly through experience.

Lawyers in all eras have had special access to courts. A limited form of access is the right to advise a litigant on how to present his case to a court. In more advanced form, called the "right of audience," a lawyer may directly address the court on behalf of a litigant. The advocate thereby can discuss a legal dispute with the judge before the judge is to reach a decision. The lawyer's exercise of the right of audience can influence how the judge understands the governing legal rules and how the judge assesses controverted evidence. The purpose of the lawyers' arguments is to inform and shape the judge's decision by giving reasons for and against a particular result.

The right of audience historically was limited to those with special training as advocates.[35] Qualifying as an advocate required a period of apprenticeship in the service of the court or with an established advocate. Apprenticeship provided opportunity for the candidate to learn the substance of the law and the techniques and lore of the profession. Apprenticeship also provided the judges and established lawyers with opportunity to assess the candidate's competence, diligence, and discretion. Some form of apprenticeship remains an element of a lawyer's training, whether by legal requirement or by practical necessity. A lawyer's vocation has intellectual foundation, but it is "practice"—that is, vocational activity learned by experience as well as academic instruction.

As the legal profession became more formalized during the Middle Ages, requirements were imposed for systematic education at a legal institute or university, or *studia* as early institutes were called. A most famous "law school" (to use a modern term) was at Bologna, where there was an imperial *studium legale* dating back to the eleventh century; others were established in Pavia, Padua, Ravenna, and Rome.[36]

The curriculum in the *studia legale* was based on a new form of comprehensive legal analysis consisting of commentary on the Justinian Code. The code, originating in the late Roman Empire and also called the *Corpus Juris*, had been recovered from obscurity in the Middle Ages. As legal text it was comprehensive, authoritative, and esoteric. Academic commentary on the code was much the same. The learning encompassed in the code and the commentaries came to constitute the special professional knowledge of the higher-level judges and lawyers. It provided rationale and rhetoric to guide or at least to embellish legal discourse, even discourse addressing such a pedestrian legal problem as the interpretation of a local charter. The commentary on the code evolved through the seventeenth and eighteenth centuries and beyond. As it did so, the culture of the commentary, as it may be called, preserved professional intellectual tradition, but it also impeded attempts to simplify the law, such as that by Louis XIV of France in 1667.

In the medieval period, one can imagine an ordinary citizen being able to navigate the legal system and effectively present a legal claim in court without the assistance of a lawyer. As political systems stabilized in the Renaissance and afterward, however, legal systems became more elaborate and court procedure more technical. Referring to the situation in England at the close of the thirteenth century, Paul Brand observes: "The new royal courts were run by judges ... who had already gained knowledge of the law from service as clerks or as professional lawyers ... This meant that litigants needed expert legal assistance in dealing with a set of rules and procedures with which they were not and could not be familiar."[37]

In all developed legal systems, such as those that evolved in Europe by the sixteenth century, it became a practical impossibility for the ordinary litigant in a major legal dispute to represent himself effectively. The procedure in such a system would be intelligible to an educated jurist but would have been baffling to an unsophisticated litigant.[38] A developed legal system therefore creates its own demand for advocates.[39]

In addition to advocacy, the other primary function of lawyers is legal counseling. Legal counseling is an important step removed from advocacy in litigation. In most litigation a practical question for participants is whether it will be useful to pursue the dispute through to the end—a judgment of the court. Obviously, it will not be useful to do so when it can be predicted that the result will be adverse, for then the litigant will suffer loss not only of the case on the merits but also of the cost of litigation (the court fees and the fees of his advocate) and, in most legal systems, the litigant will also be liable for the opposing party's costs. A prudent litigant therefore would want advice from an informed source about whether to proceed.

An advocate can provide this kind of advice. Advocates in their relationships with clients therefore are legal counselors insofar as they give advice about the prudence of pursuing litigation based on their estimates of the chance of success and the cost of carrying through the litigation.[40] However, estimations of the chance of success can be made by others who are also familiar with the behavior of courts. These include clerks of the court, assistants to judges and advocates, and others in a position to observe patterns of litigation. The knowledge of these observers is similar to that of the advocates and is the primary basis of the "lower-level" law practice whose evolution is considered below.

In the contemporary world an additional dimension has been added by "globalization" of commerce and finance. Lawyers in different countries now perform similar functions in different legal systems and under somewhat different rules of ethics. This book may contribute to an understanding of that phenomenon.[41]

Professional Knowledge and the Nature of "Law"

By the seventeenth century, an advocate's formal method of achieving professional status in continental Europe had become university study of treatises based on the *Corpus Juris*. For professionals educated in this way, "the law" formally considered was a body of written doctrines expressed in systematic form whose meaning was expounded and understood by authoritative academic interpretation. Of course, most lawyers and many judges understood that, in practice, the written texts often could be misunderstood, distorted, or ignored in deference to practical and political considerations. But the professional concept was (and still is, at least as the point of beginning) that law consists of the writings—writings that are known and understood only by those trained in law. In contrast, the average citizen or businessperson thinks of law as "things you can do and can't do"—that is, possible courses of action. In a sense, the lawyers had developed one legal system, based on writings, while ordinary citizens continued to operate on a different normative system based on custom and usage.

This difference in understanding of "law" took on much greater significance in the eighteenth and nineteenth centuries with the increasing centralization of government authority. A concomitant of government centralization was codification, the systematic formulation of basic law designed to govern throughout a national regime. The prime example of such a formulation is of course the Code Napoléon, promulgated in France at the beginning of the nineteenth century and emulated in other continental regimes. However, other forms of systematic statement of the law have a similar logic, such as the exposition of English common law in the "Commentaries" of William Blackstone, published in 1776 and succeeding years, and the definition of government structure in the U.S. Constitution, promulgated in 1787. Later developments of the same kind include the early nineteenth-century constitutions and codifications in Ibero-American countries and the later Prussian and Austrian codes.

All of these formulations are expressed in legal language, have authoritative status throughout a national state, and are legally superior to local usage. Lawyers, through their professional education and practice, acquire special knowledge of these formulations, including special knowledge of legal rules that govern their interpretation. As pronounced by the U.S. Supreme Court in its momentous decision in *Marbury v. Madison* in 1803: "It is distinctly the province of the Judicial Department [that is, the judges in interaction with lawyers] to say what the law is."[42]

The new national codifications were expressed in the traditional systematic technique that had been employed in legal treatises. Thereafter, legal scholars and jurists composed new treatises of commentary on these compilations. Jurists in common law regimes, such as Joseph Story in the United States, while also a member of the Supreme Court, produced no fewer than eight treatises on various subjects; Justice James Fitzjames Stephen of England wrote a masterly treatise on criminal law and drafted a codification of criminal law for adoption in India. Treatises on the continental codes proliferated in every European country. The medium of professional literature— the law book—thereby sustained an esoteric culture of "law" whose mastery is the foundation of law practice and the essence of academic legal study.

Legal texts expound the legal rules that govern the relationships among persons and organizations in the community (substantive law) and those that govern how the courts function (procedural law). Specialized legal knowledge or technique also includes information and insight into how the legal system actually functions, how judges carry out their judicial functions, and how particular judges are likely to decide a case if a dispute comes down to a judicial decision. This component of a lawyer's knowledge can be called "professional lore," meaning informal knowledge shared within the profession. It is acquired by observing practice, through direct experience in dealing with the courts, and in informal conversations—professional gossip—

among lawyers. John Baker suggests that this body of knowledge is a second body of law, coexisting with the written law but known only to lawyers.[43]

Lawyers have always engaged in professional gossip, some of it casual and some more systematic. Convivial discussion among opposing lawyers engenders suspicion on the part of clients, who wonder how a lawyer so friendly with an opposing lawyer in one moment can in another moment be a stalwart advocate for the client. Such worries are understandable but ordinarily unjustified. Talk between opposing lawyers ordinarily concerns the possibility of settling the matter immediately in dispute, a negotiation over the next steps in handling the matter, or idle professional gossip. Discussion of settlement possibilities or of the next stages in a litigation or negotiation is part of the lawyer's responsibility in handling a client's matter.

Engaging in professional gossip serves various other purposes: it can release tensions that arise in lawyers' work, provide an opportunity to complain about judges and clients, or simply relieve boredom. Professional gossip addresses such topics as the mental habits and inclinations of judges and court officials, ways of dealing with government agencies, the calendar in courts and agencies, the standing and reputation of fellow practitioners, recent events in the law courts, and local, national, or world issues. Professional gossip thus provides lawyers with additional insight into the ways, idiosyncrasies, and prejudices of judges and court staff and other members of an official bureaucracy. Exchanging professional gossip is an important function in meetings where lawyers gather together. Organized gatherings of lawyers evolve into bar associations.

Gossip cumulatively becomes part of the lore of the profession and helps define its culture. The resulting professional culture in turn has much force in shaping the attitude and behavior of individual lawyers. The lore is not always ethically positive and is often quite the contrary. Most new lawyers entering the profession are strongly disposed to upholding high standards of conduct but quickly absorb a more indifferent or cynical attitude if such an attitude prevails among the bar. Even in systems with high standards, young lawyers learn that there are severe constraints on what law and legal practice can do to realize justice.

Professional lore is captured in professional anecdotes and pronouncements that are handed down from generation to generation and that migrate

A HISTORICAL SKETCH OF THE LEGAL PROFESSIONS 29

from locality to locality. Many of them are funny, although usually ironic in tenor. A fair sample of the genre is contained in a treatise on the legal profession in India, including aphorisms and anecdotes not only from Indian practice but also from England and the United States.[44] Among the aphorisms are the following:

I. Law is not natural reason, but . . . the artificial reason and judgment of the law.

II. The Bar and the Bench are the joint guardians of the rule of law.

III. Every man owes some of his time to up building of the profession to which he belongs.

IV. It is not the duty of a legal practitioner blindly to follow every instruction his client gives him.[45]

One of the standard anecdotes is this:

> Judge of appellate court to counsel: "You need not cite any more authorities; you may safely assume that the Court knows something."
> Counsel in response: "The assumption that the Court knew something was the mistake I made in the Court below."

Another anecdote:

> Clergyman to lawyer: "I always understood that you gentlemen of the bar were not in the habit of charging clergymen for your services."
> Lawyer in response: "You are much in error. You clergymen look for your reward in the next world but we lawyers have to get ours in this."

Perhaps the most persistent lamentation in lawyers' professional lore is over decline in the ethics of the profession. Lamentations to that effect apparently have been uttered in every historical era. In the sixteenth century Baldesar Castiglione observed: "So old people talk about Courts in the same way they talk about everything else and affirm that those from the past were far more excellent and full of outstanding men than those we know today. They say that nowadays everything is the opposite; and that nothing prevails except envy and ill will or that our age is far more degenerate." Marc Galanter has said, "The scenario favored by lawyers . . . [is that] the profession has fallen from an earlier state of grace into an abject and debased condition."[46] The references to earlier times, together with demands for repair and restoration, have been standard pronouncements by leaders of the bar in all regimes in all ages. The invocation of lofty ideals by leaders of the bar could be considered, in Samuel Johnson's phrase, as "the triumph of hope over experience." Another interpretation is that these pronouncements endeavor to reinforce professional ideals in a profession whose ideals are perpetually under intense stress.

Upper- and Lower-Level Lawyers

The legal profession as it evolved in the Middle Ages was constituted of upper and lower levels. The boundary formally defining the upper-level lawyers is "the bar." The "bar" literally is the rail in a courtroom that separates the court proper from the benches open to the public, much as a similar rail or screen in a church marks off the area of the altar. The terms "member of the bar" and "bar association" stem from this physical separation, with the advocates and the judges on one side and the public on the other.

The upper-level practitioners were the advocates—those having the right of audience in court. In the church courts of the fourteenth century, for example, the division between upper and lower levels was between advocates and "proctors." The advocates gave formal opinions and presented argument in court. The proctors "were not expected to be legal experts and hence depended less on academic credentials and more on their practical ability to manage litigation and to guide litigants successfully through the procedural and bureaucratic labyrinths of the court."[47] The lower-level lawyers in the church courts and in other court systems performed auxiliary tasks, many of which were regarded as legally unsavory and others that simply were illegal. Exercising persuasive influence on a court clerk to see that a matter is placed on the court calendar ahead of other matters is unsavory, but it would be illegal where definite rules govern priority in calendaring. Paying a bribe to a court clerk for the same purpose is illegal in all legal systems and is considered also to be seriously wrong in most systems.

We should not suppose that in those premodern times the differentiation between upper-level and lower-level practitioners was clearer than the definition of the legal profession itself. As John Baker has said of the English legal profession in the fifteenth century:

When we contemplate lawyers as a whole, we are bound to wonder whether these diverse men of law can properly be regarded as constituting a single profession. Some lived from the profits of public office, other from private practice; many combined both. Some were in the permanent employ of great magnates or religious houses, other grubbed for work of a more *ad hoc* character among lesser folks; many had mixed practices, serving high and low as occasion offered. Some specialized in advocacy . . . including skilled draftsmanship, advice, and acting in arbitrations. Others kept to the more menial tasks associated with attorneyship, clerkship, and auditorship. Some followed both callings at once, and may even have combined them with other occupations.[48]

Nevertheless, it is possible to distinguish between upper- and lower-level practitioners in general terms even if it is impossible to do so cleanly as an empirical matter.[49] Upper-level practitioners are the lawyers called upon to appear in the appellate courts and the trial courts of general jurisdiction, as distinct from courts exercising petty jurisdiction. In court appearances the upper-level advocate is expected to employ technical discourse and exhibit a sober demeanor corresponding to that of the judges in the upper-level courts. Emulation of judicial style signifies deference to judicial authority and projects the advocate's role as the judge's subordinate colleague.

The modern model for advocates is the English barrister, where identification with the judges is particularly strong. In France, Germany, Italy, and England, lawyers when in court traditionally have worn black robes like those of the judges. Even in the United States most lawyers conduct themselves in most courts with a measure of gravity and wear dark formal clothing. The courtroom lawyer for the United States government in cases before the Supreme Court, the solicitor general, traditionally wears a cutaway and tails. In France, the upper-level lawyers were called *avocats*. In the *ancien régime,* before the French Revolution, *avocats* enjoyed something of a noble status, with attendant privileges. Concerning their status in that period a legal historian notes that "the advocate was exempted from military service; he could expel from his neighborhood any artisan who disturbed his work; the eldest members of the bar had the right to bring their cases directly to the highest courts, just as aristocrats did."[50]

Upper-level lawyers in France, Spain, and England in the sixteenth and seventeenth centuries considered themselves to be public figures and members of the governing class in great empires—an aristocracy "of the robe."[51]

In France and Spain there were official ranks of lawyers of what can be called a middling sort—*avoués* in France, *procuradores* in Spain. They were authorized to represent parties in court but with a lower professional stature than the advocates.

An advocate's direct interaction with the judges in litigation yields special insights into how the judges think, and therefore how the court might decide a legal dispute that has not yet ripened into litigation. In proportion as the advocate shares the technical and cultural viewpoint of the judiciary, an advocate's legal opinion can approximate a pronouncement of a court. This insight and technique is the basis of legal counseling performed by senior advocates and conventionally is given expression in the form of written opinions. Such an opinion can be obtained, although for a fee, more quickly and less expensively than an adjudication, and has the additional virtue of being private. Providing such opinions remains today an important function of lawyers whose legal opinions command respect among judges and other members of the legal community.

In Russia there was a somewhat different division between *prisiazhnye poverennye* (sworn advocates) and *chastnye poverennye* (private advocates). The sworn advocates had university training and were concentrated in the major cities, while the private advocates were admitted to practice only locally and were concentrated in the smaller cities and towns. There were also *podpol'nye advokati* (unauthorized practitioners), who provided ordinary people with less sophisticated legal assistance.[52]

In a court system as in every bureaucracy, however, there are discrepancies between how the system is ordained to function and how it actually works. There are people who know how the system actually works and who are ready to apply that knowledge for the benefit of litigants. The purveyors of this assistance in the operation of the courts were the lower levels of legal practitioner. Historically, the lower levels of legal practitioner in the English courts were called "attorneys" or "solicitors," in contradistinction to barristers. In Spain the division was between upper-level *abogados* and lower-level *procuradores*; in Italy the division was between *avvocati* and *procuratori*. In France there was a similar division.

These lower-level practitioners dealt with the more routine and less attractive aspects of legal procedure: helping litigants by filing papers, keeping track of their cases during pendency of litigation, making excuses to the court for delay or absence of the client or his advocate, serving as go-betweens for the lawyers, judges, and court staff. Lower-level practitioners also could convey information to the upper-level advocates about how the court actually functioned and to potential clients about the availability of and fees for lawyers' services. The following, for example, is a description of these functionaries in France:

> The litigant's first and most enduring contact with any kind of lawyer would probably be with an attorney. [The attorney's] function was to steer cases through the court and take care of the procedural details. . . . A client's best protection was sometimes endless stalling, and he could count on the skilled attorney to uncover one procedural twist after another.[53]

So also the function of lower-level lawyer in Renaissance Spain, the *solicitador*, is described by Richard Kagan:

> [O]ne of the solicitor's tasks was to act as go-between, arranging for bribes, payoffs and gifts designed to steer his client's cases through the courts. . . . [S]olicitors were a combination of legal agent and overseer for busy clients: keeping tabs on their other lawyers [the *abogado* or *procurador*], assisting in the preparation of law suits, distributing monies and otherwise making certain that their clients' cases were developing as they should.[54]

Auxiliary practitioners often developed skills in drafting routine court papers and other legal documents such as deeds and contracts. The clever and ambitious among these functionaries could also provide guidance to their professional betters in the upper level of the bar. However, lower-level practitioners faced a formidable barrier to improvement of their status as distinct from their competence. This was the strong and persistent effort of the higher-level practitioners to maintain their distinct identity and their affinity with the judiciary.[55] The upper-level lawyers emphasized, for example, their professional independence and integrity, their scruples about fees, and the principle that the practice of law was a profession and not a "business."

A sociological interpretation of this division of the profession is that it allowed the upper-level practitioners to maintain their claims to probity and intellectual sophistication in law on a plane just below that of the judiciary—professional *honneur*—while the lower-level practitioners took care of less noble but necessary details in the service of clients. Thus the complicated texts and *glossae* of the Roman law could be read and expounded only by upper-level practitioners with university training, whereas the lower-level practitioners lacked the requisite literary knowledge.[56] Until the seventeenth century, in English practice such a division separated the judges and advocates, who could use the archaic "law French" that was the language of the courts, from the lower orders of practice.[57] A similar distinction prevailed among upper-level lawyers in some Italian states, particularly Venice, Lombardy, Rome, and Naples.[58]

In the modern democratic era, formal distinctions of all kinds have become eroded and often erased. But stratification persists in many fields of human activity, such as academia and the world of art and culture, and so also in the legal profession. Thus in most modern legal systems there is formal equality among all persons admitted to practice law, but there are in fact divisions between upper-level lawyers and lower-level ones. Upper-level lawyers in modern practice are most often found in prestigious large law firms engaged in corporate and business law; lawyers who practice criminal law and domestic relations law (divorce and related matters) are often held in lesser esteem. Although these stereotypes are inaccurate and unfair, they exist. This stratification has been documented in sociological studies in the United States but is evident in most modern legal systems.[59]

The analysis in this book centers on law practice in civil matters as distinct from criminal law. From the medieval era until the seventeenth century, in most Western legal systems persons accused of a crime were not permitted the assistance of legal counsel.[60] In many authoritarian regimes in modern times—China, for example—lodging of a criminal prosecution remains "tantamount to a finding of guilt."[61] Historically, the office of prosecutor was and is an important instrument of state and in many legal systems has traditionally been distinct from that of lawyers who represent defendants accused of a crime. In the continental European legal systems, the prosecutor is still considered to be a member of the tribunal and fulfills a quasi-judicial role, as Mirjan Damaska has explained in his illuminating analysis.[62] In some legal systems the official who conducts a criminal prosecution is called a judge.

The ethical responsibilities of prosecutors in all legal systems are substantially similar to those governing lawyers in civil practice, with an important if highly ambiguous qualification. A prosecutor is held to be a "minister of justice" and hence responsible for being not only an advocate but also a guarantor of fairness to criminal defendants.[63] However, it has always been somewhat unclear how this obligation could be fulfilled other than by scrupulously observing the obligations imposed on lawyers concerning truthful evidence, candor to the court, and fairness with an adversary.[64] The concept of special responsibility of a prosecutor can also be expressed by saying that a prosecutor should look at a prosecution through the eyes of a judge as well as from the viewpoint of a protagonist. These formulations all amount to saying that the prosecutor, in the decisional process before commencing a formal proceeding, should evaluate the evidence by a more exacting standard than is required of an ordinary advocate. Accordingly, the prosecutor should determine not merely whether there is sufficient evidence to satisfy the legal standard for conviction ("beyond a reasonable doubt" in the common law formula), but whether the prosecutor, evaluating the evidence as though a judge, is satisfied that the accused is guilty.

The development of the defense lawyer's function in criminal practice has a more recent history. In all modern legal systems today, a criminal accused has a right to legal counsel.[65] Defense counsel in criminal cases are members of the bar at large and not a distinct profession. The ethical responsibilities of criminal defense counsel are largely equated with those of lawyers in civil practice and are covered by the modern codifications of legal ethics. Accordingly, the ethical obligations of criminal defense lawyers generally are the same as those of advocates in civil matters. These include avoiding conflicts of interest (for example, trying to represent codefendants whose interests may diverge), refraining from improper delaying tactics, and showing proper respect for the court.

Nevertheless, there are some modifications and important nuances in the application of these obligations to criminal practice. The American code of professional ethics, for example, recognizes that a criminal defense lawyer has wider latitude in carrying a proceeding to trial than does a lawyer in civil practice. Rule 3.1 of the ABA Rules formulates the difference as follows: "A lawyer shall not bring or defend a proceeding . . . unless there is a basis for doing so that is not frivolous. . . . A lawyer for the defendant in a criminal proceeding ... may nevertheless so defend ... as to require every element of the case be established." The idea underlying this formulation is that an accused in a criminal case has a right to demand that the prosecution establish guilt by proof and that counsel can participate in giving effect to that right. Essentially the same latitude is recognized in other legal systems.

A further nuance in the ethical obligations of criminal defense lawyers concerns the problem of perjury by a criminal accused or a witness on behalf of the accused. This problem is much discussed in American professional discourse. The rule applicable to all lawyers is that an advocate may not present perjured testimony.[66] All lawyers accept that this restriction applies in civil matters and that in criminal matters it applies to presentations by the prosecutor and by defense counsel of testimony *other* than that of the accused. But when it comes to testimony by the accused, a different view is held by most lawyers doing criminal defense work and by many judges and scholars. Under this view, it is absurd to demand that an accused facing a long term in prison be obliged to speak truthfully about his own alleged complicity, and unfair to require that the accused refrain from testifying in his own behalf. By the same token, it is thought to be pretentious and fatuous to require defense counsel to impose these obligations on their clients.[67]

This absurdity is avoided in civil law systems. In those systems, an accused is permitted to present statements that are not on oath and are not regarded as evidence in the full sense. The court is required to hear and to consider the statements, but they are not "testimony" governed by the same legal obligation of truth-telling that applies to other witnesses. (In many civil law systems the same distinction between parties and independent witnesses is also made in civil litigation.)

In common law systems, it is standard practice among criminal defense lawyers not to press the accused to "tell the whole truth and nothing but the truth" if and when the accused gives testimony in court. For one thing, the obligation to give this admonition to a client arises only when a lawyer "knows" that the client will testify falsely. Criminal defense lawyers profess that they cannot arrive at such knowledge, at least until a client has undertaken to plead guilty (typical disposition in criminal prosecutions), in which case the dilemma does not arise.[68] Many criminal defense lawyers simply avoid asking direct questions of a client that would produce embarrassing responses.

When a criminal accused gives testimony or a statement on his own behalf, in most legal systems unofficially it is assumed that, if necessary from the defendant's viewpoint, the testimony will be false. When that problem arises in the American system, the ethical code in effect transfers responsibility to the judge.[69]

The Legal Profession from the Sixteenth to the Twentieth Century: Classic Law Practice

The broad characteristics of law practice and of the legal profession persisted in substantially similar form from the sixteenth century until consummation of the Industrial Revolution in the latter part of the nineteenth century. The Industrial Revolution changed the structure of society and hence the organization of legal systems. The old socioeconomic organization was based on local communal life and production primarily for local markets by artisans working on a small scale. That pattern was gradually displaced by mass production, industrial capitalism, and global markets, which have become characteristic of the twenty-first century. The demands on the legal system slowly but inexorably evolved accordingly, and with those changes also the requirements for effective law practice.

In our discussion we treat the modern period as beginning in 1870. Any specific date for the beginning of the modern period is of course arbitrary. Moreover, the changes in law practice began at different times and emerged at different rates in various countries. In particular, the appearance of law firms, as distinct from sole proprietorships, occurred first in the United States in the period before the Civil War (1861–65) and only thereafter in solicitors' offices in England. (English barristers as such still practice independently, although in recent years many English barristers have been employed in firms of solicitors.) For a much longer period in Italy, France, and Spain, legal practitioners adhered to established traditions in the organization and conduct of practice.[70]

These traditions were based on the model of general practice by solo practitioners dependent on their personal reputations to attract clients, and on the ideal of independence from the state and from improper client interests. Not only did law firms, as distinct from solo practice, emerge much later in Europe than in the United States, but change in the subject matter of practice also emerged later in Europe. Moreover, the subject matter of office practice shifted from real estate transactions to corporate transactions much later in countries whose economies remained primarily agricultural than in countries where industrialization evolved earlier. However, until World War I, law practice even in the United States largely shared the characteristics prevailing in Europe. In all regimes, adherence to tradition was stronger in provincial cities and towns than in metropolitan centers.

The characteristics of classic law practice may be described as follows. First, the principal functions of lawyers concerned property transactions, primarily transactions concerning landed property (real estate). The focus on real estate reflected the predominance of agriculture in the economy and was manifested in lawyers' functions both as advocates and as legal counselors. Most litigation, apart from criminal matters, involved property transactions such as boundary disputes, rights of inheritance and obligations arising from mortgages, and conflicting claims to rights in use of land, water, and other resources. The functions of advocate and counselor were performed by both upper-level and lower-level lawyers according to overlapping and shifting divisions. Upper-level lawyers—the barristers and *avocats*—represented clients in major litigation before the courts of higher jurisdiction. Lower-level lawyers—the attorneys and procurators—presented litigation in petty cases before local tribunals. The two levels of practitioners competed in mid-range cases, and the boundaries between their respective spheres of dominance changed over time.

Among legal counselors there was a corresponding division of function in transactional matters. The lower-level attorneys, solicitors, and scriveners handled routine transactions, the staples of their practice being sales and leases of land and simple wills. These lawyers also assisted the upper-level lawyers in the preparation and monitoring of litigation in the higher courts; in some systems, they took care of matters at the fringe of legality, such as providing fees, commissions, and "presents" to officials. They also handled various business functions, such as collecting rents and checking on tenants. The upper level of the bar handled transactional matters that involved greater wealth and more intricate legal complexity. There was continuing competition for clientele between the two levels. In America and other places where the formal division of the bar was not maintained, lawyers nevertheless sorted themselves into roughly corresponding levels.[71]

Second, virtually all lawyers were solo practitioners until law firms began to evolve in the late nineteenth century. This was true of English barristers and their upper-level counterparts in continental Europe and also of lower-level practitioners. In England it came to be a settled custom and then a rule that barristers could not practice in firms; in most other parts of Europe it was a matter of settled custom for advocates to practice as "solos." In terms of professional status, functioning as a solo practitioner demonstrated that law was a profession and not a business, as might be implied if practice were carried out through a business association such as a partnership.

Among all levels of the profession, a lawyer's practice was considered to consist of his own work product in a very personal sense. The uncertainties of income inhibited lawyers from undertaking the complications of functioning through a law firm. That fact in turn precluded the achievement of efficiencies through internal specialization in group practice, although a lawyer usually had an apprentice to copy documents and perform other drudgery. The law firms that developed in North America were very small by modern standards—two-person or sometimes three-person enterprises, not counting apprentices.[72] The "lower branch" of the English profession (the solicitors) gained status and respectability memorialized in the Solicitors Act of 1843.[73] However, English solicitors remained a corps of solo practitioners or very small partnerships until after World War II.[74] In all parts of the world today, lawyers practicing in small cities and towns still predominantly practice alone or with one or two partners. In the current era, even in the United States about half of lawyers devoted to private practice function as solos or members of small firms.

Although most lawyers practiced alone well into the twentieth century, in many countries they often maintained their offices in commonly occupied professional quarters. Having common quarters was sometimes required by professional regulation. Indeed, in the former Soviet Union and until recently in the People's Republic of China, lawyers were required to conduct their practice under the aegis of state-run organizations. (These professional residency requirements facilitated government monitoring of lawyers' activities, particularly tendencies toward political activity.) In any event, maintaining common professional quarters was a matter of convenience, quite as tradesmen and artisans in various occupations tend to congregate in close proximity to each other. The English Inns of Court have this origin, being places where the lawyers resided when carrying on their work. In many continental countries, lawyers' chambers are in a "college" or similarly designated institution, essentially a cluster of offices. These arrangements facilitate interchange between lawyers in carrying out legal transactions, maintaining group law libraries (law books have long been a major item of a lawyer's office overhead), training apprentices. They also provide a forum for professional gossip and simple social conviviality; the opportunity to socialize with fellows cannot be overlooked. The distrust and opprobrium that have always attended law practice mean that lawyers often can find friendship primarily among their own fellows.[75]

As a consequence of being solo practitioners, most lawyers at all levels of practice traditionally have been general practitioners rather than specialists in either litigation or transaction work. A law office was predisposed to handle whatever matter a prospective client might have, because as "small businessmen" practicing lawyers do not like to turn away new clientele. Within the range of practice carried on in a specific community, every lawyer ordinarily was ready to undertake whatever business came through the door. This in turn meant that the members of the bar in any community had similar experience and knowledge of professional technique.[76] Shared professional experience resulted in lawyers' having common professional interests and made for solidarity in the face of judges and clients, although it also involved competition among themselves. John Leubsdorf observes, concerning the French legal profession:

> The solo practitioner is still the norm in France. Only one-fourth of the *avocats* in Paris, and one-tenth of those in the rest of France, practice in firms, although many other had looser forms of association. . . . [T]he number of Paris firms increased from 113 in 1974 to almost one thousand in 1993. But in France the profession places the . . . protection of each *avocat* . . . at the center of its concerns.[77]

The profession's self-image for many lawyers remains that of the solo or small-firm practitioner even though the reality is changing. Thus a member of a large international law firm may still refer to "hanging out a shingle" (meaning the sign over an office door) in reference to opening an office in a new location. Reality is changing rather slowly in France and Italy but rapidly in other countries, particularly those in the common law world. As Stan Ross notes, speaking of Australia: "Many more lawyers are working for large organizations, law firms, government or corporations. . . . Figures for New South Wales [a state in Australia] showed that 46 per cent of the profession were solo practitioners in 1948, falling to 21 per cent by 1985. . . . [As of] March 1997, 27 percent of practicing solicitors are in firms with 11 or more partners."[78]

Being a general practitioner ready to handle most kinds of law business was feasible because the subject matter of the law had a much narrower range than it does in modern conditions. The traditional subjects of litigation included conflicting claims to real property, contract disputes, bankruptcy, divorce or marital separation proceedings, administration of decedents' estates, and local legal controversies with the government. The traditional subjects of office law practice were the conveyance of real property, mortgages on real property to secure loans, contracts in unusually complicated business transactions, marriage settlements (property arrangements for prospective spouses), and testamentary dispositions. The common subject matter of law practice was thus conducive to common experience, common identity, and common interests.[79]

A general practitioner's vocation was confined to a single locality and usually a narrow set of professional connections. Most country lawyers lived out their lives in a single town. The same was true of lawyers in cities such as London and Bristol in England, Paris and Lyon in France, and Rome and Florence in Italy. City barristers and their auxiliaries occasionally traveled to the country for a trial or some other matter, particularly in England where the courts periodically went on circuit away from London. Similarly, a specific city barrister would serve the legal needs in the city of a "country cousin" solicitor. However, the difficulties of travel and communication constricted the geographic scope of transactions, with a corresponding effect on the geographic scope of a lawyer's practice. This too made for a high degree of shared professional experience among the local bar in any community.[80]

Populations before the twentieth century were mostly rural and primarily engaged directly or indirectly in agriculture. Until as late as 1900, over half the populations of Western Europe and the western hemisphere lived and worked in rural areas, and in some countries the proportion was considerably higher. An agricultural economy follows traditional patterns and involves relatively fewer transactions than an urban economy. In contrast, an urban economy involves mercantile and financial transactions which, when of unusual character, can produce legal business, such as the formation of a joint venture or the documentation of a commercial loan. Equally important, courts and other agencies of government such as the tax collector are concentrated in cities and towns. As a result of these characteristics of "legal needs," the practice of law was and remains an urban calling, more than the practice of medicine or the ministry, for example.

A lawyer's practice has always involved repeated interactions with other lawyers and with judges and other government officials. Lawyers thereby ordinarily acquire much more "inside" information about civic affairs than the average citizen. City lawyers have immediate and continuing contact with urban sources of the information such as courts, judges, and other officials. Country lawyers through their city connections receive information about official activities in the capital. Having special information about civic affairs is useful in law practice and results in an information disparity between lawyers and many of their clients, ordinarily to the lawyer's advantage. Clients have always been fearful, and rightly so, that lawyers know things that the clients do not.

Most lawyers' work was and still is inherently competitive. Traditional law practice was intensely competitive except in small towns, where a single lawyer might have a monopoly. Litigation is by definition competitive because, when a dispute goes to judicial conclusion, there is a winner and a loser. Some American academic critics, understandably dismayed by the hyper-competition in much of contemporary American law practice, think or wish that law practice could be less competitive, and often point to European practice as a model. It is true that in the civil law system of adjudication the advocate has a less visible and less active role than his counterparts in common law litigation. However, this lesser role does not mean there is not intense competition in the interaction between advocates, but only that assertiveness must be expressed in more sublimated fashion. Similar competition, although usually even less visible, pervades the office practice in transactional matters. Every client wants the best lawyer he can afford, and every lawyer wants a reputation of doing legal work that is as good as any other lawyer's, and either better or less expensive. At any rate, neither coauthor of this book has ever met an English or civil law practitioner who was not keenly on edge about the client matters for which he was responsible.

Beyond the inherently competitive nature of legal work is the fact that formal entry into the profession generally has not been very difficult. At times in some countries, effective restrictions have been maintained on entry into the legal profession, for example, in contemporary Japan. However, there has never been effective legal restriction on quasi-professional or paralegal vocations that compete with law practice, particularly in performing routine legal tasks. The ubiquitous existence of lower-level practitioners demonstrates the pervasiveness of professional competition. And there have always been unlicensed clerks and scriveners who could effectively imitate a lawyer's work.

Learning enough to become a lawyer requires no special preparatory knowledge beyond a strong facility with language, and no psychological competence beyond the ability to be firm, or stubborn if necessary. Becoming a lawyer holds the prospect of improving justice, and therefore the quality of life in the community, which has always been a social ideal of many. Being a lawyer has always been honorific in some degree, notwithstanding public suspicion of lawyers, and is therefore attractive to persons who seek upward social mobility. Many lawyers have made a comfortable living, and a few have become rich. Hence, many young people feel called to the vocation, particularly people who want to improve their station in life and who have the intelligence and drive to do so.[81]

The notion has been widely accepted in some academic disciplines that "the bar" has been resolutely successful in maintaining barriers to entry into the profession.[82] There is some truth to this, but not much. Except in some developing countries, a university education is required for admission to law practice. The requirement of a university education as a condition of becoming a lawyer is certainly a barrier to fully democratic admission to law practice. So is the economic obstacle facing a young lawyer who must establish a practice but who has neither family connections nor a strong academic record. So is the historically strong and persistent prejudice against women and religious and racial minorities. Nevertheless, analysis of the demographics of the profession suggests that law practice is relatively open to aggressive newcomers and that it is constantly threatened by practitioners in rival callings.

There certainly has been incessant competition in the practice of law among upper-level practitioners, among lower-level practitioners, and between levels of practice. There has also been incessant competition with people who were not members of the legal profession, however one defines the profession in a given historical period. For example, the modern English barristers first emerged in the fifteenth century as lower status and less expensive competitors of the elite sergeants at law, who constituted a very small and cohesive group of legal advisers to the crown. The "attorneys" in England, the *procureurs* in France, the *procuradores* in Spain, and the *procuratori* in Italy emerged as lower status and less expensive "lawyers" drawn from unofficial attachés of the courts. Much of the business available to lawyers in small towns, such as collecting rent and handling relations with agricultural tenants, could also be done by nonlawyers. In the cities, printers put out standard-form legal documents, originally drafted by some kind of lawyer. Nonlawyer advisers and lobbyists were available to conduct any public business for clients except appearing inside the bar of a court. Nonlawyers who can read closely and write coherently have always been able to perform many tasks for which lawyers have claimed special competence.

The intensity of competition among lawyers of course reflects the existing commercial mores in a society. The "guild mentality"—fraternal relations among those engaged in the same line of work—apparently was typical in the sixteenth and seventeenth centuries. Accordingly, professional competition in those settings was less intense, or at least less overt than it is today. Lawyers could properly consider themselves "gentlemen" engaged in a noble calling, rather than artisans struggling for clientele.

The patterns in general practice have remained remarkably stable, except in countries that have gone through violent revolution in the modern era, notably China, Cuba, and the former Soviet Union and its communist bloc affiliates. Lawyers everywhere have been engaged in conducting litigation or seeking to avoid litigation through legal documentation in business and property transactions. Some practitioners took on criminal cases as the law gradually enlarged the procedural rights of persons accused of crime. Lawyers operated as solo practitioners, undertook most of the kinds of practice considered to be lawyers' work, and competed constantly with other lawyers and with practitioners in functionally adjacent callings. At the same time, most lawyers shared bonds of common identity and interest that moderated competition within the profession and nurtured cooperation in efforts to suppress or control competition from without. They maintained collective undertakings through institutions such as the Inns of Court, professional "colleges," and prototype bar associations. They had affinity with, but also distance from, judges and other government officials and hoped that the public would recognize that their calling was dedicated to justice.[83]

Modern Law Practice

In the modern democratic era, the tendency has been to erase formal distinctions in all sectors of society. This tendency manifested itself in different historical periods in different countries. In the United States, by the early nineteenth century distinctions had ceased to be recognized between advocates and "attorneys" or "scriveners." A person was admitted to practice as a lawyer *simpliciter*. In some American states in this period, limitations on admission to practice were abolished; anyone could appear as a lawyer who wanted to do so and who could persuade a client to engage him.[84] In most of the English commonwealth jurisdictions, the distinction between barrister (the upper-level practitioner) and solicitor (the lower-level) was not carried over from the mother country, although the division is continued in some Australian states and barrister is an honorific title in Canada.[85] In the 1990s, the distinction in England between barrister and solicitor was substantially reduced so far as authority to appear in court is concerned, although the differentiation in titles has been continued.[86] So also in France in the same period, the historical distinction between *avocat* and *avoué* was abolished, and in Italy the distinction between *avvocati* and *procuratori*.[87]

The modern requirements for establishing competence as a lawyer include graduation from some kind of law curriculum, passing a bar examination, and, in most countries, completing a period of apprenticeship. A bar examination is a written interrogation addressing legal terminology, legal concepts, and legal analysis, and is required in many modern regimes. In other systems, notably in Latin America, passing the examinations for graduation from the law curriculum satisfies the examination requirement, an arrangement that applies in some American states. The bar examination takes at least one day of approximately six hours and in most countries more than one day. In some countries the written examination is supplemented by an oral examination. The "pass" rate varies widely. In Japan, for example, the pass rate is less than 5 percent of those sitting for the examination; in China the pass rate has been a little more than 10 percent; in many countries the pass rate is nearly 100 percent.

Bar examinations today are usually national examinations. However, in France the examination for a certificate of professional aptitude is administered locally within each *barreau*, where the pass rate is roughly calibrated to the local lawyer employment market. In federal systems such as the United States and Canada, the bar examinations are prescribed and administered by the states and provinces. A person who successfully completes the bar examination is eligible to practice throughout the jurisdiction that administered the examination.[88]

Apprenticeship systems in the modern era may be formal or informal. In a formal system, all applicants are required to pursue a fixed period of tutelage, usually a year or two years, under supervision of one or a series of mentors. The mentors may include judges and prosecutors (as in Germany) or be limited to lawyers in private practice (as in England and Ontario, Canada). Admission to practice requires satisfactory performance in the apprenticeship program as well as passing the bar exam.

An informal apprenticeship "system" prevails in many countries, including the United States and the countries of Latin America. Although an applicant may become a licensed member of the bar by passing the bar examination, the typical neophyte lawyer knows little about how to practice law. In many countries the education provided in the university law curriculum is theoretical and shallow, so law graduates in these systems, even though fully licensed to practice law, have only a fragmentary concept of their vocation. Practical legal knowledge must be acquired by working in a law firm or law department.

But there is no guarantee of employment for a new lawyer and there is great disparity in employment opportunities. A young lawyer endowed with a strong academic record or inherited wealth or family connections usually can obtain a junior position in an established law firm. Other aspirants will have to search for a place where they can "devil"—doing routine and often boring work in a law office until they learn enough through experience and observation to attract clients on their own. The quality of this kind of experience varies greatly. In many systems the competition for starting positions is so intense that law graduates take jobs as secretaries and paralegals. The same situation exists in some places in the United States.

In recent years in several countries, there has been better integration of formal legal education and apprenticeship. Several countries have established formal programs of practice instruction after university graduation and in place of apprenticeship in a law office. The aim is to supplement the theoretical legal education with practice-oriented training, and at the same time to provide more intense and systematic practice training than has been afforded in office-based apprenticeships. For example, Italy has now instituted such a program, and in England the Bar and the Law Society have long since established similar programs for apprentice barristers and solicitors respectively. The barrister apprenticeship is called "pupilage" and requires a year, the solicitor apprenticeship used to be called "articling" (after the articles of the contract of apprenticeship) and requires two years.

A continuing debate in the United States involves essentially the same issue.[89] Lawyers and judges complain that law graduates may know legal and social theory but are ignorant of the "realities of practice." Well-established law offices have in-house training programs aimed at overcoming these deficiencies. Many American law students acquire practical knowledge through internships in law firms and judicial chambers in the summers between semesters or during the school year. Other law graduates must learn through experience. Whatever the process of entry into the profession, however, the "learning curve" is very steep in a lawyer's first job.

As the modern era opened, the existing characteristics of the legal profession in Europe, and in countries absorbing European institutions, had been shaped by the mercantile-artisan character of the political economy that succeeded the previous agrarian-feudal economy. In mercantile-artisan economies, cities became the centers of politics and business, including manufacturing, trade, and finance. As cities grew, transactions burgeoned and became sufficiently important to justify the formal documentation that lawyers could supply. Legal disputes could no longer be confined to local manorial or borough courts, but found their way into tribunals maintained at a higher level of government. The transition from agrarian-feudal economy to mercantile-artisan economy, occurring at various times in various places, typically was accompanied by the emergence of the law office consisting of one, two, or perhaps three lawyers, all engaged in general practice.

The arrival of modern national government centralization and industrialism in the nineteenth century created a different legal, political, and economic environment. Modern industrialism is based on business enterprises that are constituted and sustained by investor finance and given direction by employed management. They use machinery operated in large-scale factories, transportation employing power-driven equipment such as railroads, and communication through the telegraph, later the telephone, and still later the electronic media.

The scope of state activities increased correspondingly. Governments promoted and financed business enterprises and provided legal assistance such as liberal corporation laws. In an ensuing development, government adopted laws and regulations to prevent abuses such as the exploitation of labor. Both promotion and control required legal assistance and created new roles for lawyers in government. Those developments in turn required businesses to augment their legal capabilities.

Lawyers employed by government and those employed by regulated enterprises (both businesses and nonprofit enterprises) continue to have a symbiotic relationship. In many respects the lawyers and legal staff for government and business are in antagonistic positions, the one side seeking stricter regulatory compliance and pursuing enforcement, the other seeking less onerous burdens for their clients. But the lawyers involved employ the same legal techniques, the same legal language, and mirror-image strategies. In some legal systems, lawyers specialized in regulatory fields move more or less freely from one side of the regulatory interface to the other.

Law practice in the modern era embraces much broader and more varied subject matter than traditional practice and is conducted in new organizational forms. Most of the newer types of law practice augment rather than displace the other subject matter. Thus most modern litigation practice continues to involve traditional subject matter, including disputes over money and property, but now extends to criminal defense litigation, personal injury claims, and divorce litigation. Modern transaction practice continues to include traditional subject matter, such as real estate sales, financial transactions, the organization of businesses as partnerships or corporations, and testamentary dispositions. Alongside these traditional subjects have arisen other fields of practice, most of them a consequence of increased government regulation and heavier taxation, such as tax law, securities regulation, environmental law, and antitrust law. In the organization of law practice, solo and very small law firms (two or three lawyers) continue to be characteristic, but now large organizations also provide legal services, including the law departments of government and corporate business and the large law firm.

These changes in law practice have responded to more general changes in the political and economic environment of developed countries. In most Western European countries, the state underwent two important transformations, although these occurred at varying rates and to different degrees from one country to another.

First, the activities of the state greatly expanded, either directly or through its support of favored corporate enterprises, in the fields of transportation, communication, education, manufacturing, and mining. Transportation was developed through the improvement of roads, the building of canals and straightening of rivers for navigation, and later through the construction of railways. Communication improved through expanded post roads and later through telegraph and telephone service. Education was developed through primary and secondary schools, compulsory education, the creation of technical training institutes, and the expansion of universities. Manufacturing developed in all manner of ways, particularly after steam and electricity replaced water as the power source in manufacturing. A corresponding expansion of public finance, including taxation and expenditure, necessitated the enlargement of government bureaucracies, which in turn required manifold directives and regulations. The result was an increase in the number and variety of legally defined interactions with citizens and nongovernment organizations, including business.

A second transformation was the "legalization" of the political foundations of the modern state. Until the American and French revolutions at the end of the eighteenth century, the dominant constitutional form was monarchy or a combination of monarchy and aristocracy. Beginning with those revolutions, the *anciens régimes* were replaced or diluted in favor of cabinet and parliamentary regimes. These new regimes in turn depended on legal regulation to define their own powers and the authority and responsibility of their component bureaucracies. The constitutional basis of government and the "rule of law" did not spring forth full-blown, nor did the principle that government officials were legally accountable. But by the early twentieth century the concept became accepted that officials had authority only as defined by law and could be held accountable through legal procedure. The classic exposition is by Max Weber:

> The basic idea is that laws can be enacted ... by a formally correct procedure. The governing body is either elected or appointed. ... The administrative staff consists of officials appointed ... ; the law-abiding people are members of the body politic ("fellow citizens").
>
> Obedience is not owed to anyone personally but to enacted rules and regulations. ... The person in authority, too, obeys a rule when giving an order, namely, "the law," or "rules and regulations" which represent abstract norms.[90]

The changes in the structure of business enterprise largely corresponded to the changes in the state, except they were smaller and more decentralized. Again at varying rates and to varying degrees, businesses grew in scale, and larger businesses came to be bureaucratically organized.[91] Large business enterprises were organized as corporations instead of partnerships and carried out their functions through corporate officials and employees rather than, as in earlier capitalism, through proprietors and apprentices. The complexities of the corporate organization were governed by legal documents such as corporate charters, franchises, and finance contracts with shareholders and creditors, and by quasi-legal provisions in the form of intracorporate and departmental regulations. Again, in contrast with the smaller proprietorships of an earlier era, large corporate enterprises engaged in myriad transactions and relationships with third parties, such as suppliers and customers, in relationships that were increasingly impersonal and governed by standardized documentation.

In combination, these developments have resulted in the "legalization" of the state and of economic activity. The control of governmental and business operations is accomplished not primarily through personal leadership but by rules and forms of administration prescribed either by statutes and regulations (in the case of the state) or by contracts and internal regulations (in the case of business).

The "socialist" countries—the former communist regimes in the Soviet Union and Eastern Europe and the present regime in China—have confronted variations of the "legalization" phenomenon. These regimes theoretically have operated through systematic regulation from the center—that is, as large bureaucracies with subordinate regional, local, and departmental regulations. These systems have proved very rigid, especially in the face of increasingly dynamic technical and economic change, and hence are subject to pervasive ad hoc deviation and corruption, which eventually results in chaos and crisis. From those conditions the road to reform has been very difficult. It has been particularly difficult to maintain central political direction while facilitating decentralized economic activity. Although it has been recognized that a "legal system" is required to implement this combination, developing, staffing, and energizing such a system has proved to be a formidable technical and cultural undertaking. Conceiving of the "rule of law" for the former socialist systems is not difficult theoretically, but institutionalizing it with real judges and real lawyers has proved more challenging.

In this analysis we consider the legal professions in all the modern constitutional regimes to be approximately similar. Obviously, there are differences, as will be examined, for example, between such systems as those in Germany and Mexico and Canada. And the American legal system, and hence its legal profession, may be distinctive in the depth of its involvement in business transactions and in politically controversial legal issues. The question therefore arises whether the ethical problems in American legal practice are different in kind, rather than degree, from those in other constitutional regimes.

It is clear that the nature and range of law practice in America has been distinctive. A century and a half ago Alexis de Tocqueville famously observed, "There is almost no question in the United States that is not resolved sooner or later into a judicial question."[92] A systematic comparison yielded the following observation:

> The American regimes [federal and state regulatory regimes] [are] more legally complex, more punitive, more unpredictable, and more costly to comply with than their counterparts in other economically advanced democracies. In many fields of regulation [there is] ... a more institutionally fragmented system of regulation in the United States....
>
> American citizens and advocacy groups ... generally have more access to regulatory processes and information and broader opportunities to make legal challenges to regulatory and corporate decisions.[93]

The legalistic or "adversarial" regulatory system translates into much more extensive and pervasive law practice. And, by a circular process, more extensive and pervasive law practice translates into more legalistic and adversarial governmental processes. However, we believe that the American scene has become less distinctive over the past several decades and that this trend will continue. As an Argentine colleague who is a judge observes: "In Argentina today, judges must 'solve' problems caused by bad administration. We order a public hospital to operate on a poor patient or to give medicines; we order a county to provide water to children living in poor localities." We forecast that future regimes will converge toward similar types. That prediction implicates complex factors and is certainly debatable, but rests on the following propositions.

First, as indeed Tocqueville suggested, "legalism" as a basis of social ordering is functionally related to social equality and political democracy. Most modern regimes are based on the premise of citizen equality and government's responsiveness to popular will. Such a regime cannot be based on "tradition" and hence must either be authoritarian or make political decisions through some kind of parliamentary process resulting in legislation, implemented through bureaucratic regulation. Legislation and regulation are distinctively legal mechanisms.

Second, the regulatory systems in modern regimes are, by relentless increments, becoming more pervasive. The legal regulations internal to modern regimes reflect attempts to deal with new technology, demands of new constituencies, and the forces of intense economic change and competition. "Globalization" has resulted in a continuing stream of international treaties, conventions, and implementing regulations; more and more countries have joined in binding regional commercial compacts, such as the European Union (EU), the North American Free Trade Agreement (NAFTA), and the Mercado Commun del Sur (Mercosur); international agreements increasingly govern the seas, international rivers, and the atmosphere. At the same time, there is continuing "devolution" within previously more unified national states, for example, Scotland and Wales in the United Kingdom, the regions of Spain, and the provinces of Canada. Equally important, contractual agreements governing relationships among businesses in international commerce have become more numerous, complex, and economically important as global trade continues to expand. All of these arrangements are distinctively legal.

Third, the necessity for formal dispute resolution procedures has expanded as a concomitant of these regulatory developments. Just as the modal form of substantive political policy is cast in legal terms, so is the modal form of process in applying political policy. This is not to suggest that the role of courts and judicial procedure in most parts of the world has yet approximated that in the United States.[94] It is nevertheless true that everywhere in the modern world there has been a burgeoning of litigation and arbitration in dispute resolution, both as ultimate recourse and as background for negotiated dispute resolutions.

Responsive to these developments has been the rapid expansion of large international law firms. The original model of these firms was American, but the new version is led by the English solicitor firms. These firms have taken the opportunity conferred by European Community directives that open all EU countries to professional practitioners of every member country; so a London solicitor, for example, may open an office in Rome after meeting modest local qualifications. The English firms have also followed the pathways of the British Empire, setting up shop in the Gulf states, Singapore, Hong Kong, and other old stations.

There is another perhaps less obvious tendency of convergence among systems. This has to do with public administration. As will be developed in the next section, administrative bureaucracies in the European model have been for two centuries largely staffed by law graduates of the universities. These officials usually are not counted as lawyers because they do not take the bar examination and enter law practice. But their formal training and hence their intellectual equipment is the same as those of lawyers. In their work these law-trained operatives encounter many of the same problems as a legal staff, including ethical problems.

In this same period, the field of public administration in the United States has gradually, although still incompletely, been regularized as a respectable vocation for capable people, many of them law graduates. Tocqueville noticed that "administration" in this country in 1830 was rudimentary. American public officials of that era were elected or appointed under crude patronage systems. Since the year 2000, however, there has developed a substantially merit-based public service at all levels of American government, partly the product of civil service reform, partly a necessary response to the increasingly complex demands of public service jobs. These administrative systems are constituted by law, function by very legalized processes, and employ many lawyers. In the American version, many officials in the public service are fully qualified lawyers (that is, they have taken the bar exam and hold a current license), and many of them eventually move into private law practice. During their incumbency in the public service, however, they function much like their counterparts in the European systems.

These developments, in our opinion, mean that law practice in all modern regimes will develop inevitably, if only gradually, in the same general direction.

Careers in Law in the "Legalized State"

Legal technique and legal technicians are required to facilitate the "legalization" of government and business procedures. Legal technique is a vocational skill of members of the bar and of officeholders in the state and corporate bureaucracies who have the requisite legal knowledge. However, in the career patterns in which legal technique is acquired, distinct differences have evolved between European and American practice. The European model has been adopted in Latin America and Japan and eventually will probably be adopted in China. An explanation of this difference in career patterns begins with reference to the systems of higher education.

The European educational system provides education in law at the university level—that is, after secondary school—as distinct from postgraduate education in the United States. The European law curriculum thus parallels curricula in other subjects such as philosophy, history, and economics. European university students who pursue a law curriculum acquire a knowledge of legal concepts essentially the same as that provided to students who later become lawyers. Graduates in law in the European universities who do not become lawyers therefore have a knowledge of law that would equip them to handle most "legal" matters in the government departments and in business organizations.[95]

These law-trained university graduates find employment in the bureaucracies of government and departments of corporate enterprise. Their university training in law, along with fluency and precision in the use of language, is sufficient to carry out many of the tasks of written specification and documentation required by the "legalization" of government and corporate enterprise. Moreover, in the civil law system the actions of government officials usually are not subject to challenge in the ordinary courts of law. Rather, administrative actions are the subject of specialized jurisdiction, with specialized tribunals, in what can be called administrative law.[96] It therefore can be said that Europe has evolved a distinct system of administration based on government regulations operating under the jurisdiction of specialized administrative courts, and staffed by people trained in law but who were not part of the traditional legal profession. The private bureaucracies of business companies similarly provide themselves with legal counseling through internal corporate legal staff.

In some countries the status of "in-house" lawyers is formally recognized. For example, in Germany persons trained as lawyers who have passed the bar examination, and then assume employment in a corporation, are designated by the title *Syndikusanwalt*. As such they have a legal status specified in the regulations governing the profession. The specified status includes the concept of professional independence.[97] In Japan, legal departments of business corporations are highly developed, both in number and technical sophistication. Japanese companies give intense effort to training these staffs, including special training in international commercial law. Many send staff members to the United States for legal training and subsequent admission to the bar. This development is obviously an adaptation to the severe limitation on the number of the *bengoshi*, fully admitted lawyers, in Japan.

Nevertheless, the status of in-house legal staff in Japan and in Europe is lower than that of lawyers in independent law practice. In 1982 the Court of Justice of the European Community held that a lawyer in the employ of a business corporation lacked the same authority as an independent lawyer concerning confidential matters.[98]

In England, most university programs include a curriculum in law, conferring on the student a legal background similar to that of university law graduates on the continent. University graduates who do not thereafter become barristers or solicitors nevertheless can perform work with "legal" aspects in the ministries and corporations. Also, persons trained as solicitors or barristers may migrate from private practice into service in government and in corporations, thereby becoming in-house legal staff. A roughly similar pattern has emerged in other common law countries.

The modern development in the People's Republic of China has gone a different route. The regime has wanted to expand its legal profession at a rapid rate, but lacks the university apparatus and cadres of graduates to do so. Hence it has admitted people with basic literacy and substantial experience in practical office affairs to the profession of lawyer.[99] This adaptation perhaps demonstrates the importance of experience, as distinct from formal education, as an ingredient in lawyers' technique.

In the United States, however, by the beginning of the twentieth century the training of lawyers had been transformed from university education plus apprenticeship (similar to training in Europe) into a law curriculum presented at the postgraduate level and in specialized law schools. American law schools began to offer a distinctly professional curriculum: the study of law for prospective practitioners and not for educated citizens at large. The result was that, as "legalization" in American government and corporations evolved, legal assistance has been provided by persons who had both a university education and a degree from an American law school.

Despite these differences in historical development, there is a common theme in the phenomenon of "legalization." Simply stated, legal services, particularly legal counseling in transaction matters, are necessary to the functioning of modern government agencies and business corporations.

More or less concurrent with the evolution of law departments in government and business was the evolution of the multimember law firm. This evolution has occurred at different periods in various countries, first and most rapidly in the United States, then in other common law countries, and now in Europe and Japan. The new model law firm that emerged at the beginning of the twentieth century consisted of as many as a dozen lawyers. Later, large law firms came to be constituted of dozens, then hundreds, and now thousands of lawyers, along with supporting staff of secretaries, technical assistants (paralegals), and administrative personnel.

The new model law firm is different from solo or small-firm practice not only in scale but also in organization and economics. Instead of having equal partners, each of whom is engaged in his own work, the firm carries out its work through small specialized teams, coordinated by managing partners or management committees. As the modern law firm became larger, the hierarchical structure evolved into still more complex form, with "departments" (a litigation department, a banking law department, and others), department managers, and a ranking of lawyers according to proficiency, earning capacity, and seniority. Some relatively large law firms operate as a cluster of small firms practicing under a single name. This pattern persists in continental Europe.

The modern multimember law firm first evolved in the United States in the 1890s. The innovation is attributed to the Cravath firm, whose present name is Cravath, Swaine & Moore, but the concept probably originated earlier.[100] The key elements were recognition of the importance of technical skill, particularly in complicated financial matters; differentiation of the function of maintaining client relationships from the function of performing technical legal work; and internal specialization of function within the firm.

In the traditional small firm, each lawyer handles all kinds of legal matters, except that there is usually a division of function between courtroom work and office work. A lawyer in solo practice or in a small firm receives compensation based on the clientele that he brings to the firm and for whom he performs the legal work. Apprentice lawyers have little or no earnings because they have no clients, have no clients because they have no experience, and have no experience because they lack clients through whom to develop experience. Beginning lawyers therefore necessarily depend on family connections and the like to obtain clients and thus to establish themselves in practice.

The "Cravath system" is very different from the traditional small firm in these respects. All clients are clients of the firm, not clients of any individual lawyer. Fees go into a common pot from which compensation to firm lawyers is allocated according to systematic estimation of the quantity and quality of services the lawyers render for the clientele. This method of compensation presupposes that there are significant differences among lawyers in their technical skills. Thus compensation is based on technical professional merit rather than affinity with clients. In the Cravath firm, the senior partner, Paul Cravath, in fact was by far the most successful in attracting clients and was dominant in the firm's management, circumstances that facilitated the operation of the system.[101] In effect, Cravath was an employer of other lawyers whom he recruited and continually evaluated and who were then promoted to partnership if they met his exacting standards. In legal form, however, the firm was a traditional partnership, although larger than other firms.

Because compensation in the new model law firm is based on technical proficiency rather than ability to attract clients, recruitment and apprenticeship of young lawyers proceeds on a very different basis than in the traditional law firm. In the new model, it is not determinative whether an apprentice has family connections or other means of attracting clients. Conversely, it is critically relevant whether an apprentice has technical proficiency and the capacity to develop higher proficiency. This shift in focus in turn means that the new model law firms evaluate potential recruits on the basis of merit. "Merit" is manifested by strong academic performance in law school and in the university before that, and by personal traits such as high energy, ability to concentrate, assertiveness, and ability to instill confidence in clients.

The economic organization of the new model law firm facilitates the specialization of lawyers within the firm. Firm lawyers can concentrate in different legal fields—for example, corporation law or commercial law—without being inhibited by fear that they would not share in the fees being generated by their work. A lawyer in the new model firm also does not need to worry whether he can handle a legal problem outside of his field of specialization. When a client with whom the lawyer has a relationship presents such a problem, he can simply refer it to another lawyer in the firm who specializes in that field.

The new model firm thus was an organization based on differentiated functions, a hierarchical structure (senior partners guiding and reviewing the work of subordinates), specialization of fields of practice, and personnel recruited and promoted on the basis of technical skill and performance. In short, the new model law firm is a modern bureaucracy, although smaller in scale than most government and corporate bureaucracies. A further result is that, in general, these efficiencies resulted in larger financial returns for lawyers in large-firm practice.[102]

Not coincidentally, the new model law firm is well adapted to providing increasingly specialized legal services required by increasingly complex business corporations. Hence in modern law practice the large law firm is primarily engaged in providing legal services to relatively large business organizations rather than small business proprietorships and individuals.[103]

The new model law firm developed in the United States in the period before World War II and even more rapidly thereafter. By 1970 there were firms in the new model in all large American cities, and many of them opened branches in Europe, the Eastern European countries, Russia, the Middle East, and Japan. The English solicitor firms undertook similar expansion, becoming even more aggressive in the 1990s, taking advantage in the European Community of directives that open all EU countries to professional practitioners licensed in another EU country.[104] The new model is now established in continental Europe and Asia, chiefly by merger of old-line small firms in those regions.[105] In Latin America, particularly Brazil, Argentina, and Mexico, there has been a somewhat slower pattern of development. In those countries the transformation from agricultural economy to modern production occurred much more recently, since 1950, and much more rapidly. The "traditional" forms of practice therefore have been more suddenly engulfed by larger metropolitan law firms servicing the new, explosively growing economies in these countries.

Inevitably, the differences in the modern law firm's organizational characteristics from the classic solo or small-firm practice pose special problems of legal ethics.

Persistent Grievances, Early Regulation

Grievances about lawyers are found in the Bible.[106] In early modern Europe, grievances are recorded in the earliest annals of public affairs, some dating back to the thirteenth century. In dynastic China, advocates were disparagingly referred to as *songgun*—tricksters.[107] The types of grievance have a remarkable consistency, in that statements of grievance from one location or historical period are virtually identical to statements in other locations and periods. The persistent grievances can be classified into the following general categories:

- abuse of litigation in various ways, including using dilatory tactics and false evidence and making frivolous arguments to the courts;
- preparation of false documentation, such as false deeds, contracts, or wills;
- deceiving clients and other persons and misappropriating property;
- procrastination in dealings with clients; and
- charging excessive fees.

So also regulations attempting to suppress lawyer misconduct have taken repetitive forms. One form of regulation is an oath of office. A lawyer's oath of office is a formal promise, sometimes in detail, to observe the ethical obligations of the profession. Lawyers in modern systems take such an oath, and in some circumstances the terms of the oath are subject to legal enforcement. An early example is the oath imposed on advocates in the church courts in the thirteenth century. The terms of the oath, as translated by James Brundage, suggest the ethical deviations that the oath was designed to control:

- He would faithfully execute the duties of an advocate;
- He would withhold his services from clients with unjust, desperate, or unconscionable cases;
- He would refrain from advancing [contentions] that were malicious or merely dilatory;
- He would not unnecessarily prolong proceedings before the courts;
- He would not instruct witnesses, suborn perjury, put false documents into evidence, or produce witnesses he knew to be lying;
- If he discovered that his client, his witnesses, or any of his documents were untruthful, he would so inform the court.[108]

It can be noticed that the obligations in this oath refer to the role of advocate, as distinct from legal counselor. In general, ethical norms for lawyers have focused on the role of advocate, as contrasted with office practice. This focus no doubt results from the fact that the courts have prescribed the oaths and are naturally concerned with obligations owed to the judiciary, whatever obligations the advocate might owe to clients or other parties.

For England in the medieval period the pattern is explained in a study by Jonathan Rose, who identifies the following catalogue of grievances from a thirteenth-century statutory regulation, Statute of Westminster I, chap. 29 (1375):

- deceit and collusion on the part of advocates, through forgery, false allegations, and the like, resulting in deception of the court or of opposing parties;
- bribery of and collusion with court clerks and officers;
- conspiring with real or spurious clients to foment unjustified litigation (offenses known in English law as maintenance, champerty, and barratry);
- extortion by threat of legal proceedings; and
- acting purportedly for a client but without authority, abandoning clients and cheating clients in various ways, including charging excessive fees.[109]

From the London Ordinance of 1280, Rose identifies other forms of lawyers' misconduct in the courts of the City of London, including conflict of interest by representing both sides in a dispute, or representing one party and then abandoning that client to represent the opposing party. In medieval times this vice was charmingly called "ambidexterity." In Italy in the medieval and early Renaissance periods, and in other countries, there was a similar pattern.[110]

Forms of regulation appearing in the late medieval period include the following:

- statutory prohibition of specified forms of misconduct, enforceable with penal sanctions;
- judicial control through the sanctions such as contempt of court;
- restriction of those admitted to practice on the basis of qualifications of competence and integrity;
- exercise of disciplinary authority by organizations of the legal profession, including the power to expel a lawyer from practice or to request the courts to do so (disbarment); and
- in exceptional circumstances, imposition of civil liability for malpractice.

These forms of regulation continue to be employed in the modern context.

The changes in the structure of business enterprise largely corresponded to the changes in the state, except they were smaller and more decentralized. Again at varying rates and to varying degrees, businesses grew in scale, and larger businesses came to be bureaucratically organized.

2

The Roles of Judge and Lawyer

Differences in Roles

While judges and lawyers are interdependent, there is at the same time deep conflict between the roles they perform. The relationship can accurately be described as symbiotic, in that the two roles are intensively interactive.

The structure of this conflicted relationship has had remarkable continuity in the Western tradition since the fourteenth century. By that time, the church courts had evolved a highly sophisticated procedure, which in turn became a model for the secular courts in most countries of Europe. James Brundage states the basic elements of that procedure:

- petition by the grievant, in writing;
- citation to appear directed to defendant;
- upon defendant's appearance, specific allegations by the plaintiff;
- legal objections and contentions;
- proofs by plaintiff and defendant, including testimony and possibly documents; and
- final arguments by the advocates.[1]

The same basic elements appear in modern procedure. For example, the 1994 report of the project for Approximation of Judiciary Law in the European Union sets them forth as follows: citation of defendant to appear; statement of claim; rulings on legal objections; proofs presented by the parties; final argument; and judgment.[2] These elements are essentially the same as those in late medieval canon law procedure.

In this system of procedure the lawyers take the initial steps. More precisely, the lawyer for the plaintiff takes the initial steps of consulting with the client, deliberating about strategy and tactics, drafting and presenting to the court the plaintiff's statement of claim, and then seeing to the issuance of notice (summons) to the defendant. The defendant, if he wants to defend and can afford to do so, consults a lawyer, who deliberates about strategy and tactics on the defendant's behalf and then submits some kind of response. The judge will become engaged at this point or, in some legal systems, at an earlier point when the complaint is filed. From that stage, judge and advocates interact to examine the case and move toward its resolution. In common law systems, the initiative traditionally has rested with the lawyers to move the case along, for example, by making motions and objections addressing the opposite side. In a civil law system, the initiative to move the case rests primarily with the judge. In all systems, however, the litigation process is a three-way interaction.

The interaction of judge and lawyers in a procedure with this structure is designed to yield a just result. But in the pursuit of this objective the roles of judges and lawyers are very different. Their roles are cooperative in that judge and lawyers function according to mutually understood rules, conventions, and practices. However, their responsibilities are in fundamental conflict in that each lawyer aims to achieve success for his own client, necessarily to the disadvantage of the opposing client, while the judge aims to find justice somewhere in between.

A conscientious judge aims at deciding a controversy according to the most accurate practicable assessment of the facts and most technically accurate conception of the law. To make an accurate assessment of the facts, the judge should be familiar with all of the relevant evidence, including gradations and nuances that may help the court interpret ambiguous or contradictory evidence. To make an accurate assessment of the law, the judge should know not only the literal terms of the law but also its history, purpose, and previous applications. Civil law systems have a different attitude toward precedent than do common law countries, but in both systems it is important that the judge know how a legal rule has been previously interpreted. Fundamentally, the judge wants to reach a result that is technically in accord with governing law and, if possible, a result that also is just in a moral sense.

A conscientious advocate has a different objective. Simply stated, an advocate's objective in a litigated dispute is to obtain the best possible result for the client in light of the evidence and subject to the requirements and limitations of the law. The Japanese code of ethics, Article 7, puts the advocate's responsibility clearly but indirectly: "An attorney shall not disregard the discovery of truth as a result of being overly concerned with the outcome of the matter." No advocate in any legal system can "disregard" the discovery of truth, to use the Japanese term, and indeed wants to be fully acquainted with indisputable facts and with highly persuasive evidence. An advocate cannot make unfavorable evidence "go away," except by using unethical and unlawful means. Indisputable facts therefore are a constraint with which an advocate must deal. Advocates in all systems are also "concerned with the outcome," for a favorable outcome—one as favorable as the facts and law will permit—is what an advocate is employed to accomplish. The rules in some systems more directly authorize vigorous partisanship by an advocate on behalf of a client. The American rule, for example, uses the term "zeal." [3]

From time to time there is criticism and anguish concerning this concept of the advocate's role. In the United States for the past several decades, and in other countries from time to time, debate over this issue has been intense. The criticism in essence is that the advocate, being committed to achieving the best possible result for the client, thereby commits his professional efforts, and indeed his soul, to causes that are "unjust," or worse, causes that he "knows" are unjust.

There is no question that some advocates in some cases achieve results that they themselves would consider unjust. This is true in the minimal sense that most advocates have been involved in a lawsuit against an opponent who simply failed to present the other side of the dispute effectively, or who fell below a minimum of professional competence in attempting to do so. Most practitioners can recall the peculiar sensation they have felt when an opponent has failed to present strong available evidence that should have been presented, or has failed to make a legal argument that could well have prevailed. The sensation is a mixture of relief, thankfulness, and sadness. The advocate feels relief because any litigated case can result in a loss, and the advocate who wins because of an opponent's ineptitude realizes he has escaped a loss, but not by reason of his own merit. Thankfulness is for the good luck that has come his way but which he did not deserve. Sadness ensues in the realization that the administration of justice has demonstrated its imperfection, not for the first time or the last time, through an opponent's blunder. The failure of the system is indeed a social tragedy, and a professional one for a conscientious advocate.

Contemporary criticism of partisan advocacy has been most intense in American academic circles, where a comparison is sometimes made to the more "civilized" or "justice-oriented" system of civil law. In some of this criticism, it is imagined that justice in the civil law systems is the product of conscientious, truth-seeking judges before whom the advocates and litigants submissively await the judge's discernment of truth and justice. It is envisioned that the adversary system of the common law is, in contrast, a game of hide-and-seek in which clever advocates maneuver to deceive each other and the court. In such a comparison the civil law system is obviously superior. Administration of justice in civil law systems may sometimes approximate the imagined ideal, at least in some countries. However, in our opinion this comparison of civil law procedure with common law procedure is a misleading comparison of an idealized judge-centered system with a crudely disparaged adversary system.[4] The realities are more complex.

In the first place, the advocates in most civil law systems are as intensely partisan as common law advocates. Their unashamed aim is to win, devil take the loser. They would consider it absurd for an advocate to worry whether his client's cause is just as long as it is legally admissible. They generally would agree with Robert Gordon's summary of the attitude of American advocates: "a specialized role-morality of fidelity to the goals and interests of clients that absolves the lawyers of personal accountability. . . ."[5] They believe that in the judge-centered system questions of truth and justice are, according to the law and to long-established tradition, the responsibility of the court. Judges usually hold the same view. Civil law judges typically are unsympathetic to the role of the advocates. The judicial viewpoint in civil law systems is that the judges seek to do justice, but only within the framework of the legal controversy as defined by the advocates, and perhaps in the teeth of obstructions by the advocates.

The strength of these attitudes on the part of civil law professionals probably is magnified by the fact that, in civil law procedure, the forensic powers of the advocates are limited. So far as facts are concerned, the civil law advocate is very largely dependent on the judge's conception of the relevance of the evidence. In some systems, notably in France, Germany, and the Jewish religious court (*Beit Din*), the judge may exercise initiative to develop issues for consideration beyond those preferred by the advocates. In other civil law systems, however, the judge strictly confines his attention to the issues in the pleadings and takes no initiative to extend the inquiry. This limited judicial responsibility is established in the codes of civil procedure and is mirrored in the concept of *principio dispositivo*, explained below, which defines the responsibilities of the advocates.

Under the rules of ethics in most civil law countries, an advocate supposedly cannot seek out or interview witnesses before trial. In some systems the advocates adhere to this restriction, merely nominating witnesses for consideration by the judge and suggesting questions to be asked. However, the intensity of the questioning depends on the judge. In many civil law systems the advocates may not directly address questions to witnesses. If the judge considers the questions to be relevant, the party's "right to proof" requires that the substance of the questions be asked. An advocate has no right to require the judge to pursue questioning beyond addressing issues framed by the pleadings. In some civil law systems, such as Japan's, the advocates are permitted cross-examination. In others they may ask questions directly of the witnesses, but the idea of cross-examination is alien.

In contrast, in common law systems the responsibility for searching out, organizing, and presenting proof is the advocates'. (In common law systems where there is a division between the solicitors and barristers, as in England, organizing the proof is the responsibility of the solicitors on each side, while presenting the proof is the responsibility of the barristers.) As a concomitant of these responsibilities, the advocates usually are immediately aware of the nuances, weaknesses, and potential force of items of potential evidence. The advocates present the evidence by selecting the documents and witnesses to be offered on their respective sides, usually determining the sequence of proof and formulating the substance and sequence of questioning the witnesses. Cross-examination of opposing witnesses by the advocates is a matter of procedural right and can be deeply probing. The body of evidence on which the court bases its decision is thus the product of an intense interaction between the advocates.

The dynamic of the common law adversary system has several implications for justice. First, the advocates share responsibility—indeed have primary responsibility—for the evidence on which the court will decide a dispute. This responsibility has personal moral implications. A common law advocate cannot say that an outcome was simply the work of the judge or "the system." Second, the advocates in a common law system are required as a practical matter to cooperate with each other throughout the case. In the American system of broad and often extended pretrial discovery, the interaction between opposing advocates is even longer and more intense. This pattern of "involuntary cooperation" between common law advocates commences with the exchange of documents and the scheduling of depositions. It also requires the advocates to meet with each other, outside the presence of the judge, to work out the exchange of evidence and to arrange schedules for resolving preliminary matters. In contrast, in the civil law system the advocates ordinarily deal with each other wholly through correspondence and by filing and counterfiling documents. They encounter each other directly only at hearings in court.

So far as law is concerned, the civil law presumes that the judge knows the law, a presumption that is expressed in the Latin brocard *jura novit curia*. This presumption devolves into a dynamic in some civil law systems in which the lawyers' arguments are regarded by the court as expostulations rather than expositions. The judges in some civil law systems often consider the briefs submitted by the advocates to be supererogation. In other civil law systems, notably those of Germany and France, the advocates are permitted and expected to make substantial legal expositions to the court in opening statements and, in some systems, in closing remarks as well.

Judges in the French and German systems typically maintain tight control over the progress of a case, whereas judges in the Italian and Ibero-American systems play a more passive role. In any event, the advocates cannot be sure what evidence the judge regards as especially relevant and therefore what issues should be addressed in their briefs. The style and demeanor in advocacy also varies in civil law systems. In some systems the lawyers are expected to be concise and to the point, while in others they are allowed to make long-winded orations. These expectations reflect attitudes embedded in national cultures.

In contrast, in the common law adversary systems, briefs submitted by the advocates define the legal contentions the court is to consider, although

THE ROLES OF JUDGE AND LAWYER

the judge has authority to consider and to inquire into additional legal issues. The advocates on both sides are aware that the frameworks they present can be decisive.

Whether in a civil law system or one in the common law, however, conscientious and reflective advocates recognize that the administration of justice involves the tragedy of unjust outcomes. Some lawyers are content to shrug off unjust outcomes as being simply unavoidable or the luck of circumstance. In doing so they are being morally callous and socially obtuse. However, the fact that many lawyers are morally callous does not mean that they are wrong in concluding that unjust results in the administration of justice are unavoidable consequences and that the work of lawyers often contributes to the consequences.

Not all lawyers are equally competent, and many lawyers, alas, are relatively incompetent. The blunt truth is that some decisions by the courts result from the fact that the advocate for one side was more clever, more steadfast, more patient, more diligent, or simply had a better day than the opponent. Moreover, in legal systems where a client can engage a lawyer for a fee, clients with more money, other things being equal, are more likely to have better lawyers than clients who have little money or none.

The difficult question in legal ethics is not whether the tragedy of unjust judgments can occur. Certainly unjust judgments occur every day, everywhere in the world. Injustice in the administration of justice—in the work of judges and lawyers—is systemic, meaning that it is an inevitable aspect of the system. The difficult question is what can be done about it. Unfortunately, in our estimate there are only limited means of amelioration. However, because the means of amelioration are modest, serious and sustained effort should be made to achieve whatever amelioration is practicable.

Office Lawyering

The same kind of tragedy can occur in office practice. For example, the lawyer for one side in a negotiation may realize that the proposed structure for a business transaction has very favorable tax consequences for his client but severely adverse consequences for the other client; and the lawyer also may realize that the opposite side does not appreciate these facts. Or the lawyer for the buyer of a real estate parcel may know that the parcel is likely to become very valuable if a certain public works project is approved, knows that the public project is likely to be approved in the near future, and recognizes that the seller does not know these facts. Or the lawyer for a spouse may know that his client intends to leave the marriage and seek divorce but that the other spouse has no suspicion of that fact, while the spouses are planning important financial matters. One of us had a consultation with a lawyer whose opposite number was about to agree to a contract clause that seemed favorable to the opposite side, but which the inquiring lawyer knew was legally invalid. Should the opposing lawyer be told of this? Was it relevant that the other side was being very oppressive in the negotiations?

The office lawyer in each of these situations might bring about a different course of events if he were representing the other side of the transaction. Moreover, the office lawyer often is involved in transactions in which the party on the other side is not legally represented. In modern law practice, many office lawyers draft form contracts that will be employed repeatedly in other transactions, such as leases for residential apartments, sales contracts for automobiles and home appliances, and the contracts that govern the modern form of money called credit cards. Every ordinary citizen in a developed economy routinely participates in such standardized transactions. Usually customers simply sign documents put forward by the corporate employee on the other side, sometimes wondering about the meaning and significance of the provisions in the documents. Under typical company procedures, employees who deal with customers have no authority to modify a standard form document and would refuse a request to do so.

The standard form document is drafted by an office lawyer for the corporate party, on terms typically as favorable to the company as the law permits. For example, if the law limits the amount of interest a company may charge, the lawyer may insert a clause providing for some kind of transaction fee that in economic terms effectively increases the rate of interest paid by the customer. If the law provides that a disappointed purchaser can sue the corporate party, the lawyer may insert a clause requiring that, before bringing suit, the purchaser must make a formal demand for redress within a specified time after the transaction, such as fifteen days. The lawyer and his client know that most customers will not be sufficiently alert to comply with such a "notice requirement," and they also know that failure to comply with the requirement can be an effective defense if a lawsuit is attempted by an aggrieved purchaser.

Of course, the office lawyer for the corporation also is aware that regulations have been adopted to combat or neutralize onerous contract provisions. These regulations are commonly called consumer protection legislation, much of which proliferated in the twentieth century. Similar regulations aim at protecting small businesspeople and artisans and workers in various occupations. Legislatures and government agencies have devised these neutralizing regulations in ongoing interactions with businesses, which in turn formulate new self-protective contract provisions.

The neutralizing regulatory provisions are of course drafted by lawyers employed by the government. The same interactive pattern appears in other fields of social activity, among them: land use by private owners, on one hand, and promulgation of land use controls by government, on the other hand; industrial effluent emissions from factories owned by manufacturing companies and, in response, environmental controls by government; maneuvers in corporate governance by capitalist entrepreneurs and, in response, regulatory measures requiring corporate financial disclosures.

The dialectic between private business initiative and government regulatory initiative goes on. The strategists are business executives on one side and politicians on the other. The tacticians include lawyers on both sides.

Complex and serious questions are presented as to whether and on what terms the office lawyer tacticians in these interactions have legal, professional, and moral responsibility for the results of their efforts. Debate addressing these questions has been intense in the United States, for essentially two reasons. First, in the United States (as compared with Europe and Japan), lawyers are much more salient participants in the entrepreneur-regulatory interaction because of the peculiar "legalistic" structure of American government. In the United States, therefore, lawyers will be blamed or commended for their interactive maneuvers, whereas in Europe and Japan responsibility will more likely be attributed directly to the companies and the ministries. Second, in the United States, particularly since the 1960s, there has been strong antibusiness sentiment among many law school faculties. This sentiment is widely expressed in academic scholarship concerning the legal profession.

In the foregoing respects there is substantial similarity in the roles of judges on one hand, and advocates and office lawyers on the other hand, in all modern legal systems. However, there are differences in professional career patterns between the common law systems and those of the civil law—differences that have subtle consequences. In general, there is greater professional affinity between judges and lawyers in the common law systems.

The differences in the career paths between civil law and common law systems begin in the recruitment and training of law curriculum graduates. In civil law systems, university graduates typically enter the judicial career path at or soon after graduation. In most common law systems, judges are drawn from the ranks of the legal profession. Accordingly, virtually all common law judges have had prior experience as lawyers. There are variations of these basic patterns. Argentina, for example, is a federal system in which most judges in the national system are career civil servants, but judges in the state courts typically take the bench in their senior years after careers in law practice. Other civil law systems also have pathways from law practice to the bench. In some systems former judges are permitted to assume law practice. These variations influence the degree of affiliation between the judges and lawyers in a given system.

The judicial training system in some civil law systems is intensive and effective. For example, in Germany, apprenticeship (*Referendariatzeit*) is two years for candidates for all branches of the profession—the judiciary, private practice, *notaire*, and public service. The German candidate judge therefore will have an apprenticeship in the office of a prosecutor or a private lawyer, along with his judicial apprenticeship, before becoming a junior judge. The apprentices in the German system receive a living-wage stipend, take technical courses in a broad range of subjects, and must pass a demanding final examination. A similar system has been recommended in other countries but is resisted on account of its expense. The system is questioned in Germany itself as an inappropriate subsidy.

In France, the system is similar but imposes an even sharper division between judges and lawyers:

Judging ... is a separate profession with a separate career path. Although successful *avocats* have sometimes in the past become magistrates ... today the great majority of magistrates start out as magistrates in their twenties. They usually attend law school but then—instead of joining prospective *avocats* in their postgraduate education ... they attend a special magistrates' school, the Ecole Nationale de la Magistrature in Bordeaux.[6]

Upon graduation from the Ecole de Magistrature, the candidate in the French system becomes either one of the "sitting judges" (*magistrats du siège*) who hear and decide cases, or one of the "standing judges" or prosecutors as they would be called in common law systems. Judges of the administrative courts are trained in the Ecole Nationale d'Administration. In some civil law systems, those of Italy and China, for example, a university graduate can become a junior judge by passing the judicial qualification examination without doing an apprenticeship or attending a special institute.

In most civil law systems, a judge for his entire career is a member of a statewide judicial bureaucracy that encompasses his life. Judges usually have no professional relationships with lawyers except as they meet in court, and rarely have social relationships with lawyers. Their relationship to the broader community is more or less monastic. The career advancement of a civil law judge to more senior positions in the judicial hierarchy is determined by evaluations conducted by more senior peers in the court system. In some systems the judge's salary has increments based on seniority in the system, regardless of rank in the hierarchy.

In contrast, common law judges are recruited from the ranks of advocates and become judges at about age forty, on the basis of a superior or at least a satisfactory first career as a lawyer. Accordingly, common law judges know how a legal dispute appears from the viewpoint of an advocate and perhaps also from the viewpoint of an office lawyer. Most common law judges maintain professional ties to the practicing bar, for example by participating in bar association meetings in various ways. Retired judges in the common law systems of Australia and the United States, although not in England, may return to law practice if they wish, and some do so.[7] They may also maintain social relationships with lawyers, although on a limited and guarded basis. Most of them remember what they learned as lawyers about the contingencies and ambiguities of litigation. They realize that the principal difference between a judge and an advocate is the side of the bench on which they are located and the fact that a judge has decisional authority conferred by the state. As observed by Justice Robert Jackson of the U.S. Supreme Court (who himself had long years of experience as a lawyer): "We [judges] are not final because we are infallible, but infallible because we are final."[8]

The difference in roles between that of judge and that of advocate in a civil law system is illustrated historically in the development of the legal profession in Prussia before the emergence of modern Germany. In early eighteenth-century Prussian procedure, the judge alone conducted "inquiry" into civil disputes; lawyers were not permitted. In 1781, subordinate law-trained persons were allowed to cooperate with the judges in a role of "public servant." A half-century later, in 1846, the Prussian law was reformed to recognize the office of lawyer, but it was an office with very limited powers and standing. Only in 1878, after German unification, was legal advocacy in the modern sense recognized at the national level, a recognition coinciding with a major reform in the code of civil procedure.[9]

In most civil law systems there is little possibility for a lawyer to become a judge, although some civil law systems require potential judges to serve an apprenticeship as a lawyer. In some systems, such as Japan's, strong performance in law school is necessary for entry into a judicial career and continues to be an important element of a judge's subsequent professional evaluations. There is also little possibility for a civil law judge to become a lawyer in the later stages of a career. Accordingly, in most civil law systems neither judges nor lawyers even imagine having a professional life in the other branch of the profession. Their professional selves and "life plans" are irrevocably committed to the branch of the profession in which they begin. Lawyers who have not been successful in their vocation often are envious, not only of other lawyers who have been more successful, but also of judges. The parallel opinion held by most judges is that lawyers, except those who are conspicuously successful, are intellectually and morally inferior. These career constraints and attitudes contribute to a sense of mutual isolation between civil law judges and civil law lawyers.

Role Conflict

The conflict between the roles of judge and lawyer is evident in all systems. In a case coming before a court, the judge cannot know all that the lawyers know. In particular, the judge cannot be present at the private discussions between the clients and their respective advocates, nor can the judge be informed of these discussions for, as we shall see, the discussions between client and lawyer are protected by rules that maintain strict confidence for them.

No one could suppose that a client giving testimony in court would be more forthcoming in that milieu than in previously discussing the same matter in her lawyer's chambers. In the presence of the judge, the client inevitably will be much more guarded and self-justifying. Furthermore, an advocate may sometimes discover crucial information from a source other than the client, but which the opposing side has not discovered—for example, an independent witness to a transaction or a scientific report relevant to the issues in dispute.

With few exceptions, the advocate has a duty to keep all such information confidential. Correlatively, the advocate has no duty to inform the court or opposing counsel, except as procedural rules may require disclosure after litigation has commenced. This secretive posture is inherent in the function of advocates in both the common law and civil law systems, and is probably more pronounced in the civil law systems. In those systems the lawyers have relatively weak affirmative powers in conducting litigation, so the negative power of professional secrecy is correspondingly more important. In any event, the result in both civil law and common law systems is that the judge will lack some information, perhaps crucial information, that one advocate or the other could have submitted but has withheld.

The same disparity in information can arise between the court and an office lawyer—that is, a lawyer who has structured a transaction through legal documentation. The disparity here can be even greater than in a court proceeding. An office lawyer sometimes can structure a transaction to avoid the application of the legal rules that otherwise would apply. For example, the lawyer for the seller of goods may structure a sales transaction so that formal completion of the sale occurs in some other country and thus is governed by that country's more favorable laws. The documentation may require adjudication of disputes in some other country or by arbitration.[10] The judge in the "home" country never even sees the transaction and has no occasion to realize that the substance of the transaction occurred locally.

The difference in information between what judges can see and what lawyers know is inherent in their roles and pervasive in its effects. Judges are supposed to find the truth somewhere among the presentations by the parties. Advocates are supposed to make presentations that are as one-sidedly favorable to their respective clients as is permitted by the indisputable facts and the incontrovertible inferences. However, both judges and lawyers understand that the possibility of discovering the truth is limited, often severely limited. The limitations arising from the common law adversary system are obvious and have been often explored.[11] The limitations under the judge-centered systems of the civil law are perhaps less obvious but are nevertheless real.

In the civil law systems, the judge's objective is not "the whole truth" but "procedural truth" or *verità processuale.* The term refers to the "truth" that will emerge from the judicial process: The court seeks truth, but only such truth as can be discerned through adherence to procedural regularity. Procedural truth is recognized as being at best an imitation or approximation of actual truth. The judge's full access to the truth is impeded by limitations on the types and sources of evidence that the judge is allowed to pursue under the rules of procedure; by disparity in the competence of the advocates; by disparity in the ability of the litigants to employ competent counsel; by sheer accidents in the preparation and presentation of the evidence; by other accidents such as the date of the trial (one party or the other may be having a bad day on that date, for example). In a constitutional regime the judge's discernment is obstructed by the legal rules of the attorney-client privilege and the lawyer's duty of confidentiality. Moreover, a legal culture's acceptance of the concept of *verità processuale* can become a self-fulfilling prophecy and a justification for indifference to procedures that would get closer to the real truth.[12]

Advocates in civil law systems consider that they have a right and obligation to use lawful procedural means to resist inquiry that would reveal evidence adverse to their clients. The concept is that of *principio dispositivo* (in Italian), *principe dispositif* (in French), or *Dispositionsprinzip* (in German). Strictly speaking, the concept is that the court is responsible for disposing of the matter on the basis of proofs presented by the parties in accordance with procedural law. As interpreted by advocates, however, the concept means that they have no responsibility concerning truth except to comply with procedural obligations. Moreover, those obligations are interpreted narrowly and hence can justify what is effectively obstruction of inquiry. The exercise of judicial initiative to explore new evidence is regarded as an intrusion into the lawyer's sphere of responsibility. Correlatively, the narrow concept of judicial responsibility frees the judge from obligation to go beyond the terms of dispute as it has been framed by the advocates. Many common law judges and lawyers have a similar attitude.

As a result of these attitudes, judges in both systems often confront "stonewalling" by advocates on both sides—dogmatic assertions and intransigent denials where neither side is willing to concede the slightest nuance lest it be taken as a fatal concession. In common law jury trials, contradictory narratives can be given to the jury to resolve. In the civil law systems, and in nonjury trials in common law, judges may confront diametrically opposed versions of the relevant events. In such circumstances, the judges may resort to some basis for a decision that neither side has asserted. This *terza via* (third way) evades the contentions on behalf of the parties and therefore is an indirect subversion of the right to be heard. But such an escape by the court is understandable where the advocate's arguments have simply passed each other without confronting the difficulties and uncertainties in the evidence.

Somewhat similar limitations can frustrate a judge's ability to discern and apply the proper rules of law. Judges vary in their legal experience and acuity. Simply put, some judges are not particularly perceptive, diligent, or careful. In some situations, a judge may be called on to decide a case in which one or both of the advocates are specialists who know much more about the relevant law. These and other deficiencies can limit a judge's ability to apply the appropriate legal rules. However, it is our belief that this limitation is much less severe than the difference between judges and advocates concerning access to evidence.

Both the judge and the advocates therefore can be at positions remote from ideal justice in a legal dispute. The judge is remote because he cannot fully discern the discrepancies between truth and mere evidence and between ideal justice and mere legal right. The advocates are remote because they cannot know (although they often suspect) that there are similar discrepancies on the other side and because of their duties of loyalty and confidentiality to their respective clients.

The remoteness of the judges and lawyers from ideal justice is probably greater in many civil law systems than in most common law systems, for the reasons already suggested. Chief among these causes are the career-centered character of the judiciary and the distant and relatively impotent position of the advocates. Another cause, both more fundamental and more elusive, is the skeptical attitude in a specific local culture toward the ideas of "justice" and "truth." In many "Latin" civil law systems (those of Italy, Spain, Ibero-America), judges and lawyers are deeply skeptical about achieving justice through the legal process. In any event, all systems of justice in the real world will sometimes fail to arrive at the decisions that would be made by an all-knowing God. Humankind is simply incapable of achieving that divine justice.

Quite beyond the significance of career paths and rules of ethics is the practical significance of the "legal manpower" available in a system—the number of judges and lawyers, particularly the ratio of judges to lawyers. Since the civil law system is "judge-centered," it is not surprising that the ratio of judges to lawyers in many civil law systems is large in comparison with that in common law systems. There is also a substantial contrast among legal systems in the rich Western countries—for example, France, Germany, and Italy, where there is one judge for every six lawyers, and poorer countries where the ratio is similar but there are fewer of both judges and lawyers. In rich common law systems such as England and the United States, the corresponding ratio is on the order of one to fifty.[13] In legal systems lacking a substantial cadre of lawyers, the importance of the judges is obviously even greater. In Russia in 1998, for example, there were about 15,000 judges but only about 32,000 advocates.[14] No doubt the ratio of judges to lawyers is even greater in less economically developed regimes.

This quantitative difference is an important "environmental" influence on how the judicial systems in these countries function. It is virtually inevitable that the Germany judiciary, for example, would carry greater responsibility in developing and resolving legal disputes than the judiciary in England. As Judge Posner has observed, "a high ratio of judges to lawyers enables judges to do more in cases relative to what lawyers do—to be more active and investigative."[15]

However, enablement is one thing, fulfillment something else. Many judges in many civil law systems function like tired and indifferent bureaucrats, as of course do some judges in common law systems. Judges in the civil law systems traditionally sat in panels of three, a practice that reduced the number of cases each judge could undertake. In recent years, however, the expense of maintaining the judiciary has led Germany and several other civil law systems to assign a single judge to hear each case, except in cases of unusual importance. Similar contrasts in "legal resources" exist among other civil law and common law systems.

The contrast is more poignant among economically less advanced countries, whether those of the civil law or the common law family. These countries all have serious public finance problems, and their financial privation is a disabling influence on their judicial systems.[16] A colleague of ours, reporting about the court system of a developing country in Africa, sadly remarked that it simply has no "infrastructure"—no clerks, no law books, no typewriters. And no prospect of improvement. The result of poor financing can be exaggeration of the difference between justice available to the wealthy, who can hire lawyers, and justice available to the ordinary citizens, who have resort only to overworked and understaffed courts. One of us observed the proceedings of a court in an underdeveloped country where a man was sent to prison by a court with one court clerk, no legal counsel, a judge without training in the law, and a record consisting only of the indictment.

The differences in the responsibilities of the judge and the advocates in the administration of justice are reflected in corresponding differences in the ethical concepts and rules governing judges and those governing lawyers. This book addresses lawyers' ethics, but notice should be taken of the rules of judicial ethics.[17] The differences between judicial ethics and lawyers' ethics can be stated in terms of the antinomies in Table 1.

TABLE 1
The Ethical Responsibilities of Judge and Advocate Compared

Judge	Advocate
Is impartial between disputing parties	Represents one party
Is independent from influences	Is loyal to client
Displays impartiality	Displays commitment to client
Declines to serve in a case in which impartiality might reasonably be questioned	Declines to serve in a case in which loyalty to a client might reasonably be questioned
Serves as a public official	Is an advocate for private parties or a public prosecutor; as such is both an advocate for the state and an officer of the court
Allocates efforts among various official duties as judge	Devotes all professional effort to clients
Attends to information submitted to court through regular procedure	Attends to all information, whatever its source, relevant to client's matter
Maintains confidentiality of information not publicly disclosed in court	Maintains confidentiality of all information relating to client
Refrains from using information acquired as a judge for private gain	Refrains from using information acquired as a lawyer to the disadvantage of the client

The role characteristics of judge and advocate can be summarized by saying that impartiality is the fundamental ethical concept in the judicial role, while loyalty to client is the corresponding concept for lawyers. A judge should be subjectively impartial. That is, a judge should exercise self-discipline to avoid favoring the rich over the poor, the powerful (including government officials) over the weak, and local citizens over foreigners; and a judge should avoid favoritism based on race, gender, or religious affiliation. However, because it is impossible by objective evidence to determine whether a judge is subjectively impartial, legal standards of impartiality necessarily refer to observable behavior. Judges' behavior can be scrutinized for indications of favoritism or partiality—for example, friendship with one of the lawyers or one of the parties to a dispute, or familiarity with the facts in dispute.

It is universally prescribed that a judge may not preside in a dispute involving members of his family or near relatives, involving people with whom the judge has had substantial or recent personal dealings, or involving people who previously were clients of the judge or clients of a law firm with which the judge was affiliated (in countries where judges may have practiced law before assuming judicial office). For the same reason, a judge should not preside in a case involving a person who had been instrumental in the appointment of the judge (in countries where such appointments are made by an authority outside the judiciary itself). It is lamentable but unavoidable that external manifestations of bias may not in fact be correlated with actual bias. On one hand, there are judges who harbor strong prejudices that they conceal, and, on the other hand, judges who would be perfectly disinterested even though they have an affiliation with one of the litigants.

Related to the concept of impartiality is that of judicial independence. This means freedom from interference by outside influence, particularly influence of the political branches of government and from powerful economic and political interest groups. It also includes improper influence from other judges, whether members of the same court, of a court of parallel jurisdiction, or of a higher judicial authority. The extreme case of judicial partiality is the possibility that bribes or other inducements will be offered and accepted. There is also concern about the adequacy of financial and institutional support for the courts as a whole.[18] Erosion of salaries by inflation can make judges vulnerable to a temptation to takes bribes and, in the longer term, make it difficult to recruit judges of sufficient competency and integrity.[19]

The duty of impartiality can be enforced through rules requiring recusal of a judge. "Recusal" means declining or abstaining from participation in a specific case. Recusal may be either voluntary (whereby the judge withdraws from a case) or involuntary (whereby, through a motion or other procedural initiative, a demand is made that the judge withdraw). For example, a judge assigned to a case involving a close relative properly would voluntarily withdraw and have the case assigned to another judge. When a party believes a judge should withdraw but the judge has not done so, the party may take initiative to compel withdrawal.

The procedure for recusal varies among legal systems, sometimes being accomplished through a request to higher judicial authority (typical in civil law systems), sometimes a demand addressed to the judge himself (typical in common law systems).[20] Under the latter system, the commonly accepted procedure is that the motion to compel withdrawal will be referred to some judge other than the "target" judge. In the federal courts in the United States, the target determines his own recusal in the first instance. However, under any system the "target" ordinarily will know the source of the initiative to compel withdrawal. The result can be hostile relations between the judge and the lawyer, either in the immediate case or in other matters in which they are later involved. The situation brings to mind the old folktale of the church mice planning to put a bell on the neck of the rectory cat. Fine plan, but as the saying goes, "Who will bell the cat?"

Some legal systems have elaborate codes governing the circumstances under which a judge should be recused.[21] For example, Article 23 of the Code of Civil Procedure of Japan has detailed specifications of grounds for challenging impartiality and Article 24 further provides that "any party may challenge ... where there are circumstances ... which would obstruct the impartiality of a judge's decision." In Israel there is an extensive jurisprudence on the subject of judicial impartiality.[22] Most legal systems, however, function with very general rules or simply principles based on tradition. In any event, the number of cases in which the principle of impartiality is formally applied are few and unusual.[23] No doubt that is because the governing principle is well understood and honored, except, unfortunately, by some judges in some legal systems who are indifferent or corrupt.

Judicial Corruption

Judges are aware that corruption of even a few judges results in disrespect and cynicism about the integrity of the whole judiciary. In some countries most judges feel confident and protected in these respects, but in others it is common knowledge that many judges are susceptible to improper influence.[24]

The grossest improper influence is of course bribery. In some countries it is an open secret that there is widespread judicial bribery. The honest judges know of it, the lawyers know of it, and the general public holds strong suspicion. Bribery is like a cancer in that it tends to be self-regenerating and weakens the system's ability to identify, investigate, and prosecute specific instances of corruption. The attitude is that "everyone does it."

A less overt form of corruption consists of favoritism or hostility shown by judges toward certain litigants or classes of litigants or toward certain lawyers. Judges in any legal system necessarily exercise judgment and discretion in myriad functions—scheduling hearings, granting postponements, appointing special subordinate officials such as referees and trustees. These decisions can be made systematically and impartially, but they also can be made in patterns of special dispensation. Another form of corruption is the exercise of improper influence in selecting and promoting judges. In the civil law systems, judges are supposed to be appointed, evaluated, and recognized for promotion after disinterested assessments by a higher authority in the judicial system. In some systems, however, these assessments can be influenced by "judicial politics" and by political pressure from outside the judiciary.

The problem of judicial corruption has been intensively addressed in a survey by the Open Society Institute. The survey summarizes: "[T]here is a widespread perception that corruption is endemic in the judiciary of ... Bulgaria, the Czech Republic, Latvia [and other countries] ... but supervisory mechanisms to ensure judges' impartiality—such as disclosure of assets and clear rules on recusement—... are weak...." About one of the countries the survey says: "[T]he courts are widely perceived to be corrupt and that bribery is common ... including the legal profession ... in addition to the courts *per se.*"[25] We have credible information that similar conditions exist in many legal systems, particularly those in countries that are financially weak. Unfortunately, fiscal weakness often translates into financial privation for the courts, as well as for the prosecution and police, and thereby makes them susceptible to corruption.

Another form of corruption is delay resulting from indolence, insecurity, or indifference of judges. It is an old and true maxim that "justice delayed is justice denied." Yet the problem of judicial delay is as old as the maxim. The causes of delay are many and subtle, not all of them directly the fault of most of the judges. Some judges are simply lazy; many are demoralized by overwhelming caseloads or paralyzed by delay on the part of the advocates; others cannot deal with the psychological burden of making decisions. Whatever the dynamics of delay, however, for lawyers and their clients delay is a pervasive form of injustice of which the lawyers are acutely aware but which clients often are unable to comprehend. Blame for judicial delay is often shifted to the lawyers. Unfortunately, many lawyers have the same failing in this respect as the judges. Lazy and inefficient lawyers blame the courts.

In the United States the selection of most judges is an overtly political process. Most American judges are either appointed by the executive with the concurrence of the legislature (the President and the Senate for federal judges, state governors and state legislatures for state court judges), or elected by direct popular vote. Political considerations are almost invariably taken into account and often dominate the choices. For this reason, the public, the news media, and legal professionals often suspect that political favoritism is a factor in decisions by some of those selected as judges. A conspicuous example of that kind of suspicion is the reaction among many observers to the decision by the Supreme Court of the United States in *Bush v. Gore*, the dispute over the outcome of the 2000 presidential election.[26] It was said, and in some quarters believed, that the Supreme Court's decision reflected the original political affiliations of the justices.

Where judges are elected by popular vote, financial contributions to judicial election campaigns are a practical necessity. Lawyers have special knowledge about the candidates for office and therefore are strategically positioned to assist in fund-raising and election advertising. The assistance from lawyers to a candidate in a judicial election results in at least a sense of appreciation on the part of the successful candidate, which could affect the exercise of judicial functions in favor of supporters. Conscientious judges try to exclude these events from their consciousness, but cannot be completely successful in doing so. The public, the news media, and some members of the legal profession are suspicious, or at least deeply uneasy, about these relationships. However, political relationships of some kind are unavoidable as a practical matter in systems that choose judges by popular election.

In the United States, the American Bar Association has recommended a rule that would limit financial contributions by lawyers to election campaigns of judges and other officials. However, the rule as promulgated is virtually a dead letter. It prohibits a lawyer from making financial contributions where the *purpose* of a donation is to obtain preferment from the successful candidate.[27] Lawyers are consummately capable of imagining other purposes that could animate a political contribution, for example, concern that the best candidate should be selected. In debates over the rule it was openly predicted that, for this reason, violations of the rule could not be proved. Other legal systems, since they do not have elected judges, do not have to indulge similar sophistry.

Judicial corruption or favoritism, whether induced by bribery or political affiliation or personal relationship, contradicts the basic premise of a constitutional legal system, which is that matters should be adjudicated according to law and not according to the identity or standing of a litigant. Judicial favoritism, real or suspected, is a source of chronic anxiety among members of the bar in many legal systems. Since some judicial systems are known to be corrupt, an essential question in such a system is how a lawyer who is honest or disposed to be honest can function efficiently.

On this issue, the law and official norms of ethics governing lawyers' relationships with judges are essentially the same in every legal system: a lawyer must refrain from bribery, fraud, and misrepresentation and from the exploitation of judicial favoritism. But a lawyer who insists upon being scrupulously ethical in a corrupt judicial system usually will attract fewer clients and may be limited to a marginal law practice. In our observation, most lawyers wish to be honest and try to be as honest as their professional environment will permit. How does a lawyer who is disposed to be honest cope with a situation in which being honest is a serious disadvantage?

The problem faced by an honest lawyer trying to cope with a corrupt judiciary is a specific instance of the ethical problem addressed in Reinhold Niebuhr's classically titled book, *Moral Man and Immoral Society*.[28] From that broader perspective, it must be recognized fact that many people in most societies do not conduct themselves in accord with the ethical standards that are commonly professed in their community. Thus ethically inclined children are shocked to discover that outside their family environment they will encounter cheats, liars, and trimmers, and at any rate people who make utterances they do not believe and commitments they will not fulfill. Many people in adulthood remain angry and disillusioned by that experience. All adults learn that there are discrepancies between a society's professed ethics—honesty, responsibility, and the like—and what people actually do, especially when facing difficult choices.

The conflict between ethical pretense and ethical reality is vivid and immediate for lawyers. Clients come to lawyers when they encounter conflict between their rights and obligations, or are concerned that the future will bring on such conflicts. Legal process is society's ultimate mechanism to provide corrective justice. But a corrupt legal process will systematically fail to provide corrective justice and instead favor those who facilitate or indulge its corruption. The vocation of most lawyers requires direct interaction with the system. So, where the legal system is slothful or corrupt, lawyers in the system will nevertheless have to deal with it.

The fascist regime is a good example of a systemic form of corruption. The fascist regimes of Nazi Germany, Italy under Mussolini, and Franco's Spain formally adhered to a traditional system of private property, contract transactions, and the rule of law. But these regimes subverted the traditional system with pervasive secret surveillance and intervention in matters they regarded as threats to the order. Lawyers trying to practice in such regimes could confront corruption portrayed as a "new order." Concerning practice under such a regime, in Spain under Franco, an experienced lawyer observed: "Lawyers could practice normally, but had to be cautious with clients and causes that could disturb the regime." Many clients and causes could disturb an alert authoritarian regime. An efficient authoritarian regime would easily discover litigation that might "disturb" and so also transactions that could be threatening, even those conducted under shield of confidentiality. Lawyers are by nature cautious, and in such a regime normal professional practice would be considerably constrained.

One mechanism for coping with judicial sloth and corruption is simply to leave the legal profession, or to avoid it in the first place. Many morally sensitive people reject the thought of becoming lawyers, and many law graduates leave the legal profession in disgust, repelled by systemic sloth and corruption or the sophistries improvised to deal with those deficiencies. Another escape mechanism is to find a relatively safe professional haven, for example, on the legal staff of a government bureau or a corporation, or in a branch of practice far removed from the sources of ethical pollution.[29] A mechanism sometimes available to elite lawyers is to commission other lawyers to do necessary "dirty work."[30] But for most lawyers these are not available options. For various reasons—family obligations, debts, limited imagination, love of the law, hope for a better world in the years ahead—they remain in law practice. Some lawyers simply fall in line with the system.

Many people who confront moral and ethical contradictions that they cannot resolve find recourse in "denial"—maintaining optimistic belief despite strong negative evidence. So do lawyers. Thus, when confronting corruption in a judicial system, many lawyers persuade themselves that the system is "really not so bad" or plead that "no system is perfect." Another reaction is to retreat into deep cynicism, often voiced by lawyers to clients as well as colleagues. Thus lawyers say, "The judge's decision depends on what he had for breakfast,"[31] or "You never know what they will do; the law means nothing to them."[32] These expressions often are self-protective explanations, in which the lawyers are talking to themselves as well as the clients, seeking to justify why they do not achieve more favorable outcomes. But these sentiments also reflect unattractive truths about the judiciary. It is openly acknowledged within the legal profession that the outcome of litigation often can be strongly or decisively affected by the court in which it is brought. For example, local differences in dialect and culture can translate into significant influences in this direction. In litigation strategy, a key legal maneuver may be to lodge the case in a forum considered to be friendly—to secure "home court advantage" in the sports analogy. From a moral point of view, implementing such a strategy is disgusting. From a practicing lawyer's point of view, it is a matter of professional duty.

Most lawyers learn to live with their society as it is, without denial and without disabling cynicism, and with as little complicity as possible. The experience can lead to strong personal bonds among members of the profession and in efforts to reform the system. It can also lead to varieties of religious reflection and commitment.

Ethical Justification of Advocacy

In many traditional societies, judges are regarded as accountable to some higher religious authority, and the office of the judge is closely related to divine authority. Such is the concept of justice in Islamic systems, and was the concept in Europe before the modern era. Today reliance is no longer placed on divine guidance to assure impartiality and discernment on the part of judges. Instead, rules of procedure function as a secular substitute for a religious guarantee of fairness. Among the most important rules of procedure is the rule that the parties to litigation, whether criminal or civil, may have the assistance of advocates to speak on their behalf. The theory is that the watchfulness and intervention of the advocates on either side will induce proper fulfillment of the judicial role. In most modern legal systems the right to counsel is a constitutional guarantee. The right to such assistance is perhaps the most important procedural right because an advocate has the knowledge and position to insist that the court recognize other procedural rights.

A judge who has tried to be fair can have an easy conscience, even when deciding difficult cases. A lawyer often cannot so readily have an easy conscience. The classic moral question for the lawyer is: How can you defend a person you know is guilty? The question is especially pointed when addressed to a lawyer representing a criminal accused who is charged with a heinous crime such as murder or rape. The familiar criticism of lawyers is that they should seek justice and not merely victory for their clients.[33] A weaker version of this criticism is that a lawyer should not seek victory "at all costs."

This takes us to the core of the difference in the professional responsibilities of judges and lawyers. The source of the problem is the uncertainty involved in properly interpreting the law and in organizing evidence and drawing proper inferences from the judicial proof. Legal rules cannot be made so precise and complete as to address every eventuality that may arise in specific cases. And evidence is often ambiguous and in conflict. Events resulting in litigation usually arise by accident and also are poorly remembered by the witnesses. Litigation usually finds its way into court long after the events in dispute. Litigation always involves contending parties, both of whom believe (or pretend to believe) that their cause is just. Decisions by judges therefore may rest on errors of some sort. And lawyers can be well aware that error is being committed.

At various stages of history in different societies, a simple solution has been proposed to deal with the fact that lawyers conceal some things that they know about their clients' causes: judges should inquire into the facts directly, without the intervention of lawyers. Such a rule once prevailed in most of Europe in criminal cases, and as well in inquiries concerning heresy conducted in both the Catholic church and some Protestant churches. The standard practice in such inquiries required the accused to appear before the tribunal without a lawyer and to answer questions under oath, often under threat of torture. The term "Star Chamber proceeding" is a modern pejorative term to describe that system, taking the name of the room in England where a high commission conducted inquiries into offenses of disloyalty. A less severe limitation on defense counsel in criminal cases was to permit merely formal or nominal representation: defense counsel would observe at trial but could take no initiative and would remain silent when the prosecution concluded. A modern version was the Soviet state trial, where the objective was to induce the accused to acknowledge his "errors."

A generic term for these procedures is *ex parte* justice—that is, proceedings in which one side can make presentations to the court but not the other side (typically the accused in a criminal or quasi-criminal proceeding). The ultimate justification for such proceedings has been preservation of the safety and security of the regime—in response to the fear that treasonable or subversive offenders will escape detection and retribution through artifice and manipulation by clever lawyers. That justification is strong, and often compelling, when the regime is weak or internally divided. However, regimes that consider themselves politically stable recognize that *ex parte* justice entails high social costs: invasion of individual privacy, government by intimidation, overreaching prosecution, and often unjust judgments. Avoiding or mitigating these evils is the justification for the role of the advocate.

The right of a person accused of a crime to have legal counsel is now a constitutional right in virtually all modern political systems. The Japanese provision is typical. Article 37.3 of the Japanese constitution says: "At all times the accused shall have the assistance of competent counsel who shall, if the accused is unable to secure the same by his own efforts, be assigned to his service by the State."

The justification of the role of the advocate in criminal and quasi-criminal proceedings does not justify the role of the advocate in civil litigation or that of the legal counselor (office lawyer). The justification for these roles is more complicated and, superficially at least, less compelling. The right to legal assistance in civil matters is closely tied to the social and political system of private property and private contracting—capitalism in various forms. The problem is very large, and providing a complete explanation would require a consideration of European civilization since the Renaissance. However, a justification is necessary as the constitutional and political foundation of law practice. The ultimate justification is that private lawyers facilitate maintenance of the rule of law and are indispensable to it as a practical matter.

Law practice consists to a large extent in facilitating the acquisition of property, documenting transactions for the exchange of property and for investment, and handling disputes over property and financial transactions. One approach is to provide this service through a neutral legal official. In many civil law systems, including those of France, Germany, and Japan, many property transactions, notably sales of real property, traditionally have been allocated to a distinct branch of the legal profession, the *notaires*.

Under French law the *notaire* is a private professional who performs a neutral function of public significance in formally documenting and systematically completing specified property and contract transactions, primarily real estate transfers and testamentary dispositions. The intervention of a *notaire* is obligatory in some transactions, optional in others. *Notaires* have a monopoly in the conveyancing of real estate, similar to that of solicitors in English practice, and in the documentation of marriage settlements and testamentary dispositions (wills). Under French law, the certificate of a *notaire* that the transaction was properly concluded is incontestable proof of the bona fides of the transaction, in the absence of clear proof of corruption on the part of the *notaire* (almost impossible to establish).[34] Many other civil law systems have an equivalent office. The Spanish equivalent is the *notario*.

In common law systems the techniques for conclusively establishing the bona fides of property transactions have evolved differently, but they typically involve participation by lawyers. In some systems it is customary for one office lawyer to handle the documentation of such a transaction for both parties. In others, there are solicitors on both sides. The aim in either arrangement is to establish an incontestable transfer. In any event, property rights and rights created through contracts are the essence of a system of private property, the rule of law is the essential mechanism for giving effect to these rights, and processing property exchanges in light of the rules of law is the vocational agenda of the legal profession. The complex financial and commercial transactions handled by modern lawyers are essentially (very) elaborate versions of conveyances and mortgages.

The argument concerning the relationship between private property and the rule of law can be stated in simplified terms as follows.[35]

A political system that honors the rule of law must recognize a system of private rights. Private rights by definition include rights against the government, as well as rights against other private parties. Effectively maintaining private rights against the government requires, as a practical matter, that private parties have economic resources to assert those rights. Hence a system of private rights must include rights of property. In terms of classic political theory, this could be said to be a justification provided by John Locke for a regime defined by Thomas Hobbes.[36]

A viable system of private property necessarily implies that there are constitutional limitations seriously and consistently observed that protect against trespass upon property by other persons, and against excessive interventions by government concerning the use and development of resources such as land, labor, and technology. Typical trespassers are neighboring landholders, poachers, and commercial rivals. Typical excessive government interventions are expropriation, oppressive taxation, and suffocating regulation. Enforcement of rights against these intrusions, we have learned through experience, depends on an independent authority in government, specifically an independent judiciary. The independence of a judiciary is supported by an independent legal profession, which in turn keeps an eye on the judges.

Protection of private property is often inconvenient for government (which can use the money itself) and often also unpopular. It is a widely held popular belief that private accumulation of surplus (hence wealth) is selfish and must have involved deceptive practice. Therefore, historically it has often been difficult to maintain regimes that protect property owners from intervention. The difficulty is the greater because property owners persistently succumb to temptations to manipulate government intervention for their own benefit. "Crony capitalism" is ubiquitous and is a persistent fellow-traveler with honest entrepreneurship. Some degree of cooperation between government and enterprise is necessary, however, because maintaining a political regime requires a steady flow of money. Hence a viable constitutional regime involves a delicate balance, at constant risk of instability, between private property's inviolability and its subjection to taxation and other regulation for public purposes.

The balance between privacy and regulation of property can be maintained through legal rules governing the relationship, monitored and enforced by disinterested judges. The principle that rights of property should be adjudged by a disinterested judiciary became established at different stages in various European countries but could be said to have achieved broad recognition, if not consistent implementation, by the fifteenth century.[37]

Historically, the legal protection of individual human rights evolved somewhat later than the establishment of the rule of law for property. The protection of individual human rights is epitomized in standards of fairness in criminal procedure—the rights to have a specification of charges, to confront adverse witnesses, to present defense evidence, and to receive the assistance of legal counsel. These rights became widely recognized in Western regimes in the seventeenth and eighteenth centuries.[38] In the modern context, human rights are properly accorded higher standing than property rights. Nevertheless, in a constitutional regime predicated on the rule of law, it seems evident that effective protection of property rights is a concomitant of effective protection of human rights.[39] It takes private money (that is, property) to employ the means for peaceful resistance to government prosecution of individuals or government expropriation of enterprises. At the same time, in a democratic era legal protection of ordinary citizens is virtually by definition a necessary complement to, perhaps a political quid pro quo for, protection of business property.

An independent judiciary is essential in a constitutional regime because rules concerning violations of human rights and enforcement of property rights must be applied with technical competence and disinterest. Advocates for the disputing parties are extremely useful in such a regime, if perhaps not absolutely essential. Beyond their functions as monitors of the judges, lawyers function as mediators of disputes. The possibility of settlement by compromise can be furthered if each party receives an expert estimate, from a lawyer, of the likely outcome if the dispute ripens into litigation before the judges. In transactions at a step removed from a legal dispute, parties can achieve more predictable results in a transaction that is governed by a carefully drawn contract.

It is thus no accident that the rise of the legal profession is a concomitant of the rise of capitalism, or that the practice of law is a vocation most evident in capitalist regimes, or that most lawyers are primarily engaged in the practice of business law. Neither is it a coincidence that the basic elements of private law practice consist of the law of property, trespass, contract, and government regulation and taxation.

An especially important constituency for the rule of law is the middle class or bourgeoisie—that is, the educated and technically skilled people gathered in cities. These include not only the merchants and manufacturers but also artisans skilled enough to maintain independent enterprises, operators of markets and restaurants and other service establishments, lower-level officials, and city folk in general. It is thus also no accident that the rise of the legal profession is a concomitant of the evolution of the literate and liberal urban bourgeoisie. Historically, residents of cities obtained "liberties" in return for limited submission to government and agreement to pay defined taxes, under arrangements of mutual forbearance with the neighboring feudal authority. These détentes were epitomized in the city charters of Renaissance civilization. "Cities have free air," in the classic phrase. On a larger political scale were similar concordats between the church and secular rulers.

These municipal charters and concordats were complex legal documents that can be considered the legal antecedents of modern written constitutions. Their provisions characteristically contained limitations on taxation and trade regulation, guarantees of local autonomy in specified respects, and stipulations concerning jurisdiction. Giving effect to their provisions required technical advice available from lawyers. It is thus also no accident that law practice characteristically has involved this kind of "municipal law," that is, interpretation of intergovernmental regulations.

A reasonable summary of the foregoing thesis has been set forth by Charles Taylor.[40] The elements of a constitutional regime include:

the rule of law
lawyers, the courts, and legal proceduralism
voluntary association for political participation
separation of powers, including an independent judicial system
a balance between central political authority and local autonomy. (The
    latter can take the forms of both decentralization of governmental

authority and devolution to private authority in the form of corporations and other associations.)

In the modern democratic era, the protections of the rule of law have been more fully extended to ordinary citizens. That era can be said to have commenced in the century demarked by the English Bill of Rights (1689), Rousseau's *Discourse into the Origins of Inequality of Men* (1754), the American Declaration of Independence (1776), and the French Declaration of the Rights of Man (1789). Proclaiming individual rights on a democratic basis is one thing, but fulfilling that proclamation is much more difficult. In broad perspective, since the beginning of the nineteenth century the administration of justice has confronted this fundamental dilemma: how to provide ordinary citizens with equality before the law while affording businesses and wealthy persons the liberty to retain the best available legal assistance.

Social Justice and Legal Aid

When businesses and wealthy persons are permitted unrestricted choice in legal assistance, they will seek and usually obtain the best available legal talent, just as they secure the best among other available services such as housing and medicine. The range of capability among lawyers is very great. It necessarily follows that clients with money often have more able lawyers and that people who are economically less affluent often have relatively less competent lawyers—or none at all. Insofar as legal assistance can improve a client's legal situation, the inevitable result is inequality before the law.

There is an important qualification to the economic truism stated above: many capable people become lawyers because they want to help others to get justice, and they stay in law practice helping ordinary people even though they could make more money, and perhaps achieve higher status, if employed by business enterprises. There is no economic calculus to determine the extent of this phenomenon, and many economists think it is a myth. However, we are reminded of an old joke in which the punch line is, "I have seen it done." We know lawyers who fit this description. Some of the "idealists" work for legal aid, some in modestly remunerative private practice, and others in government law departments. Many lawyers who work for business enterprises wish they could do the same.

In any event, it is not seriously disputable that middle- and lower-income individuals obtain only a relatively modest share of lawyers' services. There is substantial survey evidence concerning the situation in the United States.[41] There is little systematic information about other countries, but our knowledge of law practice suggests that the situation throughout the world is essentially the same. Individuals who are in the middle-income range, or below that level, engage lawyers only in legal emergencies, such as divorce and when they are accused of a crime, and in certain routine transactions such as real property transfer and preparation of a testament (will). Beyond this, low-income people may be eligible for legal aid, especially when accused of a crime. But most services of lawyers throughout the world are rendered to individuals of substantial wealth or to businesses.

The legal profession nevertheless proclaims that "anyone who needs a lawyer can get one." That proclamation dampens criticism and justifies the profession's claim to self-government, but it opens the way for criticism, not only about the inadequacy of legal assistance for ordinary people but also about political hypocrisy. The inadequacy of legal assistance for ordinary people is in turn the moral and political predicate of the demand for "equal access to justice," particularly publicly subsidized legal assistance for poor and middle-income individuals.

Much ink has been spilled over this issue, but, in our opinion, with little clarity of thought. We suggest the following analysis:

(1) Lawyers have valuable skills (including verbal facility, the ability to concentrate, psychological toughness) that can be applied not only in law practice but also in such services as banking, insurance, business management, and public administration. The "price" of legal services therefore is primarily determined not by what practicing lawyers are accustomed to charging, but by the income that most lawyers could gain in other employments.

(2) Legal assistance is therefore relatively expensive. Although some professional rules inflate the cost of some services, particularly ones that look complicated but that really are routine, there is little "monopoly" pricing for nonroutine services.

(3) The cost of nonroutine legal services (for example, representation in litigation) cannot be much reduced because competent performance of

those services requires complicated skills. Therefore, a decent society requires a substantial measure of subsidized legal services.

(4) The basic strategy for ameliorating the legal problems of ordinary individuals should be standardizing and simplifying commonly occurring legal transactions. Modern legislation has made useful progress in that direction, such as "no-fault" divorce, standardized mortgage financing for homeowners, and simplified pension systems. Another component is "advice bureaus" and similar arrangements under which the intelligence and assertiveness of experienced office workers are deployed on behalf of the poor. Still another is an "ombudsman" concept, whereby administrative bureaucracies respond to their own internal malfunctioning.

(5) By the same token, a strategy aimed at providing "equal access" to the legal systems as they exist must be regarded as a moral ideal rather than a policy.[42]

In the democratic era, however, this approach can be criticized as undemocratic, despairing, and perhaps even "elitist."

Many legal systems have developed programs of legal aid whereby lawyers are provided to poor people in need of legal assistance. Often the legal assistance provided in this way is of a higher caliber than could be obtained by a person of modest means seeking a lawyer from the private bar. Thus it can happen that better lawyers serve both wealthy and corporate clients as well as some of the poor, while middle-income clients often get less competent or less dedicated assistance. This peculiar distribution results from a social wish to provide for the poor, at least some of them, but under constraint against providing legal service to everyone at the high level that can be afforded by the rich.

The difficult political dilemma is how to ameliorate this inequality. The problem is most serious in countries where the economy and cultural tradition result in gross disparities in wealth. It is an outrage that the rich man can escape accountability to the law while the poor man goes to jail. Extreme measures to prevent this can be imagined. For example, severe restrictions could be imposed on eligibility for legal assistance, requiring that everyone obtain legal assistance from a government agency on a first-come, first-served basis, as in a public medical clinic. Such indeed was approximately the official system in the Soviet Union under the communist regime. However, no constitutional regime has been willing to impose such a limitation. Restrictions of this kind would contradict a constitutional regime's fundamental premise of liberty in matters of property and contract, and in any event would probably be rendered ineffective by evasive or corrupting stratagems.

Broadly speaking, two other strategies have been pursued. One is a wide-ranging strategy of amelioration through public administration by measures of social justice; the other is a more limited one of amelioration in adjudication through legal aid. Measures of social justice include public education, which reduces inequalities in dealing with the complexities of modern life; public transportation and communication, which reduce inequalities in access to economic and social opportunity; and publicly supported housing and medical services. Provisions of this kind are standard in Western Europe, and many Americans believe similar systems should be more fully developed in the United States. A legal aspect of these social services is procedures for resolving complaints about the unfairness in their administration. In civil law systems, this legal dimension consists of a separate system of justice, *droit administratif*. The common law systems have roughly equivalent "fair hearing" procedures.

The *droit administratif* of the civil law systems and "fair hearing" procedures of common law regimes can be considered judge-centered adjudicative systems. In these systems, disputes over the allocation or administration of public benefits are determined by judicial or quasi-judicial officials administering the programs of social benefits—including education, police services, and health care. Those officials sometimes are called judges and in any event function under the aegis of legal regulations that define their procedures and authority. Many of the determinations are similar to judicial decisions made in the courts.

The fairness and efficiency of such a system necessarily depends on the competence and integrity of the officials who administer it. In most of the European countries and in Japan, these systems are well established and have a high reputation. The same is largely true of the systems in Canada and other economically developed countries. The systems in the United States vary widely from one locality to another. In the absence of a strong tradition of administrative competence and integrity, such a system has all the limitations of procedures in which parties are not allowed lawyers. However, these systems are relatively inexpensive and are subject to political oversight and criticism through the parliamentary process.

The problem of inequality in social justice persists in the ordinary courts, however, in both criminal and civil proceedings and in ordinary citizens' needs for legal advice. Here, amelioration is undertaken through legal aid. By "legal aid" we mean subsidized legal assistance to people who lack adequate means to employ a lawyer. This assistance includes the court appointment of lawyers, free or low cost legal aid provided by public agencies and charitable and fraternal organizations, and the free services of lawyers serving *pro bono publico*. In criminal cases, all modern legal systems provide legal assistance of some sort. The provisions in civil litigation are more diverse and often less comprehensive.[43]

Theoretically, legal aid should be unnecessary in the judge-centered civil law systems. In those systems, the judge is responsible for just results and for making the inquiries necessary to achieve justice. This ideal is said to be substantially realized in Germany and, perhaps to a lesser degree, in France. However, it is merely a formal ideal in many other civil law systems. Theoretically, judges in the common law systems have a similar responsibility in cases where litigants appear without counsel. A litigant who represents himself is said to appear *in propria persona*, or "*pro per*" as it is called in legal slang. When a litigant has no lawyer, responsibility to some extent shifts to the judge to ensure adequate consideration of that party's side of the dispute. These cases typically are before courts of petty jurisdiction, which often have huge caseloads. For reasons explained earlier, busy or indolent judges can fail to understand a case presented by ordinary citizens, particularly citizens of limited education and sophistication. In many legal systems the judges have additional difficulty dealing fairly with cases where lawyers are unavailable to assist in the presentations. Some judges in all systems tend to treat these cases perfunctorily.

In criminal cases, under both civil law and common law, it is a universal principle that the prosecutor is a "minister of justice" and not merely an advocate for conviction. In civil law systems, indeed, the prosecutor is considered part of the judiciary.[44] Most prosecutors in most systems take very seriously the duty to be fair to a criminal suspect. Proper prosecutorial review of the adequacy of evidence in a criminal case is a substantial protection for the accused. But all modern legal systems provide lawyers for persons accused of a crime who are unable to pay for a defense advocate.

The quality of legal aid in criminal cases varies enormously. Legal aid systems must be administered through a "means test," that is, standards and procedures to differentiate between applicants who really are poor and applicants who are trying to avoid using their own money to hire a lawyer. Means tests are inherently somewhat arbitrary and often cannot identify circumstances in which need is especially great. However, without such a mechanism the system would be exploited by people who could afford a lawyer. Some countries and localities provide reasonably adequate provision for legal aid. That is, every person who can qualify under the means test is provided legal consultation, assistance in negotiation, and if necessary, advocacy at trial. But the systems in many countries are grievously underfinanced and understaffed.

The legal profession in many countries accepts the concept that lawyers should provide representation to the poor as an obligation *pro bono publico*. The Italian rules, for example, provide that a "lawyer must provide representation to a client if the judicial authorities ask him to do so in compliance with the applicable laws."[45] Most common law systems impose a similar obligation to accept judicial appointments and impose a moral obligation on lawyers to voluntarily give a certain amount of time to providing legal assistance to the poor.[46] In Japan the obligation is imposed on the bar association; Article 88 of the Articles of the Association of the Japan Federation of the Bar provides that "the bar association shall extend legal consultation and legal aid upon request of the indigent." Nevertheless, fulfillment of the obligation is merely nominal in many countries. The courts have had to acquiesce in the reluctance of the government to provide fully adequate legal aid services and do the best they can to provide justice for litigants who cannot afford lawyers.

Every judicial system must maintain a concept of adequate legal representation on the basis of which to determine whether a litigant was provided assistance below the proper professional standard. The remedy in such situations can be nullification of a judgment unfairly obtained. However, the procedure to nullify a judgment itself ordinarily involves a complicated procedure and the assistance of an advocate, often an advocate of special skill and tenacity. Nullification proceedings on the basis of inadequate counsel are infrequent in all legal systems and successful only in egregious cases. Those who cannot afford to employ an advocate thus are at risk of injustice and many in fact suffer injustice, whereas those who can afford high-caliber legal counsel do much better. This is a large and continuing tragedy in many countries.

Socialism has been an idealized alternative to capitalism since the early nineteenth century, reflecting still earlier utopian visions of human community. The ideals of socialism have been collective ownership of property, cooperative work, just distribution of the product of labor, and absence of coercion from either government or private interests. In this vision, harmony would prevail and hence organized government could be unnecessary, and law, judges, and lawyers would be superfluous. Karl Marx predicted that the state would "wither away" and with it the institutions of coercion inherent in a legal regime. In the twentieth century, the Soviet Union, China, and Cuba contended that their regimes were precursors to a harmonious Marxian society. However, if it is possible that any such society can be constructed, those regimes have not done so. The reality has been quite different. The socialist alternative as it actually evolved has been deeply sobering for all political idealists. It may also suggest why a legal system with judges and lawyers performs useful functions, and why a system of private property is a necessary basis for the rule of law. Concrete analysis of "socialist law practice" puts into clearer perspective the relative virtues of a capitalist regime and with it a system of private property, unlovely as such a system may be when viewed in some other comparison.

A system of private property is not, however, a sufficient condition for the rule of law. A serious and sustained political commitment to human rights and civil liberties is also essential.[47] The most vivid illustration of that fact in modern history is the Nazi regime. The Nazi regime called itself socialist (National Socialist) but largely maintained the preexisting capitalist system and concomitant rights of private property, except for the exclusion, expropriation, and substantial extermination of the Jews and the suppression of political opposition. The Nazis organized special administration to exterminate the Jews and imposed a system of special courts and special procedures to deal with dissidents, who were denied elementary rights in the Nazi courts as well as in their ordinary lives.[48] Similar though less intrusive systems were established in fascist Italy and Franco's Spain. Those experiences demonstrate that protection of personal rights is considered anterior to property rights in moral and political importance.

In any event, in socialist regimes—in which private property is insignificant and private business virtually nonexistent—the basis of law practice is quite different from that examined here.[49] Simply put, under socialist regimes there is no "corporate" or "business" or "financial" law practice, or a law practice of any consequence in real estate transactions and testamentary dispositions. The absence of these fields of law practice is a consequence of the absence of these forms of economic activity. In the former Soviet Union, in the former East bloc countries, and in Cuba, basic economic resources are not "property" but rather are subjects of government administration. By exclusion, therefore, law practice under socialism has consisted of providing representation in criminal and juvenile proceedings, either as prosecutors on behalf of the state or as defense counsel on behalf of individual defendants, and providing representation of private parties in divorce and custody proceeding and in petty disputes between neighbors, such as disputes over fences and hedges.

In many of the East bloc countries there was no legal right to obtain full ownership of even household residences or local garden patches, although Poland and some other countries recognized private property in farms and residences. Ownership was recognized in personal property such as clothing and automobiles, but not in shares of stock, business partnerships, or the like. In the absence of ownership rights in real property, an occupant of an apartment or farm acreage had a renewable license for residence and, in some regimes, legal power to designate at death members of family as successors in those rights of occupancy. In none of these countries were the enterprises of production—factories, utilities, transportation organizations—legally autonomous from the state. Rather, production enterprises were divisions or subdivisions of ministries in various jurisdictions. The fact that production enterprises lacked legal autonomy in turn meant that the task of coordinating production and distribution was accomplished by means other than contracts and similar legal relationships.

Business enterprises in capitalist countries operate through a complex web of contracts based on rights of property and the right to sell one's labor—supply contracts, sales contracts, service and repair contracts, wage and hour agreements with employees, contracts providing capital through loans and ownership investments, and others. All such arrangements are established through legal relationships and often are memorialized in legal documentation. They therefore involve lawyers' services, at least in drafting the prototype agreements that evolve into standard forms. The relationships between business enterprises and governmental authority in capitalist systems are administered through legal rules, constituted of legislation and implementing regulation. Traditional rules of law establish the right of an enterprise to own and manage its facilities, to recruit and employ staff, and to engage in internal governance—that is, management of the enterprise. Modern legislation permits more elaborate forms of organization, particularly the business corporation, which in turn facilitates the large-scale business enterprises characteristic of modern economies. Modern regulation imposes controls on business enterprises, such as labor laws and environmental regulations, and also requires businesses to assist in the administration of social programs such as health care and in the collection of taxes on business itself and income taxes on their employees. Government controls and regulations are in turn administered through complex bureaucratic structures that are themselves defined by legal rules and subject to supervision through legal procedures.

The situation in socialist regimes is formally similar to that in capitalist regimes, in that their production enterprises have had names and structures modeled on capitalist forms. The regimes also had a system of administrative courts formally similar to those in capitalist civil law systems. Theoretically, these courts could resolve disputes between units of the socialist enterprises, similar to arbitration proceedings between enterprises in the capitalist systems. However, experience in the system indicated that the administrative courts were largely ineffectual except in relatively minor disputes. Disputes involving substantial issues had to be referred upward for resolution, often to the highest government level.

Aside from their formal similarities, the driving incentives in capitalist and socialist systems are very different. In capitalist regimes, the driving entrepreneurial forces are hope of reward and fear of failing to realize a profit for investors in an enterprise. In socialist regimes, the driving force is compliance with (or evasion of) directives from government authority, ultimately the governing state council. Thus the structure of capitalism is inherently decentralized, while the structure of socialism is inherently centralized. Legal rules, enforced through regular procedure, are the basic coordinating mechanism in capitalism, whereas in socialism the basic coordinating mechanism is administrative direction based on systemwide plans.[50] Law and lawyers or their functional equivalents are indispensable in a capitalist regime. In a socialist regime, law and lawyers are antithetical to the society's basic economic and political concerns.

A remarkably revealing explanation of the legal profession in a socialist regime is given in a book published in China in 1990:

> Based on socialist public ownership, the attorney system serves the socialist economy and society. China's lawyers are state personnel who specialize in legal affairs. They are different from their counterparts in the Western countries. The work units of China's lawyers are accountable to the unified leadership, supervision, and management of state justice administrative institutions. They practice within a collective work system and in this respect, they are quite different from law offices freely operated in the West.
>
> The task of China's lawyers is to provide legal persons and citizens with legal assistance so as to guarantee the precise application of law and safeguard the interests of the state, communities, and the legitimate rights and interests of the citizens.[51]

The Chinese system has been undergoing modification in recent years, in the direction of a proper legal system, but it is still shaped both by a version of Marxist ideology and by China's cultural tradition:

> Contrary to the universalism of formal moral philosophy, [Chinese culture] stressed particularism and personal treatment. . . . This traditional preference for informality and particularism was later reinforced by Marxist-Leninst-Maoist thought, which emphasized a ["from the masses to the masses"] approach to the administration of justice. . . .
>
> Today, litigation in the public courts is still viewed with disfavor in China, as it represents a breakdown in relationships. . . .[52]

The regime in the now-dismantled German Democratic Republic—East Germany—exemplifies the discrepancy between socialist ideals and reality in the legal system. Inga Markovits has provided a detailed and illuminating study of the legal system in East Germany before the absorption of that regime into West Germany.[53] That system appears to be representative of the former communist regimes, except that in efficiency it was probably well above average among socialist regimes.

In the East German system the physical location of lawyers' offices was itself significant. In that regime and others in socialist systems, lawyers in nongovernmental employment were required to maintain their offices in "collectives" or "colleges," clusters in close mutual proximity. The collective was supervised by a senior lawyer chosen by the government. The senior member's function formally resembled that of the French *batonier* (senior local practitioner), and in physical terms these arrangements resembled the chambers of English barristers in the Inns of Court. However, the arrangement was legally compulsory and was used to keep members of the bar under close watch.

East German judges and lawyers were primarily engaged in ameliorating conflict arising from interpersonal disputes, not serious disputation concerning claims of legal right. Peaceful resolution of conflict has a proper place, and a large place, in sustaining a community. But people who assert legal rights are not "antisocial" if their claims are justifiable. By the same token, amelioration of conflict can be a mask for denial of legal rights: "East German judges . . . were expected to investigate thoroughly the social context of disputes . . . a defendant's entire social career beginning from childhood."[54] Resolution by noncontentious discussion became the ultimate basis of dispute resolution, instead of being a subordinate alternative to decision reached through adjudication based on rules. In a regime based on social adjustment, disputation can become a form of blackmail, and resolution of a dispute can depend on accommodation deemed prudent by the official arbiter. If a dispute has serious political implications, the arbiter might refuse even to "ameliorate" and instead will refer the problem to higher governmental authority: "[P]olitically touchy offenses were not prosecuted before the local court but in the regional capital."[55]

Legal claims in the socialist system occasionally raised issues involving the basic legitimacy of the socialist economic system, just as such issues can arise in legal matters in capitalist regimes. A set of issues fundamental to both socialist and capitalist regimes includes the legal aspects of employment. A good deal of litigation in the socialist system involved cases of employees, but along lines of dispute quite the opposite of those in Western regimes. In capitalist systems, disputes between employees and employers typically involve complaints by employees concerning wages, working conditions, or employment benefits. In the East German system, in contrast, "the vast majority of cases was not . . . brought by employees against their employers but by employers against their negligent or undisciplined employees."[56] Other economic problems involved priority in supplies, services, production levels, prices, and controversies over quality. In the socialist regime these issues were resolved by internal bureaucratic negotiation among state enterprises, not by reference to contract, property, or sales law. The "self-help" mechanism of rejection of products and services, available in a contract regime, was not available in the socialist system. It was considered that "the law should not stand between the socialist state and its citizens. East German law thus knew no judicial review of administrative decisions."[57]

The destruction of the Berlin Wall accelerated the dissolution of the East German regime. When the East German system merged with that of West Germany, the socialist lawyers of the old East German regime thereupon confronted a virtual revolution in their political and professional milieu. They lacked concepts and techniques to deal with property, contract, and legally serious disputes with government agencies—that is, the basic professional repertoire of lawyers in the Western tradition. In the capitalist reincarnation of East Germany, some East German lawyers found employment in newly established offices of West German firms, on the strength of their intimate knowledge of the local political structure. But for many others the change resulted in professional obsolescence and consequently deep personal tragedy. The depth of the tragedy, however, indicates that there is a fundamental discrepancy between the utopian dream of a society unencumbered by lawyers and a society in which there is a reasonably clear concept of legal rules.

Access to Justice for Ordinary Citizens

The primary subject matter of modern law practice, as we have seen, consists of property and contract transactions, and litigation and other forms of dispute resolution concerning such transactions. Most contract transactions are relatively routine and when in writing are based on standardized forms; only a small minority of people become involved in transactions of greater complexity. Most of the professional work of most law firm lawyers therefore concerns business transactions and the affairs of people of substantial means. Abraham Lincoln, perhaps the model of a lawyer in the mind of the average person, nevertheless earned most of his fees from representing railroad corporations.[58]

Yet law practice involves much more than the affairs of business enterprises and wealthy individuals. Perhaps most visible from the public perspective is criminal law; indeed, much of the general public thinks of lawyers in the context of criminal cases.[59] Public consciousness of the legal profession is now largely shaped by television and movies. "Media law practice" typically involves litigation, usually criminal cases or domestic relations matters (divorce, child custody, and financial support). By definition these disputes involve rights and duties of individuals, not business matters.

The emerging vocabulary for legal problems or ordinary citizens begins with "human rights" and "access to justice." Human rights refers to the idea that fundamental human needs should be defined and protected through legal rules. Access to justice refers to the idea that protection afforded by legal rules should be enforceable through legal procedure.

The concept of fundamental human rights has a long juristic tradition in Western culture, including the concept of natural law, and a political tradition going back at least as far as the English, American, and French Revolutions. Important modern articulations include the Atlantic Charter promulgated by President Franklin Roosevelt and Prime Minister Winston Churchill in World War II and the Convention on Human Rights adopted under the auspices of the United Nations in 1947.[60] In the political sphere there has been an evolution of protections of individual rights such as employee rights, consumer protection, freedom from arbitrary action by government bureaucracies, and freedom from religious, racial, and gender discrimination. A prototype of these provisions has been the Fourteenth Amendment of the United States Constitution, guaranteeing rights to due process and equal protection. Similar protections have increasingly been incorporated in constitutional provisions and "super legislation" through international agreements such as the European Convention on Human Rights.[61] Modern implementations in the economic sphere include government commitments to a minimum standard of living, full employment, and health care.

These protections have often been made legally enforceable; that is, they are implemented by the mechanism of litigation in the ordinary courts or in special constitutional or administrative tribunals, as distinct from implementation through bureaucratic enforcement. Many of these constitutional protections operate primarily against government bureaucracies. Many Eastern European countries, since the dissolution of their communist regimes, have been especially receptive to judicial protection of rights against the state, under the aegis of new constitutional provisions.[62]

Implementation of constitutional human rights through litigation poses a problem that has come to be termed "access to justice."[63] Constitutional guarantees enforceable through litigation require not only procedural pathways for conducting the litigation but also assistance in pursuing the pathways with professional technical and strategic skill. However, most individuals seeking vindication of their rights have limited financial means. The appropriate concept for implementing access to justice therefore is superficially simple: enhancement of "legal aid"—that is, public subvention of legal assistance for individuals who cannot afford the cost of necessary legal assistance.[64]

Popular consciousness throughout the world has become more sharply attuned to "legal rights," thereby increasing the demand for legal assistance. Concepts of what a legal right *is* have expanded to include such matters as protection against race and sex discrimination, immigration rights, and rights of the disabled. Concepts of fair legal procedure in the modern era have escalated, making every legal aid case potentially more complicated than it might have been one or two generations ago. Whatever definition of eligibility may be established, there are always additional worthy claimants standing beyond any boundary of eligibility and seeking to come within it. The unhappy experience in England with its legal assistance program illustrates these difficulties. The administration of Margaret Thatcher and subsequent Labour governments have been able to justify substantial reduction in support for legal assistance on the ground that the demand for services seemed nearly infinite. Providing "adequate" legal aid is a much more formidable problem than has widely been recognized.

The provision of adequate legal aid nominally has been assumed to be a professional responsibility of the bar in many systems. This sense of responsibility is expressed in the "cab rank rule" embraced by the bar in Victorian England and an article of professional faith in many other countries. The idea is expressed as follows: "Lawyers are the key holders to the legal system because they have a monopoly over legal services. Without their help many people would be unable to exercise their legal rights . . . [B]arristers, like cab drivers, must act on a first come, first serve basis."[65]

The further implication is that each barrister must accept any legally arguable case, regardless of whether the lawyer's fee can be paid. This idea has long been an element in the bar's claim to independence and self-government. The profession states to itself: "We control legal services, and accept that such control entails obligation to assist everyone who needs a lawyer." The idea that the lawyers of a community are ready, willing, and able to serve all those in local need of legal assistance was proclaimed by Thomas Erskine in the late eighteenth century: "From the moment that any advocate can be permitted to say that he . . . will not stand between the Crown and the subject arraigned in . . . court . . . from that moment the liberties of England are at end."[66]

But that lofty sentiment was a myth then, and still is. The idea that lawyers as a group have the capability and duty of providing for public legal needs is, in modern context, misleading. No one would argue that doctors as a profession could provide a national health system or that teachers as a profession could provide a system of public education. Attachment to the idea that the bar is "responsible" for providing adequate legal assistance to the poor continues to embarrass the legal profession. It also obscures the difficult and expensive policy issues involved if serious effort were made to provide universal "access to justice."

3

The Professional "Virtues": Competence

Basic Professional Virtues

Basic ethical precepts guide lawyers in the practice of their profession. These precepts can be understood as professional virtues, comparable to the personal virtues specified in classical Greek terminology and by ancient authorities such as Cicero. The classical personal virtues included courage, patriotism, and friendship.[1]

In modern professional language, particularly in Europe, the term "values" is more commonly used. The American Bar Association has come to use the term "core values." In any event, the reference is to ethical norms that should guide the lawyer in fulfilling the professional role. The professional virtues of lawyers are: competence; independence; loyalty to client; maintaining the confidentiality of client secrets; responsibility to the courts and to colleagues; and honorable conduct in professional and personal matters. The virtue of competence is addressed in this chapter, the others in succeeding chapters.

These virtues are expressed in somewhat different terms and according to somewhat different priorities in various legal systems. For example, the legal professions in France, Italy, and Spain in professional rhetoric and self-conception give priority and great emphasis to independence, meaning independence both from clients and from the state.[2] The barristers in the English profession consider themselves associates of judges, with corresponding responsibilities, but English lawyers also are admonished that "clients are free to . . . insist that cases be litigated."[3] The Japanese code of professional ethics, like Japanese law generally, expresses ethical norms as ideals and objectives rather than as precisely stated obligations. In contrast, the German profession has highly specific norms and emphasizes the lawyer's responsibility to the courts, a priority that originated historically in the concept of the German legal profession as a servant of the state.[4] The American profession gives great emphasis to loyalty to the client.[5] These differences are important ones of emphasis, certainly differences of priority. Nevertheless, essentially the same virtues have been recognized since the legal profession in the Western tradition could be identified as such, in approximately the twelfth century.

From an early period these virtues have been expressed as maxims of the profession, constituting an oral tradition of professionalism. In more recent history, the same concepts are reflected in written regulations—statutes, judicial orders, and memorializations by the bar. For example, the prohibition against a lawyer being "ambidextrous"—trying to represent a client in one matter but opposing the client in that or another matter—has an ancient pedigree and expresses the virtue of loyalty to client. Regulations of the profession imposed by the courts or by legislation substantially correspond to ethical precepts and aspirations expressed by the profession itself.[6]

Of course, not all lawyers have always adhered to these ethical precepts. Some lawyers in virtually every community engage in professional misconduct. At times in some communities many members of the legal profession have been corrupt. The practice of law inherently involves partisanship and concealment, behaviors that create opportunity for unscrupulous and deceptive conduct. Partisanship and concealment are also inconsistent with most versions of common ethical standards.[7] The practice of law unavoidably presents opportunities to cheat clients and other parties and to exploit legal procedures that inflict injury on both clients and others. Because these incentives are inherent in law practice and because deviations are inevitable, the ethical concepts that historically have governed law practice are the mirror image of the opportunities for abuse. Ethical abuses by lawyers contribute to the exploitation and denial of justice in specific cases, to malfunctions in the administration of justice, and to popular suspicion of lawyers and of the system of justice. They also undermine the very legal order upon which the livelihood of the legal profession depends.

The verbal formulations of the professional virtues, however, are at least exhortations whereby lawyers address themselves about the ethics of their calling. Like all exhortations, they invoke ideals that their audience is summoned to fulfill—seeking truth, ensuring justice for all, and maintaining unsullied probity of the profession. Yet the formulations of professional ethics also contemplate not merely the pronouncement of professional virtues but also their exercise in the course of a lawyer's professional work. Practice of law is not a theoretical existence or a vocation performed in a cloister. It is an activity performed in a real world involving uncertainties and risks, for both clients and lawyers, and it is carried out by fallible people engaged in earning a living.

This "reality constraint" becomes very apparent when ethical formulations are translated into legally enforceable rules of conduct. In this perspective, concepts of professional ethics involve tensions and contradictions that are similar to those in ordinary moral discourse. For example, in ordinary moral discourse it is a proper exhortation to say that one should always tell the truth. But it is something quite different to say that it should be illegal to fail truthfully to disclose to a storm trooper the hiding place of an innocent fugitive, such as Anne Frank.[8] A similar tension exists in the ethical concepts governing the practice of law, between moral aspirations on one hand and, on the other hand, ethical rules that take serious account of real-world conditions. Pronouncements on lawyers' ethics often mask the tension between the ideal and the exigencies of reality. Two examples illustrate this tension.

The first concerns an advocate's professional duty of loyalty to a client. A pronouncement of this duty that has become famous in the common law world was made by Lord Brougham, an English barrister (later Lord Chancellor) in the early nineteenth century. Brougham was justifying a strategic maneuver that he undertook in representing the defendant in a famous case, the trial of Queen Caroline. Brougham's client in that case was Queen Caroline of England, who was accused of marital infidelity and on that basis was sued for divorce by her husband, the king of England. The divorce proceeding was terminated in her favor when Brougham, in representing the queen, presented the following threat to the prosecution: If the prosecution on behalf of the king endeavored to prove adulterous misconduct on the part of the queen, Brougham would bring forth evidence that the king, at an early age and before marrying Caroline, had married a Catholic. That proof not only would establish the king's guilt of the crime of bigamy but also would dethrone the king, because at the time it was unlawful for members of the

English royal line to marry Catholics. The prosecution of the queen was dropped, but Brougham was strongly criticized for having threatened blackmail.[9] Brougham responded:

> [A]n advocate, in the discharge of his duty, knows but one person in all the world, and that person is his client. To save the client by all means and expedients, and at all hazards and costs to other persons, and amongst them, to himself, is his first and only duty; and in performing this duty he must not regard the alarm, the torments, the destruction he may bring on others. Separating the duty of a patriot from that of an advocate, he must go on reckless of consequences, though it should be his unhappy fate to involve his country in confusion.[10]

Under standards of professional ethics, recognized then as now, Brougham's strategy appears to us to have been proper. The evidence of the king's prior marriage was technically relevant in the divorce proceeding because that evidence would show that the king was already married at the time he purported to marry Caroline, hence that there was no valid marriage between them and therefore no basis for a divorce proceeding. As advocate, Brougham had a duty to present the evidence if the proceeding continued, unless the queen instructed him to withhold it.[11] Yet disclosure of the king's prior marriage would produce a political catastrophe for the king and "confusion" for the United Kingdom, and hence, at least arguably, constitute a violation of Brougham's obligations as a citizen.

A similar conflict between a lawyer's responsibility to a client and responsibility as a citizen often arises in modern cases of espionage and treason. The person accused of these offenses is tried in a national court with the aid of a lawyer whose efforts are dedicated to frustrating the prosecution and thereby weakening the legal controls against betrayal of one's country. In a more attenuated sense, the same conflict exists for a lawyer defending any person accused of a crime, where acquittal concretely imposes a limit on the social controls constituted by the criminal law. The same applies to a lawyer who represents a business corporation in resisting enforcement of a government regulation.

However, Lord Brougham's statement of the lawyer's position is an exaggeration. A lawyer may not use "all means and expedients" in representing a client. For example, it is illegal and professionally improper to bribe a witness or to present fabricated documents into evidence. Brougham properly used evidence he believed to be truthful, but he could not properly have used the evidence if he knew it to be false.[12] Nor could he properly have threatened to offer evidence that was inadmissible because it was irrelevant. A lawyer certainly is not required or permitted to "save the client . . . at all hazards . . . to himself." For example, a lawyer may call the police if the lawyer is threatened with death at the hands of a client. A lawyer is also not required to carry through a transaction he knows is tainted with fraud.[13] On the contrary, a lawyer must terminate participation in a transaction he discovers is tainted by fraud and may have an obligation to take corrective measures to abort the transaction.[14]

There is no hyperbole, however, in Brougham's statement that a lawyer's duty of loyalty to the client has priority over the risk that the client's cause might "involve his country in confusion." It is noteworthy, in this context, that the new regulation of the legal profession in postcommunist Russia, the Law on the Advokatura, has very similar language. Under that law, an advocate has a duty to "use all methods and means provided for by law to defend the rights and legal interests" of clients.[15] The Russian rule applies only to advocacy in court, but the concept is recognized as applicable also to transaction representation.

The risk of embarrassing the government and its officials is a concomitant of the rule of law and of the lawyer's responsibilities for a client. This risk became reality in famous instances, such as the notorious Dreyfus case in France,[16] the Profumo case in England,[17] and the investigations of presidents Nixon and Clinton in the United States.[18] Investigation of high government officials, leading possibly to their being prosecuted and convicted, is a necessary corollary to the proposition that officials in a constitutional regime are governed by law.

A second example of hyperbole concerning professional ethics is in a public address by Kenneth Starr, special prosecutor in the investigation of President Clinton. Starr, referring to the responsibilities of an advocate, said: "Truth indeed is intended to be the primary goal of our judicial system, because without truth as a foundation, justice cannot predictably be achieved . . . [T]he truth and not the service of clients, is the legal system's abiding value."[19] This statement is correct as it applies to the legal system considered as a functional whole. It is correct as it applies to the role of judges, as explained in Chapter 2. It is also correct as it applies to prosecuting attorneys, although with some qualifications, for it is a universally recognized principle that a prosecutor—that is, a lawyer for the state in a criminal case—has a duty to discern the truth and not simply to present evidence indicating that the accused is guilty. Starr's statement is also correct as it applies to lawyers in civil matters, although with other important qualifications.

However, the statement is wrong and grossly misleading as applied to legal representation of targets of criminal investigation or prosecution—which is what Starr was referring to. A lawyer for a criminal accused may not use illegal tactics, such as presenting forged documents or trying to bribe or intimidate the judge. But a lawyer in such a case may properly advise the client not to be forthcoming to the police at the investigation stage and not to testify at trial. The obvious effect of a suspect's silence is frustration of the investigation and thereby possibly the concealment of the truth.[20] But keeping silent in the face of criminal investigation is a constitutional right in modern legal regimes. In regimes where the client may refuse to give testimony, a lawyer for a suspect has both right and duty to assist the client in concealing important facts by invoking that right.[21] It is noteworthy in this connection to contrast the Law on Lawyers of the People's Republic of China, Article 45, which provides that a lawyer is prohibited from "divulging State secrets" and from "concealing important facts."

Principles of legal ethics thus sometimes contradict commonly expressed principles of civic morality. They also contradict principles pronounced by some moral philosophers and principles expressed in "folk ethics," or what ordinary people consider right and wrong. For example, folk ethics require that we be loyal to our friends, but folk ethics also require us generally to obey the law. What if a friend has violated the law and is trying to hide in my house? People in ordinary life inevitably run into dilemmas resulting from contrary indications of general ethical propositions that we fully accept. Yet we do not hesitate to affirm that we should be loyal to our friends (as a general proposition) and also that we should (generally) obey the law.

The concepts of legal ethics involve similar tensions between general propositions, to which all lawyers agree, and specific situations where the general propositions point to conflicting courses of action. Most lawyers like to think of their profession as adhering to general ethical propositions, such as the duty of loyalty to clients and the duty of candor to the courts. Yet if stated as universal obligations, these propositions must be understood as aspirational and not precise statements of governing norms. Consider, for example, the statement, "A lawyer's primary responsibility is to ensure the fair administration of justice." Such a statement necessarily ignores the fact that lawyers individually cannot provide such insurance and that the system of justice as a matter of fact often fails to do so. Accordingly, there is unavoidable tension between ethical aspiration and ethical obligation soberly and secularly considered, just as there is unavoidable tension between religion-based morality (for example, Christian standards) and the norms that people exhibit in ordinary life.[22] This book addresses the ethical aspirations in professional ethics but also focuses particularly on the tensions involved in ethical obligations soberly and secularly considered.

The first of the professional virtues is competence. Competence is independently significant and is also the basis of the other virtues: a lawyer's incompetence can be so egregious that he is unable to recognize his other professional duties. An incompetent lawyer cannot be counted on to complete professional tasks he has undertaken. An incompetent lawyer is usually afraid while doing his work and therefore is often predisposed to make mistakes. Just as an incompetent surgeon makes mistakes that have serious consequences, and so also an incompetent carpenter or nurse, incompetent lawyers make hurtful mistakes, although ones that sometimes are not visible.

Competence in law practice requires knowledge of the law. In the modern environment the web of legal rules is broad and complex. Modern law emanates from many sources—local, national, international, and a multitude of regulatory authorities at each level. In federal systems, such as Canada, Germany, and the United States, the legal sources of modern law are even more complex. The European Union also is evolving into something like a federal system, in which its constituent states are subordinate members. Moreover, administration of the law by various bureaucracies depends on the judgment or discretion of all kinds of government officials, a factor that must be understood and taken into account. Because the law undergoes continual change, a lawyer's understanding of the law can rapidly become obsolete. These conditions of the legal environment virtually require modern lawyers to specialize in one way or another. An important dimension of a lawyer's legal competence today is recognition of the limits of his competence. A lawyer competent to handle a corporate merger, for example, can easily be incompetent to handle a divorce.

Professional competence extends beyond knowledge of the law and the circumstances of its administration, however, and includes technique in making use of legal knowledge. As stated in the Canadian Code: "Competence... goes beyond formal qualification of a lawyer to practice law... and includes knowledge and skill and the ability to use them effectively in the interests of the client."[23]

Competence as a practitioner implies having realistic awareness of the possibilities and limitations of legal procedure, including the possibilities and limitations of resorting to the courts. Competence as a lawyer also implies having continuous regard for the other virtues required in the practice. A summary review of these is appropriate at this point.

The second virtue is professional independence, including autonomy from domination or improper influence of other clients or influences of the state and from interference by other interests that might impinge on the lawyer.[24] In the continental legal systems, particularly France, Italy, and Spain, independence would be considered the first virtue. As stated by an esteemed Spanish colleague: "Independence is... the constitutional characteristics of the judicial function and... the mission [of] participants in the judicial process. So for me, independence is the primary value of the lawyer."

A corollary of the principle of independence is the virtue of loyalty to client. The concept of loyalty to the client is expressed in rules against conflict of interest and signifies that a lawyer must be in a position to provide assistance to a client uninhibited by commitments to others. A conflict of interest exists if a client becomes an adverse party in litigation, but it could also arise in a nonlitigated matter. Thus Article 26 of the Code of Ethics of Japan refers to situations where "the opposite party is at the same time represented by the attorney in another matter" and "a client's interest conflicts with that of a client in another matter..." As formulated by the CCBE, the Code of Conduct for Lawyers in the European Community, this duty is as follows:

> 3.2.1 A lawyer may not advise, represent or act on behalf of two or more clients in the same matter if there is a conflict, or a significant risk of a conflict, between the interests of those clients.

3.2.2 A lawyer must cease to act for both clients when a conflict of interests arises between those clients and also whenever there is a risk of a breach of confidence or where his independence may be impaired.

3.2.3 A lawyer must also refrain from acting for a new client in cases where there is a risk of a breach of confidences entrusted to the lawyer by a former client or if the knowledge which the lawyer possesses of the affairs of the former client would give an undue advantage to the new client.[25]

It will be observed that the duty of loyalty governs both concurrent representations (representation of two or more clients at the same time) and successive representations (representation of a second client after a lawyer has completed the representation of a previous client and then is asked to oppose the former client in the same matter). It will also be observed that the duty of loyalty is expressed partly in terms of maintaining client confidences. Thus the obligations of confidentiality and loyalty overlap, although they are not entirely coextensive.

A third basic professional virtue is maintaining in confidence information received from a client or concerning the client's affairs. The duty of confidentiality requires a lawyer to withhold his client's secrets from other clients, from third parties, from government officials, and even from the lawyer's spouse. The duty rests on the lawyer's shoulders from the first encounter with a client or prospective client and continues after the engagement for the client has been concluded.[26] The lawyer's duty of confidentiality is prescribed in the civil codes of the civil law systems.[27] It is thus a rule of general law, not merely professional conduct. The principle is expressed in Rule 1.6 in the ABA ethics code as follows: "A lawyer shall not reveal information relating to representation of a client unless the client consents after consultation, except for disclosures that are implied authorized in order to carry out the representation [and certain other exceptions]."

The Japanese formulation is in Article 20 of the Japanese Code of Ethics, as follows: "An attorney shall not disclose or utilize, without any good reason, confidential information of a client which is obtained in the course of his or her practice." The lawyer's duty to maintain confidentiality of a client's affairs rests immediately and directly on the lawyer. It requires confidentiality out of court, for example in handling other matters or in casual conversation, as well as in connection with judicial proceedings.

The lawyer's duty of confidentiality is supported by rules that prohibit courts and other official agencies from inquiring into the lawyer's knowledge. In the civil law, this rule is based on the fact that a lawyer is a member of a profession. Accordingly, in civil law systems it is often referred to as a "professional secret" and technically belongs to and is exercised by the lawyer.[28] In common law systems a lawyer's duty, in a court or other legal forum, the refusal to disclose confidences imparted by a client, is referred to as the attorney-client privilege. The common law attorney-client privilege is framed as a right of the *client* (as distinct from the lawyer) to refuse to disclose communications by the client to the lawyer.[29] Both the lawyer's professional right to maintain confidences, established in the civil law, and the professional right to refuse to make disclosure, established in the common law attorney-client privilege, give effect to a more general principle: a lawyer has a right and duty not to disclose matters learned in the course of practicing his profession.[30]

The fourth professional virtue is responsibility. As previously noted, lawyers in some systems would consider independence the first virtue. In any event, the narrowest sense of the concept is that, in relationships with the courts and with other lawyers, a lawyer must not mislead the judges or other lawyers and must adhere to commitments made in such relationships. For example, the CCBE Rules state:

> 4.2 A lawyer must always have due regard for the fair conduct of proceedings...
>
> 4. lawyer while maintaining due respect and courtesy towards the court [should] defend the interests of his client honorably ... within the limits of the law.
>
> 4.4 A lawyer shall never knowingly give false or misleading information to the court.
>
> 5.1.1 The corporate spirit of the profession requires a relationship of trust and cooperation between lawyers for the benefit of their clients and in order to avoid unnecessary litigation.

These expressions in the CCBE Code are stated in guarded terms, but the same guardedness is expressed in other versions of professional ethics. The guardedness reflects the complex and ambiguous balance among a lawyer's duties to the client (loyalty), to the courts (to be strictly truthful in statements made to a judge), and to other lawyers (professional cooperation). These ambiguities will be explored presently.

THE PROFESSIONAL "VIRTUES": COMPETENCE

The fifth virtue is honor or honorable conduct and has two connotations. One connotation is that a lawyer should behave with formal correctness or proper etiquette in relations with the courts and professional colleagues. This standard is universally accepted, although it is sometimes violated in some systems, particularly in the United States. Efforts have been made in some American states to mitigate these violations by "codes of civility," which prohibit use of epithets and similar misbehavior.[31] To similar effect, although in more general language, is Article 88 of the Italian Code of Civil Procedure, which provides as follows: "Parties and lawyers have the duty to behave with ... correctness in the course of the proceeding."[32]

The other connotation of "honor" is more substantial but also more diffuse. It is the principle that a lawyer should be honest and law-abiding in all of his conduct. The American rules, characteristic in their relative specificity on such matters, provide that it is professional misconduct for a lawyer to:

- commit a criminal act that reflects adversely on the lawyer's honesty, trustworthiness or fitness as a lawyer in other respects;
- engage in conduct involving dishonesty, fraud, deceit or misrepresentation;
- engage in conduct that is prejudicial to the administration of justice;
- state or imply an ability to influence improperly a government agency or official;
- knowingly assist a judge or judicial official in conduct that is a violation of applicable rules or judicial conduct or other law.[33]

The Canadian and CCBE formulations are more general but to the same effect.[34]

The virtue of "honor" is especially emphasized in Japan, through terms such as "dignity" and "integrity" and a duty to "refine himself ... and enhance the level of his ... culture." The underlying concept in Japan is assimilation of lawyers to judges in a common professional commitment.

Competence More Fully Considered

A person who calls himself a lawyer thereby proclaims competence in the practice of law. The formulations in the ethical standards are simple but not very informative. For example, *The Guide to the Professional Conduct of So-*

licitors in England provides: "A solicitor must not act, or continue to act, where the client cannot be represented with competence and diligence."[35]

Implicitly, the standard is the prevailing level of competence in the locality in which the lawyer regularly practices. This standard can become explicit in a civil suit for legal malpractice when the court must articulate the standard for imposing liability.[36]

The concept of "locality" of practice reflects the law's accommodation to practical necessity. A general practitioner in a small regional city cannot reasonably be expected to exhibit the same level of technical acquaintance with esoteric fields such as tax law or environmental regulation as specialists in a large big-city firm made up of lawyers who are all specialists. By the same token, a big-city lawyer would often be imprudent in trying to carry through an important matter in a small regional city (for example, obtaining approval of a real estate development plan) without assistance from a local lawyer who knows how things are done in his town.

The legal rule thus reflects the very great diversity of professional knowledge and skill among lawyers in modern practice. The range of diversity is becoming ever greater as communities interact with each other in increasing degree—"globalization"—and as the legal regulatory regimes of the world multiply in depth and complexity.

There are many "horror stories" about legal incompetence. A leading case in the United States that involved litigation (and hence competence of an advocate) concerned a widow who consulted a lawyer about whether she could bring a medical malpractice case against the hospital in which her husband died. After an office consultation, the lawyer indicated he would consider whether such a suit might have merit. But he then apparently forgot about the matter for months, until the time limitation (statute of limitations) within which such a suit should be brought had expired. The widow then brought a suit for legal malpractice against the lawyer, seeking as damages the amount she would have recovered against the doctor in a medical malpractice claim.[37] Another example from the United States, arising in transaction practice (and hence the competence of an office lawyer), involved the failure of a high-level corporate law firm to notice, in a complicated financial transaction, that the monetary amount involved in the transaction was erroneously recorded in the documentation by omission of three zeros. The oversight changed the dollar figure in the transaction from $92,885,000 to $92,885.[38]

Undoubtedly there have been countless similar blunders by lawyers throughout history and throughout the world. Some of these blunders involve momentary lapses by competent lawyers, but others involve failures of competence by lawyers who got in over their heads—that is, who undertook matters that required more skill or experience than they could deploy.

Yet all lawyers and all law firms face continual dilemmas about whether the level of their competency is adequate for their practice. If a new matter is too simple or routine for their level of practice, they may be obliged to turn it down. Such a matter would waste the talents of a lawyer or a firm's lawyers and might require charging the client a greater fee than is appropriate. By the same token, a new matter may be more complex or esoteric than a lawyer can confidently handle. In that case, the lawyer will either have to turn down the new matter and refer it elsewhere, or devote uneconomical time and effort to becoming adequately acquainted with the new subject matter.

At the same time, no lawyer likes to turn away new business. Very few lawyers or law firms feel certain that their practices will be successful. They do not know, for example, whether sufficient new matters will come their way to meet the next month's expenses and the next month's family needs. In addition, rejection of a new matter is also rejection of a client who is demonstrating a wish to engage the lawyer. Such a rejection often is, in a real sense, a denial of justice for the potential client. And the potential client may never come back.

Medium-sized and large law firms often resolve these problems through a "new business" committee. Such a committee considers all new significant engagements, giving consideration to the opportunity presented and to the demands that the matter may place on the firm's personnel. Questions of actual or potential conflicts of interest will also be considered, either by that committee or by some other procedure. Solo practitioners and small firms usually make the same kinds of calculations informally. Sometimes risk is involved no matter how the decision is made.

The legal rule defining competence is expressed in very general terms. In the American Restatement of the Law Governing Lawyers, for example, the rule simply states that a lawyer must "act with reasonable competence and diligence." The standard of competence could be stated more specifically, but only to a limited degree. A more specific standard would have to address specific legal tasks, such as drafting a will or pleading in a specific type of litigation. The specifications would necessarily be mechanical and hence fail to penetrate to subtler aspects of competence. The same difficulty is presented in defining competence in any profession. The difficulty is suggested by the difference between a cookbook recipe (analogous to a legal rule) and a meal prepared by a skillful chef (the product of complex skills).

Modern regimes have enacted regulatory standards of competence. Thus a person may call himself a "lawyer" (or, depending on the specific legal system, *avocat* or barrister or other professional title) only if he has been recognized as such by official admission to the legal profession. Assuming a candidate has complied with the requirements of admission to practice as a lawyer, however, in most systems it confers eligibility to perform any kind of legal service.

But among those who have been admitted to practice there are in fact very great differences in professional skill. There is thus a discrepancy between the formal equality of lawyers under regulations governing the legal profession and the actual inequality reflected in differences among practitioners in their knowledge and acuity. A serious and ever-present problem from the viewpoint of potential clients is that, although all people legally calling themselves lawyers are formally qualified, and accordingly have been certified to undertake legal matters, the actual levels of ability among lawyers cover a wide range.

Admission to practice law is based on fulfillment of prescribed qualifications. As noted earlier, the required qualifications include legal education, a minimum age in some countries, an apprenticeship or similar practical training in many countries, and, in most countries, successful completion of a qualifying examination (the "bar examination"). A typical candidate for admission fulfills these qualifications at a relatively young age and thereby becomes fully licensed to practice. In France, Germany, and Italy, lawyers typically qualify to practice at around age thirty, partly reflecting the time requirements of apprenticeship but also the fact that many students pursue their university education at a leisurely pace. In the United States and England the age of qualification is typically about twenty-five, but many older people (for example, women who enroll in law school after having had children) qualify as well.

Lawyers in any given age group also possess different personal qualities such as thoroughness or capacity for sustained work. These personal differences magnify the differences among lawyers of the same age and experience. Moreover, most of the knowledge and technique of a successful lawyer is acquired through experience in practice. Hence, the nature and duration of lawyers' practice experience also can result in substantial differences in competence. An influential factor in the development of a lawyer's practice experience is the setting in which a lawyer begins a professional career. Some beginners obtain positions in highly competent law firms or legal departments where they receive high-level training. Other beginners must locate in relatively weaker law firms or apprenticeships or simply start by themselves. Where one begins has a substantial and long-lasting effect on the types of work a lawyer does, on the supervision and professional guidance he receives from more senior lawyers, and on his "networking" opportunities. The cumulative influence of early practice experience is a primary force in the de facto differentiation of lawyers' skill and effectiveness.

In some developing countries, young lawyers may face another difficulty at this stage. On one hand, the best training and experience is to be obtained in the local office of an international law firm. On the other hand, employment in such a firm may be regarded with suspicion by the local authorities, or indeed be prohibited except for experienced lawyers. A "solution" for a neophyte may be to work for the international firm, but to avoid publicizing the relationship.

In some environments, notably in "elite" law firms in the United States, beginners are hired on the basis of their academic achievement in law school. Family connections and "good background" (i.e., social class and network) certainly help a beginner obtain a good placement, but ordinarily they do not suffice in the highly competitive modern environment. In some other environments, however, such as Italy and many Ibero-American countries, academic achievement usually is much less relevant. Because universities are often overcrowded and the examination process a mere formality, it is difficult to identify the most capable graduates. In these circumstances, initial placement in law firms is frequently based on family connections. Of course, a beginner who is fortunately placed but turns out to be obviously incompetent will not long progress in a firm of capable lawyers. But others can survive, thus realizing professional benefit from their early connections.

There are three "models" for establishing the initial level of professional competence: the continental European, the English, and the American.

The Continental European Model

As Chapters 1 and 2 described, legal training in continental Europe is based on a combination of university education and government-supervised apprenticeship. The university curriculum is derived from Roman law and teaches classical legal concepts, with emphasis on substantive law (property, contract, and criminal law, civil wrongs, and the like). Concepts of adjective law (including procedure in civil and criminal litigation, jurisdiction, private international law, recognition of judgments) are introduced only in the latter part of the curriculum and are presented in formal terms rather than in terms of practice. In some curricula an important course is jurisprudence, the exposition of the theoretical bases of law, including natural law.

Instruction in the European university law curriculum is primarily theoretical and conceptual, presented by professors who are scholars in these fields. In general, instruction consists of statements of the rules of law as set forth in the legal codes and digests, consideration of the rules from historical and theoretical perspectives, and scholarly commentaries on the rules and their relationships to each other. The viewpoint from which law is presented thus is that of the jurist or judge, in contrast to the viewpoint of a lawyer. The pedagogical method conveys the message that the law is clear and definite. Many European professors are also practitioners and therefore well understand that the law from the viewpoint of lawyers and their clients is often quite unclear and therefore indefinite. However, in European legal education it has been considered inappropriate, indeed irrelevant, to compare the theoretical concepts expounded in the university curriculum with the "law in action" as experienced in practice. The professors consider themselves a faculty of a humane science and not instructors in professional training, to the point of typically excluding from consideration the practical aspects of law and the administration of justice.[39]

In the scholarly tradition of European university education, the curriculum therefore provides a historical and philosophical basis for understanding and appreciating law as a major element of Western civilization. This attitude is imparted both to students who will go on to other vocations and to nascent lawyers. It is an attitude of respect, possibly reverence, quite distinct from a realistic appraisal of law as it is administered in practice.[40]

In most developing countries, both those with civil law traditions and those with common law traditions, the shallow formality of legal education is made worse by the deficiencies in the instructional resources of the universities. Classes are very large and are taught by monologue lecture, with an expectation of rote learning by the students. There is accordingly little opportunity for reflection or discussion concerning the text of the law, let alone the complexities of applying law in real practice. At the same time, from a perspective of public finance there is no practical alternative for a developing country that is trying to modernize its legal system. A formalistic legal education is better than none, and introducing new cadres of poorly trained lawyers and judges is undoubtedly better than staffing the courts with people who have had no legal training at all.

The European tradition continues in both Eastern and Western Europe and has been absorbed by Spain and Portugal in Ibero-American countries and, through the German model, in Japan and China.[41] This conception of the "audience" for university legal education is coherent, having regard for the eventual careers of most students in the law curricula. Most European university students taking a law curriculum do not enter the legal profession, as either judges or lawyers. Rather, most of them enter white-collar careers in public and business administration, where general knowledge of law and the capacity for careful thought and verbal expression are valuable skills. This conception of the student audience also supports the presentation of law in logical and theoretical form, much as university curricula in economics, engineering, and accounting typically are relatively theoretical. The university law curriculum does not address the "dark side" of the law that is exposed in a "realist" approach to legal education.[42]

The conception of law as a science based in logic and classical history is expressed not only in university curricula but also in the academic and professional literature of the law. In the European and Japanese traditions, legal scholarship consists of exposition and commentary concerning the law's formal texts, as distinct from the practical circumstances of its practice and administration. Legal scholars have great influence in shaping the recognized formulations of the law, particularly in treatises on legal subjects.[43]

A substantial fraction of the graduates of the European-style university law curriculum become law professionals, some as judges, some as lawyers, and a few as notaries. The essence of law, for these prospective professionals, is the historical and philosophical specification and articulation of legal rules. The essence of legal technique consists of discourse in this mode. A formal conception of law thereby becomes a continuing self-fulfilling prophecy. Law "is" the historically and philosophically considered system of formal norms, expounded by professors specialized in the scholastic tradition, and imparted to students who achieve academic distinction by demonstrating similar skills. Whether such an education is appropriate for lawyers, or for judges, is another question.

For those who aim to become members of the legal profession in the civil law system, the next stage consists of a combination of professional examinations and professional apprenticeship. The content, sequence, and rigor of these components varies among civil law countries. Some systems have one examination upon graduation and another after apprenticeship; some have one examination, either before or after apprenticeship. Some have one system of apprenticeship for both aspiring judges and aspiring lawyers; others establish separate pathways from the beginning of apprenticeship. In some systems, the apprenticeship is tightly controlled and regulated and includes substantial formal instruction in "practice" subjects. In other systems, an apprenticeship may consist of nothing more than obtaining a position as an assistant in a lawyer's office, being then consigned to copying work and running errands. The northern European countries—conspicuously France and Germany—have traditionally maintained high standards for professional apprenticeship. In some other countries the standards are nominal, and in some they are a farce.[44] In Italy, regulatory supervision of the system has been lax, and the actual quality of apprenticeship uneven, but major reforms have been undertaken in recent years.[45]

A professional examination is required in most countries employing the continental European system. At one time, admission to practice was permitted if one had graduated from the university law curriculum, and that system still obtains in some European countries and most Latin American countries. Where an examination is required, it calls for written answers to questions concerning the rules of law. The typical examination includes a written part taken over several days that is graded according to format answers, and then an oral examination.[46] Most systems also require disclosure of an applicant's personal background to determine whether there have been disqualifying events, notably any criminal convictions.[47]

Upon completion of these requirements, an applicant is provisionally admitted as a professional, whether as judge, lawyer, or member of a specialized legal vocation such as *notaire*. Admission as a lawyer in most European countries is administered by the bar of a city or province, reflecting that historically the legal profession is a locally centered vocation. For example, in France the Centres régionaux de formation professionnelle des avocats (CRFPA) are attached to the regional courts of appeal. Admission in one locality usually results in licensure valid throughout the country.[48] Those who are admitted to judicial careers enter a highly structured system of evaluation and potential promotion, beginning in lower courts and culminating for some in appointment to the system's highest courts.

In most systems, admission as a lawyer is subject to requirements of further experience in practice or tutelage by an experienced practitioner. Those who are admitted to practice may be required to complete a probationary period before becoming full-fledged members of the bar. For example, in France a candidate must complete a one-year training program, then a two-year period of conditional admission practicing under the supervision of an established advocate, and only then does he attain full admission. Until recent years, in most European countries distinctions were maintained among different branches of the legal profession, for example, between the *avocat* and *avoué* in France. However, the modern trend is to eliminate these distinctions.

After a lawyer is admitted to practice in the civil law systems, professional success depends on unofficial recognition, or "reputation." Some legal systems maintain formal distinctions based on subsequent accomplishment. For example, in France the governance of the profession in each city is supervised by a leading member of the bar, the *batonier*, whose selection reflects recognition of high standing. Furthermore, many practitioners are also law professors, so their standing in the legal profession derives in large part from their standing in the academic world.

In light of these requirements for admission to practice, lawyers in most continental legal systems have basic intellectual competence, a high level of literacy, and a capacity for sustained attention to intellectual problems. These important elements of competency in the legal profession and in many types of practice are sufficient for competent practice. Additional qualifications are important in law practice, however—imagination, audacity, personal persuasiveness, and cold realism about human frailties, including the frailties of judges and other officials. These qualifications manifest themselves in the course of practice and yield different but "invisible" degrees of proficiency among experienced practitioners.

The English Model

The legal profession in England since the seventeenth century has been divided between barristers and solicitors, although this distinction is now being effaced.[49] From an early period, admission as a barrister has required the completion of a training program, including an apprenticeship, under the tutelage of the bar itself.[50] Admission as a solicitor was formalized in 1843 and put under supervision of the Law Society, the governing organization of the solicitors' branch of the profession. Admission as a solicitor similarly required an apprenticeship. Neither barristers nor solicitors were required to have a university degree, and until modern times many practitioners had not attended university. During the last half of the twentieth century, however, most people becoming lawyers have had a university degree, and it has now become compulsory.[51]

The historical fact that university education was not required for admission to practice in England nevertheless has had important continuing influence on the concept of education for the English profession. The essential concept in the English tradition is that of training through apprenticeship.[52] In the early Renaissance period in England, aspiring barristers obtained some practice training in the Inns of Court through moots (simulated legal arguments) in which both technique and substantive knowledge were acquired.[53]

A barrister learned practice primarily by "deviling" in a barrister's office; a solicitor learned in the same way with an established solicitor. In the modern era, professional training has been systematized through organized professional curricula provided at institutes sponsored by the professions. The training program in these institutes is one year of intensive instruction in professional techniques, such as drafting documents for solicitors and preparing and conducting legal arguments for barristers. The program follows graduation from university and is followed by a period of working apprenticeship in a lawyer's office, one year for barristers and two years for solicitors.[54]

This historical evolution also helps explain the fact that the university curricula traditionally pursued by English lawyers, which preceded the training program and apprenticeship, has no necessary relationship to law. English universities offer curricula in law that are much like those in continental European universities—historical and philosophical, rooted in Roman law as well as historic common law. Most students who go on to enter the profession will have pursued the law curriculum, but those who have pursued a different "major" can qualify by passing a professional examination.[55] English lawyers in the modern era will as likely have pursued a curriculum in the humanities—history, philosophy and politics, or science—as a curriculum centered on law. "Law" as understood by a practicing English lawyer thus is a technical vocation learned after university. This model also helps explain the characteristic attitude of English lawyers toward their profession: pragmatic, without theoretical framework or pretension.

In the English system an entrance examination is now required in each branch of the profession. Upon completing the training and apprenticeship phases of preparation, and passing the examination, the young lawyer is legally qualified to practice. However, achieving competence in the English system, as elsewhere, requires gaining sufficient experience. Barristers practicing as such are not permitted to join firms but must practice as solos.[56] Accordingly, the novice barrister acquires experience chiefly by accepting appointments made by the courts in criminal cases and in legal aid proceedings, and by getting referrals from more experienced barristers and from friends among the solicitors.[57] Novice solicitors are permitted to join law firms and do so. Those with strong credentials or connections tend to go to the larger solicitors' offices, those with lesser credentials and connections typically join smaller firms or offices of solicitors in solo practice.[58]

The professional road in England from this point is a cyclical progression as it is elsewhere: competence being achieved through experience and experience being necessary to attain competence, with reputation—favorable or otherwise—established accordingly.

The English model has been transferred to countries in the former British Empire, including Australia, Canada, India, New Zealand, Nigeria, Singapore, and the South African Republic. Indeed, the English training system is still pursued by many students from these other countries. The English system was imported into anglophone Canada (Ontario and eight other provinces), but Quebec has followed the French continental tradition. In recent years, however, the Canadian systems have absorbed elements of the American model.

As elsewhere, many people who have been admitted to practice in England leave the profession for other vocations and thereby become "alumni" of law practice. Those who have completed legal training but then leave the legal profession—for business, journalism, an academic career—are an important but often unnoticed element of the modern middle class. These alumni of the law form an important nonprofessional community that interprets and evaluates the legal profession in general and individual lawyers in particular—through gossip and folklore, the news media, and, very often, as intermediaries between lawyers and clients.

The American Model

The American model for licensure entails a university education, a three-year program of graduate professional education in law, a bar examination, and, in a few states (and in Canada), a period of apprenticeship. It is now being adopted in Japan.[59] The distinctive element is that the law curriculum is open only to students who have earned a university degree.

This system evolved in the late nineteenth century under the leadership of the Harvard Law School and became firmly established in the 1920s. Before that time and until after the American Civil War, legal training was unsystematic and virtually unregulated. Admission to practice in many states required only that a local judge, sometimes in consultation with members of the local bar, be satisfied that the candidate was "fit to practice law." (In many places the local judge was himself of dubious professional competence.) Fitness to practice law was acquired by reading law books, in the early part of the nineteenth century perhaps only Blackstone's *Commentaries on the Laws of England*;[60] serving as a practitioner's assistant; and watching proceedings in the courthouse and absorbing professional gossip.[61] In a few localities there were training institutes conducted by experienced practitioners.[62]

Several American universities in the first half of the nineteenth century offered curricula in law, usually patterned on the classic European model.[63] The course of study was designed to provide a liberal and philosophical foundation in law, and secondarily to be a basis for future law practice. University education was not required for lawyers, however, and the curriculum had no direct connection to the establishment of competence.

The Harvard Law School graduate curriculum was initiated in the 1870s and through imitation by other institutions gradually produced revolutionary change. The curriculum was based on the "case method"—that is, the study of law by analyzing judicial decisions. The case method system was premised on two ideas: first, that law, including law practice, was a science, something like biology; and second, that the science of law was properly taught by studying judicial decisions, analogous to studying biological specimens.[64] The instructional books in this system therefore consisted entirely of reprints of judicial decisions organized by subject matter (such as contracts and property) and, within that framework, a supposedly logical order of exposition. In the Harvard case method there was little or no reference to legislation, none to court practice or administration of justice, and none to broader social and historical background.[65]

It was in protest against this Harvard approach that Oliver Wendell Holmes uttered some of his most memorable dicta about law. In *The Common Law*, published in 1881, Holmes said: "The life of the law has not been logic: it has been experience. The felt necessities of the times, the prevalent moral and political theories, intuitions of public policy ... even the prejudices which judges share with their fellow men."[66] Again, a few years later Holmes observed: "It is perfectly proper to regard and study the law simply as a great anthropological document."[67]

The concepts underlying the Harvard case method—that law was a classificatory science like biology as understood at the end of the nineteenth century, and that it should be studied exclusively through specimen judicial decisions—were certainly erroneous. Nevertheless, these concepts shaped the Harvard curriculum until well into the twentieth century, and that curriculum became the model for legal education at most other institutions.

The concepts underlying the Harvard method had two very important practical implications. First, legal education was properly to be undertaken at the graduate level, following completion of the university curriculum. In this respect the American law school diploma was like the doctoral degree (Ph.D.) in the humanities and sciences. Conducting legal education as an advanced degree program severed legal education from the college curriculum and in time led to law faculties typically being functionally distant from the rest of the university. It also resulted in a law school student body whose members had diverse university educations before entering the law curriculum. American law students may have concentrated in engineering or music in their undergraduate years, as well as in the more typical subjects of history, philosophy, literature, or economics.

The second practical implication of the Harvard concept was that the law curriculum, although conceived as a science, addressed law as the subject of a profession's vocation and not as a branch of humane learning. The focus on judicial decisions concentrated on common law precedents, to the disregard of classical Roman jurisprudence. It also addressed cases by focusing on the facts of a legal dispute instead of general legal rules and principles. A critical approach to judicial decisions in American legal pedagogy could reveal confusion, inconsistencies, and contradictions, not a systematic and coherent whole.[68] Thus, American legal education became at the same time a subject of "higher learning" for postgraduate study, a technical subject for prospective practitioners, and, as sometimes taught, a critique of law and legal reasoning. The result eventually was a curriculum that was intellectually sophisticated but taught by faculty separated, indeed often isolated, from the other fields of university study and research.

The Harvard concept of a graduate professional curriculum in law was regarded as having elevated law to a level of both academic and professional prominence. As such, the Harvard case method became the program for reform of American legal education. In the first several decades of the twentieth century that model was made virtually obligatory throughout the United States.

The American graduate professional curriculum in law was disconnected not only from the undergraduate university curriculum but also from the standards and procedures for admission to practice. However, approximately concurrent with adoption of the case method the rules of admission to practice were reformed. The new requirements included a written bar examination and a more systematic review of personal character.[69] These requirements were animated both by a desire to ensure a level of competence in people entering the profession and by an animosity toward "undesirable" elements among those seeking admission, particularly immigrants and children of immigrants, such as Jews and Italians.[70] Completion of the law school curriculum, passage of the bar examination, and satisfaction of a minimal standard of "character and fitness" thereby became the necessary conditions, and sufficient conditions, for practicing law in the United States. A few states in addition imposed some kind of probationary or apprenticeship requirement. However, apprenticeship and character requirements often operated in favor of the sons and nephews of established practitioners, to the exclusion or disadvantage of dissidents, women, and racial minorities.[71] Similar challenges have been made to the bar examination and to legal education itself,[72] but these have been rejected.

Canada has evolved a combination of the English and American systems. Completion of a graduate law degree approximately like the Harvard program is now required, as is a bar examination and character review, but also required is a one-year period of apprenticeship—called "articling" because traditionally it is performed under the articles of apprenticeship.

In the United States and Canada, completion of these requirements formally certifies the fledging lawyer as competent to practice. Admission standards are "democratic" in that fulfillment is calibrated to performance at or somewhat below the average, rather than being administered as a system of exclusion. The levels of technical accomplishment among newly minted Canadian and American lawyers therefore cover a wide range. Some fledgling lawyers with very little experience can in fact carry out quite competent representation in many kinds of matters. This may be attributable to formal education that is broader and longer than in the European models. It may also be a consequence of the fact that law practice in Canada and the United States has enormous breadth in subject matter, involving not only traditional specialties such as trial advocacy and conveyancing but new ones such as computer law, environmental law, and health law. In any new field of activity, recent education and youthful intensity can be a comparative advantage relative to long experience.

Practical Competence

The mechanisms for initial testing of competence—educational requirements, a bar examination, apprenticeship—are relatively inexact. Most relevant professional skills can be acquired only through experience as a lawyer or, increasingly in modern practice, experience reinforced and extended through continuing legal education in professional lectures and seminars. A young lawyer gains experience in the practice arts by observing more experienced lawyers, "giving it a try," imitating them in adapting technique and "style," and engaging in self-critical evaluation and sometimes review and observation by others. The practice arts include, among others:

- continuing, renewed and deepened attention to legal texts in the fields in which the lawyer becomes engaged;
- observing the behavior patterns and apparent motivations of the judges, clerks, regulatory officials, and opposite-number lawyers with whom they interact;
- developing strategic sense in handling matters for clients;
- mastering technique in conducting interviews with clients, in person and over the telephone, learning to "listen with the third ear," and balancing sympathy with objectivity in dealing with clients' problems;
- mastering technique in dealing with opposing parties and their lawyers, including ones who are ill-informed, bad mannered, or unreasonable;
- learning to mask surprise at the unexpected;
- organizing priorities, focusing effort, and learning what formalities may safely be disregarded in various circumstances;
- appreciating the importance of time and timing in undertaking tasks and conducting maneuvers on behalf of clients;

- appreciating the costs at risk for clients and how much clients can afford;
- being able to submit billings without embarrassment and persuade clients to pay.

A reasonably successful lawyer must have achieved an adequate combination of these practice arts. Some lawyers achieve an exquisite combination of these arts and are brilliantly successful, much as a major league athlete will combine many practical skills of his sport. Some who have entered the profession find they lack the right combination, or find that employing such a combination is distasteful or even repugnant and depart for another vocation. But many continue, getting by with various levels of competence.

Yet once a person is admitted to practice, "demoting" him out of the profession is difficult even if he proves to be relatively incompetent. The established members of the profession have little incentive to lift standards by excluding those who are marginally competent after they have been admitted. Differences in competence above that minimum level are difficult to prove, unpleasant to prosecute, and disruptive of collegial relationships. A lawyer whom a fellow could accuse of incompetence might, while the ensuing disbarment proceeding is pending, appear on the other side in a litigation or a negotiation. From a more materialistic viewpoint, if the level of practice is mediocre, lawyers of superior ability will prosper.

The result is that mediocrity—literally, the "average"— is the prevailing standard of practice in the law, as it no doubt is in other professions and vocations. Serious criticism of this level of practice typically is addressed only by outsiders, notably academics, and by highly competent and successful practitioners who are dismayed by the prevailing low standards observed in their profession.[73]

The criticism that many average lawyers are not very competent, and that many lawyers are marginally incompetent or worse, is, in our opinion, correct and tragic but largely futile. First, the criticism has persisted through history, which suggests that the deficiency is an aspect of humanity and not a phenomenon of a specific legal system or historical period. Second, half the lawyers in any given community at any given time are by definition below average. Assuming, as we do, that effective competency in law practice covers a wide range of proficiency, this means that many clients must deal with lawyers who are not very competent. We also assume, on the basis of economic and political axioms, that clients who are wealthy or powerful will do better in finding a capable lawyer than clients who are not. Third, because law practice interacts with the system of justice, incompetence on the part of a lawyer often translates into injustice to the client.

Incompetence among lawyers, as among judges, must be regarded as a serious social evil. But remedying that social evil entails choices that are difficult to implement and which the legal profession and the larger community are reluctant to make. Above all, measuring competence in any profession is difficult.[74] Nevertheless, it is possible to identify gross incompetence. The disciplinary apparatus could identify and disbar lawyers who are grossly incompetent, at least lawyers who are repeatedly so. There are no reliable figures on the effectiveness of professional policing of incompetence, and a reliable measure of the incidence of incompetence would be difficult or impossible to construct. However, we believe that disciplinary response to lawyer incompetence is weak everywhere. For example, the disciplinary system for solicitors in England, which probably is at least as good as disciplinary systems elsewhere, deals almost exclusively with dishonesty, as distinct from incompetence.[75] In Canada and the United States, incompetence as such is rarely redressed in the disciplinary process.[76] Instead, cases of serious incompetence either go unaddressed or come to the attention of disciplinary authority when a lawyer who has bungled compounds that offense by concealing his errors and lying to the client. All our information indicates that the same situation prevails in most other systems.

The same failures are characteristic of disciplinary mechanisms in other professions.[77] A profession as a group has incentives of self-esteem and public relationships to proclaim the need for high standards, but fewer incentives to organize and mount effective policing of incompetence. Lawyers in their own practice settings are interested in hiring good apprentices and maintaining a high level of competence in their offices, but they have little practical interest in strengthening the competence of other law offices. At a more personal level, effective policing would involve investigations, contested proceedings, and disbarments that ruin the hopes and professional livelihoods of those who are found wanting. Effective policing by the profession would thus be expensive, divisive, controversial, and often occasion for regret or remorse. The historical record suggests that it has always been thus.

Long-run improvement in the technical competency of lawyers can be achieved through better basic education, better law school education, and better practice training and monitoring of professional development in the early years of practice. We, the authors, have dedicated much of our lives to some of these goals. We do not expect large returns in the short run, however.

If it is assumed that the professional disciplinary mechanism is relatively ineffective, and the occasional judicial response to incompetence is no better, the question is whether the courts should provide a remedy through a claim for damages—malpractice liability. In an earlier era, the answer to this question was negative. In some legal systems no such remedy was recognized, and in others it was recognized only to the extent of liability for fraud as distinct from negligence. Everywhere the courts were more or less inhospitable to claims of professional malpractice, and lawyers were extremely reluctant to prosecute claims against fellow professionals.

That attitude still persists in varying degrees. In many systems there is effectively no damages remedy for a lawyer's negligence, however egregious. In contrast, in the United States the remedy of legal malpractice is recognized and assertion of such claims has burgeoned. There is an established body of legal doctrine, parallel to the law of medical malpractice.[78] Malpractice liability can be asserted not only in favor of clients but also in favor of narrowly defined categories of third persons directly injured by a lawyer's negligence. In that "nonclient" category, for example, are family members who would have taken an inheritance under a will but who lost out because the will was improperly drafted. Another category includes parties to business transactions who are directly affected by a lawyer's opinion, for example, a bank that has lent money to the lawyer's client. Moreover, aggrieved clients may sue a lawyer who failed to disclose a conflict of interest, contending that the lawyer thereby created an advantage for the other client. That claim can create a question of fact as to whether the lawyer provided vigorous representation.

In England, there is a sort of middle way. Neither barristers nor solicitors can be sued for negligence in their conduct in court but can be liable for advice or assistance they provide out of court. Proving negligence for conduct in court is in any event very difficult. First, in court proceedings there is an opposing party whose very engagement is to oppose. It is therefore doubtful whether an approach different from that taken by the accused lawyer would have succeeded. Second, all in-court maneuvers (arguably) involve professional judgment concerning strategy and tactics. Surely there should be a basis for malpractice liability if crucial evidence has been ignored or a viable claim against another party overlooked. But beyond this, an accused lawyer can defend on the ground that professional strategy and judgment were involved.

But the English decisions have now somewhat enlarged the scope of what is "out of court" and hence the bases of a legal malpractice claim.[79] In a leading decision, the House of Lords reviewed the evolution of the rule of lawyer malpractice liability in England, of development of the law in Australia, Canada, and New Zealand, and reference to the law in continental Europe and in the United States. Lord Bingham of Cornhill, C. J., then said:

> Save where a claim relates to the acts or omissions of an advocate conducting a contested case in open court, forensic immunity is not to be recognized [as] a blanket rule . . . [T]here are certain forms of advice (such as decisions made on strategic or professional grounds on which witnesses should or should not be called, or whether claims or defenses should or should not be pleaded) which would be covered by forensic immunity. . . . We cannot . . . accept that a similar immunity should attach to allegedly negligent decisions made out of court. . . .[80]

In our opinion the courts should be no more hesitant to recognize civil claims for legal malpractice than claims, for example, of accounting or engineering malpractice. There are recognized standards of law practice, there can be relevant expert testimony concerning compliance with those standards, and there are techniques for measuring resulting damages. Liability insurance is now widely available and, indeed, many countries require lawyers to maintain such insurance. The notion that allowing legal malpractice claims will weaken the bonds of the lawyer-client relationship is sometimes offered as a rationale for limiting or denying liability. This apology strikes us as absurd. Most clients are somewhat uneasy with their lawyers in any event, especially a client dealing with a lawyer for the first time. Legal malpractice claims are based on the conduct of a lawyer who (allegedly) abused that relationship. Malpractice claims typically are brought only if the professional has badly handled the underlying matter or thereafter badly handled the relationship. Furthermore, recognizing the remedy gives a client who has been wronged a remedy independent of the local disciplinary mechanism, which in our estimate is often erratic or even feeble.

Finding a Good Lawyer

The differences in competence among the practicing bar in any community are reflected in "reputation." Professional reputation is the assessment of a professional in the informal collective judgment of peers within the professional community and, more uncertainly, in the opinion of a larger public. The informal collective judgment is an unsystematic distillation of professional evaluations, casual observation, hearsay, attributions based on personal background, stereotyping, and other miscellany. Every lawyer has some kind of professional reputation.[81]

Potential clients can differentiate between mediocre lawyers and highly competent ones only on the basis of reputation. Professional reputation is transmitted along pathways of social and business acquaintance. Potential clients with money or status, through their networks of acquaintances with similar status, often can identify competent lawyers much more easily than can people in other social circles. The picture in England of an ordinary citizen trying to find a lawyer is in our opinion similar to that in other countries. It has been portrayed as follows:

> In one study involving divorcing parents, by far the most popular method of choosing [a solicitor] was through recommendation of family or friends. The next largest group went to a solicitor they had used before—in many cases for their house purchase. Nearly one person in six had simply noticed a solicitor's office and walked in, or chosen a firm from the *Yellow Pages*.[82]

Under the English system of a divided profession—barristers and solicitors—a major litigation matter generally is referred by a solicitor to a barrister for presentation in court. Referral by a solicitor provides some assurance that the representation will be placed in the hands of an advocate of appropriate competence. To the extent that the division between barrister and solicitor provides a check on competence, that check is being lost through the modern reduction or elimination of the division. However, there is no such screening mechanism for what the English call "noncontentious" work—that is, office transactions—which are in the practice domain of the solicitors. Nor does the screening mechanism operate in litigation matters that solicitors are now authorized to handle. In those matters, clients without preexisting connections to the world of law practice are probably as often at sea in England as they are elsewhere.

In a client's search for an appropriate lawyer, another factor is often at work as well: unrealistic expectations on the part of inexperienced clients as to what lawyers and the legal system can do for them. Many people imagine that the court system will accept their version of the dispute, forgetting that the other side has a different interpretation and will testify accordingly. These attitudes are reinforced by popular belief that the rich and powerful always turn the law to their advantage by having a lawyer, and that a lawyer can help them in the same way. Much counseling of inexperienced clients who consult a lawyer consists of lowering their expectations. But that kind of counseling can leave the client in deep doubt about the competence of her lawyer: "How did I get into the hands of a lawyer who says that we may lose?"

The difference in practical access to a suitably competent lawyer, being related to the socioeconomic status of potential clients, means that getting a suitably competent lawyer is a risky proposition for the average citizen. As noted in the Canadian Code: "[O]ne who has little or no contact with lawyers or who is a stranger in the community may have difficulty in finding a lawyer who has the special skill required for the particular task."[83] That "social distance" in turn adversely affects the distribution of legal services among the poor and lower economic classes—beyond the already important effect of differential ability to pay. It is therefore inevitable but cruel that the distribution of legal services is fundamentally unfair.[84]

The traditional system whereby clients learn about lawyers through reputation may have worked in small communities (although we have doubts about that), but in the modern context it has become unsystematic and unreliable. These defects are increasingly apparent as modern society becomes more concentrated in large metropolitan communities. In these places, the networks through which personal reputation is transmitted become ever more disconnected from each other. In an impersonal mass society, how does one find a competent lawyer who does not already know such a lawyer?

One mechanism is the advertising of professional services. Advertising can substitute for or supplement reputation, or indeed it can create an "artificial" reputation.

Traditionally lawyers were prohibited from advertising of any kind. They could use business cards and in most countries could have their name on their office door or, classically, their "shingle." Otherwise, lawyers were limited to describing their firms in legal directories—thick books of formal listings organized by region and alphabetically. In recent years, these restrictions have been relaxed, and some kinds of advertising are permitted.[85] Lawyer advertising now appears in the telephone book "yellow pages" in every American locality and often on television.

Lawyer advertising has come to be permitted in most other legal systems, although at a slower rate and with less aggressive intensity than in the United States. The CCBE Code reflects the fact that there are variations in permissible advertising in the European countries: "A lawyer should not advertise or seek personal publicity where this is not permitted."[86] The Italian Code says: "A lawyer may honestly and truthfully inform people about his professional activity . . . through brochures, letterheads, professional or other telephone books . . . [and] may indicate the areas in which he is practicing . . . "[87] In England today, advertising by both barristers and solicitors is liberally allowed, but must be, as the solicitors' rules put it, "in good taste."[88] In France, under a decree promulgated in 1991, advertising is permitted but closely regulated. The size and style of advertising is limited, it must be approved in advance by the local bar, and it must accord with "discretion." Advertising is not permitted in news media. The Canadian Code discussion of lawyer advertising reflects the fact that regulation of advertising in Canada, as in some other countries, is decentralized into localities. The Canadian Code also has recitals that express the intense reservations about advertising that have traditionally prevailed in the legal profession everywhere.[89] In China a lawyer is entirely prohibited from advertising.

Not all advertising is successful, in that it does not yield new clientele sufficient to justify the expense involved. American law firms, through trial and error, have gained some sophistication in advertising technique. Law firms engaged in business law, dealing primarily with sophisticated clients, advertise in restrained fashion, chiefly through brochures describing litigation, commercial, and financial matters that they have handled. Law firms that represent individuals focus on such practice fields as divorce, personal injury claims, bankruptcy, and defense of charges in motor vehicle offenses.

Lawyer advertising certainly enhances public awareness that personal problems may have important legal dimensions and that the assistance of a lawyer could help in dealing with them. Legal advertising continues to be regarded with dismay by many thoughtful observers, both within and outside the profession. They are especially concerned that unsophisticated clients may be exploited, particularly if they have rights with high economic value such as personal injury claims. Obviously, law firms that continue to advertise consider the effort worthwhile. Law firms that can stay in practice long enough to reap the returns from advertising usually are at least fairly competent. Thus, by a Darwinian process of survival, law firm advertising probably results in providing average individuals with legal service that is at least average in competence.

Advertising is a technique of relatively modern vintage. A much older restriction on lawyers' efforts to get clientele is the prohibition of solicitation.

The traditional definition of solicitation included any affirmative effort by a lawyer to attract clients except with business cards, a sign over the office, and, with the invention of the telephone, a listing in the ordinary pages of the telephone book. In colloquial terminology, the prohibition was against "ambulance chasing," such as calling on injury victims in the hospital, calling relatives of a decedent to seek probate business, or hanging about the courthouse to seek out defendants in criminal proceedings. A modern form of solicitation is "parachuting" into the scene of a catastrophe such as an airplane crash, ostensibly to "investigate" but also to engage in conversation with potential clients.

All such forms of solicitation are prohibited everywhere by similar rules. The English rule is that solicitors "[may not] publicise their practices . . . by means of unsolicited visits or telephone calls."[90] The Italian rule is that "a lawyer is forbidden to offer professional services to third parties and in general to carry out any activity to promote contacts with clients . . . "[91] The Japanese Rules of Advertising of Practicing Attorneys adopted in 2000, Article 5, provide that a lawyer may not seek clients "by means of visit or by telephone." The American rule is characteristically more complicated: "A lawyer shall not by in-person or live telephone contact solicit professional employment from a prospective client with whom the lawyer has no family or prior professional relationship when a significant motive . . . is the lawyer's pecuniary gain."[92] This permits recorded telephone messages and presumably e-mail, and permits direct contacts with relatives and present or former clients. The American rule also exempts contacts where the motive is *not* pecuniary gain for the lawyer. This last exemption accommodates efforts by civil rights and other activist organizations to seek out people who might need legal help or who would be willing to participate in "test case" litigation.[93]

In the United States there have been some instances of grossly reprehensible solicitations by lawyers, such as going to the scene of disastrous accidents in pursuit of personal injury litigation. Another gambit has involved lawyers going to retirement homes to seek out estate planning engagements with senior citizens and then designating themselves as executors (supervisors) of the estate or even as will beneficiaries. These forms of misconduct are prohibited everywhere, but violations can go undetected. Virtually all competent lawyers refrain from solicitation, except through such classic forms as playing golf with potential clients.

At the intersection of advertising and public service is the problem of relations between lawyers and the media. Establishing and nurturing relationships with the media can be advertising in effect. The universally recognized norm used to be that a lawyer should have no contact with the media. Canon 20 of the ABA Canons of Professional Ethics of 1908, for example, provided: "Newspaper publications by a lawyer as to pending or anticipated litigation may interfere with a fair trial. . . . Generally they are to be condemned." The rule governing English barristers is still to the same effect:

> A barrister must not in relation to any anticipated or current proceedings in which he is briefed [i.e., retained] or expects to appear or has appeared as an advocate express a personal opinion to or in the press or other media upon the facts or the issues arising in the proceedings.[94]

However, this traditional norm has been radically eroded in some countries. In the United States, the constitutional principle of free speech in the First Amendment intrudes on all limitations on communication. The American media have been insistent that litigation is public business and as such a matter about which the media have a right and duty to inquire. In criminal cases, prosecutors, particularly those who hold office by election, have strong incentive to publicize prosecutions, especially those involving violent crime; defense counsel feel a corresponding need to neutralize adverse publicity by giving their own version of the facts.

The American Bar Association has tried to maintain a cordial relationship with media representatives, but also to preserve the legal profession's traditional stance toward trial publicity. With that objective, the ABA has promulgated rules aimed at maintaining a balance between "free press and fair trial." ABA Rule 3.6, entitled "Trial Publicity," sets forth elaborately defined protocols for public statements by lawyers, including prosecutors and defense counsel in criminal cases. However, the U.S. Supreme Court refused to bless Rule 3.6. In a split decision with a cacophony of concurrence and dissent, the court in *Gentile v. State Bar of Nevada* left the law uncertain and most analysts baffled.[95] As a practical matter, the American rule evidently is that comment is permissible if it does not poison the minds of prospective jurors. That means almost anything goes.

"Media relations" accordingly has become an intense concern not merely to prosecutors and defense counsel in criminal cases but to other "repeat players" in litigation as well. These include business companies and plaintiffs' lawyers concerning product defects (for example, claims against automobile companies), employee relations (for example, claims of race and sex discrimination), and consumer and environmental cases. Indeed, media relations regarding litigation have become something of a subspecialty in the field of public relations. Companies and their lawyers are urged, for example, to "get out there first with the truth," while many lawyers for claimants have become adept at disseminating press releases and giving "lectures" on the courthouse steps.

Legal proceedings in most other countries have remained more shrouded. However, court proceedings have always been of interest to the public, at least locally and through gossip. After all, the English judges traveling on circuit came to town in red robes, accompanied by their retinues. The ensuing proceedings could not be very secret. But modern media coverage of legal proceedings is something else. On one hand, in mass society the media are the public's only source of information about what is happening in court. Legal proceedings can be of great practical and political significance. On the other hand, media accounts are necessarily incomplete, often are "dumbed down" for popular consumption, and sometimes distort the evidence and the issues. But these deficiencies are no different from those attending media coverage of other events—parliamentary politics, business activity, and sporting events, for example.

In our estimate, the legal world simply has to become accustomed to the presence and influence of "the media." Juries can be adequately admonished to disregard what they have heard before receiving the evidence (most jurors are not unaware of media distortion). Judges have long since learned to put suitable discount on information other than evidence. Life will go on.

A more insidious influence, in our opinion, is the pressure of media opinion on the judiciary concerning controversial public issues that come before the courts, such as legal issues concerning political contributions, product liability, and control of the media itself. This problem is again most difficult in the United States because of the popular election of judges; some elections of American appellate judges have become intensely politicized.[96] The problem of politics in judicial elections has become more acute as a result of a decision by the Supreme Court in *Republican Party of Minnesota v. White*. That decision held that a candidate for judicial office had a right of free speech concerning legal issues that might come before the court—for example, abortion or the procedure in death penalty prosecutions. Judges' freedom to make speeches about judicial issues is a challenge to the independence of the judiciary, discussed in Chapter 2. However, protecting freedom of the press (as distinct from freedom of the judges themselves to make speeches) on issues of judicial performance seems to us as important as protecting the independence of the judiciary. A satisfactory détente is possible where the media are "responsible" and the judiciary is professionally steadfast. But these are behavioral standards, not susceptible of enactment as legal rules.

4

Independence

Professional Independence

A second norm of professional ethics, which for many lawyers would be the first principle, is independence. The essential idea is that, in carrying out his professional functions, a lawyer should think and act professionally and not be subservient to direction or control by others. This norm is stated in the Italian Code as follows: "In the exercise of his professional activity a lawyer has the duty to preserve his independence and to defend his liberty from any external pressure of restrictions."[1] The counterpart American rule is stated as follows: "In representing a client, a lawyer shall exercise independent professional judgment and render candid advice."[2]

The concept of independence is both central to the idea of professional ethics and necessarily ambiguous. From one perspective, it expresses an aspiration that is shared by all professions, particularly those traditionally known in Europe as the "free professions." These include medicine, law, pedagogy in both higher and lower education, and, more recently and more generally, professional scientists, accountants, financial consultants, psychologists, and others. The root term, "profess," means "affirmation of belief" and is used to describe the religious commitment being made by a novice upon becoming a priest. The definition of "profession" refers to vocations requiring a high level of special knowledge and skill. It is also linked to a professional's duty of loyalty to clients and to maintain the confidentiality of client information.[3] In the civil law tradition the concept is also linked to the right of a professional to refuse to disclose such information to others, including the courts.[4]

The relationship between independence and loyalty to client obviously is that a lawyer cannot be fully loyal to a client if there are interfering commitments to others, including the state. The relationship between independence and maintenance of confidentiality is that a lawyer could not be independent if required to disclose a client's affairs to the prosecutor or the police, for example. The obligation of confidentiality also allows a lawyer intellectual independence in assessing the facts and circumstances of a matter and in deliberating about recommendations, without fear that subsequent disclosure will result in embarrassment.

The concept of professional independence can be explored by posing the question: What are the "contaminating" influences from which a lawyer should be independent?[5] The sources of improper influence upon a lawyer can be classified into four categories: independence from the state, including independence from the courts; independence from improper influence of relationships a lawyer may have with others, including other clients and a lawyer's colleagues; independence from the client; and independence from improper influence of the lawyer's personal opinions about matters of politics, morality, and the state of society.

The sources of the feared improper influence are identified somewhat differently in various legal traditions. The French legal profession, for example, has emphasized independence from the state, an attitude shared in other "Latin" countries such as Italy and Spain. That attitude and policy goes back to the time of the powerful Bourbon kings of the seventeenth and eighteen centuries, an era in which suffocation by the state was a real threat.[6] In Italy, the virtue of "professional" independence was most strongly voiced during Mussolini's regime, perhaps as encoded language pleading for broader political freedom.[7] In postwar Germany, assertion of professional independence has obvious significance as an argument for renewal of constitutional government after the Nazi catastrophe.[8] English barristers traditionally consider themselves to be affiliated with the courts and to play a fundamental role in governing the state.

In contrast, in the People's Republic of China, lawyers' responsibility to the state supersedes their responsibility to their clients, and they can be disciplined for improperly challenging the authority of state officials.[9] The risk of state interference with professional autonomy is much less salient in American professional consciousness because the concept of the "state" is itself alien to the American experience. But legal constraints on what a lawyer may do for a client are regarded by many American lawyers as interference with the profession's independence.[10]

In systems with a "divided" profession as in England (with its barristers and solicitors), and some states in Australia, there is an added complexity to the matter of independence. It has been observed that "the livelihood of a barrister is very dependent on solicitors and what they think of the barrister. From a barrister's perspective, the goal . . . is not necessarily to win the case . . . [but] to [impress] the solicitors on both sides for future cases."[11]

The basis of lawyers' concern about independence from the state or the government is immediate. (In the common law tradition, the "state" is usually referred to as the "government.") The legal profession is a corps of persons expert in law and government but who, for the most part, are neither officials or employees of the state nor fully aligned with its interest. On the contrary, most lawyers are in private practice, and the function of lawyers in private practice is often to resist efforts of state officials, for example, in representing defendants in criminal prosecutions or in representing individuals or businesses who are subject to governmental directives or investigations.

Maintaining appropriate "distance" between the state bureaucratic apparatus and members of the legal profession is an essential element of a modern constitutional regime. Challenge of state authority often is accomplished with legal assistance, which in turn requires that the lawyer be independent of the state. Attack on the bar's professional independence from government authority was manifest in Nazi Germany, communist Russia, fascist Italy, and Peronist Argentina. A more diffuse attack, but a very real one, was felt by lawyers in the American South who challenged racial segregation from the 1950s until about 1970. Similar attacks were made against lawyers disputing apartheid in South Africa and, more recently, dictatorship in other African countries.[12]

The practice of law in this respect is similar to the "loyal opposition" provided by minority political parties in parliamentary government. Like the loyal opposition in politics, the legal profession accepts the regime's constitutional framework, but within that framework the lawyer in representation of a client is a dissident voice. Like loyal opposition in the political arena, the lawyer's voice can excite antipathy on the part of the regime and sometimes in public opinion as well. The constitutional importance of political independence of the bar also is parallel to the importance of freedom of the press, both being media for challenging government policy and for upholding freedom of religious affiliation and practice.

Instilling an attitude of independence is a salient element of professional socialization in the Western tradition. It begins in professional training for the neophyte, is sustained by professional lore and "stories" exemplifying the virtue, and is referenced in controversies with the state. However, independence is not a "natural" or easily accepted attitude. Many who were lawyers in the former communist regimes, for example, have had difficulty reorienting themselves from being almost supplicants to being fearless champions under the new constitutional ideal.

However, at some point of intensity in its exercise, professional independence can become obstruction and subversion, just as political opposition in a parliamentary regime can become destructive. This risk is particularly serious where the resources available to clients of the private bar and the resources available to regulatory authorities and private opposite parties are out of balance. In the postcommunist regime in Russia, for example, the private oligarchs enriched themselves through privatization, aided in part by their private lawyers, and in doing so ran rings around understaffed and ill-equipped government enforcement agencies. There have been similar patterns in third world countries where governments have been "kleptocracies." In the "first world" countries as well, lawyers often can drag out investigations and other legal proceedings to the point of affording de facto immunity to their clients. Similarly, the efforts of governments to trace "money laundering" in many instances are obstructed by lawyers who invoke professional secrecy to shield their clients. And yet the protection of lawyers' professional secrecy has a necessary place in a constitutional regime.

The delicate balance between the bar's independence and its public responsibility is perhaps illustrated in the relationship between the profession and the state in Russia, before and after the overthrow of the Soviet regime. The Soviet regime required lawyers to be members of collective offices called a "college." Nominally, that arrangement was patterned on the *colegios* of Western systems such as Spain's, where collective identity and professional life sustained the bar's independence. In Russia, however, the system was a means of keeping lawyers under observation and control. Since the demise of the Soviet system, the system of colleges and the requirement of compulsory membership have been continued. Some of these colleges now have a positive reputation in the professions as sources of technical assistance and professional solidarity.[13] The reconstituted Russian colleges could evolve into institutions like their Western sisters, combining elements of a bar association and a law firm, and thus support true professional independence.

An appropriate balance between professional independence from the state and professional responsibility is difficult to define and can be even more difficult to maintain. One litigant's forceful stand against oppressive authority is another's obstruction of justice. One client's private affairs are another's illegal financial operations. The difficulties are compounded in the modern context, where transactions can be centered in countries that are regulatory havens and in financial institutions whose records are inaccessible. They are further compounded as members of the practicing bar become more numerous, more dispersed, less publicly visible, and share a diminishing set of common values and attitudes. But efforts to define and proclaim common values for the legal professions across national lines, such as the CCBE Code, move in the direction of responsible professional independence.

"Self-Government" of the Profession

Maintaining independence of the bar from the state can be effective only through lawyers' collective action. Individually or in their own law firms, lawyers are relatively weak politically. Finding shelter behind powerful clients is protective, but only if the clients remain powerful, and in any event relying on clients involves the risk of compromising professional independence from another direction. Hence lawyers from earliest times have banded together in bar associations. Some of their interests are of course selfish, such as efforts to maintain fee levels and to exclude others from functions that lawyers consider their exclusive professional domain. Maintaining the bar's political autonomy from the state is also selfish, but in the same sense that the news media are selfish in asserting freedom of the press or university professors in asserting academic freedom.

A concept giving institutional form to professional independence is that the legal profession should be self-governing, or at least have a substantial role in regulating the profession. Self-government implies that the bar as a group defines and administers its standards of professional conduct such as competence and loyalty to clients. Self-governing professions were among the centers of authority in the pluralistic constitution of the Old Regime— along with the church, the clergy, the higher and lower aristocracies, and the guilds of artisans, merchants, and tradesmen.[14] The concept that a professional group such as lawyers should be beyond the reach of government regulation is much more difficult to justify in the modern era of democratic government.

The structure of bar government in some legal systems is national, while in others it is regional. For example, the English Bar Council is the governing organization for barristers in the whole of England and Wales, while the French *avocats* are organized in local associations (*barreaux*), each of which has a governing counsel (*conseil de l'ordre*) and is linked to the regional court of appeal. A French national body, the Conseil National du Barreau, endeavors to harmonize local standards and represents the profession in dealings with the government. In the United States, the basic organization of the bar is at the state level (e.g., the California State Bar, the New York State Bar Association), where there are links to the respective state court systems; a national organization (the American Bar Association) seeks to harmonize standards and represent the profession in dealings with the federal government.

The bar's claim to self-governance asserts that regulation of lawyers is largely beyond the authority of the political branches of government to modify or invade. Assertion of that right in bold terms is necessary only when the legal profession's independence is under serious attack, which historically has usually occurred as part of a broader attack on minority political parties, the free press, the church and clergy, and others. A modified claim of independence is established in American law, where the courts (whose judges were once lawyers) have claimed primary authority to regulate the bar to the exclusion of the legislature. On this basis, many American state supreme courts have held invalid attempts by legislatures to regulate the legal profession, while affirming the court's own authority over members of the bar.[15]

The independence of the bar, at least substantial independence from the legislature, is a more or less firmly established principle in all modern legal systems. Apart from protecting against political oppression directed against lawyers, the concept has effects on the conception of the norms governing the practice of law. The ethical norms governing the practice of law are not usually considered ordinary positive law, but instead a special norm that is intramural to the profession.[16] In this respect the legal profession makes a claim parallel to that traditionally made by the medical profession and, in a somewhat different way, by the clergy and by academics. Accordingly, the ethical norms governing the profession have traditionally been considered, by the bar and by the courts in giving them effect, to be customs or practices. Considered as such, the rules of the profession have long been considered a subject for study in sociology, or a problem of moral philosophy, but not one for legal analysis.

The premise that legal ethics is outside the realm of legal obligations is widely shared by many lawyers as well. Most have considered "professional ethics" to be traditions of their profession, not legal rules.[17] Vestiges of this approach are found in obsolescent judicial decisions that a lawyer should not or cannot sue for an unpaid fee,[18] that a lawyer cannot be sued for malpractice,[19] and that the rules of ethics do not impose definite obligations on lawyers.[20] From this viewpoint, it follows that disciplinary proceedings are an intrafraternal matter and outside the purview of the courts, except for utterly unreasonable or fraudulent disciplinary prosecutions. The premise is that, since the legal profession is governed by customs established by fraternal consensus and not by legal rules enforceable through legal procedures, legal analysis of the rules of professional ethics would be inappropriate, or indeed incoherent.

This traditional viewpoint is rapidly changing, however. At the most abstract level, it is coming to be recognized that "law" is a broader category than legislation promulgated by a nation. Effective government through legal norms is also exercised through other power centers, ranging from multinational corporations to international organizations such as the United Nations. At a lower level of generalization, the formulation and application of norms in all sectors of society is increasingly "legalized"—that is, codified as formal regulations and enforced by bureaucratic procedures. For example, regulation of the environment is now accomplished through detailed regulations rather than through norms concerning use of property; and consumer transactions are regulated through detailed requirements rather than through norms of contract law.

A similar transformation is occurring in the ethical norms of the legal profession. In 1970 the American Code of Professional Responsibility was promulgated and in 1974 the Canadian Code of Professional Conduct, and between 1984 and 1996 several states in Australia adopted formal codes; New Zealand did so in 1989.[21] In England today, the Law Society and the Bar Council exercise delegated authority to regulate solicitors and barristers respectively. The Law Society has an elaborate code, the Bar Council a more succinct one.[22] The Chinese Regulations of Lawyers' Professional Ethics and Business Practices were adopted in 1996, after the All-China Lawyers Association was authorized to promulgate governing rules. There has been a similar development in India under authority of the Advocates Act of 1961.[23] Several European countries have adopted codes of ethics, for example the Italian Codice Deontologico Forense adopted in 1997. The CCEB of the European Community is a body of similarly codified standards. Many more countries now have specific regulations concerning a lawyer's financial accounts, rather than relying on the norm of fiduciary duty.[24]

The formalization of legal ethics has had one definite beneficial effect: It has reduced the possibility that leaders of the bar can punish or ostracize unorthodox lawyers on the basis of supposed ethical violations. History has recorded many instances of courageous lawyers defending persons unjustly accused of crimes. History has less faithfully recorded that some of these lawyers subsequently suffered at the hands of the local professional establishment for flouting the received political consensus. Infliction of that kind of retribution is probably more difficult when the rules of professional conduct have been formalized.

The transformation of professional ethics from informal customs and practices into systematic legal codes is not an unmixed blessing, however. Law is not always and everywhere superior to custom and practice as a means of social ordering. Formalization of norms into law to some extent weakens the moral force of the rules by shifting attention from normative principles and their spirit to legalistic definition. Formalization also shifts enforcement from the mechanism of social pressure through professional colleagues to enforcement by state authority. Codification nevertheless has inspired greater consistency in the rules and greater regularity of their enforcement. But maintaining professional independence while at the same time being governed by the legal authority of the state involves a difficult balance.[25]

A special aspect of a lawyer's independence from the state is independence from the judiciary. An advocate's function, as we have seen, is to present the position of a client in ways that typically will be resisted by opposing counsel. In deciding a case, the judge necessarily will reject the presentation by one advocate or the other. If an advocate were dependent on a judge's favor, the advocate might moderate his presentation in order to preserve his standing with the judge, although doing so could weaken the force of his presentation on behalf of the client. This is the rationale of Lord Brougham's classic utterance, quoted earlier, that an advocate knows "no other duty" than to his client.[26]

In civil law systems, the relationships between lawyers and the judiciary have always been more distant than in common law systems. The fact that civil law judges follow a career path quite separate from that of lawyers maintains distance between the bench and the bar and facilitates the independence of the bar. Indeed, in most civil law countries the relationship between judges and lawyers is one of estrangement and often is somewhat hostile. In common law countries, where the judges are recruited from the ranks of lawyers, most judges maintain some social and professional relationships with the bar, particularly in ceremonial matters.

At the same time, the judiciary in all systems has important authority and responsibility concerning the conduct of lawyers who appear in matters before the courts. A judge has authority to nullify legal maneuvers that violate the rules of procedure and, in most systems, to impose penalties for gross abuse. A judge has authority to refer a misbehaving lawyer to a disciplinary body. And judges have invisible but important authority to disbelieve and reject presentations by lawyers in whom they have lost confidence.

Exercise of these forms of judicial authority can present challenges to the independence of the bar. Examples include a lawyer's refusing to obey a direction from the court or making statements out of court that criticize a judge. Contentious interchanges such as these are rare in most legal systems, but they have recurred in the United States. In many instances, American lawyers have invoked constitutional provisions by way of justification or immunity from judicial sanctions.[27] The prevailing sentiments between bench and bar in all legal systems, however, are mutual deference and, generally, mutual respect.

Other Clients and the Lawyer's Own Interests

Another source of interference with a lawyer's independent professional judgment on behalf of a client is the lawyer's concern for the interests of other clients. Virtually all lawyers in private practice (as distinct from lawyers in the employ of government or business organizations) have many clients. Indeed, having multiple clients is an important aspect of a lawyer's independence because it reduces dependency on the patronage of a single client. The typical lawyer in independent practice therefore will have several clients at any one time and many other clients over the course of time. A lawyer nevertheless must maintain appropriate loyalty to each client. The duty of loyalty is usually expressed in negative terms as the duty to avoid conflicts of interest. (The rules concerning conflict of interest are addressed in Chapter 5.) The broad principle is that a lawyer should not undertake or continue a representation that will entail a position that would be adverse to a present client, or a representation that is adverse to a former client in a matter in which the lawyer had previously been engaged.

The concepts of independence and loyalty to the client also require that a lawyer not give preference to the lawyer's own financial or personal interests over the interests of a client. Most plainly, a lawyer must deal honestly with a client in such matters as handling the client's property and setting a fee for the lawyer's service. However, the relationship between the duty of loyalty and the lawyer's legitimate interests requires some subtle distinctions.

As a practical matter, a lawyer must be concerned about his own interests as well as those of the client. All conscientious lawyers want to avoid client transactions that could implicate the lawyer in illegal conduct or fraud.[28] Many lawyers do not want to undertake matters that will require highly aggressive tactics directed toward other parties.[29] Lawyers also recognize that the reputation of a lawyer's clientele may be transferred to the lawyer himself, because, as it is said in folk wisdom, "birds of a feather flock together."

Hence, lawyers do not want to represent "unsavory" clients. But all lawyers and law firms depend on a succession of clients and a flow of fees in order to maintain their practice and livelihood. That economic pressure is a temptation to undertake tasks that may be beyond their competence or involve transactions at the boundary of illegality.

Steady fee income is a practical necessity (except for the few lawyers with independent incomes). Lawyers in independent practice are entitled to compensation for their efforts, aside from engagements in which they have agreed to serve "pro bono," without charging a fee. Arriving at an appropriate fee necessarily involves some kind of conflict of interest with the client, even when the client is eager to hire the lawyer and the lawyer equally eager to serve. Lawyers' fees are a particularly sensitive subject with clients and are subject to varying degrees of regulation.

Another problem of professional independence results from the increasing tendency of lawyers to practice in firms, particularly large firms, in contrast with solo or small-firm practice. A law firm is a type of bureaucracy, governed by internal rules, procedures, and systems of authority. Many law firms, including virtually all large firms, now have written rules and formal policies, procedures for reviewing decisions by lawyers in the firm, and hierarchical internal regimes. They must have systematic procedures for reviewing prospective new engagements to determine whether conflict of interest may be involved. If a prospective engagement will be large or protracted, the firm must assess whether it has adequate personnel to handle it; if the eventual fee for an engagement seems less than secure, the firm must determine whether the risk of nonpayment is worthwhile; if an engagement will involve political controversy or social opprobrium, the firm has to decide whether to accept it. Many law firms have a "two partner" rule concerning the issuance of written opinions: a written opinion issued by a lawyer in the firm must be reviewed and approved by at least one other partner.

Decisions concerning conflicts of interest, the terms of an opinion, and other issues of course must be made by solo practitioners as well. For a solo practitioner the decision is by and for the practitioner alone, who takes the opportunity or risk accordingly. In a firm, in contrast, decisions about such matters are made by one lawyer or a committee of the firm concerning the practice opportunities of other lawyers, with corresponding possibilities for disagreement, perhaps intense disagreement. The resolution of the issues raised in such situations affects the professional independence of the individual lawyers.

The process of deliberation and decision-making inside a law firm is sometimes extremely complex. Like many other aspects of human relationship, it can be performed more readily than it can be analyzed and explained. A thoughtful European sociologist observed that it requires "a political know-how allowing [members of the firm] to be players in a power game de-emphasizing unilateral impositions of strength and encouraging learning and mutual prescription in negotiation." He added: "[S]tructural constraints are multiple and sometimes contradictory. Members need to learn and interiorize, or at least commit themselves to, a system of rules and underlying norms and values that contribute to make these [norms] meaningful and enforceable."[30]

Of course there is a very positive aspect to these bureaucratic procedures: they usually result in better-considered decisions and more soberly considered risks. The systematic consideration of ethical problems that is typical in law firms is at least a partial explanation for the phenomenon, which appears to be universal, that law firm lawyers invite fewer disputes about their ethics than do solo practitioners. A solo practitioner by definition is personally involved in an ethical question that arises in his "firm." There is an old maxim that a lawyer who tries to represent himself has a fool for a client. There is truth in this maxim at least to the extent that a lawyer often cannot be fully objective about his own professional conduct. Yet objectivity is as necessary in resolving ethical problems as it is in resolving other legal problems.

Another kind of ethical problem arises when a law firm is being organized or dissolves. In today's legal world, it is common, for example, for two solo practitioners to form a law firm, or for an existing firm to be closed, with its members going different ways. Among the immediate issues raised by the formation or dissolution of a firm are the assignment of responsibility for existing clients, the allocation of work, and the division of revenues. (There may also be more mundane issues such as the leasehold on the firm's office.) When lawyers associate to form a firm, the usual rule is that the individual lawyers remain responsible for the matters they have been handling until a reassignment is arranged within the firm; when a firm dissolves, the usual rule is that all lawyers in the firm remain responsible for all clients until a reassignment is arranged. Through extensive experience with this problem in the United States, it has come to be recognized that a client is the client of both the firm and the lawyer personally handling the matter, and that the client may choose which lawyer should continue the representation. However, law-firm breakups have generated intense disputes.[31]

The harmonious, or at least peaceful, resolution of ethical problems is necessary for a firm's continuity. But harmonious resolution may be impossible. Law firms have dissolved over such issues as conflict of interest, such as one lawyer or department wanting to take on a new client whose engagement would conflict with the representation of another client by another lawyer in the firm. Some disputes have become public and notorious, such as internal disputes over whether the firm should continue to represent tobacco companies. A firm with which an author of this book was associated decided to terminate its representation of a client who was apparently engaged in systematic fraud against the client's customers. The result was the curtailment of a practice opportunity for one lawyer in the firm, which could be interpreted as an intrusion on that person's professional independence.

Independence from the Client

By definition, a lawyer's function is to protect the legal interests of his client. A lawyer would not have been engaged if the client had not felt a need for assistance, whether by providing advice or in prosecuting or defending a claim in court. An important aspect of loyalty to client, paradoxically perhaps, is to give a client advice that the client may well not wish to hear. A leading American lawyer of many years ago stated the point very pungently: "About half of the practice of a decent lawyer consists in telling would-be clients that they are damned fools and should stop."[32] Less blunt but equally true is a statement of the lawyer's duty to advise corporate officials, including CEOs: "Difficult as it may be, it is imperative that someone inform the emperors that they have no clothes, i.e., . . . when there is a serious problem . . . which must be dealt with."[33]

As is more fully discussed in Chapter 5, there are special complexities in dealing with a corporate officer, as distinct from dealing with an individual client. Nevertheless, the basic point holds: The highest form of loyalty to a client can be giving unwelcome advice. Baldesar Castiglione said almost 500 years ago that the principal (client) who seeks advice: "should choose the noblest and wisest and give them free leave and authority to tell him their opinion on any subject without hesitation and so behave towards them that everyone would realize he wanted to know the truth about everything. . . ."[34] Giving an "opinion . . . without hesitation" is the proper standard in law practice and requires an adequate measure of independence from the client.

Implicit in providing unwelcome legal advice is recognition that the client has legal obligations to others, including the government. The legal rights of others also establish a framework for the assistance that a lawyer may properly render to a client: A lawyer may not assist a client in violating the laws or give advice that encourages the client to do so. As Robert Gordon has observed, lawyers "have an official status as licensed fiduciaries in the public interest, charged with encouraging compliance with legal norms."[35] Thus a lawyer may not aid a client in perpetrating fraud on another party, in preparing a false tax return, in unlawfully exploiting a fiduciary relationship, and so on. So also a lawyer may not tell a client how to conduct a transaction that will defraud another. The principle is stated in Rule 1.2(d) of the ABA Rules as follows: "A lawyer shall not counsel a client to engage, or assist a client, in conduct that the lawyer knows is criminal or fraudulent." The Canadian Code provision is more discursive but also perhaps more exacting: "When advising the client the lawyer must never knowingly assist in or encourage any dishonesty, fraud, crime or illegal conduct, or instruct the client as to how to violate the law and avoid punishment. The lawyer should be on guard against becoming the tool or dupe of an unscrupulous client. . . ."[36] The same principle is stated or simply presumed in the ethical standards of other systems.[37] Another way of stating the proposition is that lawyers are not immune or given special dispensation from obligations the law imposes on citizens generally.

However, there are substantial ambiguities lurking in this principle. Some of the ambiguity springs from ambiguities in the law itself. For example, it is unlawful for a business to issue financial statements that are "misleading," but financial statements can be prepared that are extremely optimistic and therefore possibly misleading, but not clearly so. Hence it can be a matter of doubt whether the content of a financial statement is legally misleading or merely overly optimistic. To pursue this example, when a lawyer has provided advice about the financial statement, there can be similar doubt about whether the lawyer violated the law. A lawyer is not required to resolve all doubts against the client and accordingly advise that a financial statement be ultraconservative, but neither is a lawyer permitted to bless a statement that is clearly misleading.

By way of another example, it is unlawful under the tax laws to claim unjustified deductions or exemptions in a tax return, but there are deductions and exemptions that could be justified according to one's interpretation of the law. Lawyers can be fairly liberal in their interpretations of the rules governing deductions and exemptions. So also, the law may prohibit noxious emissions from a factory, but there can be argument over whether a certain level of emissions is "noxious." And so on.

Indeed, all legal rules are unavoidably ambiguous in some applications. Legal rules are constituted of words, and words are symbols, not "things." (We bypass the epistemological issue of whether things are things.) Hence the words of a legal rule do not necessarily point to specific things (such as courses of action by a client) but only signal or suggest possible courses of action. Lawyers have intimate acquaintance with legal rules and their application and accordingly have special insight into their ambiguities. One interpretation of the law may allow a client to gain an economic benefit, while a more restrictive interpretation would warn the client not to try to do so.

In providing an opinion on such issues, a lawyer substitutes the lawyer's own opinion for the hypothetical decision of a court. The client can proceed with the transaction on the basis of the lawyer's opinion. If the legality of the transaction is later questioned, the client can assert that the transaction was done in reliance on advice of counsel. In that situation, the lawyer's opinion will be subject to reevaluation by some outsider, either an opposing private party or a government official or, in eventual litigation, a judge. A reevaluation by the opposing private party or government official may result in an agreement that the lawyer's opinion was correct. In that case, the client has been enabled to achieve its objective within the boundaries of the law without a full-blown legal controversy. But if the reevaluation disagrees with the lawyer's opinion, the disputing parties thereupon must resort to some higher authority, such as a court, to resolve the conflict over proper interpretation of the law. In that case, the client may lose the appeal and also incur the cost of litigating the issue. The client may be disappointed and angry unless the lawyer had given warning that his interpretation was disputable. However, the fact that the client acted on "advice of counsel" may protect the client from certain kinds of legal penalties, particularly ones dependent on proof of wrongful intent, even though the transaction is held to be invalid.

There is a third possibility: that the transaction will not be questioned by anyone, either by another private party or by any regulatory agency. In that case, the transaction will quietly stand, and the client will have achieved its objective under the safeguard of the lawyer's opinion. This is probably the most common sequence of events. However, there is no way to estimate the statistical frequency of the various possibilities because the details that inform decision-making in most transactions remain confidential.

It will be evident that a lawyer will be subject to some pressure from the client, usually tacit, to give an opinion that will allow the client to achieve the objective at minimum cost and complication. Sometimes the lawyer's opinion involves giving the client the benefit of the doubt in interpreting the relevant legal rules. In other situations, the lawyer may suggest a procedure or structure different from that proposed by the client, but one that will achieve substantially the same objective. For example, the client may propose selling a product to a customer, but wish to retain a lien on the product (a right to repossess it) until the purchase price has been fully paid. The lawyer may recommend that, instead of selling it, the product be leased to the customer with rental payments that incorporate the sale price. A lease transaction thereby can be the economic equivalent of a sale but, in many legal systems, would be legally more secure than a sale. Furthermore, using a lease in some legal systems may avoid official publication of the transaction that would be required if a "sale" were involved. For another example, the client may contemplate lending money to a risky business venture. The lawyer may suggest that the money be made available in "tranches" (that is, rationed out in segments upon specified conditions), or that it be placed in the custody of a neutral third party (an escrow agent) for disbursement under specified conditions, or yet some other protective arrangement that reduces the risk that the loan will not be repaid.

Yet another example of "creative lawyering" has become common in contemporary globalized commerce. In Islamic countries it is a rule of law and religious obligation that money may not be loaned at interest, although it may be invested. (The same rule governed in Western countries until about the fifteenth century.) Many of the Islamic oil-producing countries have generated enormous sums that they wish to invest under terms that are the economic equivalent to a loan. Skillful lawyers have developed financial documents that are not "loans" but involve essentially largely the same economics as a loan.

Most legal interpretations or lawyer-recommended alternative courses of action are innocuous. The alternative recommended by a lawyer simply involves doing the transaction in a technically correct fashion. But legal interpretations and legal alternatives can sometimes involve substantial risk that the lawyer's approach will later be determined to be invalid. If that happens, the approach will not only fail to accomplish the objective, but also subject the client to regulatory or criminal prosecution.

It is in these risky contexts that the lawyer's independence from the client can be compromised. In the crudest form, a lawyer may give the client a favorable opinion that is simply unsupportable. An opinion that is so unreasonable may later be held to constitute fraud on the lawyer's part.[38] Short of that extreme, some lawyers are very aggressive in giving interpretations that are favorable to their clients, others are more conservative. Furthermore, most sophisticated clients can distinguish the level of risk that different lawyers are willing to assume, and accordingly seek one kind of legal advice or another. There are lawyers who are willing to take large risks. Of course, risk-taking lawyers could not sustain their practices without risk-taking clients.

Consideration of the possible legal risks involved in a transaction usually involves discussion between the client and the lawyer, with the client making the final decision. The discussions and calculations between client and lawyer are conducted in confidence and, unless they amount to fraud, cannot subsequently be probed in court. A conscientious lawyer thus carries a heavy burden of responsibility to provide advice and assistance that does not amount to merely endorsing the client's wishes.

Fulfillment of this responsibility is supported by practical considerations. A lawyer who is promiscuous in giving advice risks loss of reputation, accusation through the professional disciplinary machinery, and liability for malpractice. A lawyer who adopts a consistently conservative pattern establishes a positive reputation with other lawyers and with government officials, and transactions that have his blessing are unlikely to be challenged. A complication for lawyers practicing in law firms is that some members of the firm may have a greater propensity for taking risk than others. Law firms from time to time dissolve over that kind of difference.

A technically similar function is performed by lawyers who serve government agencies and officials. The authority of a government official is conferred and defined by law, which often is ambiguous in its terms. For example, a government fiscal officer may be concerned whether it is legally proper for revenues specified for one purpose to be disbursed for some related purpose, such as funds for the art museum being used to build a parking garage for the museum. A government lawyer can provide the necessary legal analysis. Similarly, police and regulatory inspectors need advice about the limits of their authority to enter a private residence or business or to seize contraband. The response can be latitudinarian or conservative, as in the case of advice and assistance provided to a private party.

At another level of analysis, in a civilized community most people obey the law, but it is not self-enforcing. Enforcement requires the efforts of public authorities or of people whose rights have been transgressed. Lawyers are familiar with the kinds of effort required and with the likelihood that enforcement will actually occur in various circumstances.

The condition of the law in this respect can be summarized by the concept of "discount" in law enforcement: The discount is the difference between the standards of conduct established by law and the likelihood that a specific course of conduct will be challenged. In jurisprudence, a similar concept is expressed in the term "desuetude," that is, the pervasive disregard of some legal norms. A familiar example is the posted speed limit on public highways, which many drivers interpret as a mere suggestion. A blunter expression concerning the possibilities of enforcement against a course of action is: can you get away with it?

Virtually all legal rules are subject to discount to one degree or another, and many legal rules fall into desuetude. Hence the realistic answer to whether a client could "get away with it" can often be yes. That is, it is objectively probable that government authorities are unlikely to intervene, unless the violations of law are flagrant or repeated, and that injured private parties are unlikely to respond unless the injury is serious. Lawyers in any field usually can make fairly reliable estimates of the discount rate in enforcement of the legal rules in their domain of practice. This special knowledge creates moral dilemmas on the part of conscientious lawyers and opportunities for abuse on the part of lawyers who are deficient in moral scruples. The special knowledge of an unscrupulous lawyer can serve a client whose objective is antisocial or at the border of illegality.

A central question in lawyers' ethics, therefore, is the extent to which a lawyer will give advice and assistance to clients that furthers the clients' interests but is at the expense of objective fidelity to the law. The contrast can be described as the difference between an objective or judicial viewpoint and an advocate's viewpoint. This distinction is clear in concept. An objective interpretation of the law is that which a judge would adopt if confronted with the facts or circumstances that are presented to a lawyer who is advising a client. Of course there can be some ambiguity in the concept of a judicial viewpoint, because judges do not have a perfectly uniform understanding of the law. But the idea of a judicial viewpoint is perfectly intelligible to lawyers. Indeed, it is a viewpoint a lawyer considers hypothetically in assessing the risks involved in a proposed transaction or course of action. The opposite of a judicial viewpoint is an advocate's viewpoint, which the lawyer uses to resolve all ambiguities in the facts and the applicable law in favor of the client's interests, short of giving an opinion that would be professionally embarrassing to the lawyer. (Some lawyers are not easily embarrassed.) Obviously, the judicial viewpoint involves much less latitude for exploiting ambiguity than does the advocate's viewpoint.

The problem of independence from the client revolves around this distinction between an objective viewpoint and the advocate's viewpoint. A lawyer truly independent from the client would give advice and assistance predicated on a judicial viewpoint, or something close to it. A lawyer improperly subservient to client interest would give advice and assistance up to the point where his opinion is so unreasonable as to be unprofessional.

Concerning this distinction, it is necessary to note the difference in situation between a lawyer who adopts an advocate's viewpoint while acting as an advocate in court, and a lawyer who adopts such a viewpoint while acting for a client in an out-of-court transaction. A lawyer acting as an advocate in court presents his version of the law and facts in an open forum, before a judge and opposing counsel. A lawyer acting for a client in an out-of-court transaction proceeds in the closed forum of his office. The lawyer's latitude in interpreting the law can be greater in the lawyer's closed forum. Beyond the ambiguities in the meaning of the law are ambiguities in interpretation of the relevant facts. Similar differences of perspective are presented. A lawyer can view the facts of a client's transaction from the critical viewpoint of a judge, but often can construe them from the more sympathetic viewpoint of an advocate.

The situations that lawyers address in their practice thus can involve a complex mixture of inherent legal ambiguity, differences of legal interpretation depending on viewpoint, and differences in interpretation of facts. Many situations are not seriously ambiguous, and in such situations the lawyer's responsibility to remain within the boundaries of the law is clear. In these situations, which we believe are the norm, lawyers serve the public interest by providing guidance to clients that furthers compliance with law. That service is the justification for the confidentiality that protects the lawyer-client relationship. As stated by the U.S. Supreme Court in a leading decision: the purpose of the attorney-client privilege "is to encourage full and frank communication between attorneys and their clients and thereby promote broader public interests in the observance of law and administration of justice."[39]

We have no doubt that, in consultations with clients, most lawyers do not simply look for loopholes but provide guidance that directs transactions within the contours intended by the law. Lawyers in general are predisposed to treat the texts of the law seriously. According to our estimate, a lawyer's assistance does indeed "promote broader public interests in the observance of law," as stated by the Supreme Court.

But there is and always has been public suspicion that lawyers typically are subservient to their clients' interests. In the Marxist tradition, still alive in some political and academic circles, it is a premise that corporation lawyers always conduct themselves in that mode. It is also a simple fact that many lawyers are too subservient to their clients' interests. It also is clear to us, however, that no method of inquiry exists for determining the extent to which lawyers in any regime are appropriately objective and independent in relationships with their clients.

Legal Ambiguity and Ethical Ideals

As we have seen, in the modern era, the profession's ethical norms have come to be "legalized," that is, formulated in codes of rules rather than handed down as a set of customs. There are advantages in this transformation, the same as provided in law itself—objectivity, clarity, universality, and greater equality of application. However, the legalization of professional ethics in legal rules has the result of transferring the ambiguity inherent in legal rules to the rules of professional ethics. For example, a lawyer of a conservative disposition might conclude that a conflict of interest would be involved in a proposed representation, whereas a latitudinarian lawyer would conclude that there was no conflict, or at least not one serious enough to worry about. One lawyer might consider certain communications from a client to interfere with the lawyer's professional judgment, whereas another lawyer would treat the client's admonitions as simply part of the "noise" involved in law practice.

In all such instances—which occur continually in daily practice—it is the lawyer who must make the initial decision how to proceed. In almost all cases the lawyer's decision will be conclusive. That is, the problem that the lawyer resolves will not be brought before some other authority, and indeed the client and other affected persons usually will be unaware that the problem arose. Thus the lawyer is required to make an "independent judgment" about his own judgments, including judgments about his independence!

Most lawyers are relatively conservative. Being a lawyer involves acknowledging the legitimacy of the regime in which a lawyer practices, accepting the legitimacy of the regime's procedures, and accepting the standing body of law. Revolutionaries and many radicals reject these assumptions, although some famous revolutionaries were trained as lawyers, for example, Mohandas Gandhi and Fidel Castro. Many lawyers have strong critical attitudes about the social and economic system, some inclining to the left and some to the right on the political spectrum. However, most lawyers keep such critical thoughts to themselves. To function as a lawyer requires maintaining at least an outward display of commitment to the legal system and an appreciation, if not approval, of its workings.

Some lawyers are "square" in outlook, others are iconoclasts. Lawyers have opinions not only about abstract political issues but also about social and personal issues such as religion, parental responsibility, abortion, and divorce. Opinions on such subjects often can be significant in dealing with legal problems encountered in ordinary law practice. In morally sensitive areas of the law, the meaning ascribed to a legal term inevitably reflects a person's views concerning political or social issues. Lawyers recognize that a judge's background sensibility can affect how a "boundary" case may be decided, whether in the field of employee rights or concerning divorce or on some other socially controversial subject. Yet the same is true of lawyers. A devout Roman Catholic lawyer, for example, could have difficulty engaging his professional enthusiasm in certain kinds of divorce cases.

Some of the stories of professional heroism by lawyers describe the relationship between political ideology and professional independence in a positive way. Pietro Calamandrei, an Italian lawyer and prominent legal scholar, stood up against the fascist regime of Mussolini and exercised strong influence seeking to preserve the integrity of Italian legal procedure, doing so quietly and obliquely to avoid interference from the regime.[40] Andrew Hamilton, an American lawyer in the eighteenth century, stood up for a printer accused of defaming the British colonial administration;[41] as described earlier, Henry Brougham, an English barrister, stood up for Queen Caroline in the divorce proceeding brought against her by the king; Lewis Powell, later a justice of the U.S. Supreme Court, as a lawyer helped guide the South in the United States toward a peaceful adjustment to the abolition of racial segregation.[42]

In such controversies, the lawyer must fulfill professional duty even if his personal sentiments about the client's cause are ambivalent. The basic principle is reflected in the ABA Rules of Professional Conduct: "A lawyer's representation of a client, including representation by appointment, does not constitute an endorsement of the client's personal, economic, social or moral views or activities."[43] The rule governing English barristers goes further. A barrister "must not withhold services on the ground that the nature of the case is objectionable to him or to any section of the public."[44]

The foregoing rule of ethics, and the rules of ethics generally, are a mechanism by which the profession seeks to maintain its independence from the state, from the interests of clients, and from other sources of interference.

They are statements made collectively by lawyers, addressing not only themselves but also the state and the larger political community. They express the legal profession's view of its duties and its conception of lawyers' special position in a constitutional order.

Another mechanism for maintaining the profession's independence is the activity of bar associations in professional education, in the exchange of information about legal developments, and in formal and informal discipline. In the Latin countries, the affiliation is often referred to as *confraternité*, to use the French term. In the common law countries a similar reference is made in the term professional "brotherhood"—even as women have come to increasing membership in the profession. Whatever the term, in most legal systems the collegial sentiment is strong.

In many legal systems, the bar organizations have legal authority to govern and discipline the profession, including calling for censure and disbarment. Even where the organized bar has only unofficial standing, it is nevertheless influential in disciplinary matters and in consideration of regulatory questions that affect the profession. In many developing countries, the legal profession has been an articulate force in fundamental constitutional controversies.[45] The history of the bar displays recurrent disputes between the legal profession and the state.

In all such controversies, an important force on the side of the lawyers has been their solidarity as an organization. Lawyers acting alone may be forceful in the small controversies that arise in law practice, but they would be insignificant against the state. Collectively, however, the bar can be a significant force. As a pragmatic matter, lawyers have a vested interest in maintaining the rule of law, just as journalists are deeply interested in freedom of the press. The rule of law is a lawyer's bread and butter.

"Bread and butter" is a metaphor for income. Lawyers must have sufficient income to make a decent living and maintain their independence. We trust we have been persuasive that the independence of lawyers in independent practice is an element of constitutional government. A sufficient income for lawyers in independent practice is derived from fees. Therefore legal fees, despite the discomfort they cause some clients (and some lawyers), are an unavoidable part of a constitutional scheme.

Ideally, a lawyer should feel no constraint in assisting a client by reason of the lawyer's relationships with the government, with the courts, with partners in his firm, with colleagues in the bar, with the payer of his fee (usually the client, but not always), or with the client himself. Ideally, a lawyer should feel confident that his colleagues will provide support in maintaining the independence of the profession. Ideally, the courts will administer the law with discernment and neutrality; and ideally, the lawyer can earn a respectable living in his professional calling.

Most lawyers experience their profession as something less than this ideal, often considerably less. But that realization does not diminish the ideal's attraction. The ideal draws most lawyers to their calling and sustains them in it.

5

Loyalty

Loyalty to Client: The Basic Concepts

The notion of a lawyer without a client is an oxymoron. Lawyers, meaning practicing lawyers, are people who assist clients. A client's very purpose in engaging a lawyer is to gain the advantage of assistance from someone informed and skillful in matters of the law.

In common law systems, a lawyer is understood to be an agent for the client. Under civil law, the engagement is *locatio conductio operarum*, that is, a contract that engages services. The civil law concept gives a broader range of authority to the lawyer, recognizing the lawyer's distinctive status as a professional, than is entailed in the common law client-lawyer relationship. (A common law lawyer's ordinary scope of authority can be enlarged by special agreement.) Under all regimes the relationship entails a duty of loyalty and a related duty of confidentiality on the lawyer's part. A lawyer's duties of loyalty and confidentiality are much like those of other professionals, such as a financial adviser or a broker in dealings in real estate or commodities. However, the role of lawyer is governed not only by the rules of agency but also by many special professional rules.

The obligation of loyalty to clients is the key distinction between the role of the lawyer and that of the judge in the administration of justice, as explained in Chapter 2. A lawyer serving as advocate in litigation is a partisan on behalf of the client, not a neutral party responsible for just results to other parties involved, whereas the judge has responsibility for doing impartial justice. A lawyer engaged in transactions has a similar duty to provide counsel and assistance that protect the client's interests. As explained in Chapter 2, the ultimate rationale for loyalty to the client in litigation is that it provides a check on the rectitude and proficiency of the judge. The ultimate rationale for loyalty to the client in office counseling is that a client has a right to manage his affairs with minimum adverse entanglement with the law.

The duty of loyalty to clients is subject to important qualifications. A lawyer may provide counsel and assistance only in furtherance of lawful purposes, and specifically is prohibited from giving aid to criminal or fraudulent enterprise.[1] The advocate has a duty to speak truthfully in statements and documents presented as the advocate's utterance (as distinct from the utterance of the client). That obligation applies to statements to courts, to government officials, and to third parties, even if the effect of being truthful may be detrimental to the client. As a corollary, a lawyer may refuse to carry out purposes that the lawyer considers unconscionable even though they may be within the limits of the law, and may withdraw from an engagement, originally understood to be acceptable, that develops into an unconscionable one.[2]

The duty of loyalty is also qualified by the practical necessity that lawyers in independent law practice have more than one client. Theoretically, the rule of loyalty could require that a lawyer serve only one client through his career. That would carry to its logical conclusion the biblical maxim, often invoked in proclamations about the lawyer's duty of loyalty, that "no one can serve two masters."[3] Many lawyers actually do have only one client: lawyers in the employ of government bureaus and those employed in the legal departments of business corporations. But most lawyers are in independent practice, providing legal services to several clients. If the rules governing loyalty prohibited having more than one client, dependence on that client would radically compromise a lawyer's independence, which, as seen in Chapter 3, is itself a prime ethical virtue. Practice limited to one client also would severely inhibit a lawyer's ability to see legal problems from more than one perspective, which is an element of intellectual independence and professional judgment. Clients whose needs for legal assistance are modest or occasional would have difficulty engaging a lawyer, because the engagement would disable the lawyer from any other concurrent engagements. Over the course of their careers, lawyers in independent practice typically have many clients with many different legal problems.

The principle of loyalty also operates in engagements on behalf of a succession of clients. A successive representation is involved when a lawyer has concluded one engagement and then is presented with an opportunity to represent a different client. What if the two representations involve the same subject matter? The rule is that a lawyer who formerly represented a client is prohibited from thereafter undertaking an engagement for another client that would involve attacking work that he had done for the first client, or making adverse use of confidences that had been obtained in the representation of the first client.

Thus a lawyer's duty of loyalty is not absolute, but is hedged by qualifications. Some of these qualifications protect the public, particularly the prohibition against assisting a client in unlawful undertakings. Other qualifications protect the interests of other clients and potential clients, particularly rules governing conflict of interest where a lawyer has multiple clients. The rules concerning loyalty thus permit "serving two masters," but on terms designed to avoid impairing the lawyer's effectiveness on behalf of each client.

The duty of loyalty in other vocations governed by the law of agency or its civil law counterpart—accountants, financial advisers, employees—is subject to limitations similar to those imposed on lawyers concerning criminal or fraudulent undertakings and the duty to speak truthfully to legal authorities. However, the duty of loyalty for lawyers is peculiarly delicate. A lawyer's service consists of guiding affairs for the client's private and often selfish purposes, with an eye to legal requirements that have been designed for the very purpose of limiting or regulating selfish purposes. In contemporary academic discussion of professional ethics, intense criticism has been addressed to this partisanship in a lawyer's role. Of course, criticism is warranted of lawyers who violate legal rules of professional ethics in their representation of clients. At another level, criticism is warranted of the fact that the rich have highly competent legal assistance and the poor and middle-class citizens often have little or no means of offsetting that advantage. But some of the academic criticism goes further, arguing that partisanship in matters of justice is itself wrong, even if the role of advocate fully conforms to the law and the rules of professional ethics. According to this view, a lawyer should personally and directly seek justice by acting unilaterally, and not merely by participating in the interactive legal process with regulatory officials or before the judges.

It has even been argued by William Simon that a lawyer may pursue the lawyer's conception of justice without advising the client that he has adopted that mission.[4] Simon does not directly state that a lawyer should deceive a client. However, he says that in appropriate circumstances a lawyer could make an "anonymous" disclosure of client confidences, which plainly implies that the disclosure would be hidden from the client. He gives an example of a corporate lawyer who disagrees with management's approach in a labor dispute. The lawyer, says Simon, "should form her own judgment about the substantive resolution and take reasonable steps to bring it about."[5] That guarded statement suggests, at least to us, that the lawyer could proceed to disclose client confidences or take other action unfavorable to the client (as the client understands those interests), without telling the client.

Those measures, if we understand them correctly, would involve a breach of universally recognized legal and moral duties—lying to the client (by receiving information that the client assumes will be confidential) and betraying the client. Of course, a lawyer has a right, and sometimes a duty, to tell a client what is the right thing to do and that the client should do it. As we quoted Elihu Root in Chapter 4: "About half of the practice of a decent lawyer consists in telling . . . [clients to] stop." A lawyer may well form "her own judgment about the substantive resolution" and *openly* take "reasonable steps," for example, arguing with the client or withdrawing from the representation. That course of action entails risking the client's enmity, loss of employment, perhaps loss of reputation, and perhaps also professional embarrassment. But for proper lawyers that goes with the territory.

In the academic argument, it is assumed that the measures asked of the lawyer are lawful and are in pursuit of objectives the client is lawfully entitled to pursue. (In supporting the argument, reference is sometimes made to illegal practices that some lawyers sometimes engage in, which is a different matter.) The argument typically is addressed to the representation of business enterprises, and implicitly invokes a hostility to capitalist enterprise that is widely shared in academia.

If such subversion of client purposes is acceptable in the representation of businesses, presumably it is also acceptable in the representation of wealthy individual clients, for example, concerning their tax avoidance strategies. And if acceptable there, why not also in the representation of criminal defendants, such as one accused of rape who confesses to his lawyer, or one of the "9/11" defendants? The rule of law, it seems to us, operates in all these contexts and the rules are designed to put beyond present cavil, by a lawyer who has undertaken an engagement, issues disputable on moral or political grounds. As Thomas More is presented as saying in "A Man for All Seasons," break down the law and what is left but the Devil?

Moreover, even in the corporate setting, real individuals are involved. Legal advice for a business corporation typically is provided to ordinary people in ordinary jobs inside the corporation who want to carry out their responsibilities in a legally proper manner. It is nevertheless argued that the lawyer's personal idea of justice should prevail through unilateral action, including deception of the client people. In the same vein, Duncan Kennedy of Harvard endorsed techniques to undermine corporate representation of being "[s]ly ... manipulat[ive] ... collusive, skillful and tricky. ..."[6] However, as remarked by Detlev Vagts, also of Harvard, at a merely pragmatic level such a strategy "is unlikely to work ... It certainly won't work a second time."[7]

We believe no active practitioner or responsible academician elsewhere in the world would give these arguments serious consideration. It is a legal and moral wrong to deceive a client. A lawyer ordinarily learns the critical information through confidential communication from the client, transmitted to the lawyer on the assumption that there are duties of loyalty and confidentiality and that those obligations will be honored. The idea that a lawyer would engage in deception and betrayal in order to accomplish his personal concept of a public agenda, is surely perverse. Lawyers are not obliged to undertake representation that entails objectives or means that they consider distasteful. It is open to any lawyer to insist, expressly or by suggestion, that he will not provide representation in matters he disapproves of. In fact, many lawyers hold themselves out in this way by, for example, declining to undertake criminal defense work, highly aggressive litigation, or matters involving use of economic leverage. For this very reason many lawyers go into the service of the government or adopt practice specialties that do not involve transactions that they find morally troubling.

More fundamentally, the rules of ethics permit a lawyer to withdraw from a matter that he finds repugnant, with or without the client's consent. The French rules of professional ethics, for example, contain a *clause de con-*

science, enabling the lawyer's resignation for reasons of conscience. Rule 1.16 of the American rules allows a lawyer to withdraw where the client "insists upon pursuing an objective that the lawyer considers repugnant." Of course, a lawyer ordinarily is extremely reluctant to withdraw on such a basis, for doing so will almost inevitably affect his reputation adversely; in addition, he will lose his fees and risk grievance or a malpractice claim. But the right to withdraw makes the point that there is nothing unconditionally obligatory about an undertaking to represent a client. A lawyer's professional engagement is not akin to that of an indentured servant.

There are many lawful practice maneuvers—measures that a client may properly expect his lawyer to pursue—that a lawyer may consider troubling or obnoxious. The classic example is a client who could defend a suit on a debt by pleading the statute of limitations ("prescription" in civil law usage)—that is, that the suit has been brought too late, even though the debt was lawfully incurred. Some clients might wish to forgo the statute-of-limitations defense and dispute an alleged debt only on the merits. Possibly a lawyer might have a similar inclination if he himself were the defendant in a suit on a debt. But, in our opinion, it is naive to claim that relying on the "technical" defense of statute of limitations for a client is somehow immoral. In human affairs, time has many uses, and the concept of a statute of limitations is one of them. In folk parlance, the idea is that bygones should be bygones. Moreover, a statute-of-limitations defense, when valid, works quickly and peremptorily, and thus can spare the client the cost and distress involved in defending a claim through disputed testimony about the merits. Still more broadly, a court of law is not a good forum for many kinds of moral discourse, if for no other reason than that the law, as it comes down in specific cases, works by political fiat of the state, not moral suasion.

The contentions and positions that a lawyer may interpose on behalf of a client often lie at the boundary of a legal rule designed to protect the public interest. One example is the statute of limitations. A statute of limitations, until the specified time period has run, has no effect on an alleged legal obligation and hence is legally irrelevant. On the day after the statutory period has expired, however, the statute converts a legally tenable claim into an unenforceable one. Another example is the rule of majority vote, exemplified by the 2000 presidential election in the United States. Under the rule of majority vote, a handful of votes, theoretically even one vote, determines the constitutional decision of the whole community, even the whole country. Another example is a territorial boundary, such as that between two countries, where one regime lies on one side and a quite different regime on the other. It makes no difference to fish whether they are in Miami or Cuba, or in North or South Korea, but it can make a great difference to people. Yet a national boundary is nothing more than a human (and legal) artifact.

The law is constituted of a maze of such boundaries. There is a legal boundary between a corporation and its owners, between an employer and an employee, between a loan and a gift, and so on. A lawyer's advice can facilitate compliance merely with the letter of the law, and therefore a course of action that is contrary to its spirit. A lawyer's assistance to a client is not an expression of "true" friendship any more than such friendship is expressed in assistance provided by a doctor, an employee, a broker, or a government official assisting a citizen. Instead, a lawyer's assistance is professional and is provided in the course of earning a living. In classic Aristotelian terminology, the professional relationship is an "advantage friendship," where both parties derive advantage from their respective contributions and for their respective interests.[8]

The most troublesome aspect of legal ethics is how far, and subject to what limitations, the duty of loyalty in a professional "advantage friendship" may be pursued. This issue is addressed in the rules specifying limits on the assistance a lawyer may provide to a client. But in ethical and moral terms, the issue of loyalty goes much deeper. In moral terms, the question is not simply what limits a lawyer is legally obliged to obey, but what limits a lawyer ought to impose on himself as a matter of identity and in choosing a life path. No one is obliged to become a lawyer. No one who has become a lawyer is obliged to continue in the vocation. Unfortunately, many lawyers deal with the moral problems of law practice simply by ignoring them.

Who Is in Charge?

In economic and political terms, the relationship between client and lawyer is something like a temporary partnership or joint venture. The venture is the "matter" to be addressed in the professional engagement. This interpretation of the relationship is uncomfortable to lawyers with a traditional outlook. It does not capture the fact that one of the venturers, the lawyer, is governed by special constraints and allegiance to society as an officer of the court. Legal realists, especially Americans imbued with the economic approach to law, may be inclined to disparage that qualification. But we think it is a factor, revealed, for example, in the difference between the typical products of a business school and those of a law school.

The cooperative venture between client and lawyer involves general agreement concerning what is to be done and how. The agreement usually is tacit. In any cooperative undertaking, however, disagreement can emerge over the aims or means of the venture. The issue that then arises is which of the participants has final authority to determine the course of action.

Agency law prescribes that, unless the proposed action is illegal, an agent is obliged to follow the directions of the principal. Accordingly, in the lawyer-client relationship in common law regimes, the lawyer has that obligation. In civil law regimes, in litigation matters the advocate is said to be "master of the argument"—the final authority over the contentions to be advanced before the court. A similar concept governs transaction practice in civil law systems. However, in all regimes a lawyer is a special kind of instrument by virtue of being an "officer of the court." In the ABA Rules of Professional Conduct the lawyer is described more generally as an "officer of the legal system." This phrase, vague as it is, signifies that a lawyer is a public officer in certain respects and to a certain degree. The scope of that public responsibility cannot be fully defined, except in terms that are equally vague. However, it implies that a lawyer has responsibilities, particularly in dealings with courts and with other parties, that govern the measures taken on behalf of clients.

The specific duties to the courts are positioned in a larger framework of definitions of authority between client and lawyer. The basic framework is the law itself. In that framework there are significant differences among legal systems, and further differences depending on whether the matter involves litigation, and hence interaction with the courts, or a transaction matter.

In civil law systems, the responsibility for strategy and tactics in a litigated matter is reposed in the advocates.[9] The advocate has authority to refuse to pursue a tactic that the client demands and to insist on pursuing a measure that the client disapproves. It is assumed that the advocate will discuss important procedural issues with the client. When litigation is settled by agreement in a civil law system, the client is required to sign a formal settlement agreement, called the "disposal" of the litigation. Civil law systems do not expressly address the question of who is in charge in transactions handled in office practice, but the client has authority over the final terms of any proposed transaction.

In contrast, in most common law systems the client has ultimate authority. However, there are important variations among the common law systems. The Canadian Code, for example, observes that "the lawyer should never waive or abandon his client's legal rights (for example an available legal defense under a statute of limitations) without his client's informed consent. . . ."[10] The American version leans more heavily toward the client, the general rule being that "a lawyer shall abide by a client's decisions concerning the objectives of the representation . . . and shall consult with the client as to the means by which they are to be pursued."[11] In litigation in the English system in which a barrister is engaged, the barrister must decline instructions (given by the solicitor) that "seek to limit the ordinary authority or discretion of a barrister in the conduct of proceedings in Court. . . ."[12] This rule is amplified in the Code of Conduct, General Standards, Standards, Fundamental Principle No. 306, stating that a barrister is "individually and personally responsible for his own conduct and for his professional work; he must exercise his own personal judgment in all his professional activities." The Law Society's Code for Advocacy, which governs solicitors in situations where they are authorized to act as advocates in court, is similar.[13]

Concerning final authority in transaction matters, the difference between the civil and common law systems may, as a practical matter, be very small or invisible. First, there is no clear distinction between the aims of an engagement and the means by which it is to be carried out.[14] Second, the client ordinarily selects the lawyer and often can select a lawyer whose reputation for aggressiveness corresponds to the client's own inclinations. Furthermore, the client usually pays the fee and can discharge a lawyer who refuses to undertake measures that the client considers necessary. At the same time, as noted earlier, the ethics rules allow a lawyer to withdraw if the client demands tactics that the lawyer considers highly improper. There is usually great inconvenience and sometimes actual harm to both client and lawyer if they dissolve the engagement in a difference over the proper approach.

For all these reasons, a client-lawyer relationship usually continues even in the face of serious disagreements, like an unhappy marriage. However, in the case of a "divorce," the rule governing allocation of authority can be significant. If the lawyer is ultimately "in charge," but has refused to follow a client's direction and then is fired, the lawyer will be entitled to his fee or to compensation according to law. If the client is ultimately in charge, and the lawyer refuses to follow direction and is fired, the lawyer may be entitled to no fee or to radically reduced compensation. Perhaps more important as a practical matter, in a typical divorce between client and lawyer, the participants will recall the facts in very different terms. In one version the client will be in the right, in the other the lawyer will be. Disputes over such matters are not uncommon within the confines of the office, but are rarely brought out in public.

The duty of loyalty to a client therefore is very clear as a broad concept, but often complex in fulfillment.

Concurrent Multiple Representation

The duty of loyalty is formalized in rules governing conflict of interest. Conflict of interest is simply the mirror image of the duty of loyalty. A lawyer has a conflict of interest when he cannot give loyal service to a client because of obligations to others (including obligations to other clients), or from the lawyer's personal interests (such as the lawyer's ownership of a property interest that might be affected in the transaction for the client). Not all dual representations involve a conflict of interest. On the contrary, it is often advantageous for two or more parties on the same side of litigation to employ the same lawyer, or for two parties to a transaction to have one lawyer represent both even if their interests are not perfectly symmetrical. A conflict of interest on the lawyer's part arises when the interests of two or more clients are antagonistic and efforts on behalf of one client would subvert the interests of another client.

The concept of conflict of interest is clear: a lawyer should not undertake a representation unless he can give it wholehearted professional commitment, and he cannot give wholehearted commitment to a client if he must simultaneously give heed to other interests, such as those of another client. As elaborated in the codes and in practice, however, the rules governing conflict of interest are more complicated. These complications are the consequence of real-world contextual factors that are only implicit in the statement of the concept. One contextual factor, referred to earlier, is that the vocation of an independent practitioner requires a lawyer or law firm to have several clients at the same time and many more clients over the course of time.

A second contextual factor is the great difference in competency among lawyers. Exceptionally competent lawyers are in demand by many prospective clients. An unqualified duty of "undivided loyalty" would make the engagement of a highly competent lawyer a matter of "first come, first served," and thereby preclude some clients from obtaining the services of a lawyer they need and want. This is the justification for the corollary that clients, generally speaking, may give consent to or "waive" conflicts that would otherwise be impermissible.

A third contextual factor is that the rules governing conflict of interest must be formulated in terms that apply to legal representation in all fields of the law—litigation, corporation law, family law, criminal law, and the rest. Trying to formulate different conflict-of-interest rules for different types of law practice would be virtually impossible as a practical matter, because law practice does not subdivide into sharply distinct fields. Furthermore, defining different rules for different fields of practice, with more liberal rules in some fields than in others, would engender endless debate within the profession and result in endless dispute in applying the rules. The unavoidable generality of the rules governing conflict of interest leaves wide room for interpretation.

The various ethical codes seek to accommodate these complications. The Canadian Code states the basic rule as follows:

> The lawyer must not advise or represent both sides of a dispute and, save after adequate disclosure to and with the consent of the client or prospective client concerned, he should not act or continue to act in a matter when there is or there is likely to be a conflicting interest. A conflicting interest is one which would be likely to affect adversely the judgment of the lawyer on behalf of . . . [the] client

or prospective client or which the lawyer might be prompted to prefer to the interests of a client or prospective client.[15]

The Italian Code states the obligation both affirmatively and negatively. The affirmative statement is as follows: "The lawyer has the duty to carry out his professional activity with loyalty to his client." The negative statement in the Italian Ethical Code is that:

> A lawyer shall refrain from accepting any employment that may create a conflict with the interests of a client.
>
> A conflict of interest arises if the acceptance of a new client may result in a violation of confidentiality applicable to information supplied by another client, if the knowledge which the lawyer has about an existing client's business provides an unfair advantage to the new client, or if the representation of an existing client limits the lawyer's independence in carrying out the new representation.[16]

These formulations express several elements. First, a lawyer may not represent opposing parties in litigation. The reasons for this proposition seem obvious. One rationale is indeed obvious, for a lawyer could not be an effective partisan advocate on behalf of two parties who are suing each other. A second justification is perhaps not so obvious: representation of both sides by one lawyer might deprive the court of fully forceful presentations of the contending positions, and thus impair the court's understanding of the matters at issue. As expressed in the Restatement of the Law Governing Lawyers:

> [A] tribunal properly wishes assurance that its own processes not be compromised by less than vigorous advocacy . . . if a lawyer were to represent clients opposing each other . . . the public interest in the orderly management of litigation could be seriously compromised. Thus, the same lawyer may not represent both plaintiff and defendant. . . .[17]

An interesting California case illustrates this principle as it relates to litigation.[18] A lawyer acted as mediator in negotiating a settlement agreement between divorcing spouses, who did not separately have lawyers. The propriety of this dual representation was challenged. The court held that representation in the *settlement* negotiation was not improper because the lawyer had acted as a neutral mediator, but cautioned that the lawyer could not continue to represent the parties if any issues had to be adjudicated by the court.

Second, conflict rules have somewhat different applications in transaction or office practice. A lawyer may undertake representation of two or more clients in a transaction where advancing the interests of one client would not be materially detrimental to the interests of the other client. Typical instances of potential conflicts in transaction practice include representation of both buyer and seller in a real estate transaction; representation of two or more business venturers seeking to form a partnership or become principals in a closely held corporation; representation of a corporate officer and the corporation, for example, in a contract providing retirement benefits to the officer; or drafting estate plans for a husband and wife who have separate property.

In these situations it is often problematic whether there is an improper conflict of interest. Ordinarily, there are obvious advantages in using one lawyer. From the clients' viewpoint, engaging only one lawyer is less expensive and more expeditious. Representation of both parties by the same lawyer allows closer coordination of the clients' purposes and avoids the posturing and shield-banging that some lawyers feel impelled to demonstrate in negotiations. At the same time, there are obvious risks in having one lawyer represent both sides of a negotiation, however friendly the parties may be. The lawyer can consciously or unconsciously favor one party over the other—for example, the senior partner over the junior or the corporate official over the corporation.

When any such joint representation is undertaken, the clients must be informed of the potential conflict of interest and give their consent to waive the conflict. Most laypersons are strongly inclined to give such consent, sometimes imprudently. Clients may not understand the rigor of the rule concerning conflict of interest, and some clients think that the conflict-of-interest rules are designed to spread around more work for lawyers. Clients involved in establishing coordinated objectives are, understandably, inclined to have an optimistic outlook on their venture and to discount the risk of eventual divergence of their purposes. Nevertheless, it would be categorically wrong to deny a set of clients the right to employ one lawyer to carry out their purpose. Accordingly, there must be an accommodation between securing the advantages of employing only one lawyer and the concomitant risks of doing so. This accommodation is expressed in the concept of "informed consent," discussed below.

The rule against conflict of interest also governs personal interests on the part of the lawyer. For example, a lawyer could have a financial or personal involvement in a property transaction that could impair his loyalty to the client. Similarly, if the lawyer were an investor in a business venture that he is documenting, his personal sensitivity to risk could affect how he drafts the provisions in the agreements.

There are divergent professional traditions concerning involvement of lawyers in business transactions with clients. In many systems, it is regarded simply as wrong for a lawyer to have any financial or business relationship with a client. But in the United States and to a lesser extent in Canada, lawyers are often involved in their clients' business affairs. Indeed, in those countries it has been common for transaction lawyers to provide legal services to newly organized businesses without charging immediate fees but in return for a fractional share of the enterprise—a "piece of the action," as expressed colloquially. Such an arrangement involves obvious conflict of interest, but it also permits a young business to obtain sophisticated legal assistance in its "start-up" phase. Many of the technology companies in Silicon Valley, California, obtained their initial legal assistance with this kind of arrangement.

There is another common American practice that is similar in economic terms to entering into a business transaction with a client. This is the contingent fee in representation of a plaintiff in litigation, particularly in a claim for personal injury. The lawyer who works for a contingent fee receives no fee unless there is a recovery by a court judgment or a settlement, but the lawyer is entitled to a percentage of any eventual recovery, typically one-third. The contingent fee usually aligns the lawyer's interest with that of the client. However, their interests can diverge, particularly if they are presented with a settlement proposal that the client and the lawyer evaluate differently. The client or the lawyer may want to accept the proposal, believing that "a bird in hand is worth two in the bush," while the other of them may want to reject it, believing that the claim is worth much more than the offer. The rule is that the client has final authority to decide upon acceptance, but there are many cases in which client and lawyer have fallen into dispute over such an issue.

The rule against conflicts of interest has an important corollary applicable to law firms. The corollary is called "imputation" and is to the following effect: generally, a conflict of interest burdening one lawyer in a firm is imputed to all other lawyers in a firm. This rule is stated expressly in ABA Rule 1.10 and Article 32 of the Japanese Code of Ethics for Practicing Lawyers. It is implicit in many other systems.

For example, if Lawyer A in a law firm represents one party to a negotiation, Lawyer B in the same firm could not represent the other party, except with the informed consent of both clients. It thus can happen that a lawyer in a law firm's London office can have a conflict that is imputed to other lawyers in the firm's Singapore office. The imputation rule does not apply to English barristers, who must practice as solos. Thus English barristers who physically share chambers may oppose each other in both criminal and civil matters.

The effect of the imputation rule requires a law firm to engage in careful "conflicts checking"—reviewing all existing engagements before undertaking a new representation and all previous engagements that might be implicated by the new representation. The procedure must be continually repeated because changes occur constantly in the firm's portfolio of pending matters. In some firms the "sweep" through the list of matters, and "heads up" to all lawyers in the firm, is done twice a day! In large law firms that have many clients and conduct a wide variety of transactions, the procedures for conflicts checks must be highly detailed and elaborate, and in contemporary law practice they are performed with computer assistance.

The problem of imputed conflicts of interest has become vastly more complicated with the growth of large law firms and the increasing speed of modern commercial transactions. Large law firms have literally thousands of pending matters and hundreds of former clients. A transaction can be presented to a firm on a schedule requiring substantial technical work within a few days, sometimes even a few hours. Yet the lawyers in very large law firms scarcely know what other lawyers in the firm are engaged in—except when alerted by the firm's conflicts checking system. It seems evident that some large law firms disregard many imputed conflicts, expecting that, if a question arises, they can mollify affected clients or simply ignore them. The rules are more rigorously enforced in systems where large firms have been a part of the local legal community for a long time. But many observers believe the "imputation rule" should be modified to permit a law firm to handle representations involving conflict so long as the representations are by different lawyers within the firm and the participating lawyers are isolated from each other.

There is a well-known case in American practice that demonstrates the effect of the imputation rule and the embarrassment that it can inflict. The law firm involved, a large and prominent one, was based in Chicago and had an office in Washington. The Washington office undertook representation of a petroleum industry trade association, which commissioned the firm to show how intense was the competition within that industry. The Chicago office undertook representation of a company dealing with the energy industry, alleging that there was an antitrust conspiracy among energy companies—including oil companies. The law firm had not identified its conflict of interest in these two representations until the day the antitrust suit was filed. The oil companies protested and asked the court to exclude the firm from prosecution of the antitrust case. The court's decision, disqualifying the law firm in the conflicting representations, stands as a hurtful reminder to large law firms of their need for efficient conflicts checking procedures.[19]

Isolation of the different lawyer teams within a firm can resolve such a conflict, but usually only if the affected clients give consent. Isolation is colloquially referred to as a "Chinese wall." The concept is that Lawyer A and Lawyer B in the firm can handle matters involving an imputed conflict of interest—if the lawyers do not talk to each other and if the firm maintains separate files and supporting staff for each matter. The insulation measures are the "wall." In fact, exactly this kind of arrangement is commonly employed in other kinds of enterprises, such as banking firms, brokerage firms, and insurance companies. Many international law firms try to establish that their branches in different countries are separate firms for purposes of imputed conflicts of interest. Wider use of the "Chinese wall" within law firms is coming to be permitted, but there also has been vocal opposition to any relaxation of the concept of imputed conflict.

Adversity of Interest

The key concept in the rules governing conflict of interest is "adversity of interest." The term refers to the relative likelihood of a divergence of the interests of clients involved, and the intensity of the conflict if it should eventuate. There are clear cases. A lawyer may not represent a client in one transaction while also suing the client in a related matter. At the other end of the range of possibilities, a lawyer is not precluded from undertaking to draft a will for a party who was on the other side of a real estate transfer in the past. (Indeed, new clients sometimes come to a lawyer who impressed them while on the "other side of the table" in an earlier transaction.) The concept of adversity is therefore unavoidably ambiguous, because in any kind of representation all kinds of future eventualities can be imagined.

While it is universally recognized that an advocate cannot represent opposing parties, litigation often involves more than two parties, for example, where two or more claimants are arrayed as plaintiffs or two or more parties arrayed as defendants. Several members of a family may be injured in an accident and seek reparation as co-plaintiffs. So also, in commercial litigation the defendant parties can include a primary obligor and a party who is a guarantor or someone otherwise secondarily liable for the obligation being asserted by the plaintiff. Often the co-defendants may be a corporation and some of its employees. Sometimes litigation may be originated against a defendant who subsequently seeks redress against another person by bringing him in as a "third-party defendant."

In all such situations, the question is whether one lawyer or law firm may properly represent all the parties on one side, or whether the interests of those parties involve conflict *inter sese* that requires their being separately represented. The interests of any two parties rarely are completely harmonious. Yet often it is more economical and strategically advantageous for parties with similar interests to assert a "common front." For example, all members of a family seeking compensation from the driver of the other vehicle in an automobile accident usually have a strong interest in presenting a common front. However, the defendant may not have sufficient assets (including liability insurance) to cover the full amount of all the claims. A question therefore can arise concerning the allocation of the available amount, and the resolution of that question could develop into a conflict among the claimants. On the defense side, the interests of an employer and its employees will usually be consistent, so it will be advantageous for them to establish a common front against the plaintiff. However, an employer may wish to shift primary responsibility to the employee, for financial or tactical reasons, in which event their interests will be in conflict. Litigation in commercial and financial disputes often can involve several different intersecting interests, including primary lenders, holders of security interests, and others.

Legal systems differ in their application of the concept. Whereas the Italian formulation addresses conflict of interest in terms of the influences that could affect the lawyer's loyalty, the Canadian Code expresses the concept in terms of the resulting adverse effect on the "judgment of the lawyer." The Canadian approach thus is both broader and less definite. The American Bar Association Model Rules of Professional Responsibility are much more elaborate. Rule 1.7 of the ABA Rules has prohibitions against representing both sides in litigation and a prohibition against multiple representation where the undertaking for one client may be "materially limited" by responsibilities to another client or to a third person, or where "the lawyer's own interests" would interfere with the representation. Furthermore, Rule 1.8 of the ABA Model Rules has additional rules addressing specific "conflicts" problems, including the following: business transactions between the lawyer and the client; accepting compensation from a third party for carrying out the representation without informed consent by the client; making a contract with a client that would exclude malpractice liability; and improper sexual relations with a client.[20] Thus the American version speaks both in terms of circumstances that cause or threaten conflict of interest and in terms of the effect on the lawyer's independence of judgment.

The civil law rules concerning conflict of interest are typified in the Italian formulations and are stated in more general terms, but the basic concepts are the same: protection of confidences, prevention of unfair advantage, protection of the lawyer's independent professional judgment. Article 37 of the Italian Code states:

> A lawyer shall refrain from accepting any employment that may create a conflict with the interests of a client.
>
> A conflict of interest arises if the acceptance of a new client may result in a

violation of confidentiality applicable to information supplied by another client, if the knowledge which the lawyer has about an existing client's business provides an unfair advantage to the new client, or if the representation of an existing client limits the lawyer's independence in carrying out the new representation.

The CCBE Code of Conduct is somewhat briefer, but to the same effect, and focuses on the same factors. As stated in Rule 3.2:

> A lawyer may not advise, represent or act on behalf of two or more clients in the same matter if there is a conflict, or a significant risk of conflict, between the interests of those clients.
>
> A lawyer must cease to act . . . also whenever there is a risk of a breach of confidence or where his independence may be impaired.
>
> A lawyer must also refrain from acting for a new client if there is a risk of a breach of confidences entrusted to the lawyer by a former client or if the knowledge which the lawyer possesses of the affairs of the former client would give an undue advantage to the new client.

The specifications in the ethical codes are not always definitive, however. The courts give pronouncements that may state the conflict rules in different terms. Courts, certainly those in the common law systems, have an unfortunate tendency occasionally to be loose or chatty in pronouncing their decisions, thus leaving the law unnecessarily ambiguous. They do this in all areas of the law, but the bite is directly on lawyers when the decision addresses professional ethics. An example is a decision by the Supreme Court of Canada that has achieved negative notoriety in the Canadian bar. In the case of *Regina v. Neil*, the court went through a long recitation of the sources and then quoted from a lower court decision stating: "The solicitor is in a fiduciary relationship with his client and must avoid situations where he has, or potentially may, develop a conflict of interests. . . ."[21] This might be called a "loose canon." No difficulty is presented by the proposition that a lawyer "must avoid situations where he has" a conflict of interests. But the casual phrase "or potentially may" develop a conflict is impossible to deal with. Virtually every relationship "potentially may" develop a conflict. Partners can have a falling out, spouses decide to divorce, corporate executives become estranged from the board. Such ambiguous language calls to mind the usage by some American courts of the term "appearance of impropriety" as a standard for determining conflicts of interest. "Impropriety" is in the mind of a beholder, and "appearance" is one level up in abstraction and ambiguity. Meanwhile, the lawyers have to make a living.[22]

A broadly framed rule allows lawyers, if they are so inclined, greater latitude to determine that no conflict exists and thereupon to take on an additional client. However, if there are effective mechanisms by which a client can challenge a conflict of interest, a broadly framed rule gives a client a potentially wider basis on which to challenge a suspected conflict. The more important issue often is not the precise language of the conflicts-of-interest prohibition, but instead the sensitivity with which lawyers apply the concept to themselves and the availability of effective enforcement remedies. Some recurring situations are recognized as involving improper conflict in all professional communities, while others are recognized as permissible at least with informed consent of the clients. Differences in sensitivity about conflicts of interest are the result of underlying cultural forces, within the professions of different countries and within their larger communities, rather than differences in the texts of the rules. There is no systematic evidence on the issue because most conflicts go undetected.

Consent to Conflict

In some situations, it will be apparent that the interests of parties on the same side are so divergent that they should have separate representation, even with the additional expense that incurs and the risk of possible discrepancy in the positions they assert against the common adversary or opposite number. In professional jargon this is called a "nonconsentable conflict." Some ethics systems specify certain situations that are per se nonconsentable. In some countries, for example, it is simply impermissible for a lawyer to enter into a business transaction with a client. The English *Guide to Professional Conduct of Solicitors* requires the client to have advice of another lawyer "where a solicitor in his or her personal capacity sells to, or purchases from or lends to or borrows from his or her own client."[23] In several states in the United States a similar rule has been established by decisional law.[24] ABA Rule 1.8(a) requires that, in a "business transaction" with a client, the terms must be fair and fully explained to the client, the client be given "reasonable opportunity to seek the advice of independent counsel," and then that the client consent in writing. In effect, this rule makes almost any transaction between a lawyer and client subject to rescission if the client later suffers regret. Many conscientious American lawyers simply do not enter into business transactions with clients.

Except for these prohibitions, the parties may recognize that the advantages of maintaining a concerted position outweigh the protection of their separate legal interests. That conclusion can be given effect by "informed consent" to (often referred to as a "waiver" of) the conflict by the parties whose interests are involved. In professional jargon such a situation is sometimes referred to as a "consentable" conflict of interest.

For example, in working out a deal to build a shopping center, the landowner on which the center is to be built may have a common interest with the developer in obtaining necessary government approvals, but the landowner and developer will have conflicting interests in the financial arrangements between themselves. The problem then may be whether one lawyer could represent both parties in pursuing the government approvals, but each have his own lawyer in negotiating the financial arrangement. Partners in a small business usually have the same interests in dealings with third parties, where they could use one lawyer, but may have a conflict concerning the division of responsibility and shares of profits in the business.

There are myriad possible variations. In many situations in both litigation and transactions matters, the conflict is clear and the lawyer cannot properly undertake concurrent representation of both parties. In other situations, consent by the client is proper, although the circumstances have to be carefully considered and a measure of judgment brought to bear. One practical consideration concerns the character and personality of the clients. Lawyers know that some people are likely to be hypersensitive to any possibility of what they perceive as disloyalty, whereas others are much "cooler" about that possibility.

The mechanism of consent to a conflict of interest is colloquially called "informed consent" or "conflict waiver" and is referred to in the Canadian rule as "adequate disclosure to and with the consent of the affected clients."[25] In Japan consent to a conflict is permitted only if different "matters" are involved, so a lawyer may not represent both parties to a transaction even with their consent.[26] In some jurisdictions consent on the part of a client must be in writing.[27] Even where written consent is not required, careful lawyers confirm the agreement in writing, a formalization that is more secure for the clients and more prudent for the lawyer. However, the key is not the consent as such but the adequacy of the disclosure on which the consent is predicated. The American Restatement of the Law Governing Lawyers states of this requirement as follows: "Informed consent requires that the client ... have reasonably adequate information about the material risks involved."[28]

Consent to a conflict of interest can be either general or of limited scope. For example, a client could consent to a conflicting representation in one matter but not another, or consent on the condition that certain lawyers in the firm (those affiliated with the other party) be shielded by an insulation wall. Very broad and general consents are also recognized, at least if the client is adequately cautioned. For example, to facilitate cooperation in defending asbestos litigation in the United States, the corporate defendants in these disputes entered consent agreements that allow the lawyers handling the asbestos claims to undertake any kind of hostile representations in other matters. These agreements were of indefinite duration and were relied on twenty years after they had been agreed upon. Consents of this kind as a practical matter require that the client consult with another lawyer about the advisability and terms of the consent itself. In corporate law practice, the client's inside legal department typically will provide that consultation. In modern representation of sophisticated business clients, "consent" letters can themselves be formidable documents.

Conflict of Interest in Successive Representation

The duty of loyalty, given effect in the rules concerning conflict of interest, continues on a limited basis after the lawyer has finished representing a client. There is no prohibition against a lawyer undertaking a representation adverse to a former client, for when a matter is terminated so also is the lawyer-client relationship. However, the lawyer has a duty not to compromise the matter he previously handled.

The concept governing successive representation is addressed in the following statement from the Canadian Code: "A lawyer who has acted for a client in a matter should not thereafter act against him ... in the same or any related matter...."[29]

Virtually the same language appears in the *Guide to Professional Conduct of Solicitors* in England, Principle 15.02. This concept expresses two limitations, one arising from the duty of loyalty and the other from the duty of confidentiality. In terms of loyalty, a lawyer may not undertake to represent a new client in a matter in which the lawyer had formerly represented another client, if the position of the new client will be adverse to the former client. The classic illustration is that a lawyer who has drafted a will for a client may not later, on behalf of another client, bring suit to invalidate the will. (Such a case actually occurred.) Another illustration is that a lawyer who has given advice to a business enterprise about the effects of the antitrust laws may not subsequently represent another enterprise in antitrust litigation against the former client.[30] The obligation is framed in terms of loyalty in ABA Rule 1.9(a),[31] and also in the Russian rule: "An advocate shall not accept a commission ... when he ... has previously rendered assistance regarding the particular case to persons whose interests are contrary to the interests of the [prospective client]."[32]

The rules of ethics in other systems define the lawyer's responsibility to a former client in terms of protecting confidences obtained in the previous matter.[33] For example, a lawyer who had assisted one client in assembling a parcel of real estate, and thereby gained knowledge of the client's strategy for developing the property, ordinarily could not undertake representation of another developer seeking adjacent property, except with the former client's consent. Likewise, a lawyer who previously advised a business concerning its rights of intellectual property in a trademark ordinarily could not properly advise another business concerning a directly competitive rival trademark.

Regarding protection of former clients, a difficult problem concerns the separation in time of the two representations. If a lawyer represented a client twenty years ago in a business transaction, it is improbable that information obtained in that matter could have continued relevance in a matter presently undertaken for another client. But if the representation concerned family affairs, and the subsequent representation concerns the affairs of the same family, even after a long interval of time there could be a conflict of interest.

Although no "bright line" can be drawn, it is recognized that obsolescence of information is a highly relevant factor.

These conflicts of interest concerning former clients are also imputed to all lawyers within a firm. Thus in the example concerning litigation to invalidate a will, no lawyer in the firm of the will draftsman could undertake the representation of a client who wished to challenge the will.

Conflict of interest concerning a former client can be waived by informed consent given by the former client. However, once the relationship has ended, a former client is unlikely to agree to encountering his former lawyer on the other side of the table in a transaction or on the other side of the courtroom in litigation. In anticipation that such will be the client attitude, some lawyers ask for an advance waiver (that is, one that waives conflicts in future representations) before agreeing to take on a new client. Sometimes a prospective engagement can founder over disagreement as to whether such a waiver will be given or disagreement about its scope.

The rule that conflict of interest of each lawyer in a firm is imputed to all other lawyers in the firm is of growing significance as law firms become larger and more diverse in their practice. The concept underlying the imputation rule is captured colloquially in the phrase "one for all, all for one." Lawyers in a firm share revenues, earnings, reputation, and future prospects. Hence they have similar interests in their representation of clients, or so it is presumed. If one of them is prevented from representing a client by reason of a conflict of interest, the imputation rule provides that no other lawyer in the firm may do so. Of course, the affected clients may consent, and often do so. But because the clients may refuse to consent, the risk of refusal is a deterrent to a lawyer's requesting a waiver.

As noted earlier, no other profession has such a stringent rule of imputation. Accounting firms, for example, routinely audit the accounts of competing businesses and also businesses that have continuous trading relationships—for example, the manufacturer of a product and the retailers to whom the manufacturer sells the product. Transactions in these channels of commerce are often fraught with conflict between the participants and hence the possibility of conflict of interest among the accountants servicing them. Nevertheless, as long as an accounting firm keeps the records and personnel for one client isolated from those of other clients, under the rules of the accountancy profession there is no conflict of interest on the part of the firm. The same principle of "nonimputation" is recognized in other professions such as banking, securities underwriting, and insurance. Particularly in these financial services organizations, the possibility of favoritism toward one client, to the detriment of another, is surely as strong as it is within law firms. But the firms in these other professions and vocations have greater freedom to engage clientele because they do not have an imputation rule.

In many legal systems, the rule of imputation in law firms survives largely intact, however.[34] In part, this is a matter of tradition and inertia, which are strong forces in the legal profession. A premise underlying the rule of imputation is the supposition that the typical role of the lawyer is that of advocate; on this premise the spectacle brought to mind is that of a lawyer appearing in court in litigation where his partner represents the opposing party. In transaction matters, there is an image of two or three lawyers with interconnected offices engaging in professional small talk about their clients. No confidences, it is supposed, could be secure in such an environment. These stereotypes sustain the imputation rule, but they are in tension with the evolving reality of the large law firm. In a large firm, Lawyer A in one office may learn about the involvement of Lawyer B in the same firm only upon discovering that there is a conflict regarding a client Lawyer A is eager to serve.

In many European systems, there is no rule of imputation of a conflict if the matters are unrelated in subject matter. Thus, Lawyer A in a firm may bring suit against a client of lawyer B in the same firm if the matter being handled by Lawyer B is unrelated to the subject of the lawsuit. However, one or both clients can object, and some clients will object vehemently. The law firm thereupon must choose which client to serve. It therefore can be said that imputation under the American rule operates automatically, unless consent of the clients is obtained, whereas imputation under the rule prevailing elsewhere is that imputation is a basis for client objection.

When a representation is prohibited by the imputation rule, it generates a conflict in the relationship between the lawyers—a conflict over which clients the firm should undertake—in other words, a conflict over conflicts. Most conflicts over conflicts within a firm are resolved quickly and quietly, for otherwise the firm could not survive. The resulting decision can be that there is no actual conflict, that client waivers should be sought, or that the new matter must be declined. However, some conflicts open deep divisions within a firm, particularly where a specific conflict indicates that further conflicts may develop along the same lines. For example, the lawyers in the corporate department in a law firm may wish to develop further business with banks, whereas the lawyers in the litigation department wish to develop their practice in suing banks on behalf of customers. Even if a specific conflict can be resolved, the directions of practice development in the firm will predictably produce continuing conflict.

More than one law firm has dissolved in the face of such controversies. All law firms, even many small ones, deal with conflicts of interest that are potentially unresolvable. This pressure can aggravate other pressures among high-strung professionals, such as personal jealousy, disputes over sharing compensation, and intergenerational disputes between older and younger partners.

Commencement and Termination of Representation

In the terminology of law practice, engagements on behalf of a client typically can be "on retainer" or concerning "a matter." Under a retainer arrangement, the client pays the lawyer a stipulated amount over a period, typically a year, and in return can call upon the lawyer for assistance as needed during that period. The arrangement may be more complicated, for example, through an agreement that assistance going beyond specified types will call for additional compensation. So also, the lawyer can be on retainer to provide informal advice and to handle certain customary transactions, but is to receive additional amounts for handling litigation or unusually complex transactions.

Retainer arrangements formerly were common for businesses and for wealthy individuals who needed continuous legal assistance. They are much less common today. Many small and medium-sized businesses have retainer arrangements with independent law firms rather than trying to maintain an internal legal department. However, most services provided by lawyers to larger business clients deal with specific matters on a fee basis established ad hoc. Engagements established matter-by-matter are also customary with occasional clientele, such as an individual purchasing or selling a residence or becoming involved in a lawsuit or in an interaction with a government agency.

A retainer arrangement, once established, can continue more or less indefinitely. For the client, it provides a reliable source of legal assistance, the assumption being that the lawyer will avoid other engagements that could result in a conflict of interest. For the lawyer it is a predictable source of income, free of the uncertainties involved in ad hoc engagements. So long as both sides remain content, the client looks at the lawyer as "my lawyer" and the lawyer looks at the client as "my client." Even when the arrangement is not formalized, but merely a series of engagements on various matters, it can be a source of mutual benefit and satisfaction.

In modern practice, ad hoc engagements rather than retainers have become more common. The "matter" might be a property conveyance or a business reorganization or litigation. The fee agreement may call for advance or periodic payments, or contemplate that payment will be due when the work is done. The lawyer thereupon proceeds with the work, and the engagement proceeds through consultations and conferences between client and lawyer. The typical engagement ends with the work done and payment made and everyone reasonably satisfied.

However, there can be disagreement and conflict and possibly rupture of the relationship. The client may be dissatisfied with the quality of the work or the pace at which it is being accomplished. (Lawyers are notorious procrastinators, properly so when delay is strategically useful, but in some lawyers it becomes a habit.) The client may be deeply dissatisfied with the results achieved. Or the client may frustrate the lawyer by failing to provide needed cooperation, failing to pay bills, being unwilling to undertake litigation or transactions attended by risk, or failing to accept the lawyer's recommendations for how to proceed. In such unsatisfactory circumstances, the question can arise whether the engagement should be terminated.

Termination of a client-lawyer relationship is usually by mutual agreement, expressed or merely tacit. Often, the relationship simply dissipates. A lawyer may discover that the engagement has been terminated by receiving correspondence from another lawyer announcing that the client has transferred the matter to new hands.

Such a succession involves delicacy in professional relationships between the lawyers. The rules require the departing lawyer to cooperate in the orderly transfer of responsibility to the successor. Thus ABA Rule 1.16(d) provides:

> Upon termination of representation, a lawyer shall take steps to the extent reasonably practicable to protect a client's interests, such as giving reasonable notice to the client, allowing time for employment of other counsel, surrendering papers and property to which the client is entitled and refunding any advance payment of fee that has not been earned.

The Canadian Code has rules to the same effect, adding that "cooperation with the successor lawyer will normally include providing him with memoranda of facts and law which have been prepared . . . in connection with the matter. . . ."[35] The statutes and ethical rules in most civil law systems and Japan are more elaborate and protective of the superseded lawyer's interest. The Italian code specifies that a successor lawyer may assume responsibility for a matter only upon ensuring that his predecessor's fees have been paid.

A client may fire a lawyer. A client has an absolute right to discharge a lawyer, with or without cause, except that in some systems a court's approval is required where the discharge would interfere with the court's trial schedule. If the lawyer is fired for good cause, the client may have no obligation to pay accumulated charges and may have a right to restitution of fees already paid. If the discharge is without good cause, the lawyer is entitled to be paid according to the fee agreement or, depending on the circumstances, the reasonable value of his services. However, a lawyer who has been wrongfully discharged has no right to recover his "expectation" loss—that is, the loss of revenue that the lawyer would have been earned if he had not been wrongfully discharged. This is a corollary of the principle that the client has an absolute right to discharge the lawyer. Perhaps needless to say, any termination of the relationship between client and lawyer arising from disagreement is usually traumatic. It is much like divorcing a spouse or breaking up a business partnership.

In the United States, a corollary of the rules of "divorce" between client and lawyer governs contingent fee agreements. In a contingent fee engagement, the lawyer works without pay, and often must advance costs involved in prosecuting the case, unless and until a favorable settlement or judgment is achieved. Normally these arrangements, like other client-lawyer relationships, conclude productively on both sides. But the following gambit can occur: the case is fully worked up by the lawyer and is ready for trial (no fee yet, because no recovery has yet been realized), whereupon the client fires the lawyer, hires another lawyer to sign the settlement papers, and then refuses to pay the lawyer who did the work. The rule in response to this gambit is that the client must pay the lawyer who did the work a fair share of the settlement, having regard for the contingent fee agreement.[36]

Under some circumstances a lawyer may withdraw without completing the engagement, or may be obliged to withdraw. No lawyer readily or happily takes such a step, because it results in loss of income and perhaps also loss of professional reputation. Law practice often involves profoundly unpleasant undertakings, and lawyers understand that they must carry on in an engagement even under profoundly objectionable conditions. CCBE 3.14 flatly states that a lawyer may not withdraw at a point where prejudice to the client will result. However, there are circumstances when a lawyer is justified in withdrawing or required to withdraw.

The most common occasion for withdrawal is failure of the client to pay accrued bills for the lawyer's services. Most lawyers will indulge long delays and excuses concerning unpaid bills. They want to keep the client, they want the money, and their work for the client is already a "sunk cost" for which there can be no other source of recovery. In some types of law practice, most lawyers insist on being given a deposit in advance against future fees. Sometimes the deposit is on an "evergreen" basis; that is, it must be replenished (made "green" again) as fee charges are debited against it. Advance deposits are almost always required for criminal defense work. (A defendant who is convicted is ungrateful; a defendant who is acquitted often blames the "system," of which the lawyer is the immediately present representative.) Advance deposits also are often required in divorce representation. But problems about fees are a chronic difficulty in law practice, particularly in the representation of individuals and small businesses.

Another justification for withdrawal is that the client insists on pursuing a course of action that is, in the lawyer's estimate, immoral or profoundly foolish.[37] In the civil law systems and most common law countries, the lawyer has a greater right to disassociate from a representation where, in the lawyer's opinion, continuing the representation will reflect adversely on his professional standing. As stated in the Canadian Code, a lawyer has a "positive duty" to withdraw:

> (a) if he is instructed by his client to do something inconsistent with his duty to the court and if, following explanation, the client persists in his instructions;
>
> (b) if the client is guilty of dishonourable conduct in the proceedings or is taking a position solely to harass or maliciously injure another;
>
> (c) if it becomes clear that the lawyer's continued employment will involve him in a breach of this Code.[38]

A lawyer who continues in an engagement involving illegal or fraudulent conduct runs serious risk of being charged himself as an accessory under criminal law or in civil litigation. Such a risk occurs, for example, for a lawyer who documents a transaction that turns out to involve (alleged) fraud, where the other side could later claim that the lawyer knew of the fraud and therefore wrongfully assisted in it. That situation was the basis of many controversial relationships between financial institutions and their law firms during the "S&L crisis" in the United States in the 1980s and again when the financial bubbles burst after the 1990s. The S&L crisis concerned savings and loan banks that became grossly overextended and engaged in loan transactions involving unlawful risks. In several instances, the transactions had been documented by lawyers who were aware of their unlawful character, or had information that should have made them aware. The circumstances surrounding burst financial bubbles in the 1990s were perhaps even more egregious. Another area of illegal activity in which some lawyers have become participants are currency transactions involving "money laundering"—that is, the clandestine transfer of funds to avoid regulatory controls. The European Community has issued restrictive directives addressed specifically to lawyers concerning "suspicious" financial transactions.[39]

In today's world of commerce and finance, lawyers (and accountants and investment bankers among others) engaged in transaction practice are at constant risk of this kind of involvement. Of course, statistically very few business transactions are legally improper, and in even fewer is there any basis for suspecting complicity on the part of the lawyers and other independent professionals. Lawyers who are conscientious (or simply averse to taking personal risks) are circumspect in their participation in unorthodox transactions, particularly when acting for a client with whom they are not well acquainted. Some lawyers are willing to take chances, and a few are reckless or simply crooks themselves. But for most lawyers it is personally abhorrent, and not worth it, to get involved in transactions that could be criminal or fraudulent.

Lawyers are aware that many members of the public, and some judges, distrust all lawyers and are predisposed to think that "the lawyers must have known" that the transaction was illegal. Lawyers know that becoming embroiled in an investigation or litigation concerning crime or fraud will disrupt their lives, be very expensive (they will have to hire lawyers), and damage or ruin their reputations. All these factors are very practical reinforcements of the inclination, which we believe most lawyers have, to stay away from "smelly" transactions. This combination of influences means that most lawyers, and all seriously self-respecting lawyers, will not assist in transactions that could reasonably be challenged as involving crime or fraud.

At the same time, having the assistance of legal counsel is a practical necessity in most modern financial transactions of even moderate complexity. Ordinarily, underwriters and investors will not put up their money unless documents are signed by reputable counsel, to say nothing of regulatory requirements for such certifications. Prospective investors have come to insist on legal opinion letters addressed directly to them, which accordingly make the lawyer legally responsible to the investors as well as to prospective entrepreneurs.[40] The transaction can be consummated only with an opinion from the lawyer asserting that the transaction is legal and technically proper.

Transaction lawyers become correspondingly wary—or "careful." Specifically, a transaction lawyer will require that any affirmation on the lawyer's part (for example, that an issue of stock has been registered with the regulatory authority) be based on "due diligence" conducted by the lawyer. Due diligence means a reasonably intensive inquiry into the circumstances, on the basis of which the inquirer (the lawyer) is satisfied that things are bona fide.

The complicated dynamic involved in due diligence is now standard practice. The transaction can be consummated only on the basis of a lawyer's written opinion (and similar opinions from accountants and other professionals) that the deal is bona fide and based on truthful statements; the lawyer will not issue such an opinion without careful checking; the careful checking provides assurance to investors and other third parties that the transaction is legitimate. The result in transactional matters has come to be called "transparency."

The further result, concerning the lawyer's role, is that transaction lawyers (as well as accountants who certify financial statements, and engineers who do environmental reviews) are sometimes referred to as "gatekeepers" for important transactions.[41] That term does not imply that the lawyers are police or government inspectors. Rather, it signifies that they are positioned at a critical point in the flow of events where their approval is required for the transaction to proceed to consummation. The metaphor is that they stand at the gates of places where complicated business interchanges are made and do not allow (or try not to allow) transactions to be carried out that do not conform to legal requirements, including requirements concerning factual disclosure, accuracy of financial projections, and others.

A different responsibility has been imposed on lawyers in Europe and Canada and is threatened in the United States. This has to do with money-laundering, transactions in which illegally obtained money is transferred into legally sheltered depositories where it can later be withdrawn. The prototype is money from illegal drug transactions; tax avoidance schemes are another example. The European rules now require lawyers to report "suspicious" money transfers of which they become aware, and to do so without informing the clients.[42] The term "suspicious" is obviously vague. One of us once heard a German lawyer ask rhetorically, "Isn't every transaction involving a Caribbean country suspicious?" The requirement of reporting on clients is obnoxious. The requirement that the client not be told imposes an obligation by the state that lawyers engage in betrayal.

Needless to say, the bars in Europe and Canada have been outraged and the American lawyers critical and resistant. But the governments outside the United States have been resolute, and it would not be surprising if the U.S. Departments of Treasury and Justice were to adopt a similar position. (The impetus from 9/11 has been very strong.) In regimes where the money-laundering reporting requirement is in effect, conscientious lawyers will simply have to turn down "suspicious" engagements from potential clients that they do not know and trust. It is a price paid by virtuous lawyers for the willingness of other lawyers to provide illegal help to drug dealers and other antisocial personages.

In 2002, the U.S. Congress enacted a statute, the Sarbanes-Oxley Act of 2002, which proceeded in a similar direction, but not as far. (The act already is informally called "SOX.") SOX sharpened the standards governing lawyers and accountants in financial transactions, as well as the obligations of corporate managers and boards of directors. In essence, the new act requires lawyers to be especially alert for corporate misrepresentation and to refer suspicious transactions to the company board of directors if management does not take corrective action. The Securities and Exchange Commission has adopted implementing regulations that further sharpen lawyers' obligations in securities and similar transactions. These in turn have incited turmoil and contentious response on the part of the legal profession. The net effect will be greater responsibility imposed on accountants and lawyers and heightened sensitivity to those responsibilities on the part of the corporate executives and board members, particularly independent directors (those not employed by the company).

The role of lawyers and accountants was vividly described nearly a half-century ago by Judge Henry Friendly. (Judge Friendly was in the estimate of many the greatest common law judge of his generation, especially in corporate matters, where he brought to bear his extensive previous experience in high-level corporate law practice.) In *United States v. Benjamin,* the criminal prosecution of a lawyer and an accountant for assisting in a fraudulent securities sale, he observed: "In our complex society the accountant's certificate and the lawyer's opinion can be instruments for inflicting pecuniary loss more potent than the chisel or the crowbar."[43]

Hence, a lawyer's duty of loyalty to a client must always be qualified as assistance "within the bounds of the law," to use a phrase in an earlier formulation of the American profession's rules of ethics. By the same token, if a transaction lawyer withdraws from a role in a transaction, the transaction is almost certain to abort. Any withdrawal is likely to involve distress on both sides, and often recrimination. If the dispute is addressed in some subsequent proceeding, for example, a criminal investigation of the client or a disciplinary inquiry concerning the lawyer, there is likely to be a sharp discrepancy in the testimony of the erstwhile client and the lawyer. Often the contentions become very ugly. A prudent lawyer, who believes that withdrawal is appropriate or necessary, therefore usually tries to exit quietly.

Most engagements of course begin and end prosaically, the client satisfied with loyal and effective service and the lawyer satisfied with a job adequately done and properly paid for.

6

Confidentiality

Confidentiality and the Attorney-Client Privilege

The duty of confidentiality is an article of faith in the legal profession. A lawyer is commonly thought of as "one who keeps secrets." Of course, all persons acting as agents or in another fiduciary capacity for others—financial advisers and brokers, for example—have a legal duty of confidentiality, just as they have a duty of loyalty. However, the lawyer's duty is more formally expressed, in both ethical codes and legal rules, and more rigorously observed. Some courts have recognized the duty of confidentiality, and the corresponding obligation of the lawyer not to disclose client communications even to a court, as a fundamental human right. As stated in the English case of *R (Morgan Grenfell Ltd) v. Special Commissioner of Tax*: "It is a necessary corollary of the right of any person to obtain skilled advice about the law."[1] If the duty is violated, and violation is detected, the sanctions can be severe. A lawyer's maintaining secrecy is of great practical significance when the confidences involve matters close to the boundaries of the law. In such situations, the information, if disclosed, might be used against the client by other parties or by public authority.

The duty of confidentiality supports the duty of loyalty. In some transactions, no harm to the client would result if the lawyer made full disclosure to others, but in transactions of that kind the duty of confidentiality is simply dormant. Even a client with a wholly innocuous objective can have secrets about it from a spouse/partner/assistant/boss. A client's private hopes and fears often are conveyed in "body language," which an experienced lawyer learns to "read" and thus appreciate the client's deeper wishes and concerns. By the same token, an experienced lawyer becomes skilled at *not* conveying information to others, either in words or in behavior. The classic Chinese businessman held a fan at his face to help conceal his bargaining position. So also a lawyer should be inscrutable in dealing with others.

The strong professional commitment to the sanctity of client confidences becomes a self-fulfilling prophecy. Because clients understand that communications with a lawyer are highly confidential, clients usually are more frank with their lawyer than they would be in conversations about the same topic with most others.

In litigation the lawyer's function is to present the client in a favorable light. Presenting the client's case to the court requires private exploratory and rehearsal discussions with the client. These discussions address the issues in terms that could be damaging to the client if revealed to the opposing party or to the court. Similarly, an office lawyer often carries out a transaction whose full motives and purposes are not to be disclosed to others. However, in some circumstances it is to the client's advantage to reveal communications with the lawyer, for example, to substantiate a contention that the client, having consulted the lawyer, believed on that basis that his subsequent course of conduct was lawful.

In all legal systems a lawyer has a right and a duty to maintain in confidence matters that have been learned from or concern a client. The duty governs not only communications directly from the client but also information obtained from others, such as the client's banker or accountant or friends or family members. There is some variation in the formulations, but the concept is clear as expressed in the Canadian Code: "The lawyer has a duty to hold in strict confidence all information acquired in the course of the professional relationship concerning the business and affairs of his client. . . ."[2]

In Japan, Article 20 of the Code of Ethics for Practicing Attorneys provides: "An attorney shall not disclose or utilize, without any good reason, confidential information of a client which is obtained in the course of his or her practice. The same prohibition applies to confidential information of a client of another attorney practicing at the same office. . . ."

In common law systems the principle of confidentiality is expressed as a duty of the lawyer to the client. In that framework, the client accordingly may waive or forgo the benefit of confidentiality. Confidentiality also is forfeited if the client discloses the substance of the confidential information to a third party, for example by mistakenly transmitting to an outsider a memorandum of the communication with the lawyer.[3]

In contrast, in civil law systems the principle of confidentiality is defined as a professional secret and is expressed as a professional right and duty of the lawyer. CCBE 2.3.1 states that confidentiality is "a primary and fundamental right and duty of the lawyer." So also, Article 5.7 of the Internal Rules of the Paris Bar provides that "any correspondence between the lawyer and his client is covered by professional secrecy that is general and unlimited in time. The duty to maintain confidentiality is absolutely mandatory for the lawyer, who cannot deviate even with his client's consent or upon official request."

The French provision is typical of civil law systems, not only in substance but also in its "constitutional" characteristics. A counterpart rule is enshrined in the Civil Code of some of the civil law systems and thus is part of their basic law. Decisional law in the civil law systems holds the principle of confidentiality in deep respect. A decision in the Russian Federation in 2000, for example, held that a lawyer presently representing a client could not be required to give testimony concerning knowledge gained in an earlier representation of the same client.[4] Concerning confidences obtained from a client, a Russian commentator states: "An advocate must act as if he does not know that these facts existed."[5] This Russian conceptualization has an interesting affinity with the rule of confidentiality governing confession in the Roman Catholic Church. In that protocol, the priest is justified in not reporting about the penitent, from information obtained in the spiritual confession, on the basis that the priest outside the confessional does not know what was heard by the priest inside the confessional.

In common law systems, the lawyer's duty of confidentiality is supported by a corollary known as the attorney-client privilege. This is a rule directed to courts and other official agencies that prohibits them from inquiring into confidential communications between client and advocate. The attorney-client privilege evolved through judicial decisions beginning not later than the seventeenth century. Originally the privilege attached to the lawyer rather than the client, but by the late nineteenth century it was established that the privilege belonged to the client.

Early decisions developing the rule of attorney-client privilege concerned instructions on behalf of a client transmitted by a solicitor, who had contact with the client, that were given to a barrister, who presented the case in court.[6] It was held that these instructions could not be used as adverse admissions against the client. This point of origin gave shape to the scope of the common law privilege, in that the privilege protects communications from the client to the attorney, and does not more broadly protect information acquired by the attorney from other sources. It is now settled that the common law attorney-client privilege does not apply to information garnered by the lawyer from sources other than the client. As noted above, the civil law regards secrecy as the *lawyer's* professional right, while the common law defines attorney-client privilege in terms of the *client's* right.

However, another common law rule goes a substantial way toward covering the same ground as the civil law. This is the rule known in the United States as the lawyer work-product rule and in England as the litigation privilege. It provides against disclosure of confidential information that a lawyer has assembled from various sources in anticipation of litigation, and the lawyer's analysis of that information. The rule originated in a Supreme Court decision, *Hickman v. Taylor*, decided in 1947.[7] The question presented in *Hickman* was whether notes of interviews of witnesses that had been conducted by the lawyer for one party had to be disclosed to the opposing party. The issue was provoked by the sweeping scope of discovery rules in the then recently adopted Federal Rules of Civil Procedure. The discovery provisions of Federal Rule 26 required that a party, upon demand of an opposing party, make disclosure of "any matter, not privileged, which is relevant to the subject matter involved in the pending action." That broad formula certainly included an attorney's notes of interviews with witnesses. But it seemed highly unfair that a party could capture the product of investigation conducted by the lawyer for the other side. Borrowing a concept from English practice that barred discovery of documents prepared for litigation, the Supreme Court gave recognition to what is now called the work-product privilege or immunity. As explained in a footnote in the court's opinion:

> The English courts have developed the concept of privilege to include all documents prepared by or for counsel with a view to litigation. "... Reports by a company's servants, if made in the ordinary course of routine, are not privileged

... but if the solicitor has requested that such documents shall always be prepared for his use ... they need not be disclosed." *Odgers on Pleading and Practice* (12th ed.).[8]

(This reference to English authority by an American court is an interesting instance of transfer of precedent and concept from one legal system to another.)

The work-product rule as subsequently evolved in American law is very elaborate, but generally confers immunity from disclosure of information gathered in anticipation of litigation, except information that the other party can show is vitally important in the case and which could not otherwise be obtained. For example, if one party was able to inspect a damaged automobile after a vehicle accident, and the vehicle had then gone to the junkyard before the opposing party had an opportunity to do a similar inspection, in later litigation the opposing party could obtain a copy of the inspection report if the condition of the automobile were relevant. The American rules have other important exceptions to the secrecy of work product, particularly statements given by a litigant or an independent witness to an investigator for an opposing party and information given to an opposing party's expert who will be called as a witness in the dispute.[9] But otherwise, the "internal" legal work by a party and his attorney in preparing litigation (as distinct from papers filed with the court) is protected against disclosure. Moreover, the work-product rule confers virtually absolute protection of the lawyer's "mental impressions," meaning notes expressing the lawyer's analysis of the situation, draft legal documents, and the like.

Similar protection is established in the other common law countries.[10] In litigated matters, the combination of the common law attorney-client privilege and the common law work-product privilege provides protection against compulsory disclosure that corresponds to that provided by the lawyer's professional privilege in civil law systems.

With respect to office or transaction practice, as distinguished from litigation matters, the scope of protection in the common law is considerably narrower than in the civil law. Under civil law, all such matters are covered by the rule of professional confidentiality. Under common law, communications between the client and the lawyer are protected against disclosure by the attorney-client privilege, but other information in a transaction lawyer's hands may not be thus protected. For example, if a lawyer handling a business transaction is supplied with financial information by the client's bank or accountant, that information is not protected against compulsory disclosure if there is later litigation. This is because the information did not come from the client (so is not covered by the attorney-client privilege) and was not in preparation of litigation (hence not covered by the work-product rule).

This difference in the scope of confidentiality is even sharper when account is taken of the civil law rules concerning the confidentiality of information in the hands of professionals other than lawyers. Most civil law systems confer the right and duty of professional secrecy not only on lawyers, doctors, and priests (the classic professions), but also on accountants, financial advisers, psychologists, and other professionals.[11] The total effect under the civil law, as a matter of long-established public policy, is that private information is closely shrouded. Compared with compulsory disclosure under American discovery rules, that policy represents a fundamental cultural difference.

It may be observed that this cultural difference is apparently lost (or never existed) in the thought of many American legal scholars who are critical of the partisanship of the lawyer's role, particularly the right and duty to maintain client confidences. Some of these scholars rely on European moral philosophy, notably that of Immanuel Kant, as support for this critique. But in the European professional outlook there is no contradiction between Kantian philosophy and an exacting duty of confidentiality for professionals. On the contrary, maintaining confidences is regarded as a high moral duty. As a Spanish colleague states: "There is a general duty to keep secrets ... which obliges everybody [especially lawyers] not to damage [those who have confided in them]. Some American scholarship has reached to Europe for philosophical universals that evidently are not universally embraced in European thought."

Disclosure of Client Confidences

Lawyers perform most of their functions by conveying information about their clients to others, for example, in litigation through pleadings, motions, and evidence. Information about a client is transmitted to other parties in negotiation, for example, the information implicit in a proposed term of a contract. The addressee of information about a client may be a government official, for example, in response to an official inquiry.

The lawyer shapes all such transmissions so that the message is as consistent as possible with the interests of the client. In negotiations, a lawyer may say that his client, the prospective seller of an item, will accept $1,000. That statement means that his client would accept $1,000, but it does not indicate whether the client would accept a lesser sum, even though the lawyer might know that the client's confidential "reserve price" (what the client would accept) is a lesser amount. The statement that the client would accept $1,000 is a disclosure, although only a partial one, of confidences imparted by the client to the lawyer. In a complex negotiation, the explicit and implicit disclosures to an opposite party may be extensive. For example, in the sale of a business there must be disclosures concerning the inventory, production, status of employees, revenues, and existing contracts. Typically, these disclosures are made gradually as the negotiations proceed from tentative expressions of interest toward binding formal commitment. Yet if the client had not authorized the lawyer to convey specific items of information, the lawyer would be breaching his duty of confidentiality by doing so.

Similar disclosures are made in discussions of settlement of litigation and in myriad other transactions in which a lawyer acts for a client. The legal and ethical basis of such disclosures is summarized as follows: "A lawyer has general authority to take steps reasonably calculated to further the client's objectives in the representation. . . . A lawyer may use or disclose confidential client information when the lawyer reasonably believes that doing so will advance the interests of the client. . . ."[12]

The legal concept in this formulation is that of implied authority, a concept derived from agency law. A person who acts for another (whether a lawyer or other instrumental person) has the implied authority to take measures that will accomplish the objectives contemplated in the representation. Conveying information is an exercise of that authority.

In all such communications, the lawyer's judgment is an important element. An agent cannot always gauge exactly how much of his principal's purposes and wishes ought to be conveyed. Conveying too little information might fail to bring the other party around to a possible agreement, while conveying too much might "give away the store"—that is, have a disastrous effect on the client's bargaining position. Hence, the concept is cast in terms of disclosures "reasonably calculated" to further the client's objectives. The flexibility of that concept ordinarily would allow a lawyer to defend his conduct if subjected to later recrimination by the client, even though the disclosure might have been less or more than the client would have preferred.

A client retains authority to limit the lawyer's implied authority regarding disclosures to others. Thus the client could say to the lawyer: "Tell them I'll take $1,200 and nothing less." Such an instruction binds the lawyer, even though the lawyer may clearly perceive that such a proposal is doomed to rejection. The lawyer does not have authority to suggest to the opposing party that the client might accept a smaller amount. The lawyer also would lack authority to signal such a possibility by a "wink or a nod." Nevertheless, a skillful and self-confident lawyer could intimate to opposing counsel that the proposal of other terms might yield a positive response.

In most civil law regimes and some of those in the common law, there is an important convention under which communication can be conducted among lawyers on a basis of mutual confidentiality. In these systems, lawyers on each side of litigation or a transaction may make statements and proposals to each other, on the basis that these communications are not to be disclosed to anyone else. In some systems there are specific protocols governing such communications, requiring that they be in writing and set forth under a heading of "Privileged" or "Without Prejudice" or similar terms. Article 28 of the Italian code illustrates this procedure: "Correspondence marked as confidential or any correspondence containing proposals for negotiations or settlement sent to or received from other lawyers may not be produced or referred to in judicial proceedings. . . ." The English version of this principle of confidential communication between lawyers is referred to as the "without prejudice" privilege and is highly developed in decisional law.[13]

No such rule concerning communications among lawyers is established in American practice, except concerning offers of settlement of litigation. However, parties to negotiation may make special agreements that nothing between them is to be considered a "statement" unless it is incorporated in a final agreement. The European system seems much simpler.

In many civil law systems, there is a further refinement. In these systems lawyers for opposing parties may engage in professional communications that are to be withheld from the clients on both sides. Another subsection of Italian Article 28 is illustrative: "A lawyer may not provide to his client confidential correspondence between himself and another lawyer. . . ." To some observers it may seem strange that lawyers on opposite sides have authority to conduct discussions with each other that are withheld from their clients. Yet the concept underlying this rule is clear enough: lawyers, through professional experience, recognize that clients may be unreasonable or ignorant about a matter in dispute; that ways must be found to persuade one or both of the clients to change position; and that frank talk between the lawyers may suggest ways in which that objective can be accomplished. The concept is familiar in—indeed the essence of—the function of representatives in diplomacy, labor relations, and political negotiations. The same insight is involved in the practice of mediation, in which a mediator confers separately and privately with each party to a dispute, seeking common ground for resolution of the dispute.

The CCBE statement of common principles for the legal professions in the European countries has carefully stated provisions on this subject, recognizing that different countries have different conventions. Special warning is given in the CCBE principles that a communication between lawyers in different systems may not be protected by a confidentiality rule.[14]

Underlying these differences in the rules of confidentiality are differences in basic assumptions about the lawyer-client relationship, particularly in litigation. In most civil law systems, and to a substantial degree in English common law, litigation is considered to be under the direction of the advocates and not the clients. In this conception, litigants bringing or defending a lawsuit are considered to be employing the privilege of invoking the aid of the state to resolve a private controversy. In doing so, the client may proceed only through and under the tutelage of advocates, who are themselves qualified licensees in the state's system of justice.[15] The advocate is an instrument for the client, to be sure, but one with exclusive powers and authority concerning presentations to the courts. In contrast, in most common law systems and some civil law regimes, litigation is considered to be the exercise of a legal right of the litigant.[16] In the American legal system, conducting litigation is a constitutional right.[17]

The advocate's duty of deference to the court is more fully examined in Chapter 7. However, among those duties is making proper disclosures about matters before the court. In all procedural systems, an advocate is not permitted to make a baseless denial of an allegation by an opposing party, simply because the client does not wish to admit the fact. So also, if the court requires that a pertinent question be answered, the advocate must see that a response is made even if it might adversely affect the client's case. In American procedure in civil cases, the parties have broad duties of disclosure in the pretrial "discovery" stage—producing documents and submitting to interrogations in deposition before the judicial hearing. The advocates in American procedure have a corresponding responsibility to supervise proper compliance with those procedures.[18]

As a practical matter, final authority for maneuvers in litigation usually is effectively exercised by the lawyers. This is simply because the client is dependent on the lawyer's knowledge of technique and of the legal risks in the litigation. Moreover, in some legal systems, notably those of England and Japan, the advocate's high status is such that a client simply cannot proceed with a claim or defense that the advocate considers unwarranted. Moreover, in the English system the advocate's authority is backed by a rule exposing the lawyer personally to pay costs to the opposing party if pressing the litigation is determined to have been "improper, unreasonable, or negligent."[19] In American litigation prosecuted on the basis of a contingent fee, the lawyer usually has similar influence.

In transaction matters, it is recognized in all systems that the client is the principal and as such has authority over conduct of the transaction. As principal, the client can give the lawyer broad latitude to do what the lawyer sees fit, or virtually no latitude—making the lawyer little more than a technician. This rule concerning allocation of authority is subject to important qualifications, however. A lawyer must refrain from making false or misleading statements,[20] refrain from circumventing an opposing lawyer by trying to deal directly with the opposing party,[21] and observe a standard of fairness in all dealings with third persons.[22]

Whatever the formal allocation of authority between client and lawyer, most legal undertakings function much as an informal partnership between lawyer and client. Nevertheless, situations arise where a client and lawyer deeply disagree about how to proceed, whether in litigation or in a transaction. An experienced lawyer may recommend proceeding along lines quite different from the wishes expressed by an inexperienced client. In litigation, the lawyer may believe the possibility of winning to be very strong, worthy of resolutely pressing forward, while the client is nervous about the risk of loss. Conversely, the lawyer may consider the possibility of winning to be weak, while the client has expectations that the lawyer considers unrealistic. Similar differences can emerge in transaction strategy. Resolving these differences requires skill and forbearance on the part of the lawyer and recognition that the client has final authority. However, a lawyer usually may withdraw if prepared to justify that the client's proposed course of action was foolhardy.

The traditional concept of a client-lawyer relationship contemplates a "live" human being as the client. Indeed, the stereotype client is a mature male experienced in matters involving property or business and familiar with the world around him.[23] Such a client has legal authority to give directions to another who is acting on his behalf (the lawyer) and sufficient knowledge of the world to participate competently in the discussions and decisions involved in the undertaking. Many of the governing ethical concepts implicitly depend on this assumed identity of a typical client. For example, the concept of loyalty presupposes commitment to a person, not necessarily the kind that should be owed to a bureaucratic organization such as a corporation. However, the person with whom the lawyer interacts often does not fit this traditionally assumed identity. Lawyers have occasion to represent persons who are very inexperienced in the ways of the larger world: ordinary working people; women who have spent their adult lives in the domestic vocation; children who are legally incompetent to make legally significant decisions; and senior citizens who have lost some or most of their mental and psychological strength. And many lawyers, perhaps most lawyers in some communities, ordinarily represent organizations rather than individuals, including business corporations, nonprofit corporations and associations, and agencies and bureaus of the state. Substantial adjustments in the governing ethical obligations are required for these "atypical" clients.

For clients who are inexperienced in dealing with major transactions, or who are not legally competent (children) or possibly have diminished competence (senior citizens), the governing ethical concepts are simple but unavoidably vague: such a client should be treated with special regard for the individual's personal limitations. For example, when client authorization for a contemplated course of action must be based on "informed consent," the necessary information must be given at a level of detail appropriate to the client's level of experience, age, and mental capacity. If the client has close relatives whose interests are not in conflict with the client's, the lawyer ordinarily should include them in the consultation—the spouse in the case of decisions by a married person, the parent of a child, the children of a senior citizen. These concepts are captured in the ABA Rules, Rule 1.14(a), as follows: "When a client's capacity to make adequately considered decisions in connection with a representation is diminished, whether because of minority, mental impairment or for some other reason, the lawyer shall, as far as reasonably possible, maintain a normal client-lawyer relationship with the client." The comment to this rule observes:

> [A] client with diminished capacity often has the ability to understand, deliberate upon, and reach conclusions about matters affecting the client's own well-being. For example, children as young as five or six years of age, and certainly those of ten or twelve, are regarded as having opinions that are entitled to weight in legal proceedings concerning their custody. So also ... some persons of advanced age can be quite capable of handling routine financial matters while needing special legal protection concerning major transactions.

The ethical principles in other legal systems are not so explicit, but the same concepts apply. The lawyer should possess and employ a very strong measure of sympathetic judgment. Patience, circumspection, and self-restraint are required. However, there are horror stories, unfortunately some of them true, about lawyers who have exploited naive or enfeebled clients. The classic example of exploitation is of a lawyer who makes himself the beneficiary of a senior client's testamentary disposition. If such a transaction is questioned, the law is very severe on the lawyer, and properly so.[24]

There has been some criticism in the United States that the governing rule (quoted above) does not provide sufficient guidance to or control over the lawyer.[25] Yet critics have been unable to suggest more definite standards. It is not practicable, or in the best interests of most clients, to require a lawyer to seek appointment of a guardian or conservator for a client who might be considered to be of limited capacity. Proceedings for such an appointment are expensive, not completely private, often involve delay, and can inflict additional distress on the client. The factors involved in a specific client's capabilities are multiple, interactive, and accordingly complex. The nature of the matter involved in the representation is an additional independent variable: settling a minor legal dispute is quite different from making the testamentary disposition of a substantial estate. Hence an unavoidably broad range of professional judgment must be brought to bear, one that cannot be well captured in any ethical formula. In some legal systems the state provides supportive social services for disabled people (such as medical care or retirement homes) that relieve the burden on the client, the client's family, and the lawyer. However, these services are inadequate or nonexistent in many regimes.

Corporate clients usually present the opposite problem in a client-lawyer relationship. A corporation ordinarily is under the direction of experienced managers whose vocation is to make informed decisions for the corporation. An agency or a bureau of the state ordinarily is under similar direction. However, there are two complicating factors in the ethics of the relationship.

First, the corporate management may be excessively "competent," that is, aggressive and domineering. An excessive exercise of authority by corporate management can interfere with or entirely repress the lawyer's exercise of professional judgment, to the detriment of the lawyer's responsibilities as an independent professional. Second, lurking beneath the surface of a lawyer's relationship with a corporate client is the fact that the individuals who speak for the client—particularly the corporate executives and board of directors—are *not* the client. Instead, the client is the corporate legal entity, for which the corporate executives and directors are, as a matter of law, merely spokespersons. Many of the difficulties in modern legal ethics derive from one or both of these circumstances.

Concern about overbearing corporate clients has been recurrently expressed at least since 1900. Louis Brandeis, later a justice of the U.S. Supreme Court, expressed the concern as a Boston lawyer in 1905.[26] Harlan Fiske Stone, while a justice of the Supreme Court, gave it fuller expression in a lecture in 1934.[27] A similar theme has been recurrent in academic expression since the 1960s.[28]

Of greater direct legal significance was the decision by the Supreme Court of the European Community in the *AM&S* case, a decision that has worldwide significance in law practice.[29] In that decision the court held that the attorney-client privilege (to withhold client communications exchanged with a lawyer) did not apply to in-house counsel for a corporation, but only to communications with lawyers in independent practice. The explanation by the court was that only lawyers who are subject to the professional governance imposed on lawyers in independent practice, as distinct from the status of a lawyer-employee of the client, could be entrusted to confine communications within proper professional limits. That view of in-house counsel has been rejected in common law jurisdictions,[30] but it reflects a widely held skepticism about the ability of a lawyer to deal with a powerful client on whom the lawyer is dependent for income.[31]

There is another side to the matter, however. This is the influence that right-minded legal advice can have on corporate decision-making and policy. Lawyers in a corporate law department usually enjoy high respect from corporate management: it was, after all, management that hired them. Lawyers who are employed by corporations in their law departments emphatically state that they adhere to ethical requirements in relationships with their clients. A similar position is of course affirmed by lawyers in independent practice who serve corporate clients.[32] The authors have no doubt that most lawyers for corporations, both on the staff of law departments and in independent practice, conduct themselves properly in corporate relationships. We also have no doubt that the sustained performance of professional responsibility by lawyers in representing corporations, over time and in cumulative effect, is (and has been in the past) a strong force supporting "corporate responsibility" in the capitalist constitutional regimes.

However, there are documented instances in which lawyers have colluded with serious wrongdoing by corporate officials, or at least closed their eyes to obvious legal violations.[33] "Enron" has now become familiar shorthand for the (alleged) malfeasance and nonfeasance of lawyers inside and outside of major corporations.

It is impossible to measure or quantify the net effect of the interaction between lawyers and corporate officials on fulfillment of corporate "good citizenship." The relationships of corporations to ambient legal regimes around the world are extremely varied. A major variable is the degree of fidelity to law in the local regime. Providing proper legal assistance in a country whose legal system is driven by corruption is a tricky proposition. Beyond this are situational differences among corporate clients, in a range from a small company whose chief legal matters are paying proper taxes and obtaining periodic license renewals, to large corporations that are subject to myriad legal regulations concerning employment, financial operations, environmental obligations, foreign trade restrictions, and shareholder relationships. The character and inclinations of corporate management vary widely, from punctilious to cavalier. The character and inclinations of corporate lawyers also vary widely, from strictly proper to nearly recklessly cynical. No corporation or corporate lawyer would acknowledge that he systematically evades legal requirements whenever it is advantageous. On the contrary, all corporations and corporate lawyers would affirm that they function within the requirements of the rules of legal ethics.

A complicating factor in a lawyer's representation of a corporation (or a state agency or bureaucracy, or a nonprofit organization) is that the individuals with whom the lawyer confers, and to whom legal advice and assistance are provided, are not clients. Instead, the corporation is the client and the corporation's directors, officers, and employees are functionaries of the client. Legally speaking, the directors are trustees for the corporation, and the corporate officers and employees are its agents. Correlatively, the lawyer in giving advice and assistance to these individuals does so in behalf of the corporation. There are myriad simple technical problems in differentiating corporate officials from the corporation. In normal corporate operations, the distinction between the corporation and its individual operatives presents no practical problems: the lawyer presents the legal advice and the corporate official puts it to use.

Corporation versus Corporate Official

Nevertheless, there can be tension between the legal interests of the corporation, on one hand, and, on the other hand, the personal legal interests of its directors or officers, particularly high-level officers such as the chief executive officer and chief financial officer. The tension may arise from direct financial conflict, for example, in the terms and conditions of the compensation to be paid to the executive. (Stock options, pension benefits and other "perks" can require complicated legal documentation.) Another source of conflict, particularly in smaller businesses, can arise if the top officers also are owners of other businesses to which corporate opportunities might be diverted, to the detriment of other stockholders in the principal company. There can be conflict between the ambition of top management to maintain a strong financial performance record for the company and legal requirements that the company maintain accurate financial records. There are many examples of this kind of situation, such as whether to classify shipments of goods as "sales" (with a corresponding increase in company revenues) when the shipments have not yet been paid for. Of course, this kind of manipulation may be revealed later on, as it has been since the 1990s "bubble," but the time horizon of some business executives is quite short.

In the case of lower-level company employees, the tensions are different but can nevertheless be severe. For example, the manager of a plant having environmental problems may wish to avoid remedial expenditures that would remedy the problems, because the expenditures would detract from his record of financial performance. Or an office manager may shrink from intervening in a lower-level personnel conflict because he wants to avoid the distress that a confrontation would generate. Yet the personnel conflict may involve serious legal implications, such as violation of a union contract or illegal racial discrimination. Situations such as these can come directly or indirectly to the attention of corporate counsel. And perhaps the lawyer and the lower-level executive have been personal friends.

Similar tension between the interest of the organization and its officials can arise in government. In the United States there have been famous instances, notably concerning President Nixon ("Watergate") and President Clinton ("Monica Lewinsky"), in which the "corporate" interests of the government did not correspond to the personal interests of the incumbent.[34] Less conspicuous instances of conflict between an official's personal interests and his official responsibility inevitably recur throughout the world.

The professional discourse on the problems of representing a corporation is very sparse except in the United States. Indeed, some judges and lawyers evidently have overlooked the significance of the distinction between the corporation and the corporate official insofar as it concerns the responsibility of corporate counsel. An illustration is the difference in analysis in an American case decided by an appellate court in California in 1956 and in an English case decided by the House of Lords in 1999.

The California case, *Meehan v. Hopps*, turned on whether a law firm engaged by a corporation in various transactions owed duties of loyalty and confidentiality to the chief executive officer (CEO) of the corporation, as distinct from the corporation itself. The court held, properly in our opinion, that no such duty was owed personally to the corporate officer. As the court said:

> Assuming that some of the information obtained from Hopps [the CEO] by counsel as representative of the corporation [was material in a later dispute between Hopps and the corporation], nevertheless such fact would not prevent counsel from representing ... the corporation ... in a controversy with Hopps nor from using that information against him. ... As attorneys for the corporation counsel's first duty was to it. Likewise, as an officer of the corporation, it was Hopps's duty to disclose to it all information necessary for its purposes.[35]

The case before the House of Lords, *Bolkiah v. KPMG*,[36] involved what appears to be a similar series of events. In the first stage, the corporate official, Prince Jefri Bolkiah, as chairman of the corporate entity (Brunei Investment Agency, a government agency of the monarchy of Brunei), conducted various financial transactions for the entity. KPMG, an international accounting firm, performed audits of the agency during Prince Jefri's incumbency as chairman. Later, Prince Jefri's financial management was challenged through litigation by the Bruneian government, which thereupon engaged KPMG to reexamine the financial transactions in question. Prince Jefri challenged KPMG's participation on the ground that the firm had a conflict of interest against him because he was its former client. The House of Lords upheld exclusion of KPMG on the ground that KPMG was violating its duty of confidentiality, and presumably its duty of loyalty, to Prince Jefri as its former client.

It seems appropriate for the House of Lords to have assimilated KPMG to legal counsel, inasmuch as the accounting firm was assisting legal counsel in the litigation against the former chairman of the agency. However, with respect, it is submitted that the court's analysis and conclusion from that point onward were misguided. Prince Jefri was never the client of KPMG. Rather, the client was the corporate entity and Prince Jefri merely an officer of the entity. If the analysis adopted in *Meehan v. Hopps* had been applied, as we suggest it should have, no conflict of interest would have been found to be involved on the part of KPMG.

Nevertheless, the facts of both *Meehan v. Hopps* and *Bolkiah* display the great sensitivities that can be involved for a lawyer representing a corporation. On one hand, the client is an impersonal entity—indeed, merely a legal idea—but an entity to which the duties of professional loyalty and confidentiality are owed. On the other hand, in actual operation the lawyer has interchanges with corporate officers that often are as intimate as those with an individual client. Perhaps the most difficult problem in modern civil law practice, in both analytic and practical terms, is reconciling these formally consistent but operationally contradictory propositions. Large matters of money, power, and professional reputation are often involved on all sides.

The most systematic endeavor to address the ethical problems in representation of corporations and other organizations is set forth in ABA Rule 1.13. Rule 1.13 is an interesting integration of basic corporation law, agency law, the law of torts, and guidance for exercise of judgment by lawyers representing corporations. The formulation emerged from discussions among lawyers of the Business Law Section (subdivision) of the American Bar Association, and the Kutak Commission, which was the ABA committee charged with responsibility for revising the American rules of professional ethics. For corporation lawyers, the rule provides a structure of ethical analysis rather than a prescription for action. In our opinion it could provide useful guidance to lawyers outside the United States. Rule 1.13(a) first states a truism of corporate and agency law: "A lawyer employed or retained by an organization represents the organization acting through its duly authorized constituents."[37] Although a truism, this proposition was apparently overlooked by the House of Lords in its *Bolkiah* decision. Of course, in any situation it may be disputable whether the lawyer has been engaged by the corporation or by one of its "constituents," such as a corporate officer, an employee, or the directors. And it is quite possible that a lawyer will be engaged to represent both the corporation and one or more of its constituents.[38] But in a straightforward engagement made in the name of the corporation, the inference is that the corporation is the client, not the official accomplishing the engagement on behalf of the corporation. These days careful lawyers make this explicit in the engagement letter.

Rule 1.13(d) states a corollary to this basic proposition, out of concern for fairness to an individual in the corporate family: "In dealing with an organization's directors, officers, employees . . . or other constituents, a lawyer shall explain the identity of the client when it is apparent that the organization's interests are adverse to those of the constituents with whom the lawyer is dealing." The concept here is that "fair warning" should be given to an employee who, for example, pursues a conversation with the lawyer that could get the employee in legal trouble with the corporation.[39] In the cases of *Meehan v. Hopps* and *Bolkiah*, perhaps the law firm in the *Meehan* case was at fault for not giving such a warning in its dealings with the corporate officer; and the result in the *Bolkiah* case could possibly be justified because such a warning was not given to Prince Jefri.

Rules 1.13(a) and (d) thus set the stage for the corporation lawyer's exercise of judgment in situations where conduct of a corporate "constituent" appears to proceed in a direction contrary to the interests of the corporation. Rule 1.13(b) prescribes the way in which the lawyer should address such a situation. The rule is long and complicated and can best be examined in steps. First: "If a lawyer for an organization knows that an officer . . . or other person associated with the organization is engaged in action, intends to act, or refuses to act in a matter related to the representation. . . ." This provision focuses on and limits the corporate lawyer's responsibilities to the scope of the engagement. For example, a lawyer engaged to provide securities advice to a corporation is not required, at least ordinarily, to consider whether the client is engaged in unfair trade practices or illegal employment practices.

Second: "[or if a lawyer knows] that is a violation of a legal obligation to the organization, or a violation of law which reasonably might be imputed to the organization, and is likely to result in substantial injury to the organization. . . ." This provision identifies two kinds of legal consequence. The first is an employee's breach of duty to the corporation, for example, improperly expropriating a corporate opportunity or embezzling from the company. The second is conduct violating the law that might be imputed to the corporation. This refers to a principle of agency and tort law, *respondeat superior*, according to which the conduct of a corporate agent in the course of employment that injures a third party ordinarily is chargeable also to the organization. For example, participating in illegal price-fixing discussions with officials of another company is illegal on the part of the employee but is also legally regarded as an act of the company, under both penal law and the law of tort liability. Because the act of the official is imputed to the corporation, the corporation (and not merely the official) stands liable for the consequences of the price-fixing scheme. Many forms of improper conduct by corporate employees therefore can both violate their duty to the company and result in violation of the company's obligations to third parties.

Third: ". . . [then] the lawyer shall proceed as is reasonably necessary in the best interest of the organization." It is to be noted that the corporate lawyer's obligation is to protect the *corporation*, and not to protect either the corporate official involved or a third party who might be injured. The lawyer should exhibit sensitivity and good judgment in endeavoring to protect the corporation without irreparably damaging the lawyer's relationship with the corporate official. But, if necessary, the interest of the corporate official or employee may have to be sacrificed. Measures protecting the corporation's interest may have the collateral effect of protecting third persons from harm. For example, if the lawyer's intervention terminates legally improper conduct, then there will be no further victimization of the third party. Nevertheless, the basis of the lawyer's intervention is protection of the company from adverse legal consequences and not as such protection of the third party.

Some critics of corporate law practice have asserted that a lawyer for a corporation should have an obligation to protect third-party interests, not collaterally but directly. We do not understand the legal basis of any such obligation. After all, the lawyer is an agent of the corporation and has gained information indicating the potential misconduct only by virtue of his office as lawyer for the corporation. That role includes attendant obligations of loyalty and confidentiality to the corporation. It is impossible to derive a general duty to third persons from that premise. Of course, it could be argued—and has been argued—that a corporation as such should not be entitled to the rights to loyalty and confidentiality, or that the status of a corporate client should carry only limited rights of loyalty and confidentiality. These propositions are coherent and far from absurd. But they are quite different from the proposition that, under the law as it is, a lawyer for a corporation has special duties to protect third parties.

On the other hand, some critics of Rule 1.13(b) within the legal profession complain that the rule requires a lawyer to "be a policeman of his client." That complaint is accurately founded so far as it recognizes that a lawyer must be alert to wrongdoing by the corporate personnel. But the complaint is entirely wrong in suggesting that the lawyer is being called on to "police" his own *client*. The client is the organization, and an organization sometimes may well need protection from rapacious or foolish corporate officials. That the lawyer's duty is to the corporation, rather than to the corporate officer, is the familiar legal proposition involved in *Meehan v. Hopps*, discussed earlier.

Fourth:

> In determining how to proceed, the lawyer shall give due consideration to the seriousness of the violation and its consequences, the scope and nature of the lawyer's representation, the responsibility in the organization and the apparent motivation of the person involved . . . and any other relevant considerations. Any measures taken shall be designed to minimize disruption of the organization and the risk of revealing information . . . outside the organization.

Fifth:

> Such measures may include . . . :
> (1) asking reconsideration of the matter;
> (2) advising that a separate legal opinion on the matter be sought for presentation to appropriate authority in the organization; and
> (3) referring the matter to higher authority in the organization. . . .

The enumerated measures are normal responses when serious disagreement arises between a lawyer and client. Thus a lawyer may ask, or indeed insist, that a client reconsider a course of action that the lawyer regards as imprudent or legally risky. A lawyer may informally consult a partner or some other lawyer as a check on the lawyer's own interpretation and conclusions concerning the matter. In the corporate setting, it is common procedure for a difficult issue to be sent "up the ladder" for resolution by someone with greater authority.

Rule 1.13(b)(3) continues by stating that "if warranted by the seriousness of the matter, referral [can be made] to the highest authority that can act in behalf of the corporation as determined by applicable law." That is, if the matter is important and serious enough, the lawyer can insist that a question concerning a course of action be presented to the board of directors. Such a referral necessarily would be over the head of the corporate CEO. Perhaps needless to say, such a referral ordinarily would reflect a major intracorporate dispute. Yet such disputes can arise over, for example, whether certain unfavorable facts must be included in reports required to be made to government regulatory authorities or to the shareholders; whether certain financial transactions must be reported to the tax authorities; or whether a proposed employment agreement for a high-level officer—perhaps the CEO himself—must be submitted to the board of directors.

Perhaps also needless to say, referral to the board of directors is made at the initiative of the highest-level lawyer involved in the matter. This would be the senior partner of an independent law firm or the general counsel of a corporate law department. It is not an action to be taken by junior legal staff, although the initiative may originate at that level. A similar scenario can occur at the insistence of professional accountants (it may be recalled that accountants were involved in the *Bolkiah* case), scientists, or engineers in the case of questions concerning company products, or personnel specialists in the case of employment matters. However, a confrontation between management and professionals is most intense in legal matters, precisely because the ultimate question is one of legality, not merely technical or professional judgment.

Such a scenario is an integral element of "corporate governance" in modern law practice.[40] The scenario is actually played out only rarely, however, because a corporate lawyer's threat to "go to the board" precipitates a resolution. There are no statistics on how often that threat has been made, or on how the issues are resolved, for such matters ordinarily remain in deep secrecy. It is clear that some corporate lawyers fail in their responsibility to the corporate client. They either acquiesce in serious wrongdoing, turn a "blind eye," or indeed conspire in it. The duties outlined in Rule 1.13(b) as that rule has stood for twenty years arise only when the lawyer "knows" of corporate misconduct, threatened or accomplished. A lawyer could try to ignore what seems to be happening and later say that he did not "know," despite circumstantial indications.

Nevertheless, a demand by a senior lawyer that there be board review, presented firmly to the CEO, almost always will resolve the issue as the lawyer has recommended, particularly in large corporations. High corporate officials of major corporations do not want to deal with the dissension and potential embarrassment that would be involved in a "trial" before the board of directors. At the same time, a senior lawyer knows that such a confrontation is pursued only when the matter is truly very serious.

The legal regime in the United States was substantially changed in 2002 by the adoption of the Sarbanes-Oxley Act (SOX).[41] SOX applies only to "public" corporations—that is, companies whose shares are traded on the stock exchanges. But that is large territory. SOX imposes stricter requirements on top-level corporate management, on independent directors on the corporate board of directors, on auditing firms for those companies, and on lawyers representing the companies. Most of the changes are modest, but cumulatively they are significant. Notably, a lawyer for a corporation covered by the act is required to take remedial action upon receiving "information" about corporate financial wrongdoing. This escalates the standard in ABA Rule 1.13, which is framed in terms of a lawyer "knowing" about such misconduct. The remedial response under SOX requires the lawyer to go to the independent directors if corrective action is not taken internally. Perhaps more important, these standards are now federal law, enforced by the Securities and Exchange Commission, in place of state law enforced through private lawsuits and relatively feeble professional disciplinary procedure. To make a play on words, SOX is a new ballgame.[42]

Rule 1.13 goes on to provide, in paragraph (c), as follows: "If, despite the lawyer's efforts . . . the highest authority . . . insists upon action, or a refusal to act, that is clearly a violation of law and is likely to result in substantial injury to the organization, the lawyer may resign. . . ." As described earlier, the option of simply resigning is superseded, in public corporations, by the provisions in the Sarbanes-Oxley Act.

Apart from SOX, however, a lawyer may resign in the face of such a dispute with a client, and could have resigned long before the dispute reached the stage of confrontation. Equally important from the lawyer's viewpoint, the client—or the top official of a corporate client—can discharge the lawyer. It is a universally recognized principle that a client can discharge a lawyer at any stage (except when doing so will interfere with a court proceeding in which the lawyer is acting for the client), and for any reason or no reason.

For a lawyer in independent practice, resigning or being discharged in such circumstances may be hurtful, financially and in reputation within the corporate management community. But it is not the end of the lawyer's world. For a law department lawyer ("inside counsel"), however, being discharged can be a financial and professional disaster: loss of job, loss of pay, loss of pension, loss of reputation among the very type of clients to which he has devoted his career. (This difference in consequence may indeed have been a factor in the European court's differentiation between house counsel and lawyers in independent practice, so far as confidentiality is concerned.)[43]

A lawyer's risk of being discharged is simply one aspect of the professional vocation: it goes with the territory. It is a risk that is ignored by many critics of corporation lawyers, particularly critics holding tenured positions in the academic world. Ordinarily, only a senior lawyer can precipitate the scenario of confrontation described above.[44] A lawyer does not rise to a high level of seniority in the practice of law without learning the risks and limitations that attend the office of corporate lawyer. A senior-level lawyer ordinarily enjoys the confidence of corporate officials to the extent that such a confrontation is simply unnecessary. Often there are ways in which the proper outcome can be accomplished without legal violation. And, as with so many things in life, the participants in the event will remember it differently, in terms that sustain the integrity of their respective selves.

In the United States there have been a number of cases in which a lawyer in a corporate law department has been discharged in a dispute with corporate management and then has sued for damages for wrongful discharge. (Given the unqualified right of the client to discharge a lawyer, the remedy of restoration to employment is unavailable.) Some of these disputes have concerned a lawyer's insistence on compliance with procedural law, such as fulfillment of a duty to produce documents in response to a lawful discovery demand in litigation. Some have concerned a lawyer's refusal to sign a report to a regulatory authority, on behalf of the corporation, that the lawyer believed was materially false. A number of cases have involved complaints by women lawyers of sex discrimination in employment.

The emergent American rule regarding discharge of a "house counsel" lawyer is expressed in the *Restatement of the Law Governing Lawyers*, Section 32, Comment *b*, as follows:

> [W]hen a lawyer is also an employee of a client (for example, a lawyer employed as inside legal counsel by a corporation or government agency), the client's right to discharge the lawyer does not abridge the lawyer's entitlement to salary and benefits already earned . . . for example if the client discharged the lawyer for refusing to perform an unlawful act.

Moreover, in a case involving discharge of a lawyer by a law firm, New York's highest court held that the rules of ethics are an implied term of the lawyer's employment relationship, so discharging the lawyer for unethical reasons was a breach of the employment obligation.[45]

Recognition of the remedy of damages for wrongful discharge has come very slowly in the United States. To our knowledge it has not been forthcoming anywhere else in the world. But the problem of wrongful discharge of a lawyer by officials of a corporate client is very real, if also very rare.

The Boundary of Legality

The professional virtues thus far examined are either ethically "neutral" or supportive of client interests. The ethically neutral virtues are competence and independence, while the virtues of loyalty and confidentiality by definition benefit clients. If these were the only virtues recognized in the legal profession, lawyers might indeed be only "hired guns." But proper lawyers are not hired guns and are constrained by other responsibilities. These responsibilities operate simultaneously with the duties to clients and include duties to the courts and responsibility to the legal system at large.

Their responsibility to the legal system is usually expressed in two degrees of generality. At the broadest degree of generality, a lawyer is required to be a law-abiding citizen, as discussed in Chapter 7. More specific, and connected to professional function, is a lawyer's duty to avoid furthering or participating in conduct by a client that is criminal or fraudulent or positively illegal. The definitive standards are supplied in the background general law—the criminal law and the law of civil wrongs such as fraud. That is, the general law applies to lawyers along with the rest of the community.

The Italian Code, CDF Art. 6, refers to this duty as follows: "The lawyer must carry out his professional activity with honesty and integrity." In the Canadian Code, Chap. 1, Comment 2 the duty is stated as follows: "Dishonourable or questionable conduct on the part of a lawyer in either his private life or his professional activities will reflect adversely . . . upon . . . the administration of law and justice as a whole." Rule 8.4 of the ABA Rules provides that it is professional misconduct for a lawyer to:

- commit a criminal act that reflects adversely on the lawyer's honesty, trustworthiness or fitness as a lawyer in other respects;
- engage in conduct involving fraud, dishonesty, deceit, misrepresentation;
- engage in conduct that is prejudicial to the administration of justice.

Forms of misconduct that have been found to violate these standards include tax evasion, physical assault, repeated drunk driving, and various kinds of fraud and theft such as embezzlement.

Not only is a lawyer obliged to conform his own conduct to the law, but he is required to avoid assisting a client in unlawful activities. Technically, this obligation is simply a subcategory of the lawyer's obligation to obey the law, because the larger legal system includes prohibitions against assisting others in unlawful conduct. Thus the criminal law prohibits "aiding" or "abetting" another in the commission of a crime, while the law of civil wrongs imposes liability on one who is an accessory or assistant in another's wrongful conduct. There are cases in which a lawyer has assisted a client in a transaction that the lawyer well knew was fraudulent. However, in our observation, most lawyers carefully avoid involvement in transactions that are fraudulent or otherwise illegal. This attitude is based both on personal morality and on a lawyer's well-informed appreciation of the agonizing effect of becoming a suspect in criminal investigation. But honest lawyers have clients who are dishonest. A dishonest client ordinarily does not display himself as such, but will endeavor to conceal the fraud not only from the intended victim but also from the lawyers, accountants, and others who may be called on to assist in the transaction.

A lawyer is permitted to *listen* to a narrative by a client concerning a proposed venture or course of conduct. As the narrative proceeds, it may become apparent that the proposed venture will constitute a crime, such as tax evasion or illegal money laundering. It would be extraordinary for a client to ask a lawyer whether it would be illegal to rob a bank. It would not be extraordinary, however, for a high official of a bank to ask whether it would be legal to arrange a contract between the bank and another company in which the official had an ownership interest. Also it would not be extraordinary for a lawyer to be consulted concerning whether profits from a business venture could escape income taxation if the venture were conducted through a corporation organized under the law of a "tax haven" country. Nor would it be extraordinary for a lawyer to be consulted by a party to a divorce as to whether there are means to limit or avoid financial obligations to the other spouse after a divorce.

The rules governing such communications are clear and simple. The formulation in the American rule is as follows: "A lawyer shall not counsel a client to engage, or assist a client, in conduct that the lawyer knows is criminal or fraudulent, but a lawyer may discuss the legal consequences of any proposed course of conduct with a client. . . ."[46]

Accordingly, on one side, a lawyer is permitted to listen to a client's narrative about—"discuss"—a venture or proposed course of action, even if the venture might verge on illegality. On the other side, a lawyer may not outline illegal pathways to the client or assist a client in following such a pathway.

Observing the distinction between "discussing" and "giving counsel" is not difficult for a conscientious lawyer. The conscientious lawyer will listen as long as necessary to understand the client's objectives and to think through possible pathways by which the objective could be accomplished in conformity with the law. Such a discussion could require several interviews, extensive review of documents, and prolonged deliberation by the lawyer. It could involve preparation of written hypothetical possibilities, through which to confer with other lawyers and systematically explore alternatives with the client. A conscientious lawyer could recognize that the boundaries of the relevant legal rules might be uncertain, so a course of action that the lawyer believes is lawful might nevertheless entail a degree of legal risk. All this would be proper.

Louis Brandeis, a prominent American lawyer and later a justice of the U.S. Supreme Court, explained the approach to the "boundary of legality" in the following way:

> I have been asked . . . whether [certain transactions] were legal or illegal. . . .
> If you are walking along a precipice no human being can tell you how near

you can go ... without falling over, because you may stumble on a loose stone ... but anybody can tell you where you can walk perfectly safe. ... The difficulty [with many clients is] that they wanted to go to the limit rather than ... go safely.[47]

The simple metaphor employed by Justice Brandeis incorporates several important propositions. First, there usually is extra profit to be made in a transaction that is close to the line of legality. Complying with any law usually involves expense that could be avoided by ignoring or skirting the law. The relationship is like that among a black market, a "white market," and a "gray market." A black market transaction is illegal but profitable if the participants do not get caught. A white market transaction forgoes extra profit but incurs the expense of complying with the law. A gray market transaction is "shady": It involves some of the profit of a black market transaction but less risk of getting in serious trouble with the law. Many transactions in which a lawyer is consulted involve situations in the gray area.

Second, it is clients rather than lawyers who usually have the primary interest in treading "close to the line." Of course, lawyers who are willing and inventive can earn handsome fees by contriving pathways that are close to the line but legal. And some lawyers develop reputations for being very clever in inventing such contrivances. But it is the clients who look for the pathways and who pay the lawyers to find them.

Third, the legal system often responds to inventive legal contrivances by revising the law to relocate the boundaries of legality. Some "legal gimmicks" thereby become illegal and therefore impractical. However, by the same evolution the premium is enhanced for gimmicks that remain legal. Clever but conscientious lawyers accordingly remain in high demand in the modern regulatory era.

Fourth, it is not worth the trouble for a client to engage a clever but conscientious lawyer unless the stakes in the matter are worth the cost of the lawyer's fees. Accordingly, it is only relatively wealthy clients—individuals and businesses—that have use for expensive lawyers. The rest of us pay ordinary taxes, comply with the laws and regulations, and grumble about lawyers and their rich clients. In general, the same analysis applies not only to wealthy clients but also to clients with political power. A simple example is a legal maneuver whereby contributions to political campaigns that ordinarily would be illegal can be made legal if made through another pathway, such as a charitable foundation. Campaign contributions under shelter of some legal contrivance can help a ruling party stay in office, or help a party of the opposition make a run at electoral victory.

This relationship between people with wealth and power, clever lawyers, and the boundaries of the law helps explain popular antipathy toward the wealthy, who escape or mitigate the rigors of the law as it might apply to them; toward holders of political power, who exploit the law to perpetuate themselves in power; and toward lawyers who help in these machinations. Social idealists have eternally hoped that political change can break the connection between wealth and political power and exploitive use of the law. But the political changes that can break the connection, at least thus far in history, may also enfeeble the legal system itself. The "rule of law" that lawyers may employ to shelter the wealthy and to protect political potentates is a governmental process that, when put to proper use, also protects and shelters ordinary people.

The paradox referred to by Justice Brandeis is evident to most conscientious lawyers. They recognize that the rule of law—constitutional government—is essential to the political well-being of ordinary citizens even though it is also an instrument whereby the wealthy and powerful can achieve preference from the political system. Ordinary people trudge along their paths in life far from the precipice of illegality, while holders of wealth and power often approach the line more closely and more profitably. Among other things, many conscientious lawyers who are engaged in representing "vested interests" are privately much more critical of the law than are their clients.

7

Responsibility

Multiple Responsibilities

Chapter 1 of the Canadian Code of Professional Conduct provides: "The lawyer must discharge his duties to his client, the court, members of the public and his fellow members of the profession with integrity." The Preamble to the ABA Rules of Professional Conduct is somewhat more elaborate:

> A lawyer ... is a representative of clients, an officer of the legal system and a public citizen having special responsibilities for the quality of justice.
> As a representative of clients, a lawyer [is] advisor ... advocate ... negotiator ... [and] evaluator. ...
> A lawyer should demonstrate respect for the legal system and for those who serve it, including judges, other lawyers and public officials. ...
> As a public citizen, a lawyer should seek improvement of the law, access to the legal system, the administration of justice and the quality of service rendered by the legal profession. ... A lawyer should ... help the bar regulate itself in the public interest.

The web of a lawyer's obligations begins with duties to clients, but it extends to the courts, to the legal system in a wider sense, to other lawyers, and to the public at large. Some obligations are stated in positive terms, such as the obligation to be truthful to courts in statements founded on the lawyer's own knowledge. Others are framed as limitations on conduct in behalf of clients. For example, although a lawyer may "zealously" present a client's case in court, a lawyer is not permitted to present testimony that he knows is perjured or documents that he knows to be forgeries. The obligations to the courts and to opposing counsel in litigation are of ancient origin and have been developed in great detail. Obligations addressing office practice derive primarily from the general law—that is, the criminal law, the law of civil wrongs ("torts" in common law terminology), and the myriad regulatory statutes and directives of modern legal systems. Lawyers are governed not only directly by these regulations of general law, like other citizens, but also indirectly through obligations imposed on their clients.

Beyond legal and professional obligations, lawyers have moral and ethical sentiments of personal origin—family tradition, religious affiliation, subjective sensitivities—that impose other imperatives and constraints. The practice of law, like adult life generally, is enmeshed in a web of legal, ethical, and moral obligations that often point in different directions.

Candor with the Court

An advocate has many occasions to make statements to courts. The most routine occasion is scheduling future court hearings—dates on which the advocates can be present and that are convenient for the testimony of witnesses, for example. A more complicated discussion can address whether a case may be resolved by settlement and the probability that further court hearings may therefore be unnecessary.

In settlement discussions there is tension between the principle that the client has final authority concerning the terms of settlement and the principle that the advocate speaks authoritatively to the court in matters concerning the case.[1] An advocate may believe a client has agreed to a settlement, but then encounter rebellion by the client against the proposed terms, either because there was a misunderstanding or because of a change of mind by the client.[2] Where the client is a business entity, a statement by the advocate for a party that the case has been settled will usually be accepted without question by the court, and by opposing parties, and the case will accordingly be marked down as terminated. It will be assumed that a business client understands the significance of agreeing to a compromise, that lawyers understand when a client has conveyed authority to compromise, and that, if either of these premises turns out to be inaccurate, the client will have recourse against the lawyer. But if the client is an ordinary individual, the courts usually will consider the case finally settled only when the client has signed the settlement papers. In some civil law systems, these eventualities are preempted by a rule that a settlement may not be entered except by a statement to that effect signed by the client.

Other communications between an advocate and the court can concern, for example, whether a relevant document in fact exists and the identity of its custodian; whether a prospective witness is available for testimony; whether some other litigation concerning the dispute is pending in another tribunal; or whether notice required concerning some procedural stage has been properly transmitted. Advocates are obliged to be fully truthful in such matters and in responding to inquiries concerning them.

The advocate's obligation of candor to the court in such matters is superior to any obligation to a client, except in very unusual circumstances in which the court asks an impermissible question. It can be imagined, for example, that the court in a criminal case might inquire of defense counsel whether the accused is actually guilty. That question is improper and the advocate should refuse to respond. Otherwise, and assuming the questions from the judge are proper, the advocate must respond according to his duty of candor.

The duty of candor is expressed in differently nuanced terms in the various codes. Probably most exacting is that governing the English barrister: "A barrister has an overriding duty to the Court to act with independence in the interests of justice; he must assist the Court in the administration of justice and must not deceive or knowingly or recklessly mislead the Court."[3] Japanese Code, Article 54, provides: "An attorney shall endeavor to realize a fair trial and proper procedure. An attorney shall not entice a witness into committing perjury or making a false statement, nor shall he or she submit false evidence." The Canadian Code has the following formulation: "The advocate's duty . . . must always be discharged by fair and honourable means, . . . and in a manner consistent with the lawyer's duty to treat the court with candour, fairness, courtesy and respect."[4] The ABA Rules provide as follows:

> A lawyer shall not knowingly:
> (a) make a false statement of material fact or law to a tribunal; . . .
> (b) fail to disclose to the tribunal legal authority in the controlling jurisdiction known to the lawyer to be directly adverse to the position of the client and not disclosed by opposing counsel; or
> (c) offer evidence that the lawyer knows to be false.[5]

The Italian CDF, Article 14, has perhaps more technical precision, as follows:

> Declarations made in judicial proceedings regarding the existence or nonexistence of objective facts which are a specific element for the judge's decision and with which the lawyer is directly acquainted must be true.
>
> A lawyer may not deliberately introduce false evidence . . . nor introduce declarations . . . the lawyer knows to be untrue.
>
> A lawyer is obliged to mention rulings already obtained . . . when seeking a ruling arising out of the same factual situation.

The Italian rules reflect aspects of the duty of candor that are important in all legal systems. The term "objective facts" by implication excludes rhetoric, opinion, "coloration," and other expressions falling short of definite and concrete representations. The term "specific element for the judge's decision" limits the obligation to statements concerning legally relevant issues, defined in a strict sense. (The corresponding term in common-law parlance is "material.") The term "directly acquainted" limits the obligation to statements that the lawyer presents as being of his own knowledge. The term "knows" limits the duty concerning evidence to statements about testimony or documents that are obviously false. Only when evidence is obviously false could a court or any other observer conclude that the lawyer *knew* the evidence was false, rather than merely having reason to know or to suppose.

The provision in the Italian code concerning "rulings already obtained" responds to a nearly universal problem arising in courts with a number of judges. In such cases, the advocates for the parties will be familiar with the state of the record in their case, but a judge may not be, particularly concerning rulings previously made by another judge. The advocates are not supposed to "game" the system by seeking a change of ruling when the file changes hands among judges. The opportunity to do so is greater in court systems with overcrowded calendars and a local bar so large that the judges and lawyers do not know each other. In some civil law systems the concept that a change in ruling should not be sought when the file moves to another judge is, charitably, called "procedural economy." A similar concept in common law procedure is the doctrine of "law of the case." The point is that a ruling made in an earlier stage of a case continues to govern the proceeding in later stages, even if the ruling is arguably erroneous, or was rendered by a different judge.

The CCBE Code, Section 4.4, states simply: "A lawyer shall never knowingly give false or misleading information to the court." Unfortunately, lawyers in some systems try to get away with as much evasion and dissimulation as they can. The judges come to distrust almost everything that lawyers tell them, and the duty of candor falls into desuetude. In some systems, however—those of England, Germany, and Japan in particular—the judges trust almost all the advocates. In any event, if a judge mistrusts a lawyer's statements where the lawyer speaks of his own knowledge, the lawyer will have great difficulty in future interactions with the judge, and perhaps with other judges in that court. The judges can react with various sanctions, depending on the system. For example, if the question is whether a witness is unavailable because of illness, the judge may require the lawyer to provide a doctor's certificate, whereas if the judge trusts the lawyer the lawyer's oral statement will be sufficient. This aspect of a lawyer's reputation is often referred to as a lawyer's "credit" or "credibility" in the system. Like reputation at large, a lawyer's credit with the courts is established or lost through informal interchange and experience.

A similar obligation of candor applies in a lawyer's relationships with officials other than judges, particularly staff of the courts, regulatory agencies, and tax authorities. Those relationships often involve repeated interchanges. Many lawyers specialize in dealings with specific government agencies, such as a licensing bureau or the customs collector. A lawyer who establishes a positive reputation with an agency can accomplish the client's business more quickly and securely than if each step of the transaction must be formally documented. A lawyer in a law firm with which one of us was associated once said: "The good reputation of this firm with the state regulatory agencies is one of the most valuable assets we can employ on behalf of our clients."

From an early period, obligations were imposed on advocates against such abuses as bringing unjustified suits, making needless motions, prolonging delay, and harassing witnesses.[6] The Canadian and American rules have catalogues of specific procedural abuses, the Canadian Code being as follows:

> (d) instituting or prosecuting proceedings which, although legal in themselves, are clearly motivated by malice and brought solely for the purpose of injuring the other party;

(e) appearing before a judicial officer . . . when personal relationships with such officer . . . might reasonably appear to give rise to pressure, influence or inducement affecting the impartiality of such officer;

(f) bribery, personal approach or any means other than open persuasion as an advocate;

(g) offering false evidence, misstating facts or law, presenting or relying on a false or deceptive affidavit;

(h) dissuade a material witness from giving evidence or advise such a witness to absent himself;

(i) knowingly assist a witness to . . . impersonate another;

(j) needlessly abuse, hector, or harass a witness.[7]

The counterpart ABA Rule 3.4 provides that a lawyer may not:

- unlawfully obstruct another party's access to evidence or unlawfully alter, destroy or conceal a document or other material having potentially evidentiary value;
- falsify evidence . . . assist a witness to testify falsely, or offer an inducement to a witness that is prohibited by law;
- make a frivolous discovery request or fail to make a reasonably diligent effort to comply with a legally proper discovery request by an opposing party;
- in trial, allude to any matter . . . that will not be supported by admissible evidence, assert personal knowledge of the facts in issue . . . or state a personal opinion as to the justness of a cause, the credibility of a witness, the culpability of a civil litigant or the guilt or innocence of an accused. . . .

Another ABA Rule provides more generally: "A lawyer shall not bring or defend a proceeding, or assert or controvert an issue therein, unless there is a basis for doing so that is not frivolous. . . ."[8]

These prohibitions derive from sad experience and to some extent from specific local situations. For example, the Canadian Code's prohibition on "back channel" communication between lawyer and judge indicates that, at least in some communities in Canada, there had been a worrisome familiarity between some lawyers and some judges. The American prohibition against alluding to matters "that will not be supported by admissible evidence" responds to a gambit sometimes attempted in jury cases, where the lawyer will describe proof as forthcoming, but then fail to produce it—hoping that the discrepancy will not be noticed. In China, there is evidently a long tradition of using "connections (the Chinese term is *guanxi*)," including the exchange of presents, in conducting transactions. The People's Republic of China Law on Lawyers has responded by prohibiting lawyers from meeting judges or other officials except at the court or another official place of business.[9]

The absence of a prohibition in the Canadian Code against frivolous claims and defenses contrasts with a prohibition prominent in the American codes. This difference probably reflects the fact that in Canada, as in most countries, a party making a frivolous claim will have to pay the costs incurred by the opposing party, including the opponent's attorney's fees. The cost rule provides substantial and perhaps adequate protection against procedural abuses. In contrast, in the United States the prevailing party normally must bear his own attorney's fee expense. Hence, control of frivolous procedure in the United States is attempted by means of prohibitory procedural provisions and ethics rules. In the American federal courts, for example, there can be a penalty for making factual assertions that lack an objective foundation, and the ABA Model Rules prescribe a counterpart ethical rule.[10] However, the American tradition has been that contentions in litigation are "free" unless nearly fraudulent, so resort to enforcement is rarely made except when violations are flagrant.

Procedural abuses similar to those catalogued in the Canadian and American ethics codes also occur in civil law systems, although they have somewhat different form because of the procedural differences reflected in the roles of judge and advocate in the civil law.[11] An attentive civil law judge will promptly detect and dispose of baseless contentions. However, there would be no such scrutiny where the judges are indifferent to abuses, which unfortunately is the case in many civil law systems. In any event, procedural abuses are infrequently the subject of professional disciplinary proceedings in any legal system. In well-run judicial systems with highly disciplined judges and lawyers, the dearth of complaints about procedural abuse suggests that offenses are rare. In other systems, the absence of complaints may indicate that only egregious misconduct will engage the attention of either the courts or the disciplinary authorities.

Where enforcement against procedural abuse is lax, a party who has suffered from procedural abuse has little recourse except retaliation. The courts are reluctant to become involved, and a referral to the disciplinary authority can simply mean another round of litigation. For the lawyer who has been accused, such a referral may be an attempt by the opposing party to relitigate a contention that had been previously rejected in court. Where the only practical recourse is retaliation, the result is a deterioration of procedural standards and a state of chronic procedural abuse. Many court systems are in that condition.

The fact that resort to disciplinary authority may simply lead to another round of litigation brings into focus an additional point that has been implicit in our text: any valid procedure for dealing with lawyers' ethical misconduct involves the risk that lawyers will engage in misconduct in that procedure.

In many systems the disciplinary apparatus is merely nominal. Complaints are rarely made because it is known that little or nothing will be done in response. Little or nothing will be done because there is no investigative staff to develop the evidence and no active committee of the bar to consider evidence that might be compiled. The judges in many systems regard problems of lawyer misconduct as beyond their responsibility. In most civil law systems the judge has no authority to impose sanctions directly on an offending advocate, such as contempt of court. As a consequence, the idea of "procedural abuse" as a matter of judicial concern is undeveloped or virtually nonexistent in many systems.

A formal procedure for dealing with a lawyer's misconduct must fulfill minimum standards of legal fairness. The standards vary from one legal system to another, but no system properly could punish a lawyer merely on the basis of a client's complaint. In many civil law systems, the traditional procedure is an inquiry conducted by a senior member of the local bar. In most common law systems and in Japan, the procedure is an inquiry by or supervised by a committee of lawyers. In some countries the procedure is also governed by constitutional requirements. In the United States, under the influence of these constitutional requirements, an American disciplinary proceeding now has become a full-blown trial.[12] In all systems an accused lawyer has a right to defend himself. In such a proceeding, the hearing panel of lawyers can be excessively sympathetic to fellow professionals (who may feel "There, but for the grace of God, go I!"). That attitude has now largely changed, as lawyers come to accept that some lawyers are bad actors. Unfortunately, in some legal systems—and among some members of the profession in all legal systems—judges and lawyers cynically assume that many lawyers are unscrupulous, but assume also that there are no effective measures of redress. This last attitude no doubt is widely shared in public opinion.

In all systems, a lawyer whose conduct is challenged has a right to defend himself. The defense may involve dispute as to the facts or whether the conduct constituted a violation of the applicable rules of ethics. Those defenses generate controversies that can be as complicated as litigation in court, or more so. If a lawyer's conduct is challenged in court, the lawyer is entitled to a hearing before the court according to procedure that is similar to that governing any other litigated issue.

The fact that (some) lawyers control the legal procedure for responding to misconduct by (other) lawyers no doubt helps explain the frustration of many critics of the legal profession. The critics suspect that all lawyers are motivated to take care of their own. Unfortunately, in some legal systems this suspicion is warranted. Nevertheless, in our observation, lax disciplinary enforcement is not the product of lawyers wishing to protect other lawyers. Instead, it is the product of unwillingness in many countries of either the profession or the state to commit the resources that would help achieve a higher level of enforcement. From the viewpoint of most lawyers, the cost and trouble of maintaining adequate disciplinary enforcement is a tiresome burden, even though an effective level of enforcement would be a "public" gain for the profession as a whole.

Good Citizenship

The ethical codes affirm an ideal that a lawyer should be a good citizen in the fullest sense. The Canadian Code, for example, says:

> Dishonourable or questionable conduct . . . in either his private life or his professional activities will reflect adversely . . . on the profession and the administration of law and justice as a whole. . . .
>
> The lawyer should encourage public respect for and try to improve the administration of justice. . . . His responsibilities are greater than those of a private citizen.[13]

The Japanese Code of Ethics for Practicing Lawyers, Article 1, provides: "An attorney shall be aware that his or her mission is to protect fundamental human rights and realize social justice, and shall strive to realize this mission."

The Preamble to the ABA Rules has these provisions:

> A lawyer's conduct should conform to the requirements of the law, both in professional service to clients and in the lawyer's business and personal affairs. . . .
>
> A lawyer should demonstrate respect for the legal system and for those who serve it, including judges, other lawyers and public officials.
>
> As a public citizen, a lawyer should seek improvement of the law, access to the legal system, the administration of justice and the quality of service rendered by the legal profession.

Obedience to these admonitions is supported by pragmatic considerations. A lawyer's adherence to the law supports a positive professional reputation, while violating the law can have the opposite effect, even misconduct that is unrelated to the lawyer's practice.

Lawyers in all legal systems are encouraged to participate in reform and improvement of the law. Lawyers' participation in these activities, whether for clients or out of a sense of social duty, varies among legal systems and among lawyers in a specific system. Many law reform activities are pursued collectively through bar associations. When a lawyer does participate in such activity, an audience (such as a legislative committee or a government agency) ordinarily can assume he is speaking on his own behalf as a public citizen. However, in legal systems such as those of Canada and the United States, lawyers often act as legislative advocates on behalf of clients—"lobbying" before the legislature or in administrative rule-making. The ethical rules in these systems require disclosure when a lawyer participates in that role.[14] In many legal systems specific disclosure requirements are imposed on "lobbyists" generally, including lawyers.[15]

Relationships with Other Lawyers

Lawyers continually deal with other lawyers. Their interchanges include, for example, communication of information in connection with litigation or negotiation, scheduling arrangements to confer, and presentation of proposals and counterproposals. Other instances may involve professional activities in a bar association or in dealings with government agencies. In these interchanges, lawyers are governed by ordinary standards of civility such as those that apply among businessmen, particularly truthfulness in negotiation. Dealings among lawyers often are conducted with a substantial degree of formality, reflecting the importance of the matters that typically are at issue. Within that framework, standards of civility largely depend on context, as in all "diplomatic" relationships. Professionals who have long experience with each other usually deal informally, except those who have come to dislike or distrust each other—as unfortunately sometimes happens.

These "business" standards are the backdrop of special ethical rules in many legal systems to control inevitable frictions. The Italian ethics code has an entire section on the subject of relationships among lawyers, addressing such matters as the following:

- Promptness in responding to another lawyer's request for information;
- Punctuality in attending hearings and meetings;
- Cooperation when involved in representing different clients on the same side of a matter;
- "Correspondence marked as confidential or . . . containing proposals for negotiations . . . may not be referred to in judicial proceedings" or disclosed to the client;
- When referring a matter to another lawyer, giving that lawyer complete information about the matter;
- Honoring a settlement that has been accepted by the parties;
- Disclosure of intention to terminate settlement negotiation;
- When replacing previously engaged counsel, using best efforts to see that the previously employed counsel is properly paid;
- Not electronically recording a conversation with another lawyer;
- Not expressing "negative opinions" about another lawyer or about his "alleged mistakes or incompetence."[16]

The Canadian Code speaks in more general and elevated terms:

> The lawyer's conduct towards other lawyers should be characterized by courtesy and good faith.
>
> Any ill feeling . . . between clients, particularly during litigation, should never be allowed to influence lawyers in their conduct . . . [P]ersonal animosity . . . may cause their judgment to be clouded . . . [H]aranguing or offensive tactics . . . have no place. . . .

> The lawyer should avoid sharp practice. He should not take advantage ... upon slips, irregularities or mistakes on the part of other lawyers not going to the merits or involving sacrifice of the client's rights. ....[17]

The American rules have very few provisions governing relationships among lawyers. There is a requirement that lawyers report to the disciplinary authority knowledge that "another lawyer has committed a violation of the Rules of Professional Conduct that raises a substantial question as to that lawyer's honesty, trustworthiness or fitness as a lawyer in other respects. ..."[18] This obligation is rarely fulfilled, however. Reporting another lawyer's misconduct typically will result in intense disputation about the circumstances and divert attention from the interests of the clients.[19]

Perhaps there are so few rules because relations among lawyers in some systems are so fraternal as not to require specific regulation. Alternatively, relations may be so hostile that rules could not moderate them. But in our opinion neither of these interpretations is accurate. It is more plausible that useful standards governing relationships between lawyers are difficult to state and more difficult to enforce. Most "civilizing" among lawyers is done through cooperation or retaliation. Some jurisdictions in the United States have adopted "civility" codes. These are admonitory rather than obligatory and focus primarily on litigation conduct and tactics, particularly tactics in pretrial discovery.[20] American discovery depositions usually are entirely pacific, but some counsel become grossly obnoxious. On rare occasions the courts will be asked to intervene.[21] Whether "civility" rules could moderate these abuses seems doubtful.

Lawyers in any legal system who have to deal with oppressive or dilatory misconduct by other lawyers chiefly rely on some combination of forbearance and retaliation—practicable mechanisms in an unpleasant relationship from which there is no escape.

Relationships within Law Firms

The principles of legal ethics originated before the development of law firms, particularly the large law firms characteristic of a large segment of modern practice. Accordingly, there was little necessity to address ethical issues arising from relationships among partners or associates in a firm or in corporate or government law departments. The emergence of multilawyer practice settings has required attention to those matters.

The most common ethical issue within a law firm is "imputed" conflict of interest. As previously noted, the governing principle in most systems is that a conflict of interest on the part of one lawyer in a firm will be imputed to all other lawyers in a firm. Thus, if Lawyer A in a law firm is currently representing X corporation, it will be improper for Lawyer B in that same firm to undertake litigation against X corporation, even though the matters are not related and even though A and B are not in adjacent offices, or even if their offices are separated by thousands of miles.[22] The concept is that lawyers in a firm have bonds of professional and financial interest that could affect the vigor and loyalty with which lawyers represent those whose interests are legally adverse. This concept is expressed in the Canadian Code, as follows: "[I]t will be appreciated that [in applying the rules concerning conflict of interest] the term 'client' includes a client of the law firm of which a lawyer is a partner or associate whether or not he handles the client's work."

"Conflicts" problems can also arise when a lawyer changes law firm affiliation—that is, resigns from one law firm and joins another. These problems are colloquially known as "lateral move" conflicts and pose the following questions: First, does a lawyer moving from one law firm to another firm, who would be burdened with a conflict of interest imputed from some other lawyer in the firm from which the lawyer is exiting, carry the "taint" of that imputation into the new law firm? The answer to that question in the ABA Rules is no, unless the lawyer making the lateral move was involved personally in the engagement from which the conflict arose. Second, can lawyers remaining in a firm, from which a "tainted" lawyer has departed, thereafter undertake matters against the departing lawyer's clients if none of the remaining lawyers had been previously involved? The answer to that question in the ABA Rules is yes—the firm no longer is subject to imputed "taint." The rules in other systems have not reached this level of detail.

The complications and permutations of these rules are of little general interest in an analysis of lawyers' ethics. Indeed, they are of special interest only to relatively large firms, to business clients that engage law firms, and to litigants who can employ the rules in litigation tactics. Nevertheless, the rules of imputation require that careful attention be given by every lawyer in a law firm to the identity and interests of clients being represented by other lawyers in the firm.

Another set of relationships addressed in the ethics rules concerns responsibilities of partners toward junior associates in the firm. The American rules are again characteristically elaborate. ABA Rule 5.1 provides: "A partner in a law firm shall make reasonable efforts to ensure that the firm has in effect measures giving reasonable assurance that all lawyers in the firm conform to the Rules of Professional Conduct."[23]

These provisions impose a personal obligation on lawyers who have supervisory authority over the conduct of other persons in a law firm. The obligation is not one of *respondeat superior*, whereby the supervisor would have direct legal responsibility for any ethical failure of the subordinate. Instead, the obligation is to exercise reasonable efforts concerning the law firm's procedures, for example, its system for checking conflicts or for handling trust fund accounts.[24] These provisions do not impose responsibility on the law firm as an organization. However, some jurisdictions make a law firm liable for ethical derelictions, for which the penalty could be a reprimand or a monetary penalty.

The Italian rules take a different approach to ethical responsibilities in a law firm: "Where lawyers are associated with each other, only the lawyer or lawyers to whom a case has been specifically referred is subject to disciplinary responsibility."[25] This provision expressly excludes the responsibility of a supervisor.

The Italian rule has two other interesting provisions, one concerning full-fledged colleagues and the other concerning apprentices. Concerning colleagues it is provided: "A lawyer must allow his collaborators to improve their professional preparation, remunerating them in proportion to their contribution to the lawyer's work." This requirement applies to "collaborators" with junior standing and responds to an endemic problem in law firms, that of allocating authority and responsibility in the firm's practice and in sharing its fee revenues. In law firms in which one or a few lawyers are dominant, the dominant lawyers incline to handle relationships with the clients and with the courts in important transactions, while subordinate lawyers do the drudgery. In professional argot, a law firm may consist of "finders" (lawyers who bring in clients), "binders" (lawyers who orchestrate important transactions), and "grinders" (lower echelon lawyers who do the unpleasant detail work). Law firm revenue is allocated with corresponding inequality. The dominant lawyers allocate the firm's revenues according to negotiations among themselves. Junior lawyers who (in the estimate of the dominant lawyers) lack the intellectual ability, personality, or energy to succeed at a higher level can become locked in low-level status.

The Italian rule quoted above attempts to ameliorate this pattern, but it may be doubted whether it has much effect. The position of junior associates in law firms in many countries is notoriously insecure, in terms of both compensation and advancement. The Italian rules seek to ameliorate another source of abuse, the overwork and inadequate training of law graduates, in their apprenticeship training. The Italian rules require that an apprentice be provided adequate training, an adequate workplace, due oversight, and remuneration "proportional to his contribution."[26] These requirements are unavoidably vague, inasmuch as the circumstances of apprenticeships are widely different. But they codify an important professional ideal, which we wish were systematically fulfilled. Apprenticeships are not of uniform quality —some are very good, most are mediocre, some are exploitive. Where more generous treatment of juniors is afforded, it may be the result of professional conscience on the part of leaders of the firm, but more likely it is in response to the forces of competition. In times of prosperity for the legal profession, a competent junior lawyer can be in demand by other law firms, or can go out in independent practice, and will leave if dissatisfied with the treatment from a firm. In lean times, even a very competent junior lawyer may be consigned to an indefinite period of professional drudgery.

Legal Aid: An Obligation?

Lawyers traditionally have owed some kind of obligation to people who cannot afford to pay a lawyer's fee—the poor and near poor. The basis of obligation is perhaps twofold. First, the legal profession is considered to be like a public utility, such as a water or electric power company, in which members of the profession have a monopoly on the right to practice law. On the basis of this supposed monopoly, it is said that there is a corresponding obligation to provide legal service to all who are in need. Second, the legal profession provides an essential service in gaining access to justice and, in a democratic society, every citizen, being entitled to justice, should have that means of access. The underlying moral and political concept is "equal justice for all."

Skeptics remain skeptical about these propositions. As for "monopoly," it is true that lawyers as a group have an exclusive right to appear in court and, generally, to provide legal advice in transaction matters. But no lawyer or law firm has anything like an economic monopoly in providing legal services. Hence no lawyer or law firm can garner the excess profits of a monopoly that could finance services provided to people who could not pay the market rate. On the contrary, law practice is conducted by relatively small organizations (even large firms are economically small enterprises in comparison with most businesses) that often are in intense competition with each other. The fact that most lawyers earn a relatively comfortable living could be a basis for an income tax to support legal and other services for the poor, but that would not be a justifiable basis for a tax on lawyers alone.

As for the right of access to justice, there is no explanation why lawyers (and their other clients) should bear the cost of fulfilling such a right. Primary education, for example, is a right in modern regimes, yet no serious public policy analyst would say that teachers should provide tutelage at their own expense. A similar point applies to medical care. If equal justice for all should be public policy, there should be corresponding public subvention of adequately funded legal aid for services provided by lawyers who are adequately compensated.

In most modern legal systems the state pays for legal representation of indigent persons accused of crimes. Since most criminal defendants are relatively indigent, and lawyers' services universally are relatively expensive, most criminal defendants in most countries are represented by lawyers whose compensation is provided by public subsidy. The subsidy may take the form of stipends paid to lawyers in private practice who are assigned to represent the defendants, or in the form of salaries paid to public defenders—staffs of lawyers who perform that function. Originally, all systems operated through the appointment of private lawyers. In many countries, public defenders' offices have been found to be more efficient, particularly in metropolitan areas with high volumes of criminal matters.

In the civil law countries, the system for providing representation of criminal defendants is accepted as a state function, similar to the provision of medical services and public education. In common law countries the responsibility for taking care of "the less fortunate," whether for health care or education or legal assistance, originated as a matter of charity. Hence the term "legal aid."

Providing legal aid to criminal defendants from time to time has been a politically controversial issue. Thoughtful people would agree that a criminal accused should have a lawyer, and that opinion is an article of professional faith for most lawyers. But most citizens and many lawyers would also agree that the typical criminal has brought his plight on himself and that he is morally less deserving than other claimants of public assistance, such as poor people who need better schools and health care. In most countries the level of legal aid in criminal cases reflects this sentiment. The subsidy is adequate for a modest but minimally competent level of assistance. However, in some regimes the system is more or less pro forma, or indeed a charade.

The legal profession has been supportive of public financial subvention of legal aid in criminal matters and of the duty of individual lawyers to accept appointments in such matters. All ethical codes refer to this obligation. The Italian code states that a lawyer "must provide representation to a client if the judicial authorities ask him to do so in compliance with applicable laws."[27] The Canadian Code and the Chinese and Russian law impose a similar obligation.[28] The ABA Rules provide that "a lawyer shall not seek to avoid appointment by a tribunal to represent a person except for good cause."[29] There is also a moral obligation to provide legal aid, which is broadly defined to include providing service without fee to organizations "designed primarily to address the needs of persons of limited means."[30] A few American states impose an obligation on every lawyer to contribute a specified number of hours per year to legal service to the poor, or to make compensating financial contributions to legal aid services.

It seems clear that receiving legal assistance is the universally recognized right of an indigent criminal accused, even if the quality of service is often inadequate owing to parsimonious public financing. In the United States there is intense political criticism of the inadequacy of defense representation in many criminal prosecutions, particularly in death penalty cases. The criticism in our opinion is justified as the system operates in many states. And the level of funding for representation in criminal prosecutions other than death penalty cases also remains very poor.[31]

Publicly funded legal assistance in civil matters is a different matter. An important underlying issue is the extent to which, in a specific legal system, civil litigation is employed not merely to correct individual instances of injustice but to achieve larger objectives of political or social justice. In most regimes the courts have been unreceptive to legal aid that is "activist," while in the United States social justice through litigation has been standard practice for at least a century. In legal systems in which legal services traditionally are limited in scope and effects, civil legal aid can be a noncontroversial social service like public health. In France, for example, there is an *aide juridique* scheme to provide legal advice to people of limited means through government grants to the local *barreaux*.

In contrast, in the United States legal services have wide potential scope, such as class actions and "test cases" that will affect legal interests of hundreds or thousands of people. This potential has generated acrimonious debate over the level of funding for legal aid in civil matters and over the types of matters in which publicly funded legal assistance is provided. The U.S. Congress has prohibited use of federal legal aid funds to support class actions against local governments and in other specified matters, but the Supreme Court held the restriction to be unconstitutional.[32] Conservatives in the legislature can respond by reducing the available funding. In England, a broad provision for legal aid has foundered on experience that use of the service is upwardly very elastic, rising to levels of unpopular public expense. In many European systems, "advice bureaus," ombudsmen, and similar mediating services are available to average citizens, but not general legal aid in civil matters.

Effective legal aid could be provided through publicly financed legal assistance offices that specialize in legal problems of the poor and near poor, and that work on a mass production basis. The English experience, however, suggests that any such system would become politically unacceptable if an "adequate" level of assistance were provided. The first problem is cost. All modern social intervention services are expensive, because their provision requires competent operatives who themselves are paid reasonable salaries, as in the case of health care and education. Second is the problem of democratic equality. It is politically very difficult to provide a social service for the poor at a level substantially different from what the middle classes obtain. Third, and a consequence of these economic and political factors, if legal aid is "activist," it generates legal rights for even more social services—"equal" and therefore better (compared to what the poor have had) schools, health care, and other services. The actual provision of social services to the poor in most countries runs far below the level promised at the political level. Therefore, if "access to justice" requires legal assistance to obtain full legal rights to these other services (for example, health care or education), then legal assistance compels great public expenditure.

The ideal of legal aid is uneasily poised at this point. Reasonably adequate legal representation is provided in criminal cases, including juvenile matters, but in civil matters full legal aid is not an obligation of either the state or the bar. Many academics nevertheless continue to argue that the bar should do more, invoking the "monopoly" argument described above. We wonder why the argument should not focus on public subvention of specialized legal aid offices. Be that as it may, we predict that the ideal of universal legal aid will encounter political resistance when "access to justice" begins to affect conventional social service levels, or is conspicuous on behalf of disparaged groups such as immigrants and gypsies.

Legal aid by private lawyers to indigent clients on the basis of moral obligation—*pro bono publico*—can have only modest effect on either commutative or distributive justice. In that sense the legal profession's commitment to legal aid is symbolic. But the experience of many lawyers who have provided such service makes a deep impression on them that is morally rewarding in itself. Perhaps more important, it causes lawyers to realize vividly the difficulty and distress encountered by ordinary people in trying to deal with the legal system. As a colleague of ours in South America recalls: "I had this experience many years ago. A former professor organized a group of young lawyers to provide criminal defense to poor people. I took part in this group. The experience of those days never abandoned me."

Self-Government through the Bar Association

Another element of professional citizenship is participation in the governance of the profession itself. The ideal is an aspect of the virtue of independence, addressed in Chapter 4. It contemplates the profession as fully self-regulating—that lawyers themselves should establish ethical conduct norms, encourage conformity to the norms, induce ethical conduct through informal interaction, and, if necessary, enforce the norms through disciplinary proceedings for reprimand, suspension, or disbarment. The ideal cannot be fully realized by lawyers themselves. Effective enforcement of the ethical norms requires at least some participation by the courts and, in our opinion, recognition of the civil remedy of malpractice. However, the courts in many legal systems assume that the bar is exclusively responsible for monitoring professional conduct. Judges sometimes respond to an ethical violation that adversely affects a specific case, but rarely go beyond that. In some legal systems the courts are inattentive even to that responsibility and the bar is equally inert.

Self-government is an article of faith for doctors, journalists, and other professionals as well as lawyers. The clergy, or the central church in the Roman Catholic Church and similarly organized faiths, has claimed autonomy under the principle of duty to God or, in modern constitutional regimes, on the basis of a right to free religious expression. The claim by the legal profession is made on the basis of equality with other professions and the obligation to provide clients independent legal assistance. In the United States, independence of the bar is often asserted in terms of independence of the judiciary as against the legislature, on the underlying premise that judges (being former lawyers) will be relatively benign.[33]

In civil law systems, the state asserts general authority over the professions. The legal profession in concept exercises self-government by delegation within the state-prescribed framework. In common law systems, legal regulation is an accumulation of specific remedial measures. Bar associations exercise such authority as they have been able to establish through their own efforts, subject to ad hoc legal controls imposed by the courts and other organs of government. In modern context, these two different approaches have come to approximate each other. The organizations of the profession therefore have substantial autonomy but are subject to external regulation, particularly as regards legal education, apprenticeship, and conduct before the courts.

Concerning legal education, the law curriculum has been primarily determined by the universities and law faculties. The traditional university curriculum has simply been accepted as sufficient formal education for prospective lawyers. Requirements of apprenticeship or special technical training are imposed by the state, or by the bar with state regulatory sanction, and are a supplemental requirement after the university curriculum. In the United States, where legal education is in specialized graduate schools, the bar with support from the judiciary has imposed some requirements concerning the content of legal education, but these requirements are modest and are largely consistent with the ideas of law school faculties.

In many countries there has been sustained criticism of the adequacy of legal education provided in the universities.[34] The reform strategy has been to avoid confrontation with the universities and instead to impose more exacting requirements for practical training after university. In our opinion many complaints about legal education have merit. Legal education generally is too theoretical and long (in the United States, three years in law school following four years of college). But devising a legal curriculum that would be "adequate" is fraught with difficulties.

One difficulty of devising an "adequate" legal curriculum is that law practice is increasingly diverse, involving numerous specialties and subspecialties. No curriculum of tolerable length can address all of these topics.[35] The relatively theoretical content of the university law curriculum may be a consequence of attempting to span the whole subject matter of the law, which can be done only at a high level of abstraction. Thus, for example, there is a course in the general theory of contracts, but not full compulsory courses for all students in franchise contracts or building-construction contracts; a course in the theory of civil wrongs (torts), but not in the law of defamation or unfair competition. More fundamentally, much of what is important in law practice has always been best learned through experience. By definition, that kind of education cannot be provided in an academic atmosphere, although "clinical" training goes a long way in that direction. Perhaps there is little that can usefully be changed about formal legal education, except shortening the course and providing additional exercises in writing and public speaking. Apprenticeship perhaps might also be more rigorously standardized. Movements to that effect are being pursued in several European countries.

Bar examinations everywhere are administered not by the bar but by the state, although typically in cooperation with the bar. In many common law jurisdictions, the written examinations and inquiries into "good character" are administered by committees of lawyers under supervision of the courts. In civil law systems these functions are administered by the state. The participation of the bar in apprenticeship programs is pervasive, but in many countries those programs are supplemented by organized practice training programs run by professional staff (see Chapter 2).

The third element of professional governance consists of formulating and administering the rules of professional conduct. In civil law systems, all professions, including the legal profession, are subject to regulations prescribed in the civil codes. Within that framework, bar associations in civil law countries have adopted more or less comprehensive codes. In France and some other countries, the professional codes are promulgated locally. In Italy the *Codice deontologico forense* is national. Most common law systems now have formally prescribed norms of professional conduct. In England, the Law Society is the primary author of regulations for solicitors, while the Bar Council has a parallel set of regulations for barristers. In the United States there were formulations of "canons of ethics" by state bar associations beginning at the end of the nineteenth century, then the American Bar Association Canons of Professional Ethics in 1908, and then the modern American codes of 1970 and 1983. These norms remained largely admonitory until the 1970s,[36] and such is still the status of the CCBE Code and the Canadian Code. Over the course of time, however, the direction of development has been from admonition to legal rule.

Enforcement of the rules of professional conduct is primarily by a disciplinary process of the bar, or an agency monitored by the bar. Strictly speaking, disciplinary authority refers to the power to disbar, suspend, or reprimand a lawyer. Traditionally the disciplinary authority was wholly intramural within the bar. In common law systems, it was administered by a bar committee, but in recent years administration has been reinforced by full-time staff. In the civil law systems, authority usually is exercised in a locality through the person of the *batonier*. The *batonier* is a senior member of the bar who has achieved office either through seniority or by election by members of the local bar. He is the official spokesman for the bar in dealings with civic authority and on ceremonial occasions and is *paterfamilias* for the local profession. Among his responsibilities is addressing complaints about misconduct of the lawyers in his purview, inquiring into the circumstances, and, where appropriate, taking punitive or remedial measures.

In all systems the disciplinary process begins at an office for receiving complaints, perhaps an office of the *batonier* or of the chairman of the disciplinary committee. When a complaint is received, a preliminary inquiry determines whether it is merely a "crank" complaint. If the complaint appears to have substance, the matter is submitted to a hearing panel (either a standing committee or one constituted ad hoc) that will review the documents, listen to the grievant, interrogate the accused lawyer, and then reach a decision as to guilt and, if necessary, sanction.

The disciplinary system has been modernized in many regimes, particularly in larger cities, chiefly through a professionalized staff and formal investigative and adjudicative procedures. For example, many systems in major urban centers have an office staff that conducts the preliminary inquiries and pursues a quasi-criminal prosecution in cases warranting action. In some systems the trial of a disciplinary accusation is conducted before a special session of the regular courts. However, history is manifested in participation by members of the bar in at least an oversight capacity. Sanctions ordered through the disciplinary process are directly enforceable in some legal systems, but in others they are enforceable through a subsequent proceeding in the courts, where the disciplinary determination will be given weight of varying gravity.

The authority to impose professional discipline is to be contrasted with the authority of the courts to impose sanctions for forensic misconduct (misconduct in court). It is a general principle of judicial procedure that a judge may exclude a lawyer from participation in a case if the lawyer does not behave properly. Courts have the lesser authority to impose special requirements (for example, foreshortened deadlines) and, in some systems, to impose fines or other monetary sanctions. Common law courts have the authority to punish lawyers for contempt of court. The state's prosecutorial authority to enforce the criminal law may also be brought to bear against a lawyer. It is possible for a lawyer to be subject to disciplinary proceedings, judicially imposed sanctions for forensic misconduct, civil liability for malpractice, and criminal prosecution. For example, a lawyer who embezzled funds from an estate that was under court supervision (such as a guardianship) could be excluded from the case by the court, suspended or disbarred from practice by the disciplinary authority, prosecuted for the theft under criminal law, and required to disgorge the funds through a suit for restitution.

In the traditional practice of law there was another disciplinary process, much less visible and systematic but often practically effective. In a small and closed professional community, unofficial disapproval can result in professional "distancing" or ostracism. Since most law practice requires interaction with other lawyers, these informal sanctions can be very effective, even if unsystematic and sometimes very unjust. Historically, the paucity of official proceedings addressing lawyer misconduct suggests that the informal mechanism ordinarily was, as a practical matter, the only sanction system. There is no reason to think that it was ineffective in small urban communities. But the old-fashioned system works only if members of the bar can be continuously observed by their colleagues.

In the modern urban context, the traditional system can work only among a small, close-knit group of specialist practitioners. It is said that the English barristers remain such a group. As one commentator has put it:

> [I]n the small world of English courts, a barrister caught bending the truth, or even neglecting to inform the court of an unfavorable precedent, would be discredited among the colleagues and judges. . . . Word . . . could also be expected to spread to the fairly small circle of solicitors from whom any given barrister probably draws the bulk of his or her work.[37]

In many other modern localities there are subspecialties whose practitioners regularly interact with each other—real estate conveyancers, probate lawyers (who handle decedents' estates), sometimes litigation specialists, and others. Within those groups the informal system is a strong constraint. But law practice increasingly is conducted in major urban centers and adjacent suburbs and also is increasingly balkanized into subspecialties. These social forces have made law practice increasingly "impersonal" in a most literal sense. That is, a typical lawyer has infrequent interchange with most other professional colleagues and functions at a physical and social distance from clients. Instead of the "local bar," the law firm has increasingly become the center of professional colleagueship and hence the determining influence in an ethical climate.

In this emerging milieu the bar association nevertheless remains an important institution. It symbolizes the legal profession's conception of self-government. It is a forum for discussion and debate not only about technical legal issues but also about issues of legal ethics. It can be a bridge between lawyers and the judiciary and other agencies of the state concerned with the conduct of lawyers. To an increasing extent the activities of bar associations have become international, such as the work of the CCBE and the International Bar Association. However, bar associations themselves also have become large and impersonal.

Equally important, concepts of legal due process have come to be applied in matters of professional regulation and discipline. Thus inquiry and discipline not only for lawyers but also for doctors, accountants, and financial fiduciaries is increasingly governed by legal regulations and judicial-like inquiries and determinations. In such a law-based regulatory system, it is impermissible to ostracize a lawyer because he has acquired a reputation for unreliability or even dishonesty. Due process requires norms formulated as definite legal standards, not merely "traditions of the profession," and proof of specific wrongdoing, not mere suspicion. What formerly were problems of professional ethics, addressed within a fraternal circle, therefore have become problems of compliance and enforcement of legal regulations, to be addressed as problems of public law. The old concept of professional responsibility must be modified accordingly.

8

Fees and Other Issues of Legal Economics

Regulation of Fees

A final obligation of a lawyer—perhaps it should be a first obligation—is to treat clients fairly in charging fees. The very idea of a lawyer's fee contradicts other political ideals. If all legal disputes could be resolved justly at the hands of judges, advocates would be unnecessary. If all property and financial transactions were conducted fairly and equally, the governing terms could be stipulated by regulation, and assistance from lawyers would not be required to "hand tailor" a transaction. If all human activities were governed by one legal regime, international lawyers would be unemployed. However, as soon as a community expands beyond being a small city, the informal mechanism of social regulation—one might call it the "prelegal" system—ceases to be adequate. Laws and lawyers become necessary, and justice can be had only for a price.

Lawyers are often in a position to exploit clients. Clients who regularly enter the "legal services market," particularly large businesses, can usually avoid exploitation, but most other clients deal with lawyers at a disadvantage. The typical client does not fully understand his legal problem or the various strategies for dealing with the problem (including not employing a lawyer); most clients do not know what legal service would be appropriate to deal with the problem or what that service should cost. Very often the client is in a state of acute distress, having been arrested or suddenly sued. The relationship between the typical lawyer and the typical client therefore does not conform to market theory, in which a "reasonable" buyer and seller are free to deal with each other or not. All of these circumstances create a justification for the regulation of lawyers' fees.

The fees lawyers may charge clients have always been regulated in all regimes, civil law and common law. The governing regulations have ranged from generally stated requirements that the fees be "reasonable" to highly detailed prescriptions of the charges for various tasks. The requirement that fees be reasonable covers all types of legal representation, including office counseling and advocacy in litigation. However, the very generality of the rule leaves room for dispute over whether a fee in a specific instance is reasonable. In such disputations the lawyer often prevails, to the distress of the client.

A highly detailed prescription of fees therefore has appeal but also important limitations. As a practical matter, detailed regulation cannot address all types of legal services. This difficulty is increasingly severe in modern law practice owing to the wider range of available services and the intensification of specialization. Detailed prescriptions of fees typically address only routine litigation practice, leaving unusual litigation and nonroutine transactions in office practice to be governed only by the general rule of reasonableness. Another limitation of a highly detailed prescription is obsolescence. With the passage of time and the effects of monetary inflation, any set of price controls becomes unrealistic. Obsolete fee schedules are ignored or evaded in practice, resulting in an empty regulatory regime.

Commentary in the Canadian Code concerning "fair and reasonable" says that:

Fair and reasonable fee depends on such factors as:
- the time and effort required and spent;
- the difficulty and importance of the matter;
- whether special skill or service has been required . . . ;
- the customary charges of other lawyers of equal standing . . . ;
- the amount involved or the value of the subject matter;
- the results obtained;
- the tariffs or scales authorized by local law;
- such special circumstances as loss of other employment, uncertainty of reward, and urgency.[1]

Similar formulations have been established in other common law jurisdictions. The "factors" in the Canadian rule point to circumstances that ordinarily will justify increasing a fee. No mention is made of factors that would call for decreasing a fee, for example, that the matter turned out to be much simpler than expected. These "reduction" factors are only implicit in the rule. The general rule in civil law systems is similar, such as the rule in Italy: "A lawyer may not request compensation which is obviously out of proportion to the work undertaken or otherwise excessive."[2] The term "obviously" in the Italian rule signifies that only an egregiously excessive fee is subject to legal challenge. As a practical matter that is the norm in many systems.

The Canadian Code, quoted above, refers to "the tariffs or scales authorized by local law." In some jurisdictions by statute, and in others by rules of court or by customary practice, there are rules specifying amounts that lawyers may charge for various services. For litigation, the rules are linked to those governing the amount that the winner in litigation can charge against the loser. For example, in English litigation the "costs" that may be charged against an opposing party are determined by a court official according to regular practice or established rules of thumb, and include attorneys' fees. The amount so determined is added to the judgment in favor of a plaintiff and becomes a judgment against the plaintiff when the judgment on the merits is in favor of the defendant. There is a similar procedure in most legal systems, but not in the United States, China, or Japan. In the United States, however, fee limits are imposed in specified types of cases, for example, claims for recovery of workers' compensation for injuries in industrial accidents.[3]

In most legal systems, the amount a lawyer for the winning side may charge his client is distinct from the losing party's obligation, and ordinarily is determined by private agreement between lawyer and client. Thus a successful litigant in a typical common law system could recover (for example) $5,000 in litigation costs from the losing party but be obligated to pay his own lawyer a total of $15,000 in accordance with the fee agreement between them. In the United States, the American "cost" rule in litigation is that a winning party ordinarily must pay his own lawyer and that a losing party generally has no obligation for the opposing party's lawyer fees.

Fees for office services may also be specifically regulated. In some common law systems, the bar associations have promulgated schedules of recommended fees for common office legal services, such as documenting the sale of real estate or drafting a will. The fees prescribed in these schedules are not legally binding but are a solemn pronouncement by the bar, and a lawyer proceeds at his peril in charging more. Schedules of recommended fees are illegal in the United States, where they were held to be price-fixing and hence a violation of the antitrust laws.[4] This judicial ruling gave little weight to the fact that fee schedules afford some protection for clients against outrageous gouging.

The rules governing fees in civil law systems are much more elaborate and prescribe either a specified amount or a range of permissible charges. The level of detail in civil law fee schedules is indicated in the Italian Code of Civil Procedure.[5] Section 90 of that code provides an elaborate list of litigation steps for which specific "piece work" remuneration is prescribed. In litigation matters, the permitted payments are correlated with specific litigation tasks, such as filing a motion or attending a hearing. Fee regulation based on specific litigation steps unfortunately creates perverse incentives for lawyers, who can convert litigation into superfluous interchange of papers and multiplication of court hearings, because their compensation is determined by the number of these events. Germany has recently adopted a revision of its fee regulations in which the basic idea is that fees will increase as the matter progresses; there no longer needs to be an initial agreement to cover the entire engagement. The civil law also has a supervening general rule that fees must be "reasonable."

"Reasonableness" of a fee in all systems depends primarily on the prevailing rates in local practice for similar matters. These prevailing rates can be readily determined for matters of ordinary legal practice, for example, drafting a will or organizing a corporation. However, in highly specialized work, particularly in matters in which large sums are at stake, ordinarily there is no "prevailing rate." In such situations, the fee will be determined either by prior agreement between the client and lawyer or by negotiation at the conclusion of the representation.

In transactions not covered by regulation or fee schedules, the fee is a matter of contract between client and lawyer. When large sums are involved in a litigation or transaction, the legal fee can be very substantial. Clients involved in large-scale transactions usually are sophisticated in financial matters and experienced in dealing with lawyers. Disputes over the fees in such cases are rare and usually arise as an incident to deeper disappointment or conflict between client and lawyer concerning the results. Decisional law in the United States has upheld fee contracts that provide for large returns to the lawyer but which were very clear in their terms and had been negotiated by corporate clients with assistance from their own in-house lawyers.[6]

Sophisticated clients, particularly those regularly employing lawyers, are in a position to bargain over fees. For example, insurance companies that insure motorists against liability in automobile accidents must engage lawyers to defend claims against their insureds, and in doing so often "shop" for advantageous rates. The same is true of other businesses that frequently employ lawyers. Large and medium-sized businesses have the alternative of establishing an in-house legal department for most of their legal work and employing independent law firms only on special occasion. In the modern globalized economy, the cost of legal services is one of many factors that influence where and how transactions will be structured. These competitive forces are a constraining influence on legal fees. Businessmen grumble about legal fees in general but rarely complain about the fees charged by their own lawyers.

Unsophisticated clients are a different matter. Most people employ a lawyer on only a few occasions in a lifetime and have little experience in transactions with lawyers.[7] Except in small communities, relatively few people are personally acquainted with a lawyer, and fewer still are in a position to evaluate a lawyer's competence or the complexity of their legal matter. When in need of legal assistance, the ordinary citizen usually finds a lawyer through family, church, neighborhood, or workplace connections. Where lawyer advertising is permitted, a person searching for a lawyer may find pages and pages of similar advertisements in telephone directories, leaving little basis on which to make a choice.

The problem of the lawyer's fee encapsulates the disadvantage that burdens most clients in their encounters with lawyers. Indeed, the common feeling of being overcharged may be an expression of more complex distress on the clients' part. Speaking of the relationship between lawyer and client in divorce matters, Sarat and Felstiner observe:

> Lawyer-client interaction . . . takes place in a familiar space and a space of privilege [for the lawyer]. The law books on the lawyer's shelves are books the lawyer has read or knows how to read; the language spoken is a language in which law-

yers are trained and with which they are comfortable; the rituals performed give special place to the lawyer even as they are forbidding and unwelcoming to the uninitiated.[8]

There is not much that outside authority can do to intervene in these relationships, except indirectly. But regulation of lawyers' fees is practicable. In some countries, notably Germany and France, the controls against exploitation of unsophisticated clients are close and substantially effective, by means of strict fee schedules that are carefully observed and readily enforced through the local bar associations. In other countries the fee schedules are easily evaded, enforcement is weak, and there is a tradition of indifference by the bar and the courts.

In the absence of effective public regulation, the best solution is to encourage relationships whereby prospective clients could be channeled to competent and trustworthy lawyers through intermediaries such as labor unions, professional associations, employers, and financial institutions such as banks and insurance companies with which people deal frequently. The legal profession generally has resisted such arrangements on the ground that they hamper free choice of independent counsel. These arguments, although often no doubt sincere, in our opinion avoid the real objection, which is fear of further competitive pressure on independent practitioners.

In any event, there is an inherent difficulty in fairly regulating legal fees. The price of a standard commodity or service, such as a pair of shoes or an electrical repair, can be objectively estimated. This is true also of routine legal services, such as preparing a typical residential real estate conveyance or drafting an ordinary family will. Fees for these kinds of ordinary legal services are already constrained by competition and are more or less well known in a local community. It is in nonroutine legal matters that an unsophisticated client is least able to gauge whether a fee is reasonable. But determining a fair fee in such a matter is also objectively difficult from any viewpoint. For that reason, in unusual transactions lawyers ordinarily charge on an hourly basis.

The hourly rate has now become generally standard except for contingent fee matters. However, even an hourly fee basis is not wholly reliable. There are "horror stories" of law firms billing grossly excessive hours, and in many law firms there is continuous pressure on lawyers to record a high number of "billable hours." Up to 2,500 hours per year is a common expectation in the United States, which is equivalent to 200 hours per month or 50 hours per week. Anyone who has kept track of time in a working day can appreciate the temptation to inflate reports. Inflated hourly reports of course can translate into inflated bills for legal fees.

In our opinion, most lawyers' fees are reasonable. By this we do not mean inexpensive, but instead refer to the "substitution" value of the lawyer's work. That value is the income level available in alternative types of work for which legal training is helpful and to which lawyers transfer if they cannot "make it" in law practice—banking, insurance, business management, public administration. In any event, many lawyers find themselves doing "involuntary" pro bono work, meaning that they do the work for a client in the expectation of being paid, but then cannot collect their fee. Nevertheless, ordinary clients face some risk of being overcharged and also some risk that a matter will be handled perfunctorily that should have been given greater attention. These risks continually regenerate popular fear and suspicion of lawyers.

Contingent Fees

People who cannot afford an outlay for a lawyer's fee sometimes have legal claims that are potentially large in amount but uncertain in outcome. In some countries such a client may agree to a fee that is contingent or dependent on success in the litigation. A "contingent fee" was traditionally unethical in virtually all legal systems and is still prohibited in many systems. For example, the Italian rule is that: "It is forbidden to make any agreement in which compensation for professional services is based on a certain percentage of the disputed property or the value of the controversy."[9]

Contingent fees are not expressly prohibited in some other systems, but the convention among lawyers in those systems—in Japan, for example—is that they are improper. However, contingent fee arrangements have been legitimate in the United States for many years, and more recently have been recognized in several other countries. Contingent fees are a matter of practice in many countries even while being nominally prohibited. A clandestine contingent fee is involved when a lawyer quotes a large fee for a plaintiff's case upon a tacit understanding that a much lower fee—or no fee at all—will be charged if the outcome is unfavorable.

Contingent fee arrangements are the usual basis for the prosecution of claims for personal injury in the United States. The legal rules governing personal injury claims, particularly liberal American rules of damages, result in the possibility of very large verdicts. These claims typically are made by ordinary working people or householders whose existing financial resources would not permit them to retain counsel. The possibility of a large verdict induces defendants to defend with great effort, which in turn requires corresponding effort by the lawyers prosecuting these claims. As a result, these claims are at the same time highly valuable, relatively expensive to prosecute, and usually attended by risk of failure. The contingent fee lawyer commits time and expenses for presentation of the litigation in return for a large share of any recovery, but receives no compensation if the case is lost.

The typical contingency percentage is one-third of the "gross recovery." This is the amount before deduction of litigation expense, so the client's share can sometimes be less than half of the judgment. For example, under a contingent fee of one-third in a personal injury claim, the expenses could be $50,000 (for such things as pretrial depositions and expert testimony on medical and economic loss). If the settlement or judgment is $150,000, the lawyer is entitled to $50,000 as the fee and to reimbursement of $50,000 in expenses, or a total of $100,000, leaving the client $50,000. A variation of the contingent fee is an arrangement in which the lawyer is paid some fraction of a usual hourly rate plus some percentage of recovery. Although most contingent fee representations involve personal injury claims, some commercial litigation and most class actions in the United States are also conducted on contingency fee.

The legitimacy of the contingency fee is generally accepted in Canada and, in modified form, has gained recognition in England.[10] Under the English "conditional fee," the lawyer is to receive a specified fee, not a percentage of the recovery, but only if he wins or achieves a positive settlement. Apparently in England there has now grown up a traffic in personal injury claims, which are assignable (transferable) under English law, whereby the potential claimants engage "claims handlers" to prosecute their claims. The system seems to have become subject to serious abuse.[11] In Australia, the courts have now recognized a "speculative fee," under which the lawyer gets an "uplift" of 50 or 100 percent above the agreed upon fee for a favorable result and refrains from charging if the result is unfavorable. The special name permits the bar to continue to disdain "contingent" fees. In France, a 1991 statute modified the previous prohibition on contingent fees to the extent of permitting a portion of the fee to be dependent on the result. However, the award is subject to determination by the court in which judgment is obtained.

Contingent fee agreements in the United States are subject to special regulation, the requirements being that:

- The contingent fee agreement must be in writing and must explicitly define the basis for the percentage.
- The plaintiff's attorney upon obtaining a recovery must submit a detailed accounting to the client.
- The fairness of the fee is subject to reconsideration by the court upon application by the client.[12]

Controversy over contingency fees has occurred on two levels. Within legal systems that recognize contingent fees, it is protested that lawyers often exploit clients by obtaining one-third fee agreements in cases where there is little risk of loss. This abuse is sometimes inflicted on naive clients, many of whom think that fees in a personal injury case are *required* to be on a contingent basis.[13] At another level of controversy, it is complained that the contingent fee system is an inducement for lawyers to bring suits that otherwise would not have been brought. This is true, but it is also true that many of these cases are meritorious and could not be brought except on the basis of a contingent fee. Whether and to what extent nonmeritorious cases are thereby given undue encouragement remains an unresolvable issue. What is "undue"?

The contingent fee system results in very large returns for some lawyers, particularly those capable of dramatizing serious injuries and wrongs. It also results in cases being prosecuted, often successfully, that would not have been brought if the claimant had to bear the risk of paying a lawyer's fee in a losing cause. The system is especially attractive in the United States because of the American rule concerning costs of litigation. Under that rule, as we have seen, the loser does not have to pay the winner's expenses, so a plaintiff's loss results in the loss of the plaintiff's lawyer's investment of time and effort and expenses, but no financial obligation is imposed on the client. It is false, however, to suggest that contingent fee cases typically are brought recklessly. To prosecute a large and risky claim, the plaintiff's lawyer ordinarily must make a substantial investment of effort and usually must also underwrite substantial litigation expenses. Plaintiffs' lawyers thus are entrepreneurs in risk ventures, accepting cases that have promise but turning down cases that either have a remote chance of winning or have only modest prospects in the form of damages.[14]

In any event, the contingent fee gives the "average person" who has a valuable but risky claim an opportunity to obtain representation by highly competent counsel. In the democratic era, where "access to justice" is a salient public policy concern, the contingent fee arrangement has much to be commended. Prosecuting litigation of a serious controversy requires skillful advocates, assistance that is expensive and always has been so. A contingent fee system requires plaintiffs' lawyers to perform a critical evaluation of cases they will accept. A plaintiff's lawyer thereby becomes de facto a judge of a case even before a claim can be commenced.[15] Justice in the real world unfortunately comes at a price.

Fee Disputes

Lawyers have an obligation of restraint in asserting claims for their fees. In England, it has been a matter of honor that a barrister may not sue a "lay client" for his fee, but instead looks to the "professional client," the solicitor that engaged the barrister. A solicitor may sue the lay client for the solicitor's fee and also for the fee the solicitor is obligated to pay the barrister. In civil law countries there was a similar tradition that a lawyer would not sue a client for a fee that had not been paid. In today's commercialized milieu, however, lawyers can sue a client for unpaid fees and sometimes do so, but only as a last resort.

Some clients simply are unable to pay fees that they acknowledge are owed. Some clients simply ignore obligations, including those to their lawyers. Some clients refuse to pay a fee because they believe they have been inadequately represented or otherwise abused. A client's refusal to pay a fee may be backed by a threat to sue for malpractice if the lawyer tries to collect the fee. In bygone days, it was rare for a lawyer to sue for a fee, and the courts typically proceeded from an assumption that the lawyer's claim was justified. Today the courts are more sympathetic to client contentions in fee disputes. In the United States, fee disputes and client counterclaims for malpractice may be determined by juries that are notoriously unsympathetic toward lawyers. No lawyer could relish the prospect of a legal dispute with a client. In all countries a fee dispute typically is resolved simply by the lawyer abandoning the claim.

Various alternative dispute resolution procedures have been established to avoid litigation over fee disputes. In most civil law systems a dissatisfied client may appeal to the bar association for mediation. In such a mediation a lawyer is obliged, legally or as a practical matter, to accept the recommendation of the bar president or mediation committee. In several American states a lawyer is required to submit to arbitration of a fee dispute if the client so demands, although the client retains the option of maintaining his claim in the courts.[16]

Litigation of fee disputes is adjudicated like ordinary civil disputes. However, the ethical requirement that a fee be reasonable can be the basis for a disciplinary proceeding against a lawyer who has charged an outrageous fee.[17] Unfortunately, that kind of exploitation often goes without redress where bar discipline is not rigorous.

The Economics of Justice

Every sober person recognizes, sadly perhaps, that real-world justice must involve some cost. That implies accepting the fact that justice for all is an elusive ideal. But the cost of litigation in many legal systems is very high. In England, by tradition a relatively small number of highly skillful barristers handle most of the major lawsuits, ordinarily for very high fees. Under the regime where the loser must pay the winner's lawyer fees, barrister fees and other litigation costs in England are a formidable deterrent to litigation by parties who cannot afford the risk of having to pay if they lose.[18] The cost allocation rule in the United States, under which the loser does not have such an obligation, avoids this deterrent. However, American procedure is very expensive for other reasons, particularly in cases involving high stakes. In American cases of substantial amount, typically there are elaborate pretrial document reviews and witness depositions as well as very liberal rules concerning damages and broad scope for punitive damages. In combination, these provisions can escalate the stakes to high levels. Defendants often pay substantial amounts to settle claims they believe lack merit, in order to avoid paying the high costs of pretrial procedure and risking a large adverse jury verdict.

The English justify their practice concerning engagement of barristers and allocation of costs on the ground that competent representation produces high-quality justice and that allocation of costs properly compensates the winner. These justifications make sense on their own terms. The Americans justify their elaborate pretrial discovery procedures on the ground that they are a necessary means of getting at all the facts. Americans justify jury trials as a mechanism whereby average citizens influence the administration of justice, and justify punitive damages as a means of constraining large corporations and government bureaucrats from imposing their will on a defenseless public. These justifications also make sense, but they impose a heavy cost as the price.

Justice in the civil law systems is generally less expensive. However, many civil law systems in our opinion give inadequate weight to the need to seek the truth in adjudication. The typical judge in many civil law systems simply responds to what is offered by the parties, and the parties usually have poor mechanisms for penetrating the issues in dispute. Much civil law litigation is an exercise in paper shuffling punctuated by hearings in which little energy is devoted to getting to the merits. A client in the civil law system can be inclined to view litigation as merely a professional exercise for the judges and lawyers. (This predisposition on the part of clients is often reinforced by the remarks of lawyers themselves.)

The English and American systems, in different ways and with different justifications, also give inadequate weight to the factor of cost. In the common law systems the intensity of effort on one side often is simply matched by escalation on the part of the opponent, running up expenses on both sides. A client in the common law system therefore is also likely to view litigation as a professional exercise for the lawyers, in which the influence of the judge is remote.

No legal system provides adjudication free of charge. We surmise that any system that attempted to do so would quickly be submerged in litigation, because human beings in modern impersonal societies are not subject to the restraints against asserting grievances that operate in small intimate societies. On the contrary, the impersonality and "alienation" characteristic of modern society apparently create limitless potential for asserting grievances. The fact that administered justice imposes costs, both financial and psychological, is a "rationing" device that restrains the demand for "access to justice." Many modern reformers recommend arbitration and mediation as mechanisms to ameliorate the burden of cost. Most of these procedures are more streamlined than litigation, and are for that reason usually less expensive. However, arbitration itself carries administrative costs, often very high costs. And mediation provides no remedy against a recalcitrant party.

Providing justice is a basic purpose of a decent society, as recognized by the ancient Greeks and in the Bible. Yet in modern impersonal society the ideal of justice—personified by the blindfolded maiden of justice holding forth equally balanced scales—is inseparably connected with the brute fact of lawyers' fees, a subject that is always distasteful and sometimes sordid. The contradiction in the link between justice and lawyers' fees is at the heart of many other controversies over legal ethics.

The legal profession has always been a competitive vocation and in modern context is becoming increasingly so. Attempts to moderate or eliminate competition among lawyers have been only partially successful, and the same is true of efforts to eliminate competition from others, such as banks and real estate companies. Modern lawyers and law firms are having to reorganize their work patterns and techniques to provide better and faster service.

The economic necessity to be competitively effective is deeply troubling to many lawyers. A lawyer who does not accept the challenge to become efficient runs the risk of losing clientele. A lawyer who accepts that challenge also submits to the implication that legal representation is a commodity and that justice can be bought. The idea that justice can be measured on an economic scale contradicts the idea that justice should not be for sale. Sentiments such as these involve profound confusion of categories, but they echo popular and philosophical discourse on the nature of justice. The ideal of justice is embraced by most lawyers, notwithstanding that all lawyers know privately that doing justice involves unavoidable costs. But the bar has employed the ideal of justice as a basis for ethical restrictions designed to moderate competition.

The provisions on advertising and solicitation are illustrative. As recounted in a treatise commenting on the rules in India and in England, a barrister traditionally could not:

- use the word "barrister" on a sign or shingle at his chambers;
- identify himself as a barrister on his business card;
- advertise in a professional directory aimed at other lawyers;
- identify himself as a barrister in a newspaper article;
- give a media interview concerning a case in which he participated.[19]

The modern rules in most countries are more liberal. Lawyers in the United States are allowed to advertise in newspapers, on billboards, on office signs, on radio and television, and in the "yellow pages" of telephone directories. Advertisements must be truthful, and "outreach" may not be made to accident victims, or their families, in the period immediately following an accident.[20] There is little question that lawyer advertising greatly enhances public awareness of legal claims and the possibility of retaining a lawyer. Advertising also enhances a lawyer's chance of being approached by potential clients, for otherwise lawyers would not continue to spend money on advertising. However, pervasive lawyer advertising no doubt reinforces the public impression that lawyers solicit clientele, not always discreetly or tastefully.

Seeking out clients is called "solicitation" and traditionally was entirely prohibited. The justification for the prohibition has been to inhibit "vexatious" litigation—that is, the assertion of claims by persons who would not otherwise be motivated to sue. There are indeed instances where lawyers have instigated litigation. On the other hand, the potential clients who might be persuaded by a lawyer to sue usually are the poor, the isolated, and the semiliterate. The prohibition on solicitation is not a serious impediment to more sophisticated or well-connected clientele, most of whom are quite able to connect with a lawyer when necessary. The prohibition is thus an obstacle to wider "access to justice" in a large impersonal society.

In the United States the prohibition against solicitation was employed against the civil rights movement, particularly efforts by activist organizations to encourage blacks to bring litigation challenging racially discriminatory practices. In resisting these restrictions it was argued that the principle of access to justice allowed lawyers to approach potential clients who may have civil rights claims. In a decision in *In re Primus* the United States Supreme Court pronounced an uneasy and perhaps unintelligible compromise, holding that solicitation of legal clientele was constitutionally protected when it was not for the lawyer's "pecuniary gain," although solicitation otherwise could validly be prohibited.[21] Solicitation in civil rights controversies remains specially permitted in this way.

Yet some lawyer groups recognize that restrictions on solicitation are difficult to justify in mass society, where people often do not know their own neighbors. As recognized in the Canadian Code:

> In a relatively small community . . . [a potential client] will usually be able to . . . select a qualified lawyer in whom he has confidence. However in large centres . . . and as the practice of the individual lawyer tends to become [specialized] . . . a stranger in the community may have difficulty in finding [an appropriate] lawyer. . . .[22]

The expense of lawyers' services induces efforts to provide substitutes—that is, services that achieve a similar effect but less expensively. These services have different names, such as "debt counseling" and "divorce counseling." But the term "legal services" is carefully avoided, because its use will stir hostile response from the bar.

In many countries the practice of law may be undertaken only by persons who have been admitted to the bar. In a few countries, notably Sweden, anyone can provide advice and assistance in legal matters, but only lawyers admitted to the bar may call themselves lawyers.[23] Where only lawyers are permitted to give legal advice or assistance, it becomes necessary to define "the practice of law." Finding a satisfactory definition is difficult, perhaps impossible.

The practice of law clearly includes the function of advocacy in courts, a readily identifiable and publicly visible activity. Representation in other tribunals, however, is not so obviously the practice of law. In most regimes, people other than lawyers can serve as advocates in certain kinds of proceedings, such as labor arbitration. Beyond litigation in court, the definition of law practice becomes increasingly elusive. Many of the services provided by office lawyers are hard to define as distinctively "legal." This is true, for example, of estate planning, assistance with tax matters, and business compliance with government regulations.

The difficulties of definition are compounded in the modern context, as the scope and depth of legal regulation has intensified. For example, most modern countries have elaborate regulations governing the employment relationship, but is a person who monitors compliance with those regulations on behalf of an employer providing "legal" advice? Most countries now impose elaborate restrictions for protection of the environment, but is someone who monitors compliance with those regulations engaged in "law practice"? What about compliance with insurance regulations? Consumer protection laws? More generally, most middle- and upper-level managers in public and private bureaucracies must have substantial knowledge of some field of law to carry out their functions, and they routinely make decisions that take legal regulations into account. It cannot be that all these activities constitute the practice of law.

The matter has been especially vexed in the United States.[24] In the early part of the twentieth century, bar organizations succeeded in obtaining legislation prohibiting the "unauthorized practice of law." This concept was clear as applied to an advocate in court proceedings, but vacuous as applied to many other activities. A definition commonly employed in the legislation was "activity requiring the knowledge and skill of a lawyer," but that definition obviously is circular. The boundary between the work of lawyers and the work of other vocations in the United States therefore usually has been worked out locally by tacit negotiation through move and countermove. Détente is unstable, however, in the face of rapid changes in regulation and in the responsibilities undertaken by nonlawyer corporate officials. The American Bar Association in 2002 undertook another try at a definition, but gave up.[25]

The prohibitions against the "unauthorized practice of law" have been an inviting target for social critics. The critics infer from the existence of the regulations, and from some of the self-serving rhetoric of the profession, that the bar has a monopoly and that successful lawyers are monopolists. Skeptical analysts infer that the restrictions on competition generally have failed.

Recent Regulatory Controversies: MDP and MJP

MDP is the abbreviation for multidisciplinary practice. It refers to professional service firms constituted of lawyers as well as other professionals, for example, accountants and financial advisers (in offices devoted to financial transactions and litigation) or social workers (in offices devoted to divorce and juvenile law practice). Some American law offices for years have employed professionals in these and other disciplines, such as nurses and doctors (offices devoted to personal injury claims), environmental engineers (environmental regulation compliance and litigation), and public relations and "public policy" counselors.

Under the American lawyers' rules of ethics, members of these other professions could be employed by a law firm, but they could not become partners.[26] At the same time, the major accounting firms, such as PriceWaterhouseCoopers and Ernst & Young, for many years have employed lawyers to provide assistance in accounting problems involving the tax laws. Lawyers employed in accounting firms are called "tax consultants" and not "lawyers," a denomination responding to the rule that an accounting firm cannot engage in the "practice of law." There is no functional difference between what these accounting firm lawyers do and the work done by tax lawyers in law firms, but there is a great nominal difference. As long as the operatives in the accounting firms are not called lawyers, the accounting firms are not engaged in the practice of law.

The situation could have remained this way perhaps indefinitely. However, in the 1970s the big accounting firms expanded the scope of their activities to include management consulting and financial consulting, thus ceasing to be distinctively engaged in accountancy. In the 1990s these firms became still more aggressive by merging or establishing close working relationships with other professional firms, including law firms, in Europe and other parts of the world. These arrangements are permissible in most civil law countries.

These competitive changes were considered by traditionalists in the legal profession to be both an economic threat and a threat to the integrity of the profession. These changes came on top of a sharp increase in law firm mergers, more "lateral" moves by lawyers ((from one law firm to another), and law firms establishing branches in other parts of the country and throughout the world. Bar associations in various countries had to confront whether MDPs that included lawyers would be compatible with the ethical responsibilities of lawyers.[27]

The American legal profession generally has been very resistant to multidisciplinary practice.[28] In contrast, the Australian Competition and Consumer Commission in its 1994 Final Report on the Study of the Legal Profession concluded:

> In all jurisdictions, rules preventing lawyers from sharing profits from legal practice with non-lawyers ... should be repealed to permit formation of MDP ... subject to adoption of appropriate rules of ethical and professional conduct to protect the interests of clients and the system of justice.

However, we are informed that virtually no MDPs have actually been formed in Australia. Perhaps the underlying explanation is that people who want lawyers want lawyers who are confident in calling themselves such, and not "full service" help.

The controversy therefore probably will turn out to be "sound and fury, signifying nothing," except in Europe, and there only over whether law firms can be attached to accounting firms. In the United States, affiliations that meet client needs can be established by what are now known as "strategic alliances" between law firms and other professionals. A strategic alliance is a contractual agreement between two professional services firms, such as a law firm and an accounting firm, to cooperate as separate organizations on a continuing basis, and to cross-refer clients. In the meantime, law firms can continue to employ whomever they please, as long as the nonlawyers are not made partners, and firms of other professionals can employ lawyers as they see fit, as long as the employees do not call themselves lawyers. We expect that changes in the configuration of professional practice will be driven by technological and competitive forces, not by the hopes of the accounting firms or the fears and wishes of the legal profession.

Nevertheless, there is an important point that has been obscured in the debates. This is the fundamental change in the structure and therefore the character of law practice that has taken place over the past century. The essence of the change, which we have referred to at various points, is the bureaucratization of legal services. A large fraction of lawyers today are employed in law firms, often large law firms, or in law departments of public and private businesses and government organizations. Most legal work now is done in teams under managers according to organized schedules. The clientele of modern lawyers increasingly is constituted of corporations and other organizations, so the people with whom many lawyers work are counterpart staff members in corporate and government bureaucracies. Lawyers today increasingly work not as lone operatives but in interaction with all kinds of different professionals, whether in the same professional firm or corporate entity or in working arrangements among firms. These changes have been evolving for more than a century and are now deeply and irrevocably entrenched. We therefore wonder whether it would really make much difference if lawyers worked with other professionals in yet another organizational configuration such as an MDP.

MJP is the abbreviation for multijurisdictional practice. The issue posed is the extent to which a lawyer admitted in one jurisdiction may engage in law practice in, or with respect to legal matters occurring in, another jurisdiction.

In the countries of Europe, traditionally a lawyer admitted to practice in one country could not practice elsewhere. (Indeed, in many countries admission was even more local, to the bar of a city or a province.) In the United States, admission to practice is granted by each state, not nationally. A lawyer's admission to practice in one state therefore does not entitle him to practice regularly in some other state. At the same time, the United States is highly integrated economically and socially, and Europe is rapidly becoming so, so many transactions occur across jurisdictional boundaries. The needs for legal assistance have become "transborder." Accordingly, problems can arise, for example, when the assistance of a lawyer admitted in France is required in Brazil, or when a lawyer admitted in New York has a client who moves to New Jersey or California and requires legal assistance there.

One might think that accommodating this problem would be more complicated in the European international context than in the United States. By a quirk of history, however, the problem of multijurisdictional practice today is governed much more parochially in the United States than it is within the European Union. In the European Union today, a lawyer admitted to practice in one member country may practice as a lawyer in any other country by observing a few fairly simple rules. This concept of reciprocity was established through the combination of a 1975 judicial decision by the European Court of Justice, interpreting the European Community Treaty, and a Council Directive (Legal Services Directive) adopted in 1977. In general, the directive authorizes lawyers from one EU country to practice in another country so long as they use their home-country title (for example, *avocat*), observe the ethical requirements of the host country, maintain malpractice insurance as required in the host country, and limit their practice in the host country to occasional activity rather than establishing a continuing presence in that locality. Where litigation is involved, the foreign lawyer may be required to associate with a local lawyer, but the local lawyer need not be given precedence in presentation of the matter to the court. (Of course, most lawyers would want to give primary responsibility to local counsel in litigation in a foreign court, except in very simple or routine matters.)[29]

In the United States, the situation is liberal functionally but restrictive legally. An important distinction is drawn between participating in litigation and providing transaction legal services. In litigation, the rule is that an out-of-state lawyer must obtain permission from the court in the "foreign" state in order to appear in court. The procedure is called *pro hac vice* admission.[30] Often the out-of-state lawyer will serve as primary advocate with the local lawyer being "second chair" or performing merely formal functions. With regard to transaction practice, it was accepted that, under the concept of "unauthorized practice of law," an out-of-state lawyer could not "set up shop" in a state in which he was not admitted, although a few lawyers tried to do so.[31] Beyond this the law has been unclear and rarely enforced. Many lawyers in high-level practice simply wheeled around the country when and where the needs of a transaction required; for example, lawyers based in New York or Chicago met and negotiated anywhere in the country. Also, house counsel for corporations (that is, full-time employees) went where their companies assigned them, treating their original admission to practice in a state as sufficient to permit them to practice on behalf of their corporate employer in other states as well. Attorneys for agencies of the federal government proceeded in the same way.

However, an abrupt interference in this pattern resulted from a decision by the California Supreme Court in *Birbrower, Montalbano, Condo & Frank, P.C. v. Superior Court*.[32] In that case, a New York law firm provided legal services for a New York client involving a California corporation and then undertook an arbitration in California of a dispute arising from the transaction. The client sued the law firm for malpractice, and the firm claimed fees that had not been paid. The firm's fee claim was rejected by the court on the ground that the lawyers, not being admitted in California, had been engaged in unauthorized practice in that state. The decision caused immediate shock, both because the California Supreme Court is highly respected and because the lawyer was only doing what thousands of others had been doing for decades.

The task in the United States since the *Birbrower* decision has been to delineate and modify the effects of the decision. The *Restatement of the Law Governing Lawyers*, Section 3, has propounded a definition of permissible interstate practice that is fairly liberal, as follows:

> A lawyer currently admitted to practice in a jurisdiction may provide legal services to a client ... before a tribunal ... in compliance with requirements for temporary ... admission to practice before that tribunal ... at a place within a jurisdiction in which the lawyer is not admitted to the extent that the lawyer's activities arise out of or are otherwise reasonably related to the lawyer's practice [in his home jurisdiction].

The *Restatement* observed, in Comment *e* to Section 3, that "there is much to be said for a rule permitting a lawyer to practice in any state, except for litigation matters or for the purpose of establishing a permanent in-state branch," but recognized that the precedents did not go that far. The *Restatement* also observed that "states have permitted practice within the jurisdiction by inside legal counsel for a corporation or similar organization, even if the lawyer is not locally admitted ... when all of the lawyer's work is for the employer-client ... and does not involve appearance in court." This last observation accurately reflects current attitudes.

The American Bar Association has now adopted a recommendation to modify the rules governing multijurisdictional practice. The recommended rules are not as liberal as those now in effect in the European Union, and it is unlikely that greater liberality will be embraced by many of the states. This is paradoxical because the functional basis of law practice today is specialization by type of legal work (commercial litigation, personal injury litigation, securities practice, employment law, tax law) and not by location of admission (in New York, California, or wherever). But the practice of law has always been regulated locally, and professional parochialism remains a strong force.[33]

9

Concluding Reflections

The "New Model" Lawyer

There is both "the" legal profession and a variety of legal professions. "The" legal profession includes judges and lawyers in all modern legal systems—judges of the high courts and ordinary courts; judges of courts of general jurisdiction and those in specialized tribunals such as commercial courts, labor courts, and those presiding in *droit administratif*. The profession includes barristers, advocates, solicitors, and notaires; "general practitioners" and specialists; lawyers in high-profile international law firms and those in small firms in small cities and towns.

All judges are responsible for rendering disinterested decisions, and all lawyers are responsible for providing professionally correct assistance to their clients, but there are important differences in the relationships between judge and lawyer in the various legal systems. The common law adversary system (better described as a "party presentation" system) contemplates a strong affirmative role for the advocates, while civil law systems contemplate the judge playing a more dominant role. In common law systems, the advocates must exercise initiative and interact with each other, not only in trial but also in the preparatory stages. Advocates in civil law systems typically have estranged relationships among one another, while, paradoxically, advocates in the adversary system are relatively cooperative. In some civil law systems, notably Germany and also (in somewhat different form) Japan, the judges give strong direction to the proceedings. In contrast, if an Italian judge were to exercise the authority he formally enjoys, the judge probably would meet resistance and hostility from the advocates.

The characteristics of the two basic "families"—common law and civil law—and of specific systems are perpetuated through distinctive institutions and traditions. These include the systems of education, including legal education; the systems of bar examination and apprenticeship; the typical career paths; the structure and functions of the bar associations; and the geographic basis of typical practice. The distinctive institutions include other elements as well, such as the typical office location and decoration, the types and functions of supporting staff, the pattern of social interaction (or its absence) between judges and lawyers, and the standing of lawyers in the community. No less important are still other social characteristics, such as the typical lifestyle of lawyers, including their mode of dress, their patterns of personal socialization, and the extent to which they involve themselves in the daily life of the community. A contributing influence is the portrayal of lawyers in literature, including the theater, cinema, and television, where the image of a lawyer becomes the model for new cohorts entering the profession.

There were important similarities among Western lawyers through the end of World War II and the immediate period of recovery thereafter. Most lawyers, except for those in a few larger U.S. law firms, worked as solos or in small firms, engaged in general practice, and centered their work in a single locality. In their home cities, many were public citizens of some standing, documenting important transactions, resolving local controversies (sometimes through litigation), and providing legal guidance and wise counsel to people of wealth, officials of government, and managers of businesses. They derived their positions from the superior level of their education, their relationship to the judiciary, their deep knowledge of the local environment, their professional solidarity, and the mysteries of the law itself. Life for many practitioners was economically marginal, but for most of them the work was comparatively interesting, the rewards sufficient, the status generally high.

In the nineteenth century, Tocqueville, surveying democracy at work, identified the legal profession as an "aristocracy":

> The separate knowledge that lawyers acquire in studying the law assures them a separate rank in society; they form a sort of privileged class among persons of intelligence....
>
> Hidden at the bottom of the souls of lawyers one therefore finds a part of the tastes and habits of aristocracy. They have its instinctive penchant for order, its natural love of forms; they ... secretly scorn the government of the people.[1]

A century later that description was still largely accurate for most of the legal profession in the industrialized world.

There were of course differences from one country to another. Some differences were simply of "image"—wigs for English barristers, robes for continental lawyers as well as judges, dark blue suits for lawyers in less formal traditions. Other differences were more basic. Legal education in the continental European tradition was highly theoretical and addressed students mostly from the upper middle class who were not obliged to be serious in their academic work. In the Latin countries of Europe and Hispanic America, the faculty were part-time, being chiefly engaged in law practices that occupied a wholly different compartment of their minds. In the European tradition, professional acculturation was an event subsequent to legal education and centered in the profession itself. The separation of legal education from legal practice was partly a consequence of the fact that most graduates of a legal curriculum pursued vocations other than the law, so legal education was not distinctively an entry into the profession. Subsequent entry into the profession was based primarily on family connections, not academic performance. Once a neophyte entered the profession, the entrenched seniority system postponed serious technical and professional maturation. Many new lawyers remained "young" lawyers well beyond forty years of age, advancing beyond journeyman status only upon the death or retirement of the senior for whom they worked. Subordinacy based on family and age persists in many European systems.

Beginning in the 1950s, however, there has been continuing evolution in all regimes. Career paths have become more open, merit-based, and competitive. Social standing and family connections still count, and in many regimes count heavily. But in many countries the grading system of the universities now identifies differences in performance of the students and thereby creates a merit basis for preferment in employment. Under the compulsion of intensified professional competition, the incumbent professionals give greater weight to technical competence in evaluating and advancing their juniors. The chances for women, members of racial minorities, and people from less privileged backgrounds to join the profession are better than they used to be, considering that in many countries they previously had no chance at all.

A concomitant development has been the change in legal education, particularly in the United States and Canada. Fifty years ago legal education even in those countries was relatively formalist. Some realism was imparted through the case method and through the distinctively professional character of law schools. Nevertheless, until two generations or so ago, American legal education was substantially detached from practice. Today, legal education in the United States and Canada is very much engaged with the realities of practice from an intellectually sophisticated viewpoint. There is competition among law schools in Australia, Canada, and the United States to provide effective clinical training. The result is legal education that is even more distinctively *professional* even while critical of the practicing bar, certainly as compared with the European model.

There is an apparent paradox here. American law schools, and perhaps Canadian ones as well, are often criticized by members of the bench and bar for failing to train people "who can practice law." Yet compared with the European model of legal education, which still functions much as it did a half-century ago, the American law schools are centers of professional training and socialization. Perhaps the truth is that the American law schools are indeed even more "professional" than they formerly were, but the expectations of established practitioners have escalated further.

Another development has been the evolution of the law firm, particularly the large urban law firm. The characteristics of this kind of professional association have been described in Chapter 2.

A third development has been the ascendancy of transaction practice, as distinct from litigation. Transaction practice includes myriad forms of contract—among them agreements for purchases and sales, mergers and acquisitions, licenses and franchises, and mortgages and indentures. Arbitration can be considered an aspect of transaction practice rather than a variation in litigation procedure. The legal basis of arbitration is the contract—a transaction—and the typical arbitration proceeding is a private event rather than a public one. Most modern legal systems have established arbitration on a par with ordinary civil litigation as a means of authoritative dispute resolution.

It is in this environment that the "new model" lawyer pursues a vocation with ancient roots.

The legal profession generally has been impervious to criticism concerning its ethics. In Europe, what criticism exists has been through intramural discourse within the profession, with very little emanating from law faculties or from social critics outside the profession. The criticism has been diffuse, lacking both specificity and any distinct direction of proposed reform. One could say that critical discourse about the European profession has been "lost."[2]

In contrast, the American legal profession has been under almost continuous attack on ethical grounds since the 1960s, chiefly from members of American legal academia and from lawyers of liberal political sentiment. Criticism is asserted in terms of professional ethics, thus isolating the subject of legal ethics from any comparison with business ethics or political ethics or from the normative standards that operate in everyday life. The arguments nevertheless are often cast in terms of supposedly universal ethical analysis, referencing Aristotle, Kant, and modern ethical philosophers.

The criticism is essentially that lawyers act in accordance with the amoral ethical norms of the adversary system, not in accordance with the ethical norms recognized by the general community. These criticisms have had little effect on the content of the rules of professional ethics either in the United States or in other common law countries. The "basic virtues" that we have identified are codified in largely the same terms in all common law countries, today as they were a generation ago and earlier.[3] The American Bar Association Model Code of Professional Responsibility of 1970 and its Model Rules of Professional Conduct of 1983, revised in 2002, reflect these standards, as does the American Law Institute's *Restatement of the Law Governing Lawyers*.

The Canadian bar, as we have seen, adopted a code of ethics generally resembling the American version, although with greater emphasis on traditional understanding and encumbered with less technical detail. The Bar and the Law Society of England continue to rely much more on tradition than on codification. The formation of the European Union has obliged the legal professions on the continent to undertake greater formality in the expression of professional ethics, as demonstrated in the CCBE Code. The task of drafting the CCBE Code revealed differences among countries and has stimulated efforts at local codification. Allowing for these variations, however, the same basic professional virtues are still recognized—loyalty, confidentiality, competence, and independence.

Not only has the bar resisted criticism but the legislatures, parliaments and the courts have not been much impressed by the critics. The ineffectiveness of criticism is partly attributable to the fact that most critics have not followed through with specific proposals that would gain broad support. For example, a few critics have suggested that corporations, as distinct from individuals, should not be entitled to the attorney-client privilege. However, the practical consequences of that suggestion do not seem to have been explored. If the privilege were denied to corporate entities, it seems very likely that legal counsel would be paid by corporations to provide representation on an individual basis to high-ranking corporate officers and other employees exposed to legal risks. The result would be additional complication and expense, but not a cessation of legal advice to corporate officials or necessarily any enhancement of "corporate responsibility." Other American critics have asserted that lawyers should have a firm legal obligation to provide free legal services to the poor. Again, the practical consequences of that suggestion have been ignored, specifically that poor people often have legal problems requiring specialized knowledge that most lawyers lack. Most ordinary "office lawyers" could not become "street lawyers."

A criticism more frequently voiced is that lawyers should make disclosures adverse to their clients, even when the client's conduct is lawful, where disclosure is necessary to accomplish "justice." Here, too, there is often a disjunction between the criticisms and the "facts on the ground." In the first place, American lawyers already are effectively obliged to make potentially adverse disclosures in a wide range of circumstances. These legal requirements obligate lawyers for businesses to monitor their clients' compliance with the law and to withdraw from representation if a serious violation is apparent. Whether corporate lawyers properly comply with these obligations is another question, but that is not a basis for criticizing the rules involved. Moreover, if lawyers were required to seek "just" results regardless of the wishes of their clients, lawyers would have to pretend that confidences would remain secure but report wayward clients to the authorities. If such deception were officially permissible, it is a safe guess that corporations would respond by more closely scrutinizing the political outlook of lawyers they might engage. Representation of corporations by ideologically conservative lawyers would be unlikely to make for "gentler, kinder" corporate behavior.

In any event, the cumulative effect of this kind of criticism has made many lawyers and judges more sensitive to problems of distributive and social justice. A central problem of American social justice was recognized dramatically in the momentous decision of the Supreme Court in 1954 in *Brown v. Board of Education*.[4] That decision, as many readers will know, held that legally imposed racial segregation in public schools, prevalent in all the southern states, was constitutionally impermissible under the equal protection clause of the Fourteenth Amendment. The decision was later applied to other public facilities such as libraries, recreation facilities, and places of public accommodation such as restaurants.

The decision in *Brown* was quintessentially a *legal* decision—a regulation produced by the legal process through the pronouncement of judges on the basis of lawyers' arguments. In *Brown* the legal process was invoked to "lift up" blacks—the most severely repressed and widely disparaged minority in the United States—to a position of legal equality. Questions of equal and decent treatment of other "minorities" thereby were necessarily put on the social agenda: rights of women, youth, the aged, and especially the poor and low-income people who constitute the majority of any society.

The constitutional significance of the principle in the *Brown* decision is difficult to overestimate. Legal equality of all persons had been given lip service in many regimes, but serious commitment to legal equality has at least two difficult implications for the law and its administration. One is how to implement the idea. A wide range of redistributive measures is implied through public subsidy (for example, fuller provision of public education) or regulation of private conduct (for example, the prohibition of invidious discrimination in employment). Measures such as these have obvious legal dimensions. A second implication of legal equality concerns authority itself: Forms of authority are of doubtful legitimacy if they cannot be justified by the "merit" of those who exercise it. Since the legal system is quintessentially one of authority, the principle of equality pervasively challenges every legal system, including of course the authority of judges and lawyers.

Much of the political turmoil in the late twentieth century and today involves issues arising from these implications of the principle of human equality. All members of the legal professions are caught up in it, in one way or another.

Pretension and Practice in Ethics

Most criticism of the legal profession based on ethical theory disregards the difference between theory and the practices of ordinary people. American public sentiment in particular is very moralistic. But most ordinary people, when confronted with actual ethical problems, will dissimulate, evade, and sometimes lie or cheat to protect themselves and their families. And this is to say nothing of the ethics practiced in business relationships and in relationships among politicians. Thus, criticism of "partisanship" on the part of lawyers gives little heed to the fact that most people are partisan when it comes to their own interests.

The criticisms of the American legal profession also ignore the fact that ethical issues are not specific to the "adversary system." The term "adversary system" in this connection is a conflation of two different connotations. One connotation is a technical one, the difference between the common-law method of party presentation of evidence and the judge-centered civil law method. However, as we have endeavored to show, this contrast is grossly misleading. In the first place, in civil law systems the parties define the dispute through their pleadings, within procedural requirements that are generally more constricting than those in the common law systems. Second, in civil law systems the judges rely, ordinarily and often entirely, on suggestions from the advocates as to what evidence should be received and considered. Only exceptionally do judges take initiative to consider other evidence, and even then only within the framework presented in the parties' pleadings. Put differently, in these terms there is no real-world "other system" in apposition to the "adversary system." In fact, in some supposedly judge-centered civil law systems, the receipt of evidence is determined by negotiation between the advocates out of the presence of the judge, whereupon the court is presented with a stipulation for the record! The intensity of the partisanship in this kind of negotiation can be imagined.

There is a different sense in which the term "adversary system" is used to criticize lawyers' ethics. The implication is that lawyers, specifically American lawyers, are improperly hyperaggressive and oblivious of the interests of "justice." The classic examples given are as follows: hostile cross-examination of a helpless witness (the paradigm witness is a little old lady); facilitating a client's perjured testimony; and concealing "smoking gun" documents in discovery. Each of these situations deserves comment.

Regarding hostile cross-examination of a helpless witness, we believe the criticism is justified in concept but only infrequently applicable in practice. Many people bring to mind the intense cross-examination that is seen on television dramas, or in exceptional real cases such as the examination of the police officers in the O. J. Simpson case. (Surely the police officer witnesses in that case were anything but helpless.) In contrast, the examination of the "neutral" witnesses in the O. J. Simpson case (people who were bystanders to the events) was orderly and controlled, reflecting prudent self-restraint of the lawyers. Common law lawyers in fact do not ordinarily engage in hyperaggressive examination of neutral witnesses. They know that tactics of that sort will offend the tribunal, whether judge or jury, and therefore will usually backfire. Of course, if an old lady witness is grossly exaggerating or confabulating, the cross-examination can be intense, but why not? A civil law judge, reacting from the bench, would exhibit similarly effective skepticism of the testimony of a dissembling witness.

A short answer to the criticism that lawyers facilitate their clients' perjury is that doing so is against the law and against the rules of professional conduct everywhere. Of course, some lawyers do facilitate presentations of testimony that they have every reason to believe is consciously false. More often, they present evidence that they suspect is false or grossly inaccurate. But there are several responses concerning that issue.

First, no rule can result in faithful obedience by everyone to whom the rule is addressed. Lawyers know the rules, but some lawyers nevertheless disregard them. Second, we believe that advocates are wary of presenting testimony that they suspect is consciously false, for a very practical reason: if the advocate suspects the testimony is false, so will the tribunal. Nothing is more devastating than the perception that a key witness is improperly lying. We say "improperly lying" because in the religious and cultural traditions of many societies, it is simply accepted that self-interested dissimulation and outright lies are normal on the part of a witness who has an interest in the case. In contrast, in strongly moralistic cultures, Germany, for example, lying and dissimulation violate basic social norms and are regarded as especially reprehensible in court.

Advocates, and also usually the parties, are aware of differences in local norms of moral sensitivity and conduct themselves accordingly. In societies with mixed and more ambiguous "background" norms concerning truthfulness, the problem of false testimony is correspondingly more ambiguous in legal and ethical terms.

On the subject of "smoking gun" documents, there is indeed a serious set of problems. A "smoking gun" document is one that is highly damaging. The prototype is a confidential internal corporate or government document revealing culpable knowledge on the part of responsible officials. The problems associated with smoking gun documents are salient in the United States largely because of the very broad pretrial discovery procedure in American litigation. Under the American discovery procedure, parties are required, upon demand from an opponent, to produce all documents that might contain relevant evidence, including circumstantial evidence. In practice, the advocates are responsible for carrying out the parties' obligation to produce documents, including documents that can be very damaging to the client's position. Substantially similar but somewhat narrower requirements are imposed in Australia and Canada. As a result, the advocate for a party that is the target of a document discovery demand can be under a difficult, often excruciating conflict of inclination. On the one hand, the advocate owes a clear duty of cooperation with the court and with the opposing party to comply, fully and faithfully, with a sweeping document discovery demand. On the other hand, the advocate has an obligation to the client to produce nothing that is outside the terms of the demand. Moreover, clients believe that the advocate has a duty to protect them against "self incrimination" —that is, responding to damaging discovery demands. Many American lawyers have commented on the technically difficult and ethically painful situation that results. And some American lawyers succumb to the temptation to cheat.[5]

In most civil law systems the corresponding obligation of an advocate is much more limited. It is called the "duty of exhibition." The rule is invoked through an order of the court (as in France), or through application for a court order (as in other civil law systems), that an opposing party or a third party produce—"exhibit"—a specified document. The rule has different scope in various civil law systems and varying sanctions and standards of compliance. For example, the sanction in France is severe, but in Italian procedure there is no sanction. In any event, in all civil law systems the right to require "exhibition" of a document is very narrow. The document must be specifically identified and must be directly relevant, and even then the court has a measure of discretion whether to order its disclosure. The pressures on the civil law advocate are correspondingly much less severe than in the American procedure.

Generally speaking, in common law systems other than the United States, the obligation of an advocate to produce documents in discovery approximates that in the civil law systems. The duty extends only to specifically identified documents that are directly relevant to the controversy. As a practical matter, an opposing party ordinarily does not know of the existence of a smoking gun document, and hence could not identify it to compel disclosure. Hence in common law systems outside the United States, as in the civil law systems, the advocate is unlikely to confront the problem of producing documentary evidence that is highly damaging to his client.

The disclosure of smoking gun documents, we believe, will not long be a peculiarly American problem. The principle of legal equality implies equal access to information, particularly access for a grievant to information controlled by a bureaucracy. At the beginning of the twenty-first century there were many episodes of such access, for example: the disclosure of crimes under apartheid in South Africa and the "disappearances" under the Argentine military dictatorship; the scandals over contaminated blood in France and mercury poisoning in Japan; the complicity of German and Swiss financial institutions with the Nazi regime; the "Stasi" files of the former East German Republic. We believe these events will generate broader and more readily enforceable standards of "freedom of information." At the same time, we expect bureaucracies, public and private, to exercise increasingly diligent internal discipline against creating smoking gun documents. There is no duty to produce documents that, on the basis of legal advice, were never created.

Similar problems arise from disclosure responsibilities in transaction law practice. For example, corporations whose stock is traded on the stock exchanges must make accurate financial reports to the government and, in some countries, to their stockholders. The accuracy of such a report can involve a legal judgment by a lawyer. There are similar requirements for disclosure in tax law, environmental regulation, employment law, and endless other regulatory requirements. In the first instance, the issues involved are for resolution by corporate managers and employees. But legal questions arise requiring legal advice about compliance, which in turn present questions of ethics for the lawyers involved.

These ethical problems have not been conspicuous in legal systems outside the United States, but we expect they will emerge in the future. Governments are increasingly relying on reporting requirements as mechanisms of regulatory enforcement. Regulatory enforcement emanates from ever-increasing government sources, including international ones. Popular government must meet rising expectations about compliance with regulation. These political forces are expressed in intensified regulatory requirements. For the present, however, there has not been much criticism of lawyers in other legal systems. We suggest the following explanations.

First, most other regimes do not have as many reporting requirements. They rely instead on direct public administrative scrutiny of business activity. In many systems, however, actual regulation is exiguous. Second, in other regimes lawyers normally are not involved in the reporting process and become involved only if a formal legal dispute arises. Instead, corporate officials—many of whom have had basic legal education—take direct responsibility in dealings with the government. Third, particularly in the European tradition, ethical and social criticism of capitalism—of businesses as such and those in their service, including lawyers—has become passé. The typical attitude, at least in many academic circles, is, "Of course corporations cheat and are helped in doing so by their professional advisers (accountants, lawyers, etc.)." The European tradition of social criticism has thus been Marxian, whereas the counterpart American tradition can be called "civic" or "moralist." In our opinion, however, neither the European nor the American critical tradition addresses the complex facts, the bureaucratic intricacies, and the contradictory social values arrayed along the boundaries of law in modern regimes.

Rules and Roles

The web of rules and traditional norms that govern a social role largely defines the identity of people who perform the role. The web governing lawyers includes law, ethical codes, recognized standards and conventions of practice, and everyday "nonlegal" ethical norms as adapted to the role of lawyers in a specific society. Admonitory and aspirational norms are influential, for they project an idealization of the lawyer's role and a model of professional conduct. It may be regretted that lawyers do not give more time to legal aid, for example, but saying that they should do so is some kind of an inspiration. The ideal of candor to the court is an important ideal even if it is not fulfilled.

The admonitory norms also are semantically linked to ones that are legally obligatory. An example is the phrase "honesty and integrity" in the Italian code.[6] That phrase also implies its opposite—conduct that is *dis*honest—and therefore connotes the law against fraud and theft. In a skeptical world it is worth remembering that ethical admonitions and aspirations still count, even though lawyers everywhere know that compliance is incomplete.

Akin to ethical codes are pronouncements at professional meetings and similar public utterances. It will be said, for example, that the lawyer's obligation of secrecy is "sacred," that the lawyer's dedication to client interest is "unwavering," that a lawyer's character is one of "complete integrity," and that the quality of justice is "equal." Lawyers are strongly given to such pronouncements, inasmuch as making pronouncements is a skill in the practice of law. These pronouncements are part of the profession's vocabulary (anthropologists perhaps would use the term "tribal rites"), reinforcing professional virtue in a vocation that is subject to intense pressures to go in other directions.

Another layer of ethical norm consists of what may be called "workplace rules" or "shop norms." These are practices recognized in and about a court, a bureau, or a law firm. In some courts, for example, all important documents are to be presented to the chief clerk and not to a subordinate clerk (a document not so presented may become "lost"); in some agencies, officials at a certain level are to be addressed as "your honor" even though they are not quite judges. Among members of a local bar the senior active practitioner has certain prerogatives. In some law offices all finished documents pass through a senior clerk before being sent outside. Learning the local norms in a court, bureau, and law office is an important part of a young lawyer's experience.

Beyond these shared norms, each individual has a personal set of ethical values, such as candor, diplomacy, courage, and good citizenship. An individual seeks so far as possible to give effect to his own privately held set of ethical values, and must take account of the corresponding values of others.

Human Rights and Business Interests

Law and lawyers in the modern period have responsibilities to ordinary citizens. In modern conversation, "justice" signifies freedom of conscience, protection of privacy, fair trial, and shelter from exploitation by employers and landlords. Yet most lawyers' services in the modern era, and certainly most legal services provided through private practice, are devoted to the affairs of business and wealthy individuals, including employers and landlords. There is thus a discrepancy between the rhetoric of justice as generally understood and the activity of law practice as generally conducted.

One aspect of this discrepancy is the question of legal aid, discussed in Chapter 8. Of greater importance to ordinary citizens are rights in employment, housing, health care, and education, and the right to fair treatment generally. In modern political systems, protection of these rights is primarily the responsibility of the state bureaucracies, and most ordinary people do not depend on enforcement through legal assistance, but on the responsible behavior of government officials (particularly the police), employers, landlords, the schools, and others. Lawyers for government and business, in the background, can influence how those individuals and organizations fulfill their responsibilities.

Political discourse in constitutional regimes proceeds on the silent assumption that business interests can obtain whatever assistance may be advantageous, including legal assistance. That assumption is usually correct except for business conducted by small proprietorships. But the result is that there is little discussion, except from social critics, of the political and constitutional significance of the fact that lawyers work primarily for business and business interests. In some critical circles, it is stated that legal representation of business interests is borderline antisocial, or even morally corrupt.

Since the "desocialization" in Russia and Eastern Europe, there has perhaps been a reluctant realization that private business enterprise is the most effective mechanism for the production of goods and services needed or wanted by ordinary citizens: housing, transportation, communication, leisure services such as entertainment, and at least some aspects of education and health services. Capitalist enterprise is therefore recognized as being necessary to the welfare of ordinary citizens, notwithstanding that it involves undemocratic allocations of authority and undemocratic allocations of earnings and profits.

Perhaps the central issue in modern politics is the accommodation of democratic politics with capitalist economics. In the parliamentary systems in the Western tradition, that issue is addressed at the policy level primarily through political parties representing the left and the right, and implemented through the administrative offices of the state. In the United States, to a much greater extent the issue is also addressed in legal controversies, hence in the professional work of lawyers. We think these two forces will converge over time. The administrative state has become a stabilized part of the government apparatus in the United States, as it is elsewhere, while in other systems issues of social justice are more often being formulated as legal issues, as Tocqueville predicted. The legal profession will be an instrument for giving voice to issues of social justice, even though most lawyers will continue to be engaged primarily in the service of capitalism.

These are all strands in the web of rules and norms governing of the modern lawyer's professional role. As summarized in the Preamble to the CCBE Code of Conduct:

> A lawyer must serve the interests of justice as well as those whose rights and liberties he is trusted to assert and defend and it is his duty not only to plead his client's cause [to act as advocate] but to be his adviser [to give the client confidential advice].
>
> A lawyer's function therefore lays on him a variety of legal and moral obligations (sometimes appearing to be in conflict with each other) towards:
>
>> the client;

the courts and other authorities . . . ;
the legal profession in general and each fellow member in particular.

In our opinion, the obligations that the CCBE Preamble describes as "sometimes appearing to be in conflict with each other" are in fact often in conflict with each other. There often is no simple answer as to how a lawyer should proceed, any more than there is a simple answer to many ethical dilemmas in ordinary life. One connotation of professional independence is that a lawyer should not be dominated by a single norm or interest, whether duty to the courts or the interests of a client or by his own interests in earning adequate returns from practice. All of those interests are relevant, and none of them is invariably superior to all of the others. A lawyer too deferential to the interest of the courts may fail in asserting his client's interest with adequate zeal or fervor. A lawyer not attentive to charging fees and getting properly paid—and many lawyers are not—may fail in fulfilling responsibilities to associates in the lawyer's office and to the lawyer's family. Another connotation of professional independence refers to the position of lawyers in the larger community. The sense here is that the lawyer should be politically independent, not subservient to the interests of the state although respectful of the law that is the state's creation and instrument. In this vision of the profession, lawyers individually and the bar as a profession occupy a position of neutrality regarding the interests of the state, something like the "loyal opposition" in politics. Such a position is impossible in a lawless regime and very difficult in authoritarian regimes. Indeed, a fair index of whether a regime *is* authoritarian is the degree of autonomy exhibited by members of its legal profession.

Yet most lawyers are largely occupied with representing the dominant elements of capitalist regimes, government and business. The representation of business corporations, and the corollary that professional loyalty and client confidentiality extend to business corporations, has been the underlying issue in the discourse on legal ethics for perhaps a century. It is accepted that defendants in criminal cases should have the right of confidentiality, even though this results in the acquittal of some defendants who are actually guilty. It is acceptable, or at least endurable, that legal assistance be provided to individual property owners and business entrepreneurs. However, when the client is a large corporate entity, the typical attitude is highly critical.

Law practice on behalf of corporate entities consists mostly of making and arguing technical distinctions, quite the opposite of invoking the "spirit of the law." From a lawyer's perspective, the spirit of the law is usually vacuous. Modern legal regulations express not a clear moral spirit but finely wrought compromises among competing social values and conflicting political interests. A vehicle speed limit of seventy kilometers per hour, for example, reflects a balance between ensuring safety on the highway and facilitating rapid travel. A regulation of effluent at 10 PPM (parts per million) means 10, not 1 or .1. The taxes on "income" are based on elaborate distinctions between revenue and gain. In the real world there is no such thing as perfect safety or perfect purity, or a perfectly fair tax system. Legal regulations incorporate the very conflicting ethical considerations at issue in matters of social policy. To borrow the title of a book by a judge and a professor, all of law involves "tragic choices."[7] According to the ethical precepts shared in the community at large, the practice of law is merely technical, and it is ethically suspect because it pretends engagement with broad issues of justice. Morally most challenging is the shroud of secrecy concerning a client's relationship with the law. Secrecy is for the protection of clients, but it also allows lawyers to give advice based on what they know about law and justice.

What lawyers know about law and justice is that legal systems are not wholly reliable, and very often they are worse than that—incompetent, insensitive, sometimes corrupt. Lawyers know that law often is unable to ascertain the truth and that the system sometimes may not even try to do so. Learned Hand, a great American judge, observed almost a century ago: "[A]s a litigant I should dread a lawsuit beyond almost anything else short of sickness and death."[8] A good lawyer as advocate can sustain a client through the ordeal of a lawsuit. A good lawyer as counselor often can save the client from such an ordeal.

REFERENCE MATTER

Notes

REFERENCES TO ETHICAL CODES

In this work we quote from or make reference to codes of professional ethics of various countries. Our most frequent references are to the Code of Conduct for Lawyers in the European Community, the Canadian Bar Association Code of Professional Conduct, the American Bar Association Model Rules of Professional Conduct, and the Italian *Codice Deontologico Forense*. The abbreviated citations we use in these references are as follows:

CCBE	Code of Conduct for Lawyers in the European Community
Canadian Code	Canadian Bar Association Code of Professional Conduct
ABA Rules	American Bar Association Model Rules of Professional Conduct
CDF	*Codice Deontologico Forense*

We also frequently refer to the American Law Institute *Restatement Third of the Law: The Law Governing Lawyers*. That work is referred to as *Restatement*.

INTRODUCTION

1. William J. Baumol, *The Free Market Innovation Machine* (Princeton, N.J.: Princeton University Press, 2002), p. 68.

2. We appreciate that there is a distinctive Islamic legal tradition, one that is integral to the Islamic religious tradition. However, we have found little academic or professional literature in English or Italian concerning the professional ethics of lawyers in that tradition. For a skeletal analysis, see "Comment, Bridging Ethical Borders: International Legal Ethics with an Islamic Perspective," 35 *Texas Int'l L. J.* 289 (2000). Inquiry with professional colleagues in Egypt indicated that there were no useful sources in English and few in Arabic. We hope that this situation changes in the future, as we assume it will. In the meantime, however, we can only assume that lawyers in Islamic countries are alert and sensitive to the norms of the regimes in

which they live and govern themselves accordingly. See generally Michael Cook, *Commanding Right and Forbidding Wrong in Islamic Thought* (Cambridge: Cambridge University Press, 2002).

3. See Austin Sarat and Thomas Kearns, "The Cultural Lives of Law," in Sarat and Kearns, *Law in the Domain of Culture* (Ann Arbor: University of Michigan Press, 1998), and sources cited there.

4. John H. Baker, *The Law's Two Bodies: Some Evidential Problems in English Legal History* (New York: Oxford University Press, 2001).

5. See generally Isaiah Berlin, *Karl Marx: His Life and Environment*, 4th ed. (Oxford: Oxford University Press, 1978); idem, *Vico and Herder: Two Studies in the History of Ideas* (New York: Viking, 1976).

6. A recent study of the Americans is Louis Menand, *The Metaphysical Club* (New York: Farrar, Straus & Giroux, 2001).

7. See, e.g., Ernest Gellner, *Nations and Nationalism* (Ithaca, N.Y.: Cornell University Press, 1983).

8. See, e.g., Berlin, supra note 5. In contrast, Alexis de Tocqueville, the other great political analyst of the nineteenth century, had identified religion and race as important factors in democracy. See Alexis de Tocqueville, *Democracy in America*, trans. and ed. Harvey C. Mansfield and Delba Winthrop (Chicago: University of Chicago Press, 2000), pp. 282, 302; Tocqueville, *The Old Regime and the Revolution*, ed. François Furet and Françoise Melonio, trans. Alan S. Kahan (Chicago: University of Chicago Press, 1988).

9. See, e.g., Friedrich A. Hayek, *The Fatal Conceit: The Errors of Socialism*, ed. W. W. Bartley III (Chicago: University of Chicago Press, 1988).

10. See Edward Rubin, "Getting beyond Democracy," 149 *U. Pa. L. Rev.* 711 (2001), and sources cited therein.

11. See Peter Schuck, *The Limits of Law* (Boulder, Colo.: Westview, 2000).

12. Donald Nicolson and Julian Webb, *Professional Legal Ethics: Critical Interrogations* (Oxford: Oxford University Press, 1999), chap. 2 and passim.

13. Martin Redish, "The Adversary System, Democratic Theory and the Constitutional Role of Self-Interest," 51 *DePaul L. Rev.* 359, 367 (2001).

14. For a valuable study of the development of legal representation in criminal prosecution in England, see John Langbein, *The Origins of Adversary Criminal Trial* (Oxford: Oxford University Press, 2003).

15. See also Richard Posner, "The Problematics of Moral and Legal Theory," 111 *Harv. L. Rev.* 1637 (1998).

16. See Immanuel Kant, *The Metaphysics of Morals*, trans. and ed. Mary Gregor (New York: Cambridge University Press, 1991).

17. A recent exposition of ethical philosophy in this vein is Ronald Dworkin, *Sov-*

ereign Virtue: The Theory and Practice of Equality (Cambridge, Mass.: Harvard University Press, 2000).

18. See Baldesar Castiglione, *The Book of the Courtier* (London: Penguin, 1967), p. 131: "What you must do is to obey your Lord in everything that redounds to his profit and honour, but not as regards things that bring him loss and shame. Therefore, if he were to order you to commit some treacherous deed not only are you not obliged to do it but you are obliged not to do it."
See generally Peter Burke, The *Italian Renaissance: Culture and Society in Italy*, 2d ed. (Princeton, N.J.: Princeton University Press, 1986), esp. chap. 8.

19. José Ortega y Gasset, *The Revolt of the Masses* (New York: Norton, 1932), p. 76.

20. "We hold these truths to be self-evident: that all men are . . . ," Declaration of Independence, para. 1.

21. Sir Edward Coke, "Prohibitions Del Roy," *Coke Reports* 63, 65 (pt. 12, 4th ed. 1738), 77 Eng. Rep. 1342, 1343.

CHAPTER 1

1. Perhaps the best example is an American treatise by a distinguished academic lawyer that is infused with professional mythology: Roscoe Pound, *The Lawyer from Antiquity to Modern Times: With Particular Reference to the Development of Bar Associations in the United States* (St. Paul, Minn.: West, 1953).

2. See, e.g., Robert J. Bonner, *Lawyers and Litigants in Ancient Athens: The Genesis of the Legal Profession* (Chicago: University of Chicago Press, 1927), p. 104 and passim; Douglas M. MacDowell, *The Law in Classical Athens* (Ithaca, N.Y.: Cornell University Press, 1978).

3. See Stephen Usher, *Greek Oratory: Tradition and Originality* (New York: Oxford University Press, 1999).

4. Cynthia Baraban, "Inspiring Global Professionalism: Challenges and Opportunities for American Lawyers in China," 73 *Indiana L. J.* 1247, 1253 (1998).

5. See Derk Bodde and Clarence Morris, eds., *Law in Imperial China* (Cambridge, Mass.: Harvard University Press, 1967), passim; Jingshan Wang, "The Role of the Law in Contemporary China: Theory and Practice" (Ph.D. thesis, Cornell University, 1988).

6. See Alison Conner, "Lawyers and the Legal Profession During the Republican Period," in Kathryn Bernhardt and Phillip C. C. Huang, eds., *Civil Law in Qing and Republican China* (Stanford, Calif.: Stanford University Press, 1994).

7. See Peter Wesley-Smith, *An Introduction to the Hong Kong Legal System*, 3d ed. (New York: Oxford University Press, 1998), passim.

8. Stanley Lubman, *Bird in a Cage: Legal Reform in China after Mao* (Stanford,

Calif.: Stanford University Press, 1999), p. 29. See also William Alford, "Tasselled Loafers for Barefoot Lawyers: Transformation and Tension in the World of Chinese Legal Workers," in Stanley Lubman, ed., *China's Legal Reforms* (Oxford: Oxford University Press, 1996), p. 22.

9. See Standing Committee of the Eighth National People's Congress, Order of the People's Republic of China no. 67 (May 15, 1996), Law of the People's Republic of China on Lawyers (hereinafter: PRC, Law on Lawyers). There has also been adopted a set of Regulations on Lawyers' Professional Ethics and Business Practices (translation by Thea Rozman, on file with authors). See also Standing Committee of the Eighth National People's Congress, Order of the People's Republic of China no. 64 (March 17, 1996), Amended PRC Criminal Procedure Law.

10. Gordon B. Smith, *Reforming the Russian Legal System* (New York: Cambridge University Press, 1996), pp. 3–5.

11. William E. Butler, *Russian Law* (New York: Oxford University Press, 1999), p. 27.

12. See Smith, supra note 10, p. 15; W. E. Butler, *Soviet Law*, 2d ed. (London: Butterworths, 1988), pp. 22–25.

13. See Smith, supra note 10, p. 5.

14. See Michael Cook, *Commanding Right and Forbidding Wrong in Islamic Thought* (Cambridge: Cambridge University Press, 2002).

15. A classic exposition is Arthur Engelmann, *A History of Continental Civil Procedure*, trans. Robert Millar (Boston: Little, Brown, 1927), Book III, chap. 1, topic 3.

16. Ibid., pp. 341–42.

17. Hans Julius Wolff, *Roman Law: An Historical Introduction* (Norman: University of Oklahoma Press, 1951), pp. 96–97.

18. See Vincenzo Arangio-Ruiz, *Storia del diritto romano* (Naples: E. Jovene, 1977), p. 149 et seq.

19. See Mario Bretone, *Storia del diritto romano*, 4th ed. (Rome: Laterza, 1991), p. 155; Jean-Michel R. David, *Le patronat judiciaire au dernier siècle de la République Romaine* (Rome: Ecole Française de Rome, 1992), p. 367.

20. See Emilio Betti, *Diritto romano*, vol. 1, p. 458 (1935); Emilio Betti, "La creazione del diritto nella iurisdictio del pretore romano," in *Studi in onore di G. Chiovenda* (Padua, 1927), p. 100; Fritz Schultz, *History of Roman Legal Science* (Oxford: Clarendon Press, 1946), pp. 19, 53, 117, 132, 268; Leopold Wenger, *Istituzioni di procedura civile romana* (Italian trans.) (Milan: Giuffrè, 1938), p. 150; Max Kaser, *Das römische Zivilprozessrecht*, 2d ed. (Munich: C. H. Beck, 1976), p. 200; and see esp. Giovanni Pugliese, *Il processo civile romano II—Il processo formulare* I (Milan: Giuffrè, 1963), p. 100; Gener Murga, *Derecho romano classico II: El processo*, pp. 159, 287 (Zaragoza, Spain: University of Zaragoza, 1980).

21. For such as is known about the function of lawyers in the Roman Empire, see Tony Honore, *Emperors and Lawyers* (London: Duckworth, 1981).

22. See John Anthony Crook, *Legal Advocacy in the Roman World* (Ithaca, N.Y.: Cornell University Press, 1995), pp. 13, 16; David, supra note 19, p. 49.

23. See David, supra note 19, pp. 593, 642.

24. John 18:31: "Take him yourselves and judge him by your own law" (Revised Standard Bible).

25. Antonio Pertile, *Storia del diritto italiano—dalla caduta dell'Impero Romano alla codificazione*, vol. 6, part 1 (Turin: Unione Tipografico Editrice, 1900), p. 270; Giuseppe Salvioli, *Storia del diritto italiano* (Turin: Unione Tipografico Editrice, 1930), p. 728.

26. See, e.g., Stephen Burbank, "The Architecture of Judicial Independence," 72 *S. Calif. L. Rev.* 315 (1999).

27. The classic formulation is by Max Weber, discussing the distinctive features of "bureaucratic" government. See "The Types of Legitimate Domination," in Max Weber, *Economy and Society*, vol. 1, ed. Guenther Roth and Claus Wittich (Berkeley: University of California Press, 1978), p. 212. (Essay originally published in 1922.)

28. See Grant Gilmore and Charles L. Black Jr., *The Law of Admiralty*, 2d ed. (Mineola, N.Y.: Foundation Press, 1975); Joseph W. Bishop Jr., *Justice under Fire* (New York: Charterhouse, 1974) (military law).

29. Regarding U.S. rules on foreign legal consultants, see Carol A. Needham, "The Licensing of Foreign Legal Consultants in the United States," 21 *Fordham Int'l L. J.* 1126 (1998). For France's rules governing the practice of foreign lawyers, see Roger J. Goebel, "Professional Qualification and Educational Requirements for Law Practice in a Foreign Country: Bridging the Cultural Gap," 63 *Tulane L. Rev. 443*, 464 (1989).

30. See Butler, supra note 11, pp. 123–28.

31. See Lennart Lindstrom and Carl Michael von Quitzown, "The Legal Profession in Sweden," in Allen Tyrrell and Zahd Yaqub, eds., *The Legal Profession in the New Europe*, 2d ed. (London: Cavendish, 1996).

32. See PRC, Law on Lawyers, arts. 5–14.

33. The ambiguity of the definition of "lawyer" corresponds to the ambiguity of the term "practice of law." The latter term is significant in regimes that confine "practice of law" to "lawyers." See Deborah Rhode, "Policing the Professional Monopoly: A Constitutional and Empirical Analysis of Unauthorized Practice Prohibitions," 34 *Stan. L. Rev.* 1 (1981).

34. See Arrigo Solmi, *Contributi alla storia del diritto comune* (Rome: Soc. Ed. del "Foro italiano," 1937), pp. 230, 235; Gaines Post, *Studies in Medieval Thought: Public Law and the State, 1100–1322* (Princeton, N.J.: Princeton University Press, 1964), pp.

18, 80; Heinrich Mitteis, *Le strutture giuridiche e politiche dell'età feudale* (Brescia: Morcelliana, 1962), p. 262.

35. See Giuseppe Salvioli, "Storia della procedura civile e criminale," in Del Giudice, *Storia del diritto italiano*, vols. III–II(Turin: Unione Tipografico Editrice 1930), p. 220.

36. Arrigo Solmi, *Contributi alla storia del diritto comune* (Rome: Soc. Ed. de "Foro italiano," 1937), pp. 235, 257, 287, 304; Giovanni Tamassia, "Bologna e le scuole imperiali di diritto," *Arch. Eiur. XL* (1888), pp. 267 et seq.; Heinrich Mitteis, *Le strutture giuridiche e politiche dell'età feudale* (Brescia: Morcelliana, 1962), p. 441; Manlio Bellomo, *Saggio sull'università dell'età del diritto comune* (Rome: Il Cigno Galileo Galilei, 1996), pp. 25, 52, 61, 132, 229; Giuseppe Ermini, "L'educazione del giurista nella tradizione del diritto comune," in *Atti del convegno di studi in onore di G. Ermini* (Perugia: Libreria Universitaria, 1980), p. 121; Danilo Seglioni, "'Practica,' 'Practicus, 'Practicare,' in Bartolo e in Baldo," in *L'educazione giuridica* (Perugia: Libreria Universitaria, 1979), pp. 40, 52; Gian Paolo Massetto, "Gli studi di diritto nella Lombardia del secolo XI," in *Lanfranco di Pavia e l'Europa del secolo XI* (Rome: Herder, 1993), passim.

37. Paul Brand, *The Origins of the English Legal Profession* (Oxford: Blackwell, 1992), p. 32.

38. See, e.g., the description of French civil procedure in the seventeenth century in Engelmann, supra note 15, Book IV, chap. 3, topic 3.

39. See, e.g., Deborah L. Rhode, *In the Interests of Justice: Reforming the Legal Profession* (New York: Oxford University Press, 2000), passim.

40. On the problem of estimating the chances of success in litigation, see, e.g., Fleming James, Geoffrey Hazard & John Leubsdorf, *Civil Procedure*, 4th ed. (Boston: Little, Brown, 1992), §6.4.

41. See also John Toulmin, "A Worldwide Common Code of Professional Ethics?" 15 *Fordham Int'l L. J.* 673 (1991–92); Detlev Vagts, "The International Legal Profession: A Need for More Governance?" 90 *Am. J. Int'l L.* 250 (1996); "Symposium: Ethics and the Multijurisdictional Practice of Law," 36 *So. Texas L. Rev.* 657 (1995).

42. *Marbury v. Madison*, 5 U.S. (1 Cranch) 137 (1803).

43. John H. Baker, *The Law's Two Bodies: Some Evidential Problems in English Legal History* (New York: Oxford University Press, 2001).

44. A small sample of maxims are sprinkled throughout C. L. Anand, *Professional Ethics of the Bar: Popularly Known as Legal Ethics*, 2d ed. (Allahabad, India: Law Book Company, 1987). See also Marc Galanter, infra note 46.

45. Baldesar Castiglione, *The Book of the Courtier* (London: Penguin, 1967).

46. Marc Galanter, "The Faces of Mistrust: The Image of Lawyers in Public Opinion and Political Discourse," 66 *U. Cincinnati L. Rev.* 805, 810 (1966).

47. James A. Brundage, *Medieval Canon Law* (London: Longman, 1995), pp. 137–38.

48. John Baker, "The English Legal Profession: 1450–1550," in Wilfred Prest, ed., *Lawyers in Early Modern Europe and America* (New York: Holmes and Meier, 1981), p. 17.

49. For the situation in continental Europe, see, e.g., Antonio Pertile, *Storia del diritto italiano dalla caduta dell'Impero Romano alla Codificazione*, vol. 6, part 1 (Turin: Unione Tipografico Editrice, 1900), pp. 270, 274; John P. Dawson, *The Oracles of the Law* (Ann Arbor: University of Michigan, 1968), pp. 125–27; Gino Gorla and Luigi Moccia, "A 'Revisiting' of the Comparison between 'Continental Law' and 'English Law' (16th–19th Century)," 2 *J. Legal History* 143, at 152 (1981). Concerning the English bar, see Brand, supra note 37, p. 117.

50. Leonard Berlanstein, "Lawyers in Pre-Revolutionary France," in Prest, supra note 48, p. 164.

51. For the outlook of the governing circles in general, see Norbert Elias, *La società di corte* (Bologna: Il Mulino, 1980), p. 198 (Italian translation of *Die höfische Gesellschaft*, 1975); Norbert Elias, *Civiltà: The Civilizing Process, II. Power and Civilization* (New York: Pantheon, 1981); Paul Benichou, *Morales du grand siècle* (Paris: Gallimard, 1988), p. 143. Concerning the legal profession, see Gallimard E. Amkiewicz, *Histoire des institutions 1750–1914* (Paris: Ancienne Librairie Thorin et Fils, 1992), pp. 61, 144; Jean Brissard, *Histoire du droit privé* (Paris: Ancienne Librairie Thorin et Fils, 1908), p. 534; Berlanstein, supra note 50; Bernard Sur, *Histoire des avocats en France des origines à nos jours* (Paris: Dalloz, 1998), pp. 22, 30.; Richard Kagan, "Lawyers and Litigation in Castile: 1500–1750," in Prest, supra note 48, p. 181.

52. See Eugene Huskey, *Russian Lawyers and the Soviet State: The Origins and Development of the Soviet Bar, 1917–1939* (Princeton, N.J.: Princeton University Press, 1986), pp. 15–20.

53. Berlanstein, supra note 50, pp. 165–66.

54. Kagan, supra note 51, p. 190.

55. See Pasquale Del Giudice, *Storia del diritto italiano*, vol. 2 (Milan: Univ. Hoepli, 1923), pp. 113, 122. Nineteenth-century American expressions reflecting similar concerns emphasized the importance of universal high ethical standards rather than differentiation according to status. See David Hoffman, *A Course of Legal Study* (Baltimore: Coale and Maxwell, 1817); George Sharswood, *Professional Ethics: Lectures on the Aims and Duties of the Profession of Law* (Philadelphia: 1854).

56. See Antonio Padoa-Schioppa, *Il diritto nella storia di Europa* (Padua: CEDAM, 1996), p. 168.

57. On the use of law French, see Sir William Holdsworth, *A History of English Law*, vol. 2, 4th ed. (London: Methuen, 1936), pp. 479–82.

58. See references in note 36 supra.

59. See John P. Heinz and Edward O. Laumann, *Chicago Lawyers: The Social Structure of the Bar*, rev. ed. (Evanston, Ill.: Northwestern University Press, 1994).

60. For England, see John Langbein, *The Origins of Adversary Criminal Trial* (Oxford: Oxford University Press, 2003); Theodore F. T. Plucknett, *A Concise History of the Common Law*, 5th ed. (Boston: Little, Brown, 1956), pp. 434–35. For canon law, see Brundage, supra note 47, pp. 147–49.

61. See Lubman, supra note 8, p. 164.

62. See Mirjan R. Damaska, *The Faces of Justice and State Authority: A Comparative Approach to the Legal Process* (New Haven, Conn.: Yale University Press, 1986).

63. See generally American Bar Association (ABA), *Standards for Criminal Justice: Prosecution Function and Defense Function*, 3d ed. (Washington, D.C.: ABA, 1993); ABA, *Canons of Professional and Judicial Ethics*, rev. ed. (Chicago: ABA, 1957), p. 3. The ABA Canons of Ethics, originally promulgated in 1908, stated in Canon 5: "The primary duty of a lawyer engaged in public prosecution is not to convict, but to see that justice is done." That this duty was envisioned as not extending very far, however, is implied in the sentence immediately following this pronouncement: "The suppression of facts or the secreting of witnesses capable of establishing the innocence of the accused is highly reprehensible."

64. See Fred Zacharias, "Structuring the Ethics of Prosecutorial Trial Practice: Can Prosecutors Do Justice?" 44 *Vand. L. Rev.* 45 (1991).

65. The same has been true in the People's Republic of China since 1996. See Lubman, supra note 8, p. 166; Ronald C. Brown, *Understanding Chinese Courts and Legal Process: Law with Chinese Characteristics* (The Hague: Kluwer, 1997), pp. 14, 375.

66. A classic statement is in *Nix v. Whiteside*, 475 U.S. 157, 166 (1986) ("counsel is precluded from assisting the client in presenting false evidence"). See ABA Rules, Rule 3.3(a)(4) ("A lawyer shall not knowingly offer evidence that the lawyer knows to be false.").

67. A strong and well-known statement of this viewpoint is Monroe H. Freedman, *Understanding Lawyers' Ethics* (New York: Matthew Bender, 1990).

68. See Kenneth Mann, *Defending White-Collar Crime: A Portrait of Attorneys at Work* (New Haven, Conn.: Yale University Press, 1985) (based on extensive empirical study).

69. ABA Rules, Rule 3.3(a)(4), after imposing the duty to avoid offering false testimony, provides that a lawyer, upon learning that perjured testimony is involved, "shall take reasonable remedial measures." Comment [11] to this rule states that the lawyer should advise the court and that "it is for the court then to determine what should be done."

70. See Piero Calamandrei, *Troppi avvocati!*, p. 34 and passim (Florence: 1921).

71. See Heinz and Laumann, supra note 59; Jerome E. Carlin, *Lawyers on Their Own: The Solo Practitioner in an Urban Setting*, rev. ed. (San Francisco: Austin & Winfield, 1994); Joel F. Handler, *The Lawyer and His Community: The Practicing Bar in a Middle-Sized City* (Madison: University of Wisconsin Press, 1967) (field studies of American law practice in the twentieth century, demonstrating similarities to the division of practice described in the text).

72. See Lawrence M. Friedman, *A History of American Law*, 2d ed. (New York: Simon & Schuster, 1985), pp. 311, 640.

73. See Solicitors Act of 1843: 6 and 7 Victoria c. 73 (conditions for admission as attorney or solicitor), discussed in Sir Richard Holdsworth, *A History of English Law*, vol. 15 (London: Methuen, 1965), p. 224. For a brief history of the division of the English profession between barristers and solicitors, see Judith Maute, "Alice's Adventures in Wonderland," 71 *Fordham L. Rev.* 1357 (2003), and sources cited there.

74. Richard L. Abel, *The Legal Profession in England and Wales* (Oxford: Blackwell, 1988), pp. 199–200. See also A. H. Manchester, *A Modern Legal History of England and Wales, 1750–1950* (London: Butterworths, 1980), pp. 53, 57.

75. See Gherardo Ortalli, *Scuole e maestri tra medioevo e rinascimento—Il caso veneziano*, passim (Bologna: Mulino, 1996).

76. The courthouse served as a center for the development and sharing of this professional knowledge. See Gorla and Moccia, supra note 49, p. 148; Dawson, supra note 49, p. 222.

77. John Leubsdorf, *Man in His Original Dignity: Legal Ethics in France* (Burlington, Vt.: Ashgate, 2000), p. 29.

78. Stan Ross, *Ethics in Law: Lawyers' Responsibility and Accountability in Australia*, 2d ed. (Sydney: Butterworths, 1998), pp. 464–65.

79. See, e.g., Pier Luigi Rovito, *Respublica dei Togati—Giuristi e Società nella Napoli del Seicento* (Naples: Jovene, 1982), p. 152; Richard Scott Eckert, *The Gentlemen of the Profession: The Emergence of Lawyers in Massachusetts, 1630–1810* (New York: Garland, 1991), pp. 147–48; Hoyt P. Canady, *Gentlemen of the Bar: Lawyers in Colonial South Carolina* (New York: Garland, 1987), pp. 282–83; Philip Aylett, "A Profession in the Marketplace: The Distribution of Attorneys in England and Wales, 1730–1800," 5 *Law and History Rev.* 1 (1987); Geoffrey Holmes, *Augustan England: Professions, State and Society, 1680–1730* (London: George Allen & Unwin, 1982), p. 157.

80. See David Lemmings, "Blackstone and Law Reform by Education: Preparation for the Bar and Lawyerly Culture in Eighteenth-Century England," 16 *Law and History Rev.* 211 (1998), pp. 217–18 and sources cited therein.

81. See David A. Bell, *Lawyers and Citizens: The Making of a Political Elite in Old Regime France* (New York: Oxford University Press, 1994), pp. 26–38; Andrew Abbott, "Status and Status Strain in the Professions," 86 *Am. J. Sociology* 819 (1981);

Alexis de Tocqueville, *Democracy in America*, ed. and trans. Harvey C. Mansfield and Delba Winthrop (Chicago: University of Chicago Press, 2000), vol. 1, part 2, chap. 8 (the legal profession as the "American aristocracy"); Pierre Bourdieu, "La force du droit: Eléments pour une sociologie du champ juridique," in LXIV *Actes de la recherche en sciences sociales* 3 (Paris: Maison de la science de l'homme, 1986), p. 355.

82. See, e.g., Jerold S. Auerbach, *Unequal Justice: Lawyers and Social Change in Modern America* (New York: Oxford University Press, 1976); Magali Sarfatti Larson, *The Rise of Professionalism: A Sociological Analysis* (Berkeley: University of California Press, 1977); Richard L. Abel, *American Lawyers* (New York: Oxford University Press, 1989).

83. See Giovanni Tarello, *Storia della cultura giuridica moderna—Assolutismo e codificazione del diritto* (Bologna: Il Mulino, 1976), p. 33.

84. See Friedman, supra note 72, pp. 315–18.

85. Albert Kenneth Roland Kiralfy, *The English Legal System*, 8th ed. (London: Sweet & Maxwell, 1990), p. 288; Gerald L. Gall, *The Canadian Legal System*, 4th ed. (Scarborough, Ont.: Carswell, 1995), p. 59; Donald James Gifford and Kenneth H. Gifford, *Our Legal System*, 2d. ed. (Sydney: The Law Book Co., 1983), p. 64.

86. See "Higher Courts Qualification Regulations, 1992" (published in the Law Society's *Professional Standards Bulletin*, no. 10) (March 1994).

87. See Roger Perrot, *Institutions judiciaires*, 5th ed., pp. 385, 403 (Paris: Montchrestien, 1993); Emmanuel Blanc, *La nouvelle profession d'avocat* (Paris: Librairie du Journal des Notaires et des Avocats, 1973); Christophe Charle, "Pour une histoire sociale des professions juridiques à l'époque contemporaine: Note pour une recherche," in *Actes de la recherche en sciences sociales* 117 (Paris: Maison de la science de l'homme, 1986), p. 76 et passim.

88. See Hans-Jürgen Ahrens, *Anwaltsrecht für Anfänger* (Munich: C. H. Beck, 1996); Hartung Holl, *Anwältliche Berufsordnung* (Munich: C. H. Beck, 1997).

89. Compare, e.g., ABA Task Force on Law Schools and the Profession, *Legal Education and Professional Development—An Educational Continuum* (a.k.a. The MacCrate Report) (Chicago: ABA, 1992); and Harry Edwards, "The Growing Disjunction between Legal Education and the Legal Profession," 91 *Mich. L. Rev.* 34 (1992); with Richard Posner, "The Deprofessionalization of Legal Teaching and Scholarship," 91 *Mich. L. Rev.* 1921 (1993).

90. Max Weber, "Three Types of Legitimate Domination," in Richard Swedberg, ed., *Max Weber: Essays in Economic Sociology* (Princeton, N.J.: Princeton University Press, 1999), p. 99.

91. Weber, supra note 90, p. 100.

92. Tocqueville, supra note 81, p. 257.

93. Kagan, supra note 51, p. 23 (systematic comparison of American legal system with legal systems in other constitutional democracies).

94. See Geoffrey C. Hazard and Michael Taruffo, *American Civil Procedure: An Introduction* (New Haven, Conn.: Yale University Press, 1993).

95. Hannes Siegrist, "Gli avvocati e la borghesia: Germania, Svizzera e Italia nel XIX secolo," in Jürgen Kocka, ed., *Borghesie europee dell'ottocento* (Venice: Marsilio 1989), p. 357; idem, "Profilo degli avvocati italiani dal 1870 al 1930," in *Polis* 7 (1994), 223; Maria M. Malatesta, ed., *Society and the Professions in Italy 1984–1914* (Cambridge: Cambridge University Press, 1995), passim; Geoffrey Hazard, "Japan's Legal Profession Slowly Accepts Change," *National Law Journal* (June 15, 1998), p. A25; Michele Taruffo, *La giustizia civile in Italia dal '700 a oggi* (Bologna: Il Mulino, 1980), p. 107; in general, for a thoughtful consideration of these aspects, see Marco Santoro, "La trasformazione del campo giuridico: Avvocati, procuratori e notai dall'Unità alla Repubblica," in *Storia d'Italia—Annali 10—I professionisti* (Turin: G. Einardi, 1996), p. 81.

96. See, e.g., Christian Dadomo and Susan Farran, *The French Legal System* (London: Sweet & Maxwell, 1993), chap. 3.

97. See §46 of German BRAO (the German Federal Attorneys Act).

98. Case 155/79, *AM&S Europe v. Commission of the European Communities*, E.C.R. 1575 (1982) (see subheading 21 of opinion on LEXIS). In sharp contrast, in the United States a corporate law department lawyer is treated as equivalent to a lawyer in independent practice. See *Upjohn Co. v. United States*, 449 U.S. 383 (1981).

99. See PRC Law on Lawyers, Art. 7.

100. See Howard Abadinsky, *Law and Justice: An Introduction to the American Legal System*, 4th ed. (Chicago: Nelson-Hall, 1998), pp. 117–28; Robert T. Swaine, *The Cravath Firm and Its Predecessors: 1819–1948*, vols. 1–3 (New York: Cravath, 1946–48); Carl M. Brauer, *Ropes & Gray: 1865–1990* (Boston: Ropes & Gray, 1991).

101. Swaine, supra note 100, vol. 2. For an illuminating analysis of technique in law practice in New York in the Nineteenth Century, see Bruce Kimball and Blake Brown, "'The Highest Ability in the Nation': Langdell on Wall Street 1855–1870," 29 *Law & Social Inquiry* 39 (2004).

102. Associates have clearly prospered financially under the big-firm model. It would seem to follow that the changing nature of the firm has been similarly remunerative for partners (who, after all, make the decision to keep growing). But some have questioned this assumption. See Marc Galanter and Thomas Palay, *Tournament of Lawyers: The Transformation of the Big Law Firm* (Chicago: University of Chicago Press, 1991).

103. Ibid., p. 5.

104. See, e.g., *R. (Van Hoogstraten) v. Governor of Belmarsh Prison* (2003), 1 WLR 263.

105. The larger and internally specialized law firm has begun to appear in the

People's Republic of China. See Yujie Gu, "Note, Entering the Chinese Legal Market: A Guide for American Lawyers Interested in Practicing Law in China," 48 *Drake L. Rev.* 173 (1999).

106. Luke 11:46: "Woe to you lawyers also! For you load men with burdens hard to bear, and you yourselves do not touch the burdens with one of your fingers" (Revised Standard Bible).

107. See Alford, supra note 8, pp. 22, 26.

108. See James A. Brundage, "The Calumny Oath and Ethical Ideals of Canonical Advocates," in Peter Landau and Joers Mueller, eds., *Proceedings of the Ninth International Congress of Medieval Canon Law*, Monumenta Iuris Canonici, vol. 10 (Vatican City: Biblioteca Apostolica Vaticana, 1997). We are indebted to Jonathan Rose of Arizona State University for this reference.

109. Jonathan Rose, "The Legal Profession in Medieval England: A History of Regulation," 48 *Syracuse L. Rev.* 1 (1998), pp. 49–63; See also James A. Brundage, "The Medieval Advocate's Profession," 6 *Law and History Rev.* 439 (1988), p. 450.

110. See Del Giudice, supra note 55, pp. 113, 122; and Brundage, supra note 109, pp. 446–54.

CHAPTER 2

1. James A. Brundage, *Medieval Canon Law* (London: Longman, 1995), pp. 129–34.

2. See Marcel Storme, ed., *Approximation of Judiciary Law in the European Union, Final Report* (Dordrecht: Kluwer, 1994); American Law Institute-Unidroit, "Principles and Rules of Transnational Civil Procedure" (Discussion Draft no. 4, 2003).

3. ABA Rules, Preamble, para. [2].

4. John Langbein, "The German Advantage in Civil Procedure," 52 *U. Chi. L. Rev.* 823 (1985).

5. Robert Gordon, "The Ethical Worlds of Large-Firm Litigators: Preliminary Observations," 67 *Fordham L. Rev.* 709, 733 (1998).

6. John Leubsdorf, *Man in His Original Dignity: Legal Ethics in France* (Burlington, Vt.: Ashgate, 2000), p. 101.

7. Thomas Bingham, "Judicial Ethics," in Ross Cranston, ed., *Legal Ethics and Professional Responsibility* (Oxford: Clarendon, 1995), p. 51.

8. *Brown v. Allen*, 344 U.S. 443, 540 (1953) (Justice Jackson concurring).

9. See Dietrich Rueschemeyer, "State, Capitalism, and the Organization of Legal Counsel: Examining an Extreme Case—the Prussian Bar, 1700–1914," in Terence C. Halliday and Lucien Karpik, eds., *Lawyers and the Rise of Western Political Liberalism:*

Europe and North America from the Eighteenth to Twentieth Centuries (New York: Oxford University Press, 1997), p. 220; see also Foster, supra note 5, p. 21.

10. See *The Bremen v. Zapata Off-Shore Oil Co.*, 407 U.S. 1 (1972) (contract between German company and American company requiring adjudication of disputes in London).

11. A now classic analysis is by former judge Marvin E. Frankel in his book *Partisan Justice* (New York: Hill & Wang, 1980).

12. See Michele Taruffo, *La prova del fatti giuridici—Nozioni generali* (Milan: Giuffrè, 1992), pp. 8, 35 et seq.

13. See Richard Posner, *Law and Legal Theory in England and America* (Oxford: Clarendon, 1996), pp. 27–29. Judge Posner compiled these statistics from various sources, including: the Court Service of the Lord Chancellor's Department; *World Factbook*; England's 1995 *Annual Abstract of Statistics*; and Marc Galanter, "News from Nowhere: The Debased Debate on Civil Justice," 71 *Denver U. L. Rev.* 77 (1993), pp. 104–7.

14. William E. Butler, *Russian Law* (New York: Oxford University Press, 1999), pp. 116, 155.

15. Posner, supra note 13, p. 29.

16. The chief justice of China has recognized that inadequate funding has had "serious impact on the normal process of judicial work . . ." BBC Worldwide Monitoring, "China's Chief Justice Delivers Supreme Court Work Report" (March 22, 2001).

17. See, e.g., American Bar Association (ABA), *Model Code of Judicial Conduct* (Chicago: ABA, 2002); Council of Europe Committee of Ministers, *Independence, Efficiency, and Role of Judges* (Strasbourg: Council of Europe, 1995).

18. Stephen Burbank and Barry Friedman, eds., *Judicial Independence at the Crossroads: An Interdisciplinary Approach* (Thousand Oaks, Calif.: Sage, 2002).

19. In the People's Republic of China, the financial privation of the judicial system has led some courts to participate in profit-making ventures with local governments or business enterprises. See William Alford, "Tasselled Loafers for Barefoot Lawyers: Transformation and Tension in the World of Chinese Legal Workers," in Stanley Lubman, ed., *China's Legal Reforms* (Oxford: Oxford University Press, 1996).

20. For U.S. procedure, see 28 U.S.C. §144.

21. The American rules are particularly elaborate. See ABA, supra note 17, Canon 3(E); 28 U.S.C. §455.

22. See Shimon Shetreet, *Justice in Israel: A Study of the Israeli Judiciary* (Dordrecht: M. Nijhoff, 1994).

23. See *Liljeberg v. Health Services Acquisition Corp.*, 486 U.S. 847 (1988) (setting

aside a judgment in a case where the judge was indirectly affiliated with one of the parties).

24. See generally, Roberto O. Berizonce, "Recientes tendencias en la posición del juez," Int'l Ass'n of Procedural Law, *Procedural Law on the Threshold of a New Millennium* (Baden Baden: Nomos, 1999), and sources cited therein; Mauro Cappelletti, "Who Watches the Watchmen? A Comparative Study on Judicial Responsibility," 31 *Am. J. Comp. L.* 1 (1983).

25. *Monitoring the EU Accession Process: Judicial Independence* (Budapest: Central European University Press, 2001), p. 394. We are grateful to Professor Gerhard Casper for this reference.

26. *Bush v. Gore*, 531 U.S. 98 (2000). Compare Alan M. Dershowitz, *Supreme Injustice: How the High Court Hijacked Election 2000* (New York: Oxford University Press, 2001), with Richard A. Posner, *Breaking the Deadlock: The 2000 Election, the Constitution, and the Courts* (Princeton, N.J.: Princeton University Press, 2001).

27. See Brian Buescher, "ABA Model Rule 7.6: The ABA Pleases the SEC, But Does Not Solve Pay to Play," 14 *Geo. J. Legal Ethics* 139 (2000). See also ABA Rules, Rule 7.6.

28. Reinhold Niebuhr, *Moral Man and Immoral Society* (New York: Scribner, 1932).

29. In the United States this has been a pathway to careers in academic law for a small minority of brilliant law graduates. Many of them present to their students a vision of law practice informed by disillusioning experience.

30. See Jerome E. Carlin, *Lawyers on Their Own: The Solo Practitioner in an Urban Setting*, rev. ed. (San Francisco: Austin & Winfield, 1994), p. 210; John P. Heinz and Edward O. Laumann, *Chicago Lawyers: The Social Structure of the Bar*, rev. ed. (Evanston, Ill.: Northwestern University Press, 1994), p. 10.

31. Jerome Frank, while still a law professor, made this a principal theme of a book: Jerome Frank, *Law and the Modern Mind* (Garden City, N.Y.: Doubleday, 1963). Frank eventually became a judge himself.

32. For examples of this sentiment, see Austin Sarat and William L. F. Felstiner, *Divorce Lawyers and Their Clients: Power and Meaning in the Legal Process* (New York: Oxford University Press, 1995), pp. 99–102 (field study of lawyer interactions with clients in divorce matters).

33. See, e.g., William H. Simon, *The Practice of Justice: A Theory of Lawyers' Ethics* (Cambridge, Mass.: Harvard University Press, 1998).

34. Jean Louis Halperin, *Avocats et notaires en Europe—Les professions judiciaires dans l'histoire contemporain* (Paris: LGDJ, 1996), passim.

35. For an analysis and extensive references, see Frank B. Cross, "Law and Economic Growth," 80 *Texas L. Rev.* 1732 (2002).

36. See Thomas Hobbes, *Leviathan*, ed. Richard Tuck (Cambridge: Cambridge University Press, 1991), pp. 171–75; John Locke, *Second Treatise of Government* (Indianapolis, Ind.: Hackett, 1980), chap. 5.

37. See Harold J. Berman, *Law and Revolution: The Formation of the Western Legal Tradition* (Cambridge, Mass.: Harvard University Press, 1983), p. 30.

38. See, e.g., Lucien Karpik, "Builders of Liberal Society: French Lawyers and Politics," in Halliday and Karpik, supra note 9, p. 101; J. S. Cockburn, *A History of the English Assizes: 1558–1714* (Cambridge: Cambridge University Press, 1972); compare Rueschemeyer, supra note 9, p. 207.

39. But compare the analysis in Terrence Halliday and Lucien Karpik, *PostScript: Lawyers, Political Liberalism, and Globalization*, in Halliday and Karpik, supra note 9, pp. 367–70.

40. Taylor's arguments are summarized in Halliday and Karpik, supra note 9, p. 21.

41. See George Harris and Derek Foran, "The Ethics of Middle-Class Access to Legal Services, and What Can We Learn from the Medical Profession?" 70 *Fordham L. Rev.* 775 (2001). The authors review national survey evidence developed by the American Bar Foundation and other regional surveys. See also Roger Cramton, "Delivery of Legal Services to Ordinary Americans," 44 *Case Western L. Rev.* 531 (1994).

42. See Edward Blankenburg, "The Lawyers' Lobby and the Welfare State: The Political Economy of Legal Aid," in Francis Regan, A. Paterson, T. Goriely, and D. Fleming, *The Transformation of Legal Aid 113* (Oxford: Oxford University Press, 1999). On legal aid generally, see Mauro Cappelletti, J. Gordley, and E. Johnson, eds., *Towards Equal Justice: A Comparative Study of Legal Aid in Modern Societies* (Dobbs Ferry, N.Y.: Oceana Publications, 1975).

43. Michele Taruffo, ed., *Abuse of Procedural Rights: Comparative Standards of Procedural Fairness* (The Hague: Kluwer, 1999) (proceedings of the International Association of Procedural Law International Colloquium, Tulane Law School, 1998).

44. See generally, Mirjan Damaska, *The Faces of Justice and State Authority: A Comparative Approach to the Legal Process* (New Haven, Conn.: Yale University Press, 1986).

45. Italian CDF, Art. 11.

46. ABA Rules, Rule 6.2 ("a lawyer shall not seek to avoid appointment except for good cause"); Rule 6.1 ("a lawyer should aspire to render at least 50 hours of pro bono publico legal services per year").

47. A now classic exposition of this relationship is Piero Calamandrei, *Procedure and Democracy*, trans. John Clarke Adams and Helen Adams (New York: New York University Press, 1956).

48. See, e.g., Michael Stolleis, *The Law under the Swastika*, trans. Thomas Dunlap (Chicago: University of Chicago Press, 1998).

49. This analysis is based primarily on Inga Markovits, "Children of a Lesser God: GDR Lawyers in Post-Socialist Germany," 94 *Mich. L. Rev.* 2270 (1996), p. 2279 and passim.

50. The best explication of this difference remains F. A. Hayek, *The Road to Serfdom* (Chicago: University of Chicago Press, 1944).

51. Du Xichuan and Zhang Linguan, *China's Legal System: A General Survey* (Beijing: New World Press, 1990), p. 184.

52. Margaret Y. K. Woo, "Law and Discretion in the Contemporary Chinese Courts," 8 *Pac. Rim Law & Policy J.* 581, 588 (1999).

53. Markovits, supra note 49.

54. Ibid., p. 2279; see also 2282: "[M]ost trials at which a judge departed from the prosecutor's suggested penalty resulted in only marginally different sentences. Complete acquittals were practically unheard-of."

55. Ibid., p. 2274.

56. Ibid., p. 2279.

57. Ibid., p. 2278.

58. See Albert A. Woldman, *Lawyer Lincoln* (New York: Carroll & Graf, 1994), pp. 172–85.

59. At the Yale University Law School, for example, the facade of the school's main entrance has figures depicting the architect's idea of "law." Most prominent among these figures is a policeman in pursuit of a thief.

60. See also Frank Donovan, *Mr. Roosevelt's Four Freedoms* (New York: Dodd, Mead, 1966), pp. 25–46.

61. See the United Nations Universal Declaration of Human Rights and the European Convention on Human Rights, reprinted in Ian Brownlie, ed., *Basic Documents on Human Rights*, 3d ed. (New York: Oxford University Press, 1992), pp. 21 and 326, respectively.

62. See, e.g., Gabor Halmai and Kim Lane Scheppele, "Living Well Is the Best Revenge: The Hungarian Approach to Judging the Past," in A. James McAdams, ed., *Transitional Justice and the Rule of Law in New Democracies* (Notre Dame, Ind.: University of Notre Dame Press, 1997), p. 155.

63. See Taruffo, supra note 43.

64. See Deborah L. Rhode, "Access to Justice," 69 *Fordham L. Rev.* 1785 (2001).

65. Stan Ross, *Ethics in Law: Lawyers' Responsibility and Accountability in Australia*, 2d ed. (Sydney: Butterworths, 1998), p. 173.

66. Quoted in the English case of *Rondel v. Worsley*, 1 AC 191 at 274 (1969), and reported in Ross, supra note 65, p. 173.

CHAPTER 3

1. See Aristotle, "Nicomachean Ethics," in Jonathan Barnes, ed., *The Complete Works of Aristotle*, vol. 2 (Princeton, N.J.: Princeton University Press, 1984), pp. 1762, 1826; Cicero, "On the Commonwealth," in James E. G. Zetzel, ed., *Cicero: On the Commonwealth and On the Laws* (Cambridge: Cambridge University Press, 1999). Comparable basic virtues in the Christian tradition have been expressed as "faith, hope, and charity." See, e.g., *St. Augustine, Faith, Hope, and Charity*, trans. Louis A. Arand (Westminster, Md.: Newman, 1955).

2. See John Leubsdorf, *Man in His Original Dignity: Legal Ethics in France* (Burlington, Vt.: Ashgate, 2000), passim; Bernard Sur, *Histoire des avocats en France des origines à nos jours* (Paris: Dalloz, 1998), pp. 22, 30 et seq.

3. Re A Company (No. 006798 of 1995) [1996] 1 WLR 491, 506 (Chadwick Jr.), cited in Neil Andrews, *English Civil Procedure: Fundamentals of the New Civil Justice System*, § 401 (2003).

4. See Mark Osiel, "Book Review: Lawyers as Monopolists, Aristocrats, and Entrepreneurs," 103 *Harv. L. Rev.* 2009, 2035 (1990) (reviewing Richard L. Abel and Philip S. C. Lewis, *Lawyers in Society*).

5. See, e.g., Monroe Freedman, *Understanding Lawyers' Ethics* (New York: Mathew Bender, 1990).

6. Some academic writing in the United States has suggested that it is inappropriate, because it is self-serving, for the legal profession to formulate its own ethical standards. See, e.g., Richard L. Abel, "Why Does the ABA Promulgate Ethical Rules?" 59 *Texas L. Rev.* 639 (1981); and Deborah Rhode, "Why the ABA Bothers: A Functional Perspective on Professional Codes," 59 *Texas L. Rev.* 689 (1981). These observations are surely misdirected. It would be bizarre for the concerned members of a profession to ignore their ethical standards or to feel crippled by guilt in addressing them. Furthermore, if ethical standards for the legal profession are to be expressed in writing—as has become convenient if not essential in the modern era—such an undertaking would be hardly feasible except with a competent legislative draftsman, who would for that reason be a "lawyer." A quite different question is whether one or another ethical rule promulgated by a professional group expresses proper public policy, as distinct from being self-serving.

7. See Geoffrey C. Hazard Jr., "Law Practice and the Limitations of Moral Philosophy," in Deborah L. Rhode, ed., *Ethics in Practice: Lawyers' Roles, Responsibilities, and Regulation* (New York: Oxford University Press, 2000).

8. See Anne Frank, *The Diary of A Young Girl*, ed. Otto H. Frank and Mirjam Pressler (New York: Doubleday, 1995).

9. See David Mellinkoff, *The Conscience of a Lawyer* (St. Paul, Minn.: West, 1973), p. 188.

10. 2 Trial of Queen Caroline 8 (1821), ed. by J. Nightingale (London: J. Robins & Co., 1820–21).

11. See ABA Rules, Rule 1.2(a) ("A lawyer shall abide by a client's decisions concerning the objectives of representation . . .").

12. See ABA Rules, Rule 3.3(a)(4) ("A lawyer shall not knowingly . . . offer evidence that the lawyer knows to be false . . .").

13. See ABA Rules, Rule 1.2(d) ("A lawyer shall not . . . assist a client in conduct that the lawyer knows is criminal or fraudulent . . ."). See, e.g., *Robinson v. Volkswagenwerk AG*, 940 F.2d 1369 (10th Cir. 1991) (improper concealment of relationship between parent corporation and subsidiary).

14. The duty to terminate participation in a fraudulent transaction is explicitly prescribed. See, e.g., ABA Rules, Rule 1.2 Comment [7] ("When the client's course of action has already begun . . . a lawyer may not continue assisting a client in conduct that . . . is criminal or fraudulent. Withdrawal from the representation . . . may be required."); Italian CDF, Art. 36(I) ("A lawyer shall not counsel any conduct . . . that is unlawful (or) fraudulent . . .") and Art. 47 ("A lawyer is entitled to withdraw from representation of a client"); see, e.g., Remo Danovi, "Dei doveri dell'avvocato nel processo," *Rassegna Forense*, 2001, p. 839 et seq. The need to take remedial measures results from a legal rule and a practical exigency. The legal rule is that a lawyer, like everyone else, can be liable criminally and civilly if the lawyer assists another, such as a client, in committing fraud. The practical exigency is that if a lawyer has assisted in a transaction that is fraudulent, the lawyer may come under suspicion of having been not an innocent instrumentality of a fraudulent client, but an accomplice. Taking remedial action is usually the best means of avoiding such a suspicion.

15. RSFSR, Law on the Advokatura, Art. 16.

16. The anniversary of this event has brought forth a new round of books. See, e.g., Martin P. Johnson, *The Dreyfus Affair* (New York: St. Martin's, 1999); Michael Burns, *France and the Dreyfus Affair: A Documentary History* (Boston: Bedford/St. Martin's, 1999).

17. See Lord Alfred Thompson Denning, *The Profumo–Christine Keeler Affair* (New York: Marc, 1962); Clive Irving, Ron Hall, and Jeremy Wallington, *Anatomy of a Scandal: A Study of the Profumo Affair* (New York: William Morrow, 1963).

18. An interesting account of the Nixon saga—one that covers a labyrinth of legal ethics issues—is Robert Woodward and Carl Bernstein, *The Final Days* (New York: Simon & Schuster, 1976). Regarding the Clinton situation, see the debate between Judge Posner and Professor Dershowitz: Alan M. Dershowitz, *Sexual McCarthyism: Clinton, Starr and the Emerging Constitutional Crisis* (New York: Basic Books, 1998); Richard A. Posner, *An Affair of State: The Investigation, Impeachment, and Trial of President Clinton* (Cambridge, Mass.: Harvard University Press, 1999).

19. Kenneth Starr, remarks at Mecklenburg Bar Foundation (Charlotte, N.C.: June 1, 1998), Federal Information Systems Corp., Federal News Service.

20. The privilege against self-incrimination has been incorporated—sometimes begrudgingly—into the criminal procedure of many legal systems. See Amann, "A Whipsaw Cuts Both Ways: The Privilege Against Self-Incrimination in an International Context," 45 *UCLA L. Rev.* 1201, 1251–1261 (1998).

21. A notorious case in the United States is *People v. Belge*, 83 Misc.2d 186, 372 N.Y.S.2d 798 (N.Y. Crim. Ct. 1975). In that case, a person charged with murder confessed the crime to his lawyer and also admitted that he had killed another victim, who had been reported missing but whose body had not yet been found. The lawyer withheld this information from authorities until after negotiating a concession that the client would be prosecuted as insane, rather than as fully competent.

22. See Geoffrey Hazard, "Doing the Right Thing," 70 *Wash. U. L. Quarterly* 691 (1992).

23. Canadian Code, Chap. 2 (Comment 1). See also CCBE Rules, Rule 3.1.3 ("A lawyer shall not handle a matter which he knows or ought to know he is not competent to handle . . ."); ABA Rules, Rule 1.1 ("A lawyer shall provide competent representation . . . [competency] requires legal knowledge, skill, thoroughness and preparation . . .").

24. See Canadian Code, Chap. 5 (Comment 1) (". . . [T]he client . . . may be seriously prejudiced unless the lawyer's judgment and freedom of action . . . are as free as possible from compromising influences."); CCBE Rules, Rule 2.1.1 ("The many duties to which a lawyer is subject require his absolute independence . . ."); ABA Rules, Rule 5.4 (outlining requirement of independent professional judgment).

25. CCBE Rules, Rule 3.2.1, Rule 3.2.2 and Rule 3.2.3. See also Canadian Code, Chap. 5 ("The lawyer must not . . . act or continue to act in a matter where there is or there is likely to be a conflicting interest . . .").

The ABA Rules are more complicated, dealing in separate provisions with conflict of interest where a lawyer represents two clients concurrently (Rule 1.7), representation of a new client that follows previous representation of a former client (Rule 1.9), and with the question of imputation of a conflict among two or more lawyers in the same law firm (Rule 1.10).

26. In the common law, the duty of confidentiality is conceived as a right of the client, which a lawyer has an obligation to safeguard. See *Restatement*, §60. On the duty of confidentiality to a prospective client see *Restatement*, §15, Comment c. The civil law rule is framed differently but has the same consequence. Under the civil law the lawyer as a professional has a right and duty to maintain confidentiality of all matters learned in the course of professional work. See CCBE Rules, Rule 2.3.1.

27. See, e.g., German BRAO para. 43.

28. The German rule, for example, is ZZP para. 383(6). See also BRAO paras. 4/a/2 and 56/1.

29. *Restatement*, §§68–76.

30. The difference in the civil law concept, that the right is that of the professional, and the common law concept, that the right is that of the client, can result in differences in the scope of permissible inquiry by a court. See Chap. 6. In most contexts, however, the two concepts have the same scope of application.

31. See, e.g., the Civility Code adopted by the Pennsylvania Supreme Court, 30 Pa. B. 6541 (Dec. 6, 2000). An example of an "aspirational" civility code is the Maryland State Bar Association Code of Civility (MSBA, 1997). The civility debate has been long-running; see, e.g., Warren E. Burger, "Opening Remarks," in *ALI Proceedings: 1971* (Philadelphia: ALI, 1972), p. 21; United States Court of Appeals (7th Circuit), Interim Report of the Committee on Civility of the Seventh Federal Judicial Circuit (Chicago: 1991).

32. See Federico Carpi and Michele Taruffo, *Commentario breve al codice di procedura civile*, 4th ed. (Padua: CEDAM, 2002), p. 127.

33. ABA Rules, Rule 8.4.

34. Canadian Code, Chap. 1 ("The lawyer must discharge his duties . . . with integrity."); CCBE Rules, Rule 2.2 ("[P]ersonal honour, honesty and integrity . . . are professional obligations").

35. Law Society, *Guide to Professional Conduct of Solicitors*, 8th ed. (London: Law Society, 1999), Rule 12.03. (hereinafter: *Law Society Guide*).

36. See *Restatement*, §52, especially Comment b. For a leading Canadian decision on legal malpractice, see *Central Trust Co. v. Rafuse*, 2 S.C.R. 147 (1986) (legal malpractice turns on the common law negligence duty of reasonable care, which demands "sufficient knowledge of the fundamental issues or principles of law applicable . . .").

37. *Togstad v. Vesely, Otto, Miller & O'Keefe*, 291 N.W.2d 686 (Minn. 1980).

38. *Prudential Ins. Co. v. Dewey, Ballantine, Bushby, Palmer & Wood*, 80 N.Y.2d 377 (N.Y. 1992).

39. See John Henry Merryman, "Legal Education There and Here: A Comparison," in *The Loneliness of the Comparative Lawyer* (The Hague: Kluwer, 1999), p. 66.

40. Ibid., p. 61; Mary Ann Glendon, Michael Wallace Gordon, and Paolo G. Carozza, *Comparative Legal Traditions in a Nutshell*, 2d ed. (St. Paul, Minn.: West, 1999), pp. 75–77. Compare the sketch of German legal education offered by Hans Leser, "Legal Education in Germany," in Peter Birks, ed., *Pressing Problems in the Law*, vol. 2: *What Are Law Schools Good For?* (New York: Oxford University Press, 1996), p. 91.

41. See, e.g., John Henry Merryman et al., *The Civil Law Tradition: Europe, Latin America, and East Asia* (Charlottesville, Va.: Michie, 1994).

42. Silence about the "dark side" of professional life in the United States invites other criticism. See, e.g., Richard Zitrin and Carol M. Langford, *The Moral Compass of the American Lawyer: Truth, Justice, Power, and Greed* (New York: Ballantine, 1999).

43. See John Merryman, *The Civil Law Tradition—An Introduction to the Legal Systems of Western Europe and Latin America* (Stanford, Calif.: Stanford University Press, 1986).

44. For an overview of the German apprenticeship requirements, see Gerhard Manz and Anne MacGregor, "The Legal Profession in Germany," in Allen Tyrell and Zahd Yaqub, eds., *The Legal Profession in the New Europe* (London: Cavendish, 1996), p. 150. Regarding the (optional) apprenticeship program in Spain, see Luis Algar Calderón, "The Legal Professions in Spain," in idem, p. 294.

45. Angelo Dondi, "Il regolamento istitutivo delle scuole forensi—Rilievi minimi in tema di riforme e di formazione delle professioni legali, in *Dir. pen. e proc.* 2000, p. 803 et seq.; Guido Alpa, "L'accesso alla professione forense—Nuove prospettive per l'avvocatura," in *La Nuov. Giur. Civ. Comm.* 1999, p. 193; Francesco Miraglia, "Formazione selettiva e scuole forensi—Risposta concreta al problema dell'accesso alla professione," in *Arch. Civ.* 2001, p. 289.

46. In France the examination is called the CAPA (Certificat d'Aptitude à la Profession d'Avocat); see Christian Dadomo and Susan Farran, *The French Legal System* (London: Sweet & Maxwell, 1993), p. 118. In Germany there is a two-tiered system of examination. The first state examination marks the end of university legal training; the second state examination is rather rigorous and follows a two-year period of professional training. See Nigel G. Foster, *German Legal System and Laws*, 2d ed. (London: Blackstone, 1996), pp. 84–87; Glendon, Gordon, and Carozza, supra note 40, p. 79. In Italy the process also involves numerous examinations, as explained in Thomas Glyn Watkin, *The Italian Legal Tradition* (Aldershot, England: Ashgate/Dartmouth, 1997), pp. 109–17.

47. There are various standards and procedures for determining personal suitability for admission to practice. See, e.g., Canadian Code, Chap. 1; PRC, Law on Lawyers, Art. 8(3).

48. Thus admission in France and Italy is to the bar of a city; in Germany it is to the bar of the *Lander*. Regarding France, see Dadomo and Farran, supra note 46, p. 120. For Italy, see Watkin, supra note 46, p. 114. The admission practices of the various German *Länder* are marshaled by Foster, supra note 46, pp. 81–89.

49. The breakdown of the barrister/solicitor dichotomy received extensive analysis in Andrew Boon and Jennifer Levin, *The Ethics and Conduct of Lawyers in England and Wales* (Portland, Ore.: Hart, 1999), chaps. 2 and 3.

50. The Inns of Court were professional residences and places for professional training of candidates. They have been referred to as institutions of higher learning

equivalent to universities. See J. H. Baker, *The Common Law Tradition* (London: Hambledon, 2000), pp. 69–76.

51. Boon and Levin, supra note 49, pp. 145, 152.

52. Ibid., pp. 157–62.

53. See Baker, supra note 50, p. 22.

54. Boon and Levin, supra note 49, p. 152.

55. Mary Seneviratne, *The Legal Profession: Regulation and the Consumer* (London: Sweet & Maxwell, 1999), p. 102. Even the undergraduate law curriculum tilts toward a classical humanities education. The direction of undergraduate education is a factor in the periodic tension between England's practicing bar—calling for a more practical focus—and the academy. As in the United States and elsewhere, this issue is far from resolved. See, e.g., Boon and Levin, supra note 49, pp. 154–57; Birks, supra note 40, passim.

56. See Marcel Berlins and Clare Dyer, *The Law Machine*, 5th ed. (London: Penguin, 2000), pp. 34–50.

57. See Boon and Levin, supra note 49, chap. 3.

58. On the situation of women and ethnic minorities among solicitors, see Boon and Levin, supra note 49, pp. 145–52; Neil Kibble, "Access to Legal Education and the Legal Professions in England," in Rajeev Dhavan, Neil Kibble, and William Twining, eds., *Access to Legal Education and the Legal Profession* (London: Butterworths, 1989), p. 132.

59. See Yoshiharu Kawahata, "Reform of Legal Education and Training in Japan: Problems and Prospects," 43 *So. Texas L. Rev.* 419 (2002).

60. Blackstone's *Commentaries* had enormous influence in the United States, probably more than in England. Blackstone was a concise compendium of all the common law, a convenient and economical law library unto itself, suitable for a developing country. William Blackstone, *Commentaries on the Laws of England* (Buffalo, N.Y.: William S. Hein, 1992). See Lawrence M. Friedman, *A History of American Law*, 2d ed. (New York: Simon & Schuster, 1985), p. 112 (commenting on the "ubiquity" of Blackstone during the formative years of American law).

61. Abraham Lincoln learned law in this manner. See also Joseph G. Baldwin, *The Flush Times of Alabama and Mississippi: A Series of Sketches* (New York: D. Appleton, 1854), p. 324 (discussing the apprenticeship of a thirty-five-year-old man who one day decided to become a lawyer despite being "unencumbered with any learning" up to that point).

62. The earliest such institute was the Litchfield School in Connecticut, founded in approximately 1784; Friedman, supra note 60, p. 279. For more on the Litchfield School, see Marian C. McKenna, *Tapping Reeve and the Litchfield Law School* (New York: Oceana, 1986). Another early university legal program was established in 1779

by Thomas Jefferson and George Wythe at the College of William and Mary; see E. Lee Shepard, "George Wythe," in William H. Bryson, ed., *Legal Education in Virginia: 1779–1979* (Charlottesville, Va.: University Press of Virginia, 1982).

63. At Columbia College (now University) in 1794, James Kent began delivering lectures in law that stressed the classics, logic, mathematics, and moral philosophy. See Anton-Hermann Chroust, *The Rise of the Legal Profession in America*, vol. 2 (Norman: University of Oklahoma Press, 1965), pp. 181–85. In 1799, Transylvania University in Kentucky began another university law program. See Alfred Z. Reed, *Training for the Public Profession of the Law* (Boston: Merrymount, 1921), p. 118. Harvard initiated a program in 1817, although the program did not rise to prominence until Joseph Story became a professor in 1829. See, e.g., Arthur E. Sutherland, *The Law at Harvard* (Cambridge, Mass.: Belknap, 1967).

64. For various perspectives on the origins and impact of the Harvard Law School concept, see, e.g., Robert Stevens, *Legal Education in America from the 1850s to the 1980s* (Chapel Hill: University of North Carolina Press, 1983), chaps. 3–4; William P. LaPiana, *Logic and Experience: The Origin of Modern Legal Education* (New York: Oxford University Press, 1994); Anthony Chase, "The Birth of the Modern Law School," 23 *Am. J. of Legal History* 339 (1979); Bruce Kimball and Blake Brown, "'The Highest Legal Ability in the Nation': Langdell on Wall Street 1855–1870," 29 *Law & Social Inquiry* 39 (2004).

65. See, e.g., James Bradley Thayer, *Select Cases on Evidence at the Common Law: With Notes* (Cambridge: C. W. Sever, 1892).

66. Oliver Wendell Holmes Jr., *The Common Law* (Boston: Little, Brown, 1946), p. 1.

67. Oliver Wendell Holmes Jr., "Law in Science and Science in Law," 12 *Harvard L. Rev.*, 443, p. 444 (reprinted in Richard A. Posner, ed., *The Essential Holmes* [Chicago: University of Chicago Press, 1992], p. 186).

68. A few "legal realist" skeptics in the American academic community published casebooks composed of decisions selected for their incoherence and inconsistency. For example, in 1937, Thurman Arnold and Fleming James of Yale published a casebook that, in the opinion of one reviewer, showed the law to be "an ass." See Laura Kalman, *Legal Realism at Yale: 1927–1960* (Chapel Hill: University of North Carolina Press, 1986), p. 81.

69. Admission to practice in the United States is a matter of state law and administration, not national law; see Chap. 1. Many states continued to allow admission on the basis of self-study and apprenticeship, and a few still do so today. See ABA, *Comprehensive Guide to Bar Admission Requirements* (Chicago: ABA, 1995).

70. See Stevens, supra note 64, chaps. 6–7.

71. For a summary of the rise and fall of character standards, see Richard L. Abel, *American Lawyers* (New York: Oxford University Press, 1989), pp. 69–73.

72. See Deborah Rhode, "The Future of the Legal Profession: Institutionalizing Ethics," 44 *Case Western Res. L. Rev.* 665, 690 (1994) ("no showing has ever been made that performance ... on bar exams ... correlates with performance in practice").

73. An example of this criticism from above is Warren Burger, "Some Further Reflections on the Problem of Adequacy of Trial Counsel," 49 *Fordham L. Rev* 1 (1980). The stratification of the profession—and the corresponding possibility that the elite may promulgate self-serving rules—should be considered whenever calls for "competence" or "professionalism" are made by "upper-level" lawyers. On this internal class conflict, see Roger C. Cramton, "Symposium, The Future of the Legal Profession: Delivery of Legal Services to Ordinary Americans," 44 *Case Western Reserve L. Rev.* 531, 538 (1994).

74. See the analysis in David Wilkins and G. Mitu Gulati, "Why Are There So Few Black Lawyers in Corporate Law Firms? An Institutional Analysis," 84 *California L. Rev.* 493, at 499 (1996) (referring to law firms' internal valuation of apprentice lawyers, "the inherent subjectivity of quality assessments and the difficulty and expense of monitoring").

75. Boon and Levin, supra note 49, pp. 128–34.

76. For the situation in Canada, see Allan C. Hutchinson, *Legal Ethics and Professional Responsibility* (Toronto: Irwin, 1999), p. 15. For that in the United States, see, e.g., Roger Cramton and Erik Jensen, "The State of Trial Advocacy and Legal Education: Three New Studies," 30 *J. Legal Education* 253 (1979); H. Russell Cort and Jack Sammons, "The Search for 'Good Lawyering': A Concept and Model of Lawyering Competencies," 29 *Cleveland State L. Rev.* 397 (1980). See also American Bar Association, *Lawyer Regulation for a New Century: Report of the Commission on Evaluation of Disciplinary Enforcement* (Chicago: ABA, 1992), p. 47 and passim.

77. See, e.g., Rosemary Stevens, *American Medicine and the Public Interest* (New Haven, Conn.: Yale University Press, 1971).

78. See, e.g., Ronald E. Mallen and Jeffrey M. Smith, *Legal Malpractice*, 5th ed. (St. Paul, Minn.: West, 2000). See also *Restatement*, §§48–58.

79. Seneviratne, supra note 55, pp. 55–62.

80. *Arthur J S Hall & Co. (A Firm) v. Simons Barrat v. Woolf Seddon (A Firm)*, [2002] 1 A.C. 615, 644.

81. There are systematic efforts by private organizations associated with the legal profession to identify and publish professional reputation. In the United States the Martindale-Hubbell company lists all lawyers and publishes "ratings" of "a" (good), "b," and no rating. See Martindale-Hubbell, *Law Directory* (New York: Martindale-Hubbell, 2001). For a discussion, see Manuel Ramos, "Legal Malpractice: No Lawyer or Client Is Safe," 47 *Florida L. Rev.* 1, 24–39 (1995).

82. Berlins and Dyer, supra note 56, p. 8.

83. Canadian Code, Chap. 13 (Comment 1).

84. This fact is the basis of persistent and justified social criticism that the law as administered favors the rich and powerful. It is a central element of Marxist criticism of law. It is the basis for calls to abolish "the system" or at least exterminate the legal profession. As Shakespeare has it in "Henry VI," part 2, act IV, scene 2: "First thing we do, let's kill all the lawyers." Yet abolishing lawyers would not only lead to arbitrary decision-making by judges, and hence subversion of the rule of law, but also, as a consequence of that instability, to a new class of apparatchiks serving as go-betweens within the power system. See Milovan Djilas, *The New Class: An Analysis of the Communist System* (New York: Praeger, 1957). Of course, government itself could be abolished, but that is a still larger project.

85. The salient American legal event was the decision of the Supreme Court of the United States, *Bates v. State Bar of Arizona*, 433 U.S. 350 (1977), holding that truthful newspaper advertising of legal clinic services was protected by the First Amendment guarantee of free speech. See Ronald Rotunda, "Professionalism, Legal Advertising, and Free Speech in the Wake of *Florida Bar v. Went For It*," 49 *Arkansas L. Rev.* 703 (1997).

86. CCBE Rules, Rule 2.6.1.

87. Italian CDF, Art. 17 (I and II). See Remo Danovi, "La pubblicità, la doppia deontologia e le modifiche del codice deontologico forense," in *Rass. For.* 2000, p. 41 et seq.; Luca D'Auria, "Avvocati e pubblicità—la riforma dell'art. 17 del codice deontologico," in *For. Amb.* 2002, p. 259.

88. *Law Society Guide*, supra note 35, Annex 11A(1)(b) (General Council of the Bar, *Code of Conduct of the Bar of England and Wales*, 7th ed. (London: Bar Council, 2000).

89. Canadian Code, Chap. 13 (Comment 4).

90. *Law Society Guide*, supra note 35, Annex 11A(3).

91. Italian CDF, Art. 19. The PRC, *Law on Lawyers*, Art. 44(3), prohibits "soliciting business by unfair means."

92. ABA Rules, Rule 7.3(a).

93. See *In re Primus*, 436 U.S. 412 (1978).

94. General Council of the Bar, *Code of Conduct of the Bar of England and Wales*, §709.

95. 501 U.S. 1030 (1991). See also Kevin Cole and Fred Zacharias, "The Agony of Victory and the Ethics of Lawyer Speech," 69 *So. Cal. L. Rev.* 1627 (1996) (focusing on the media coverage of the O. J. Simpson case).

96. See David Barnhizer, "On the Make: Campaign Funding and the Corrupting of the American Judiciary," 50 *Cath. U. L. Rev.* 361 (2001).

CHAPTER 4

1. CDF, Art. 10. See, e.g., Remo Danovi, *Commentario al codice deontologio forense* (Milan: Giuffrè, 2001), p. 70 et seq.; Douglas L. Parker, "An American Perspective on the Codice Deontologico of the Consiglio Nazionale Forense: Understanding the Independence of the Advocate," in *Rass. For.* 1999, p. 575.

2. ABA Rules, Rule 2.1. The ABA code elsewhere prescribes specifications concerning interference with independent professional judgment, including Rule 5.4(c), which provides that "a lawyer shall not permit a person who recommends, employs or pays the lawyer to direct or regulate the lawyer's professional judgment."

3. For a thoughtful analysis of professionalism, with particular reference to the legal profession, see Herbert Kritzer, "The Professions Are Dead, Long Live the Professions: Legal Practice in a Postprofessional World," 33 *Law & Society Rev.* 713 (1999). This article has an extensive bibliography.

4. See., e.g., Angelo Dondi, *Effettività dei provvedimenti istruttori del giudice civile* (Padua: CEDAM, 1985), p. 252 et seq.

5. See Geoffrey C. Hazard, "Per l'indipendenza professionale dell'avvocatura," in *Riv. Trim. Dir. Proc. Civ.* 1997, p. 407 et seq.; Parker, supra note 1, p. 570 et seq.

6. See John Leubsdorf, *Man in His Original Dignity: Legal Ethics in France* (Burlington, Vt.: Ashgate, 2000), chap. 6.

7. See, e.g., Piero Calamandrei, *Troppi avvocati!* (Florence: La voce, 1931), p. 36 et seq.

8. See Udo Reifner, "The Bar in the Third Reich: Anti-Semitism and the Decline of Liberal Advocacy," 32 *McGill L. J.* 96 (1986).

9. PRC, Law on Lawyers, Arts. 33 and 45(1). See Stanley Lubman, *Bird in a Cage: Legal Reform in China after Mao* (Stanford, Calif.: Stanford University Press, 1999), p. 159.

10. See, e.g., ABA Working Group on Lawyers' Representation of Regulated Clients, "Laborers in Different Vineyards? The Banking Regulators and the Legal Profession" (ABA Draft, Jan. 1993); "Symposium on Kaye Scholer," in 66 *So. Cal. L. Rev.* 977 (1993).

11. Karen Miller, "Zip to Nil? A Comparison of American and English Lawyers' Standards of Professional Conduct" (Philadelphia: ALI-ABA, August 16, 1995), p. 225.

12. For a chilling account of the widespread state brutality inflicted on all members of the anti-apartheid movement in South Africa—including lawyers—see Richard L. Abel, *Politics by Other Means: Law in the Struggle against Apartheid, 1980–1994* (London: Routledge, 1995), chap. 7.

13. See William E. Butler, *Russian Law* (New York: Oxford University Press, 1999), pp. 114–20.

14. See, e.g., Vittorio Olgiati, *Saggi sull'avvocatura—L'avvocato italiano tra diritto,*

potere e società (Milan: Giuffrè, 1990), p. 12 et seq.; Franco Cipriani, "La professione di avvocato," in *Storia d'Italia*, XIV (Turin: Einaudi, 1996) passim; for an early historical sketch, see, e.g., F. Carrara, "Il passato, il presente e l'avvenire degli avvocati in Italia," in *Opuscoli di diritto criminale* (Lucca: 1876), p. 3 et seq.; Massimo La Torre, *Il giudice, l'avvocato e il concetto di diritto* (Rubbettino: Soveria Mannelli, 2002), p. 95 et seq.

15. See, e.g., David Wilkins, "Who Should Regulate Lawyers?" 105 *Harvard L. Rev.* 801 (1992); Charles Wolfram, "Lawyer Turf and Lawyer Regulation—The Role of the Inherent Powers Doctrine," 12 *U. Ark. Little Rock L. J.* 1 (1989); Bruce Green, "Conflicts of Interest in Litigation: The Judicial Role," 65 *Fordham L. Rev.* 71 (1996).

16. See Susan Koniak, "The Law between the Bar and the State," 70 *No. Carolina L. Rev.* 1389 (1992).

17. For an overview of the evolution of professional ethics in the United States—from an informal fraternal practice to something resembling positive law—see Geoffrey Hazard, *Ethics in the Practice of Law* (New Haven, Conn.: Yale University Press, 1978), pp. 15–20.

18. See, e.g., *Law v. Ewell*, 15 Fed. Cas. 14 (C.C.D.C. 1817). Early American cases were founded on the English rule that barristers cannot sue to collect a fee.

19. English barristers traditionally were immune to suit for malpractice, as discussed in Chapter 3. The English tradition influenced malpractice law in the United States, so during the nineteenth century American attorneys were typically subject to malpractice suit only in cases of "gross negligence." Ronald E. Mallen and Jeffrey M. Smith, *Legal Malpractice*, 4th ed. (St. Paul, Minn.: West, 1996), pp. 9–17.

20. See Geoffrey Hazard, "The Future of Legal Ethics," 100 *Yale L. J.* 1239 (1991).

21. See Stan Ross, *Ethics in Law: Lawyers' Responsibility and Accountability in Australia*, 2d ed. (Sydney: Butterworths, 1998), pp. 56–57. In Australia several states have adopted formal codes of ethics. See, e.g., Law Society of Australian Capital Territory, *Rules of Professional Conduct*. Also, specialized practice groups have developed supplemental regulations.

22. See Mary Seneviratne, *The Legal Profession: Regulation and the Consumer* (London: Sweet & Maxwell, 1999), pp. 70, 75.

23. See Nirmalendu Dutt-Majumdar, *Conduct of Advocates and Legal Profession: A Short History* (Calcutta: Eastern Lawhouse, 1974), pp. 45–55.

24. See, e.g., ABA Rules, Rule 1.15; CCBE Rules, Rule 3.8.

25. In many states in the United States, grievance tribunals now include lay members as well as lawyers. See Mary M. Devlin, "The Development of Lawyer Disciplinary Procedures in the United States," 7 *Geo. J. L. Ethics* 911, n. 214 (1994). This can be considered a corollary of the fact that the rules have become "public" law rather than simply a matter of internal regulation in the legal profession.

26. See Chapter 2.

27. See, e.g., *Gentile v. State Bar of Nevada*, 501 U.S. 1030 (1991) (lawyer challenging disciplinary sanctions on First Amendment grounds).

28. See ABA Rules, Rule 1.2(d) (prohibiting assistance to a client committing a crime or fraud).

29. See ABA Rules, Rule 1.16(b)(3) ("a lawyer may withdraw if a client insists on pursuing an objective that the lawyer considers repugnant or imprudent").

30. Emmanuel Lazega, *The Collegial Phenomenon: The Social Mechanisms of Cooperation Among Peers in a Corporate Law Partnership* (Oxford: Oxford University Press, 2001), pp. 8–9.

31. Robert W. Hillman, *Law Firm Breakups: The Law and Ethics of Grabbing and Leaving* (Boston: Little, Brown, 1990).

32. Elihu Root, quoted in Phillip C. Jessup, *Elihu Root* (New York: Dodd, Mead, 1938), p. 132.

33. L. Kuslansky, "Who's the Boss? CEOs in Litigation: Problems and Solutions," 40 *Int'l. Commercial Litigation* 10 (1999).

34. Baldesar Castiglione, *The Book of the Courtier* (London: Penguin, 1967), p. 306.

35. Robert Gordon, "The Independence of Lawyers," 68 *Boston U. L. Rev.* 1, 73 (1988).

36. Canadian Code, Chap. 3 (Comment 6).

37. See Italian CDF, Art. 36 (I) ("A lawyer shall not knowingly suggest unnecessarily onerous actions, nor counsel any conduct, action or transaction that is unlawful, fraudulent or legally invalid."). See Danovi, supra note 1, p. 179 et seq. See also People's Republic of China, Regulations on Lawyers' Professional Ethics and Business Practices, Chap. 1 note 9, at Art. 8.

38. See *United States v. Benjamin*, 328 F.2d 854, 862 (2d Cir. 1964) (conviction of a lawyer involved in a fraudulent stock scheme: "defendant [the lawyer] deliberately closed his eyes to facts he had a duty to see").

39. *Upjohn Co. v. United States*, 449 U.S. 383, 389 (1981).

40. See Alessandro Galante Garrone, *Calamandrei* (Milan: Garzanti, 1987), p. 220 et seq.

41. See Paul Finkelman, ed., *A Brief Narrative of the Case and Trial of John Peter Zenger, Printer of the New York Weekly Journal* (St. James, N.Y.: Brandywine, 1997).

42. Powell conducted quiet opposition to a political movement of "massive resistance" to the decision of the U.S. Supreme Court in *Brown v. Board of Education*, 347 U.S. 483 (1954).

43. ABA Rules, Rule 1.2(b).

44. General Council of the Bar, Code of Conduct of the Bar of England and Wales, §601.

45. See, e.g., Amy L. Chua, "Markets, Democracy, and Ethnicity: Toward a New Paradigm for Law and Development," 108 *Yale L. J.* 1 (1998).

CHAPTER 5

1. CDF, Art. 36, provides that: "A lawyer shall not knowingly suggest unnecessarily onerous actions, nor counsel any conduct, action or transaction that is unlawful, fraudulent or legally invalid." On this subject see, among many, Remo Danovi, *Commentario al codice deontologico forense* (Milan: Giuffrè, 2001) passim; Douglas L. Parker, "An American Perspective on the Codice Deontologico of the Consiglio Nazionale Forense: Understanding the Independence of the Advocate," in *Rass. For.* 1999, passim. ABA Rule 1.2(d) provides that "A lawyer shall not counsel a client to engage, or assist a client, in conduct that the lawyer knows is criminal or fraudulent"; the Canadian Code, Chap. 3 (Comment 6), provides that: "When advising his client the lawyer must never knowingly assist or encourage any dishonesty, fraud, crime or illegal conduct or instruct his client as to how to violate the law and avoid punishment."

2. CDF, Art. 14 (I) provides that "A lawyer may not deliberately introduce false evidence into the trial. In particular, an attorney shall neither put on record nor introduce declarations of persons concerning facts which the lawyer knows to be untrue." See Remo Danovi, "Dei doveri dell'avvocato nel processo," in *Rass. For.* 2001, p. 839 et seq.; Pasquale Franco, "Doveri di verità e difesa del colpevole," in *Rass. For.* 2000, p. 309. More or less the same are ABA Rules 3.3 and 3.4. The Canadian Code, Chap. 8 (Comment 1), is more detailed and elaborate.

3. Matthew 6:24 (Revised Standard Bible).

4. See William Simon, *The Practice of Justice: A Theory of Lawyers' Ethics* (Cambridge, Mass.: Harvard University Press, 1998).

5. Ibid., pp. 140, 163.

6. Duncan Kennedy, "Rebels from Principle: Changing the Corporate Law Firm from Within," 36 *Harvard Law School Bulletin*, 1981, pp. 39–40

7. See, e.g., Detlev Vagts, "Response," 38 *Harvard Law School Bulletin* (Spring), 1982. Some of the responses to the Kennedy article—found in the Spring 1982 issue—reached a high level of vitriol. For a philosophical critique, see W. Bradley Wendel, "Civil Disobedience," 104 *Columbia L. Rev.* 363 (2004).

8. On the concept of "advantage friendship," see John M. Cooper, "Aristotle on Friendship," in A. O. Rorty, ed., *Essays on Aristotle's Ethics* (Berkeley: University of California Press, 1980), passim; applying the concept of friendship to the client-lawyer relationship, see Charles Fried, "The Lawyer as Friend: The Moral Foundations of the Lawyer-Client Relation," 85 *Yale L. J.* 1060 (1976).

9. See, e.g., the discussion in Dietrich Rueschemeyer, *Lawyers and Their Society: A Comparative Study of the Legal Profession in Germany and in the United States* (Cambridge, Mass.: Harvard University Press, 1973), p. 127.

10. Canadian Code, Chap. 8 (Comment 5).

11. ABA Rule 1.2(a).

12. See Code of Conduct of the Bar of England and Wales, §603(c). See Andrew Bonn and Jennifer Levin, *The Ethics and Conduct of Lawyers in England and Wales* (Oxford: Oxford University Press, 1999), passim; Donald Nicolson and Julian Webb, *Professional Legal Ethics: Critical Interrogations* (Oxford: Oxford University Press, 1999), passim.

13. Law Society, *Guide to Professional Conduct of Solicitors* (hereinafter: *Law Society Guide*) (London: Law Society, 1999), Rule 7.1.

14. See Judith Maute, "Allocation of Authority Under the Model Rules of Professional Conduct," 17 *U.C. Davis L. Rev.* 1049 (1984).

15. Canadian Code, Chap. 5.

16. CDF, Art. 7. For another formulation of the rule see, PRC, Law on Lawyers, Art. 34.

17. See *Restatement*, §128.

18. *Klemm v. Superior Court*, 142 Cal. Rptr. 509 (Cal. Ct. App., 1977).

19. *Westinghouse Elec. Corp. v. Kerr & McGee Corp.*, 580 F.2d 1311 (7th Cir. 1978).

20. Other subdivisions of ABA Rules, Rule 1.8, prohibit a lawyer from drafting an instrument by which a client makes a gift to the lawyer (the classic example being the drafting of a will for a client with such a provision); from giving financial assistance in litigation for a client, except advancement of litigation expenses; from settling claims on behalf of multiple clients unless the terms of the settlement are disclosed to all the clients; from appearing against a lawyer who is a close relative, including a spouse; and from obtaining a "proprietary interest" in a claim in litigation. This last prohibition has an exception that recognizes the legitimacy of a contingent fee arrangement.

21. 218 D.L.R. (4th) 671 (2002).

22. See Bruce Green, "Conflicts of Interest in Legal Representation: Should the Appearance of Impropriety Rule Be Eliminated in New Jersey?" 28 *Seton Hall L. Rev.* 315 (1997).

23. See *Law Society Guide*, Rule 15.04(1), supra note 13.

24. See, e.g., *In re Neville*, 708 P.2d 1297 (Ariz. 1985); *Committee on Professional Ethics v. Mershon*, 316 N.W.2d 895 (Iowa, 1982).

25. Canadian Code, Chap. 5.

26. See Code of Ethics for the Japanese Bar, Art. 32.

27. Consent to conflict of interest must be in writing according to the rules of

ethics in some American states. The American Bar Association recommended in 2002 that written consent to a conflict of interest be required in all of the states.

28. See *Restatement*, §122. Comment c(i) elaborates as follows: "[T]he information normally should address the interests giving rise to the conflict; contingent, optional, and tactical considerations and alternatives that would be foreclosed; the effect upon confidential information of the client and the consequences of a future withdrawal of consent by any client."

29. See Canadian Code, Chap. 5 (Comment 11).

30. See *United States Football League v. National Football League*, 605 F. Supp. 1448 (S.D.N.Y. 1985).

31. ABA Rule 1.9(a) states: "A lawyer who has formerly represented a client . . . shall not thereafter represent another person in the same or a substantially related matter in which that person's interests are materially adverse to the interests of the former client unless the former client consents after consultation."

32. See RSFSR, Law on the Advokatura, Art. 16.

33. See also CDF, Art. 37: "A conflict of interest arises if acceptance of a new client may result in a violation of confidentiality applicable to information supplied by another client."

34. Modification of the imputation rule in the United States has been allowed if the personally burdened lawyer is "screened" from other lawyers in the firm. See ABA Rule 1.11 (outlining limitations on a lawyer who has left government service for private practice). In 2002 the American Bar Association adopted a recommendation relaxing the imputation rule, ABA Rule 1.10, as it applies to lawyers who move from one firm to another. Several states had already adopted similar provisions. For a discussion and criticism of this change, see Lawrence Fox, "All's OK between Consenting Adults," 29 *Hofstra L. Rev.* 701 (2001).

35. See the Canadian Code, Chap. 11 (Comment 9).

36. See *Restatement*, §40 (Illustration 4); in case law, see, e.g., *Searcy, Denney, et al. v. Scheller*, 629 So.2d 947 (Fla. Dist. Ct. App. 1993) (attorney can be awarded fees, even following discharge for breach of fiduciary duty); *Vaccaro v. Estate of Gorovoy*, 696 A.2d 724 (N.J. Super. Ct. 1997) (fee recovery following attorney discharge is based on *quantum meruit*).

37. See ABA Model Rule 1.16(b).

38. See Canadian Code, Chap. 11 (Comment 4). Chapter 1 (Comment 2) of the Canadian Code provides that "dishonourable or questionable conduct" is inconsistent with the duty of integrity and hence would require withdrawal under the provision quoted from Chap. 11.

39. See Salvatore Orestano, "Il segreto professionale nell'Unione europea: La direttiva sul riciclaggio del denaro," in *Rass. For.* 2001, p. 259; Mario Santaroni, "L'eser-

cizio della professione di avvocato nell'Europa Comunitaria," in *Le Nuov. Leg. Civ. Comm.* 1998, p. 1072; Vittorio Olgiati, *Le professioni giuridiche in Europa—Politiche del diritto e dinamica sociale* (Urbino: Quattro Venti, 1996), p. 1 et seq.

40. See *Restatement*, §51, which provides that: "[A] lawyer owes a duty of care . . . to a nonclient when and to the extent that . . . the lawyer . . . invites the nonclient to rely on the lawyer's opinion . . . and the nonclient so relies. . . ."

41. See, e.g., Reinier Kraakman, "Gatekeepers—The Anatomy of a Third-Party Enforcement Strategy," 2 *J. L. Econ. and Org.* 53 (1986); "Symposium on Professional Responsibility and the Corporate Lawyer," 13 *Geo. J. L. Ethics* 2000, p. 197 et seq.

42. See, e.g., Sally Baghdasarian, "Gatekeepers: How the Broad Application of Anti-Money Laundering Statutes and Strategies May Open an Attorney's Gates to Prosecution," 32 *Southwestern U. L. Rev.* 721 (2003); Katrina Abendano, "The Role of Lawyers in the Fight against Money Laundering," 2001 *J. of Legislation* 463 (2001).

43. 328 F.2d 854, 863 (2d Cir. 1964).

CHAPTER 6

1. [2002] 2 WLR 1299, Lord Hoffman, J., quoted in Neil Andrews, *English Civil Procedure: Fundamentals of the New Civil Justice System*, §622 (2003). In the leading European Court decision in *AM&S Europe Ltd. v. Commission of the European Communities*, 155/79 [1982] ECR 1575, 1610–13, the rule is considered part of the privacy right established in Article 8 of the European Convention.

2. See Canadian Code, Chap. 5.

3. See *Restatement*, §79.

4. Decision of the Constitutional Court of the Russian Federation regarding Patrushkin's Complaint, no. 128 (July 6, 2000), available at www.consultant.ru.

5. See Vitzlii Leonenko, *Professionalnaia etika uchastnikov ugolovnogo sudoproizvodstva* (Kiev: Akademiia Nauk Ukrainskoi SSR, 1981), p. 135.

6. See Geoffrey Hazard, "An Historical Perspective on the Attorney-Client Privilege," 66 *Calif. L. Rev.* 1061 (1978); *R v. Derby Magistrates' Court, ex parte* B, [1996] AC 487 (Lord C. J. Taylor).

7. 329 U.S. 495 (1947). For a discussion of the impact of this case in the European legal culture, see Angelo Dondi, *Effettività dei provvedimenti istruttori del giudice civile* (Padua: CEDAM, 1985), p. 125 et seq.

8. For the contemporary formulation of the English litigation privilege, see Andrews, supra note 1, §27.21–27.41 (2003).

9. Federal Rules of Civil Procedure, Rule 26(b)(3) and (4).

10. See David F. Partlett, "Attorney-Client Privilege, Professions and the Common Law Tradition," 10 *Journal of the Legal Profession* 9 (1985).

11. See, e.g., Ugo Formari and Silvia Coda, "Deontologia e responsabilità in psichiatria e psicologia forensi," in *Riv. It. Med. Leg* 2000, p. 1175; Piermaria Corso, "Verifica fiscale nei confronti del professionista e tutela del segreto professionale," in *Corr. Trib.* 2001, p. 1135; idem, "Delitti tributari e segreto professionale del comercialista," in *Corr. Trib.* 2002, p. 2110.

12. *Restatement*, §113, Comment b.

13. See Andrews, supra note 1, chap. 25.

14. See Explanatory Memorandum and Commentary on the CCBE Code, Rule 2.4(4).

15. An implementation of this approach is the requirement in most civil law systems that parties to litigation must participate through attorneys. See, for instance, Luigi Paolo Comoglio, "Valori e ideologie del giusto processo—Modelli a confronto," in *Riv. Trim. Dir. Proc. Civ.* 1999, passim. In common law systems an individual litigant may participate in *propria persona* or "*pro se*"—that is, without counsel. However, corporations and other jural persons must participate through an attorney.

16. See, e.g., the Russian PRC, Law on Lawyers, Art. 28.

17. In *Faretta v. California*, 422 U.S. 806 (1975), the Supreme Court held that a criminal accused had a constitutional right to conduct his own defense. In federal courts in civil cases, 28 U.S.C. §1654 gives parties the right to "plead and conduct their own cases personally." State courts recognize the same principle.

18. See Federal Rules of Civil Procedure, Rule 11, and the corresponding ethical requirements in ABA Rules, 3.1 and 3.4. See generally Thomas Willging et al., *Discovery and Disclosure Practice, Problems and Proposals for Change: A Case-Based National Survey of Counsel in Closed Federal Civil Cases* (Washington: 1997), passim.

19. See Andrews, supra note 1, §37.73.

20. See Canadian Code, Chap. 1 (Comment 2 and Note 3); CDF, Arts. 6 and 14.

21. See ABA Model Rule 4.2; Canadian Code, Chap. 8 (Comment 4) and Chap. 16 (Comment 7); CDF Art. 27.

22. ABA Model Rule 4.3; Canadian Code, Chap. 17 (Comment 8); CDF Arts. 6, 56, and 59.

23. The background substantive law, in both civil law and common law systems, reflected these assumptions, particularly with regard to the legal status of married women. The civil law recognized that property acquired during a marriage was community property, in which the wife had an equal vested interest, but conferred on the husband the authority to manage the property. Under the common law system until modern times, property acquired during marriage was owned by the husband, and property owned by the wife before marriage was, upon marriage, subject to management by the husband.

24. Examples include *In re Mulrow*, 670 N.Y.S.2d 441 (N.Y. App. Div. 1998) (lawyer disbarred). See generally William M. McGovern, "Undue Influence and Professional Responsibility," 28 *Real Property, Probate and Trust J.* 643 (1994).

25. See, e.g., James Devine, "The Ethics of Representing the Disabled Client," 49 *Missouri L. Rev.* 493 (1984).

26. Brandeis expressed his concerns in a speech entitled "The Opportunity in the Law," presented to the Harvard Ethical Society in 1905. For commentary, see David Luban, "The Noblesse Oblige Tradition in the Practice of Law," 41 *Vand. L. Rev.* 717 (1988).

27. See Harlan F. Stone, "The Public Influence of the Bar," 48 *Harv. L. Rev.* 1 (1934) (lawyers have become "tainted with the morals . . . of the marketplace in its most antisocial manifestations").

28. See, e.g., Robert Gordon, "The Independence of Lawyers," 68 *Boston U. L. Rev.* 1 (1988); see also William Simon, "Symposium on the Practice of Justice," 51 *Stan. L. Rev.* 867 (1999).

29. Case no. 155/79, *AM&S Europe Ltd. v. Commission*, 1982 E.C.R. 1575 (1982) (attorney-client privilege does not exist for in-house counsel).

30. See *Upjohn Co. v. United States*, 449 U.S. 383 (1981). For a comparative overview, see Mary Daly, "The Cultural, Ethical, and Legal Challenges in Lawyering for a Global Organization: The Role of the General Counsel," 46 *Emory L. J.* 1057 (1997).

31. For an analysis of the significance of the *AM&S* case, see Joseph Pratt, "The Parameters of the Attorney-Client Privilege for In-House Counsel at the International Level: Protecting the Company's Confidential Information," 20 *J. Intl. Law and Bus.* 145 (1999).

32. For a justification and formal statement of the rationale, see American Law Institute, *Principles of Corporate Governance* (Philadelphia: ALI, 1993), passim.

33. See, e.g., *United States v. Benjamin*, 328 F.2d 854 (2d Cir. 1964); *In re American Continental Corp./Lincoln Savings and Loan Securities Litigation*, 794 F. Supp. 1424 (D. Ariz. 1992).

34. See Michael Paulsen, "Who 'Owns' the Government's Attorney-Client Privilege?" 83 *Minnesota L. Rev.* 473 (1998).

35. *Meehan v. Hopps*, 144 Cal. App. 2d 284, 292–293, 301 P.2d 10, 17–18 (Calif. Ct. App., 1956).

36. *Bolkiah v. KPMG*, 1 All E.R. 517 (1999). The *Bolkiah* case is interestingly discussed in Charles Hollander and Simon Salzedo, *Conflicts of Interest and Chinese Walls* (London: Sweet & Maxwell, 2000), passim.

37. The reference to "organization" in ABA Model Rule 1.13(a) signifies that the rule applies to representation of associations, government agencies, and other organizations. For application of the concept to a municipal corporation (a public

school corporation), see *Cole v. Ruidoso Municipal School*, 43 F.3d 1373 (10th Cir. 1994).

38. See ABA Model Rule 1.13(e), which refers explicitly to this possibility: "A lawyer representing an organization may also represent any one of its . . . constituents, subject to the provisions of [the rules governing conflict of interest.]" In 2003 the American Bar Association adopted amendments to Rule 1.13 that gave greater emphasis to the lawyer's responsibility to take action when confronting illegal conduct by corporate personnel. The amendments do not change the basic approach analyzed in the text.

39. In the jargon of the American legal profession, this provision is said to call for a "Miranda warning." The reference is to the warning that American police are required to give to a criminal suspect before commencing an interrogation, imposed as a matter of due process by the decision of the Supreme Court of the United States in *Miranda v. Arizona*, 384 U.S. 436 (1966).

40. In the United States, the structure and sequence of responsibility is now incorporated in federal legislation, the Sarbanes-Oxley Act of 2002, H.R. 3763, January 23, 2002.

41. Ibid.

42. See generally Report of the American Bar Association Task Force on Corporate Responsibility, March 31, 2003. The report is informally referred to as the Cheek Report, after the chair of the ABA committee that developed it, James H. Cheek III, a highly respected corporate lawyer.

43. See *AM&S* case, supra note 29.

44. A very rare instance involving a junior lawyer occurred in *Meyerhofer v. Empire Fire & Marine Ins. Co.*, 497 F.2d 1190 (2d Cir. 1974). The junior lawyer resigned and then gave information to the government regulatory authority. The court held the lawyer's conduct to be proper, but the lawyer was ostracized in the local professional community (New York City) for several years.

45. *Weider v. Skala*, 80 N.Y.2d 628, 609 N.E.2d 105 (N.Y., 1992).

46. See ABA Model Rule 1.2(d).

47. See, e.g., Brandeis, Hearings before Senate Committee on Interstate Commerce, S. Res. no. 98, 62nd Congress, 1st Session, 1911, p. 1161.

CHAPTER 7

1. See Jeffrey A. Parness and Austin W. Bartlett, "Unsettling Questions Regarding Lawyer Civil Claim Settlement Authority," 78 *Oregon L. Rev.* 1061 (1999) (analysis of American law concerning authority of a lawyer to agree to a settlement on behalf of a client).

2. Compare *International Telemeter Corp. v. Teleprompter Corp.*, 592 F.2d 49 (2d Cir. 1979) (business corporation bound by settlement announced to the court), with *Auvil v. Grafton Homes, Inc.*, 92 F.3d 226 (4th Cir. 1996) (determining that lawyer had no actual or apparent authority to agree to settlement).

3. See Code of Conduct of the Bar of England and Wales, Rule 302.

4. See Canadian Code, Chap. 8 (Comment 1).

5. See ABA Model Rule 3.3(a)(1, 3, 4). Comments 5 and 6 to this rule state: "When false evidence is offered by the client a conflict may arise between the lawyer's duty to keep the client's revelations confidential and the duty of candor to the court. ... [T]he lawyer should seek to persuade the client that the evidence should not be offered. ... If the persuasion is ineffective, the lawyer must take reasonable remedial measures. ... [I]f necessary an advocate must disclose the ... deception to the court or to the other party."

6. See Chap. 1.

7. See Canadian Code, Chap. 8 (Comment 1).

8. See ABA Model Rule 3.1.

9. See PRC Law on Lawyers, Arts. 44(8) and 45(2).

10. Federal Rules of Civil Procedure, Rule 11; ABA Rule 3.1, quoted in the text.

11. See Angelo Dondi, "Abuse of Procedural Rights: Comparative Standards: Regional Report for Italy and France," in Michele Taruffo, ed., *Abuse of Procedural Rights: Comparative Standards of Procedural Fairness* (The Hague: Kluwer, 1999), passim.

12. The seminal decision is *In re Ruffalo*, 390 U.S. 544 (1968). See generally Charles Wolfram, *Modern Legal Ethics* (St. Paul, Minn.: West, 1986), §3.4.1 et seq. For a historical analysis of the American system, see Geoffrey Hazard and Cameron Beard, "A Lawyer's Privilege against Self-Incrimination in Professional Disciplinary Proceedings," 96 *Yale L. J.* 1060 (1987).

13. Canadian Code, Chap. 1 (Comment 2); Canadian Code, Chap. 12 (Rule) and Chap. 12 (Comment 3).

14. See the Canadian Code, Chap. 12 (Comment 5); a similar provision is ABA Model Rule 3.9. Presumably a similar obligation in Italy derives from the lawyer's general obligation to be fair.

15. See, e.g., Lobbying Disclosure Act of 1995, 2 U.S.C. §160 et seq.

16. CDF Title II (contacts with other lawyers). See, e.g., Remo Danovi, *Commentario al Codice deontologico forense* (Milan: Giuffrè, 2001), p. 103.

17. See Canadian Code, Chap. 16 and Comments passim.

18. See ABA Model Rule 3.4, 4.1 and 8.3(a).

19. An exceptional instance is in the case of *In re Himmel*, 125 Ill.2d 531, 533 N.E.2d 790 (Ill. 1988). As the facts in that case indicate, reporting another lawyer's misconduct is often a tactic of professional retaliation.

20. See, e.g., ABA, Guidelines for Litigation Conduct, Lawyers' Duties 20–22 ("... will not engage in any conduct during a deposition that would not be appropriate in the presence of a judge"). A number of state civility codes are based on these ABA guidelines, which are available at www.abanet.org/dispute/lawcivil.html.

21. See *Paramount Communications v. QVC Network*, 637 A.2d 34, 60–75 (Del. 1994).

22. See *Cinema 5, Ltd. v. Cinerama, Inc.*, 528 F.2d 1384 (2d Cir. 1976); *Image Technical Services, Inc. v. Eastman Kodak*, 820 F. Supp. 1212 (N.D.CA 1993).

23. See also ABA Model Rule 1.10.

24. For American judgments imposing discipline on a partner for dereliction on this basis, see *In re Bonanno*, 135 N.J. 464, 640 A.2d 846 (N.J. 1994); *FDIC v. Nathan*, 804 F. Supp. 888 (S.D. Tex. 1992).

25. CDF, Art. 34 (I) (responsibility of collaborators, substitutes and associates).

26. CDF, Art. 26 (contact with trainees).

27. CDF, Art. 11 (duty to act as counsel).

28. Canadian Code, Chap. 13 (Comments 3 and 9); PRC, Law on Lawyers, Art. 42; RSFSR, Law on the Advokatura, Art. 22.

29. See ABA Model Rule 6.2.

30. ABA Model Rule 6.1 provides that "[a] lawyer should aspire to render at least 50 hours of pro bono legal services per year."

31. On legal services for the poor in the United States, see Geoffrey Hazard, Susan Koniak, and Roger Cramton, *The Law and Ethics of Lawyering*, 3d ed. (New York: Foundation Press, 1999), pp. 176–202 (criminal cases), pp. 1091–1121 (civil legal aid); "Symposium," 19 *Hofstra L. Rev.* 739 (1991).

32. *Legal Services Corp. v. Velazquez*, 531 U.S. 533 (2001).

33. For strongly worded claims of exclusive judicial authority to regulate lawyers, see *Mississippi Bar v. McGuire*, 647 So.2d 706 (Miss. 1994); *State ex rel. Fiedler v. Wisconsin Senate*, 454 N.W.2d 770 (Wis. 1990).

34. See generally Chapter 2. For critiques of the European model, see John Merryman, "Legal Education There and Here: A Comparison," 27 *Stanford L. Rev.* 859 (1975); Michele Taruffo, "L'insegnamento accademico del diritto processuale civile," in *Riv. Trim. Dir. Proc. Civ.* 1996, pp. 551–56; Angelo Dondi, "Il regolamento istitutivo delle scuole forensi: Rilievi minimi in tema di riforme e di formazione delle scuole legali," in *Dir. Pen. e Proc.* 2000, pp. 803–7; Francesco Miraglia, "Formazione selettiva e scuole forensi: risposta concreta al problema dell'accesso alla professione," in *Arch. civ.* 2001, pp. 289–91.

35. Dean William Prosser, a great teacher and legal scholar, once sardonically suggested that the ideal law school curriculum would require ten years. See Prosser, "The Ten Year Curriculum," 6 *J. Legal Education* 159 (1953).

36. On the status of the ethical codes in American law see Charles Wolfram, *Modern Legal Ethics* (St. Paul, Minn.: West, 1986), sec. 2.6.

37. Marion Schwarzchild, "Class, National Character, and the Bar Reforms in Britain: Will There Always Be an England?" 9 *Conn. J. Int'l L.* 185, 197 (1994).

CHAPTER 8

1. Canadian Code, Chap. 11 (Comment 1).
2. CDF, Art. 43, I, II, III.
3. See *Mack v. City of Minneapolis*, 333 N.W.2d 744 (Minn. 1983). Compare *Walters v. National Association of Radiation Survivors*, 473 U.S. 305 (1985) (upheld federal statutory limit of $10 for fees in representing claimant for veterans' benefits).
4. *Goldfarb v. Virginia State Bar*, 421 U.S. 773 (1975).
5. See also Federico Carpi and Michele Taruffo, *Commentario breve al codice di procedura civile* (Padua: CEDAM, 2002), passim.
6. See, e.g., *Ryan v. Butera, Beausang, Cohen & Brennan*, 193 F.3d 210 (3d Cir. 1999) ($1 million advance payment for extended litigation representation; engagement then canceled by client); *Brobeck, Phleger & Harrison v. Telex Corp.*, 602 F.2d 866 (9th Cir. 1979) ($1 million fee for filing petition in appellate court; further contemplated assistance preempted by client settling the litigation).
7. See Roger Cramton, "Symposium: The Future of the Legal Profession: Delivery of Legal Services to Ordinary Americans," 44 *Case Western Res. L. Rev.* 531, 541 (1994). In other countries, ordinary citizen interaction with lawyers is even less frequent.
8. Austin Sarat and William Felsteiner, *Divorce Lawyers and Their Clients* (New York: Oxford University Press, 1995), p. 23.
9. CDF, Art. 45.
10. See John Evans, "England's New Conditional Fee Agreements: How Will They Change Litigation?" 63 *Defense Counsel J.* 376 (1996).
11. See "100,000 Winners Are Still Waiting for Their Money," *The Times* (London), June 30, 2001, p. 12.
12. See ABA Rule 1.5; *Restatement*, §§34–35.
13. See generally, "Symposium: Contingency Fee Financing of Litigation in America," 47 *DePaul L. Rev.* 227 (1998).
14. See Herbert Kritzer, "Contingency Fee Lawyers as Gatekeepers in the Civil Justice System," *Judicature* (July–Aug. 1997): 22–29. A proposal for closer supervision of contingent fee arrangements in the United States is set forth in Michael Horowitz, "Making Ethics Real, Making Ethics Work: A Proposal for Contingency Fee Reform," 44 *Emory L. J.* 173 (1995).
15. Ibid.

16. See *Anderson v. Elliott*, 555 A.2d 1042 (Me. 1989) (upholding state bar rule requiring lawyer to submit fee dispute to arbitration).

17. See, e.g., *Committee on Legal Ethics v. Gallaher*, 376 S.E.2d 346 (W.Va. 1988).

18. See "Access to Justice: Final Report to the Lord Chancellor on the Civil Justice System in England and Wales" (1996) (the Woolf Report). The report is discussed in Lord Woolf, "Civil Justice in the United Kingdom," 45 *Am. J. Comp. L.* 709 (1997). See also Neil H. Andrews, "English Civil Procedure: Three Aspects of the Long Revolution" (2001) (paper on file with authors).

19. C. L. Anand, *Professional Ethics of the Bar*, 2d ed. (Allahabad, India: The Law Book Company, 1987), pp. 79–82.

20. See *In re R.M.J.*, 455 U.S. 191 (1982); *Florida Bar v. Went for It, Inc.*, 515 U.S. 618 (1995).

21. *In re Primus*, 436 U.S. 412 (1978).

22. Canadian Code, Chap. 13 (Comment 1).

23. The rule in China is approximately the same. Only a person admitted to law practice may call himself a lawyer or represent another for compensation. PRC, Law on Lawyers, Art. 14.

24. See Barlow Christensen, "The Unauthorized Practice of Law," *Am. Bar Foundation Research J.* 159 (1980) (historical analysis). See also Deborah Rhode, "Policing the Professional Monopoly," 34 *Stan. L. Rev.* 1 (1981). See also *Unauthorized Practice of Law Committee v. Parsons Technology, Inc.*, 1999 WL 47235 (N.D. Tex. Jan. 22, 1999) (subsequently, the Texas legislature passed a statute that effectively overturned the Parsons holding); *Perkins v. CTX Mortgage Co.*, 969 P.2d 93 (Wash. 1999). For an entertaining opinion on the subject of unauthorized practice, see *United States v. Bradley*, 896 F.2d 284 (7th Cir. 1990).

25. ABA, "Task Force on the Model Definition of the Practice of Law: Report to the House of Delegates" (April 29, 2003).

26. The key provisions in the ABA Rules are Rule 5.4(a), which provides that a lawyer may not "share legal fees with a nonlawyer," and Rule 5.4(b), which provides that a lawyer may not "form a partnership with a nonlawyer if any of the activities of the partnership consist of the practice of law."

27. See Mary Daly, "Choosing Wise Men Wisely: The Risks and Rewards of Purchasing Legal Services from Lawyers in a Multidisciplinary Partnership," 13 *Geo. J. Legal Ethics* 217 (2000) (Professor Daly was the reporter for the ABA commission that recommended some relaxation of the rules to facilitate MDPs); New York State Bar Ass'n, "Preserving the Core Values of the American Legal Profession: The Place of Multidisciplinary Practice in the Law Governing Lawyers" (Report of the N.Y. State Bar Ass'n Special Committee on the Law Governing Firm Structure and Operation) (2000) (opposing change). Both studies have extensive documentation.

28. See generally Symposium, "The Brave New World of Multidisciplinary Practice," 50 *J. of Legal Education* 469 (2000), and especially Phoebe A. Haddon, "The MDP Controversy: What Legal Educators Should Know," 50 *J. Legal Education* 504 (2000).

29. See generally Roger Goebel, "The Liberalization of Interstate Legal Practice in the European Union: Lessons for the United States?" 34 *International Lawyer* 307 (2000); Detlev Vagts, "Professional Responsibility in Transborder Practice: Conflict and Resolution," 13 *Geo. J. Legal Ethics* 677 (2000).

30. See *Leis v. Flynt*, 439 U.S. 438 (1979).

31. See *Ranta v. McCarney*, 391 N.W.2d 161 (N.D. 1986).

32. *Birbrower, Montalbano, Condo & Frank v. Superior Court*, 949 P.2d 1 (Cal. 1998).

33. See ABA Model Rule 5.5(c); Mary Daly, "Resolving Ethical Conflicts in Multijurisdictional Practice," 36 *S. Tex. L. Rev.* 715 (1995); Roger Goebel, "Legal Practice Rights of Domestic and Foreign Lawyers in the United States," 49 *Int'l. and Comp. L. Q.* 413 (2000).

CHAPTER 9

1. Alexis de Tocqueville, *Democracy in America*, trans. and ed. Harvey C. Mansfield and Delba Winthrop (Chicago: University of Chicago Press, 2000), p. 252.

2. We borrow this image from the title of a book on the legal profession: Anthony Kronman, *The Lost Lawyer: Failing Ideals for the Legal Profession* (Cambridge, Mass.: Belknap Press, 1993).

3. For a recent review of ethics codification in the United States, see Charles Wolfram, "Toward a History of the Legalization of American Legal Ethics-II: The Modern Era," 15 *Georgetown J. Legal Ethics* 205 (2002).

4. *Brown v. Board of Education*, 347 U.S. 483 (1954).

5. Charles Renfrew, "Discovery Sanctions: A Judicial Perspective," 67 *Calif. L. Rev.* 264 (1979); Marvin Frankel, *The Search for Truth: An Umpirial View* (New York: Association of the Bar of the City of New York, 1975).

6. CDF, Art. 6.

7. Guido Calabresi and Lucian Bebchuk, *Tragic Choices* (New York: Norton, 1978).

8. Learned Hand, "The Deficiencies of Trials to Reach the Heart of the Matter," Lecture before the New York City Bar Association, in *Lectures on Legal Topics, 1921–1922* (New York: Macmillan, 1926), p. 89.

Bibliography

Abel, Richard, and Philip Lewis. *Lawyers in Society*, 3 vols. Berkeley: University of California Press.
American Bar Association. *Model Rules of Professional Conduct*. Chicago: 1999, 2003.
American Bar Association, Center for Professional Responsibility. *Annotated Model Rules of Professional Conduct*. 4th ed. Chicago: 1999.
American Law Institute. *Restatement Third of the Law: The Law Governing Lawyers*. 2 vols. Philadelphia, Pa.: American Law Institute, 2000.
Anand, Chuni Lal. *Professional Ethics of the Bar*. 2d ed. Allahabad, India: Law Book Company, 1987.
Andrews, Neil. *English Civil Procedure: Fundamentals of the New Civil Justice System*. Oxford: Oxford University Press, 2003.
Auburn, Jonathan. *Legal Professional Privilege: Law and Theory*. Oxford: Hart, 2000.
Auerbach, Jerold. *Unequal Justice: Lawyers and Social Change in Modern America*. New York: Oxford University Press, 1976.
Baker, John H. *The Common Law Tradition*. London: Hambleton Press, 2000.
———. *The Law's Two Bodies: Some Evidential Problems in English Legal History*. New York: Oxford University Press, 2001.
Bar Council of Bar of England and Wales. *Code of Conduct of the Bar of England and Wales*. 7th ed. London: Bar Council of England and Wales, 2000.
Baumol, William. *The Free Market Innovation Machine*. Princeton, N.J.: Princeton University Press, 2002.
Berlins, Marcel, and Claire Dyer. *The Law Machine*. 5th ed. London: Penguin Books, 2000.
Boon, Andrew, and Jennifer Levin. *The Ethics and Conduct of Lawyers in England and Wales*. Oxford: Hart, 1999.
Brand, Paul. *The Origins of the English Legal Profession*. Oxford: Blackwell, 1992.
Burbank, Stephen, and Barry Friedman, eds. *Judicial Independence at the Crossroads*. Thousand Oaks, Calif.: Sage, 2002.
Canadian Bar Association. *Code of Professional Conduct*. Toronto: 1974.

Castiglione, Baldesar. *The Book of the Courtier.* Original in Italian, 1528. George Bull, trans. London: Penguin Books, 1967.

Daly, Mary, and Roger Goebel, eds. *Rights, Liability, and Ethics in International Legal Practice.* Deventer, the Netherlands: Kluwer, 1994.

Dawson, John. *Oracles of the Law.* Cambridge, Mass.: Harvard University Press, 1968.

Giuffrè, ed. *Codice deontologico forense.* Milan: 1999.

Halliday, Terrence, and Lucien Karpik, eds. *Lawyers and the Rise of Western Political Liberalism.* Oxford: Clarendon, 1997.

Handler, Joel. *The Lawyer and His Community: The Practicing Bar in a Middle-Sized City.* Madison: University of Wisconsin Press, 1967.

Hazard, Geoffrey, and William Hodes. *The Law of Lawyering.* Gaithersburg, N.Y.: Aspen Law and Business, 2001.

Hazard, Geoffrey, Susan Koniak, and Roger Cramton. *The Law and Ethics of Lawyering.* 3d ed. St. Paul, Minn.: Foundation, 1999.

Hollander, Charles, and S. Salzedo. *Conflicts of Interests and Chinese Walls.* London: Sweet & Maxwell, 2000.

Hurlburt, William. *The Self-Regulation of the Legal Profession in Canada and in England and Wales.* Calgary, Alberta: Law Society of Alberta, 2000.

Hutchinson, Allan. *Legal Ethics and Professional Responsibility.* Toronto, Ontario: Irwin Law, 1999.

Law Society of England and Wales. *The Guide to the Professional Conduct of Solicitors.* 8th ed. London: The Law Society, 1999.

Lazega, Emmanuel. *The Collegial Phenomenon: The Social Mechanisms of Cooperation among Peers in a Corporate Law Firm.* Oxford: Oxford University Press, 2001.

Ledford, Kenneth. *From General Estate to Special Interest: German Lawyers 1878–1933.* Cambridge: Cambridge University Press, 1996.

Leubsdorf, John. *Man in His Original Dignity: Legal Ethics in France.* Burlington, Vt.: Ashgate/Dartmouth, 2001.

Lubman, Stanley. *Bird in a Cage: Legal Reform in China after Mao.* Stanford, Calif.: Stanford University Press, 1999.

Nicolson, Donald, and Julian Webb. *Professional Legal Ethics: Critical Interrogations.* Oxford: Oxford University Press, 1999.

Regan, Francis, Alan Paterson, Tamara Goriely, and Don Fleming. *The Transformation of Legal Aid.* Oxford: Oxford University Press, 1999.

Règlement Intérieur of the Paris Bar. *Règlement Intérieur.* Trans. J. Hazard, 1995. (Translation on file with Geoffrey Hazard.)

Rose, Jonathan. *The Ambidextrous Lawyer: Conflict of Interest and the Medieval and Early Modern Legal Profession.* 7 *University of Chicago Law School Roundtable* 137 (2000).

Ross, Stan. *Ethics in Law: Lawyers' Responsibility and Accountability in Australia.* 2d ed. Sydney: Butterworths, 1998.
Rhode, Deborah. *In the Interests of Justice: Reforming the Legal Profession.* New York: Oxford University Press, 2000.
Sarat, Austin, and William Felstiner. *Divorce Lawyers and Their Clients.* New York: Oxford University Press, 1995.
Sarat, Austin, and Thomas Kearns. *Law in the Domain of Culture.* Ann Arbor: University of Michigan Press, 1998.
Schuck, Peter. *The Limits of Law.* Boulder, Colo.: Westview, 2000.
Seneviratne, Mary. *The Legal Profession: Regulation and the Consumer.* London: Sweet & Maxwell, 1999.
Slapper, Gary, and David Kelly. *English Legal System.* London: Cavendish, 1993.
Smith, Beverley G. *Professional Conduct for Lawyers and Judges.* Fredericton, New Brunswick: Maritime Law Book, 1998.
Stager, David, and Harry Arthurs. *Lawyers in Canada.* Toronto: University of Toronto Press, 1990.
Tyrrell, Alan, and Zahd Yaqub, eds. *The Legal Profession in the New Europe.* Cambridge: Blackwell, 1993.
Watkin, Thomas. *The Italian Legal Tradition.* Aldershot, U.K.: Ashgate, 1997.
Wolff, Hans Julius. *Roman Law.* Norman: University of Oklahoma Press, 1951.
Wolfram, Charles. *Modern Legal Ethics.* St. Paul, Minn.: West, 1986.
Xichuan, Du, and Zhang Lingyuan. *China's Legal System: A General Survey.* Beijing: New World Press, 1990.

Index

In this index an "f" after a number indicates a separate reference on the next page, and an "ff" indicates separate references on the next two pages. A continuous discussion over two or more pages is indicated by a span of page numbers, e.g., "57–59."

ABA, *see* American Bar Association
Abogados, 32
Accounting firms, 193–94, 274–75
Accused, the, 36–37, 98–99. *See also* Clients
Adams, John, 13
Ad hoc arrangements, 196
Administrative law, 55
Admission to practice, 122–23, 321n69
Admonitory norms, 292
Adversary system, 68–69, 287–88
Adversity of interest: in conflict of interest, 186–89
Advertising, 271; of professional services, 140–42, 323n85; and solicitation, 142–43
Advice: to clients, 158–62, 164–65
Advocates Act, 153
Advocates, advocacy, 16, 19, 22ff, 30, 32, 45, 289–90; judges and, 9–10, 73; roles of, 25, 64–65, 69, 88; ethics of, 65–66, 79–80; civil law, 66–67, 76–77, 89–90; common law, 67–68; loyalty to clients of, 111–13; lawyers as, 164–65; client-lawyer relationship and, 177–78
Agency law, 177
Agriculture, 41–42
Aide juridique, 250
All-China Lawyers Association, 153
AM&S case, 217
Ambidexterity, 61
Ambiguity, 164–65
Ambulance chasing, 142
American Bar Association (ABA), 84, 109, 151, 215, 235, 242, 249, 254, 273, 279, 306n63, 329n34; professional ethics, 35–36, 117; media and, 143f; Rules of Professional Conduct, 159, 177, 233, 284, 306n69, 317n25,

324n2, 337n26; Rules of Professional Responsibility, 187, 284, 332nn37, 38, 335n30; on conflict of interest, 187, 329nn27, 31; nonconsentable conflict in, 189–90; on corporation law, 221–25; on procedural abuses, 238f; on law firm relationships, 245f
American Restatement of the Law Governing Lawyers, 121–22, 191
Apartheid, 148, 324n12
Apprenticeships, 24, 45, 46–47, 72f, 126, 128, 253, 321n69
Approximation of Judiciary Law (EU), 63
Argentina, 52, 59, 72, 148
Articling, 47
Aristocracy: upper-level lawyers as, 31–32
Aristotle, 10
Asbestos litigation, 191
Aspirational norms, 292
Assistants, 25–26
Association of the Japan Federation of the Bar, 99
Atlantic Charter, 106
Attorney-client privilege, 206–9, 217
Australia, 2, 41, 45, 73, 130, 138, 148, 153, 275, 283, 289; fees for services in, 265–66
Australian Competition and Consumer Commission, 275
Austria, 27
Authority, 15f; judicial, 21, 87–88, 154–55; in client-lawyer relationship, 177–78, 213–15; to disclose information, 210f; of corporate clients, 216–17; disciplinary, 239–40
Avocats, 31, 38, 45
Avoués, 32, 45
Avvocati, 32, 45

Baker, John, 28, 30–31
Bar and Law Society (England), 47
Bar associations, 168, 256f, 275; *pro bono* requirements in, 99, 335n30; professional conduct, 254–55. *See also* American Bar Association
Bar Council (England), 153
Bar examinations, 45–46, 254. *See also* Examinations
Barreau, 46
Barristers, 22, 31f, 38f, 44f, 47, 56, 67, 108, 137, 139, 325n19; training of, 128–29
Batonier, 104, 127–28, 254–55
Beit Din, 67
Bengoshi, 22
Bentham, Jeremy, 12f
Bill of Rights (England), 94
Bingham of Cornhill, Lord, 138
Birbrower, Montalbano, Condo & Frank, P.C. v. Superior Court, 278
Blackstone, William: *Commentaries on the Laws of England*, 27, 131, 320n60
Bodin, Jean, 13
Bolkiah, Jefri, 220–21
Bolkiah v. KPMG, 220–21, 222
Bologna, 24
Boundaries: territorial, 176
Bourgeoisie, 93
Brandeis, Louis, 216, 230–31
Brazil, 59
Bribery: judicial, 82–83
Briefs: in common law adversary systems, 68–69
Bristol, 41
British Empire, 53, 130
Brougham, Henry Lord, 111–13, 167
Brown v. Board of Education, 286
Brunei Investment Agency, 220
Bulgaria, 83; Bulgarian code, 17
Bureaucracy, 51, 55, 290; government, 49–50; law firm, 156–57
Bureaucratic government, 5, 13
Bush v. Gore, 84
Businesses, 6, 48, 53; corporatization of, 50–51; in-house lawyers and, 55–56; legal interactions, 71–72; capitalist systems, 101–3; client-lawyer relationships in, 183–84, 189–90; conflict of interest in, 189–90; retainer arrangements, 195–96; legal representation of, 293–94, 296

Calamandrei, Pietro, 167
California, 181, 220
California Supreme Court, 278
Canada, 2, 45f, 53, 97, 115f, 136, 138, 140f, 183, 201, 242, 265, 289; legal training in, 130, 133–34, 283; conflict of interest in, 187f, 190–91
Canadian Code of Professional Conduct, 141, 153, 159, 197, 205, 235, 241, 245, 249, 254, 272, 317nn23, 24, 329n38; client-lawyer relationship, 178, 199; conflict of interest, 180–81, 187; successive representation in, 191–92; professional responsibility in, 229, 233; on procedural abuses, 237–38, 239; professional relationships in, 243–44; on fees, 259–60
Candor: duty of, 234–37
Canon law, 17
Canons of Professional Ethics (ABA), 143, 254, 306n63
Capitalism, 5, 13, 91, 93, 291, 294; business enterprises and, 101–3
Caroline, Queen, 111–12, 167
Case method: of education, 131f
Castiglione, Baldesar, 29, 159, 301n18; *Il Cortegiano*, 13
Castro, Fidel, 166
Categorical imperative, 11
Catholic church, 89
CCBE (Code of Conduct for Lawyers in the European Community), 116, 118, 141, 150, 153, 188, 198, 206, 212, 237, 254, 257, 284–85, 294–95
Centres régionaux de formation professionnelle des avocats (CRFPA), 127
Chastnye poverennye, 32
China, 1, 34, 44, 46, 51, 55, 73, 125, 153, 249; legal system in, 15, 16–17; judicial system in, 22–23, 311n16; lawyer-court relations, 238–39. *See also* People's Republic of China
Chinese Regulations of Lawyers' Professional Ethics and Business Practices, 153
Christianity, 11
Church courts, 63, 89
Churchill, Winston, 106
Cicero, 19f, 109
Citizenship: good, 241–42
Civil affairs, 42
Civil cases: Roman Empire, 20
Civil Code (French), 206
Civil law, 18, 34ff, 98, 154, 261, 275, 280–81, 287, 318n30, 331n15, 331n23; European, 2f, 22; procedures, 64, 66–67, 68; judges, 72–73, 74; conflicting roles in, 76–77; ideal justice in, 77–78; judge-lawyer ratio in, 78–79; advocates in, 89–90, 289–90; confidentiality in, 118, 206, 208–9, 317n26; client-lawyer rela-

INDEX

tionship in, 177–78, 198–99; professional communication in, 211–12; case settlement, 234–35; defendant representation, 248–49; self-governance in, 252, 254–55
Civil liberties, 100
Civil rights movement, 272
Class actions, 250
Clerks of the court, 25
Client confidentiality, 10
Client-lawyer relationship, 176, 179, 203, 326n20; authority in, 177–78, 213–15; conflict of interest and, 180–82; and business transactions, 183–84; successive representation and, 191–92; commencement and termination of, 195–202; corporations, 216–28
Clients, 157, 205, 334n5; loyalty to, 8–9, 110, 111–13, 116–17, 170–76; and lawyers, 42f, 75, 168–69; and ethics, 86, 316n14; and judges, 88–89; advice to, 114, 142, 158–62, 164–65, 167; selection of lawyers by, 139–41; and lawyer representation, 155–56; joint representation of, 182–83; responsibility to former, 191–93; conflict of interest, 193–94; termination of representation and, 198–99; transmission of information about, 209–10; of limited capacity, 215–16; corporations as, 216–18; and lawyers' responsibility, 229–30; case settlement and, 234–35; fees and, 258–59, 262–63, 267–68
Clinton, William, 113, 219
Code for Advocacy, 178
Code Napoléon, 3, 26
Code of Civil Procedure (Italy), 119, 261
Code of Civil Procedure (Japan), 82
Code of Conduct, General Standards, Standards, Fundamental Principle 306 (England), 178
Code of Ethics for Practicing Lawyers (Japan), 65, 116–17, 184, 205, 242
Codice Deontologico Forense, 153, 254
Coke, Lord, 14
Collectives, colleges, 104
Commentaries on the Laws of England (Blackstone), 27, 131, 320n60
Common law, 3, 27, 41, 64, 129, 188, 249, 252, 254, 280–81, 287, 290, 332n23; judges, 7–8, 68–69, 73–74, 79; accused in, 36–37; as adversary system, 67–68; judges and lawyers in, 72, 154; legal transactions, 90–91; client loyalty in, 111–12; client-lawyer relationship and, 178, 198–99; confidentiality in, 205–6, 317n26; attorney-client privilege in, 206–9; litigation costs, 269–70

Common Law, The (Holmes), 131
Communication, 49, 217; professional, 210–12
Communist Party, 18
Competence, 109; professional, 115–16, 119–24, 133, 180; practical, 134–39
Competition: lawyers, 42–43, 44
Concrete realities, 3–4, 6
Conduct: professional, 254–55
Confidentiality, 117–18, 147, 204–6, 208, 317nn21, 26; lawyer-lawyer communication, 209–18; and responsibility to legal system, 229–30
Conflict, 9, 104; nonconsentable, 189–90
Conflict of interest, 179, 193, 329nn27, 31, 33; ethical codes for, 180–82; joint representation and, 182–83; law firms and, 184–85; adversity of interest, 186–89; business transactions, 189–90; informed consent/conflict waiver and, 190–91; imputation, 194–95; corporations and, 220–21
Conflict waiver, 190
Confucianism: legal system and, 16–17
Conscience, 174–75; legal, 230–31
Conseil National du Barreau, 151
Constitutional government, 1, 6, 50, 93–94
Constitutional rights, 89
Contracts, 70f, 105–6
Convention on Human Rights, 106
Core values, 109
Corporations, 22, 174; development of, 50–51; in-house lawyers and, 55–56; and client-lawyer relationship, 216–28; ABA rules regarding, 221–25; lawyers, 277–78, 285–86, 296, 309n98
Corpus Juris, 24, 26
Corruption: in legal system, 82–87
Cortigiano, Il (Castiglione), 13
Cost allocation rule in, 268–69
Council Directive (Legal Services Directive) (EU), 277
Court of Justice (European Community), 56
Courts, 61, 67, 118; legal access to, 23–24; church, 63, 89; structured transactions and, 75–76; competence in, 137–38; malpractice claims, 138–39; duty of candor with, 234–41; forensic misconduct in, 255–56
Court structure, 79
Cravath, Paul, 58
Cravath, Swaine & Moore, 57
Cravath system, 58
CRFPA, *see* Centres regionaux de formation professionalle des avocats
Crime, 10, 258

Criminal law, 20, 27, 34, 89, 106, 314n59, 317nn20, 21, 333n39; ethics in, 35–36; accused testimony, 36–37; prosecutors in, 98–99; client-lawyer relationship, 114, 316n14; media and, 143–44; lawyer's responsibility in, 229–30; adequate representation, 249–50
Criticism: of profession, 283–86, 323n84
Cuba, 44, 100f
Curriculum, see Education
Czech Republic, 83

Death penalty cases, 249
Deception, 174
Declaration of Independence (American), 14, 94
Declaration of the Rights of Man, 94
Defendants, 36, 64
Defense lawyers, 35, 36–37
Delay: judicial, 83–84
Democracy: liberal, 14, 281, 300n8
Demography: and legal practice, 41–42; legal profession, 43–44
Descartes, René, 13
Developing countries, 79, 123
Dictatorships, 148
Discipline, 136, 168, 254; for procedural abuses, 239–40; for professional misconduct, 255–56
Disclosure: transaction law, 290–91
Discourse into the Origins of Inequality of Men (Rousseau), 94
Discovery: pretrial, 68
Dispositionsprinzip, 77
Dispute resolution, 53
Divorce: of English royalty, 111–12
Dress, 31
Dreyfus case, 113
Droit administratif, 97
Due diligence, 200–201
Due process, 106, 257

Eastern Europe, 294
Ecole Nationale d'Administration, 73
Ecole Nationale de la Magistrature (France), 73
Economic systems, 51, 102f; mercantile-artisan, 47–48; law firm, 58–59; legal claims and, 104–5
Education, 49, 137, 168; legal, 43–44, 45f, 55, 281ff, 320–21nn61, 62, 69; judges, 72–73; European curriculum, 124–28; English, 128–30; American, 130–34; curriculum, 252–53, 319n55
Egypt, 2
Elections: in United States, 84, 145

Eligibility, 107
Employees: corporation, 218–28
Employment: legal, 47, 55, 105
Empowering rights, 9–10
England, 13, 25, 27, 37, 46f, 53, 56, 59, 61, 67, 73, 79, 94, 109, 136, 141ff, 148, 153, 167, 189, 204, 211, 325n19; law in, 2f, 22; upper-level lawyers in, 31–32; legal practice in, 34, 40f; legal practitioners in, 38f, 44; lawyers in, 45, 104; legal assistance in, 107–8; client loyalty in, 111–13; legal training in, 128–30; negligence in, 137–38; professional reputation in, 139–40; client-lawyer relationship in, 178, 192; litigation privilege, 207–8; corporation law, 220–21; duty of candor, 235, 237; fees for services, 260, 265, 267; litigation costs in, 268f
English Bar Council, 151
Enlightenment, 13
Equality: legal, 290
Equal protection: rights to, 106
Ernst & Young, 274
Erskine, Thomas, 108
Ethics, 11, 20, 80(table), 109, 152, 305n55, 315n6, 316n14; professional, 2, 29–30, 35–37, 109–19; legal, 7f, 10, 283–86; prosecutors, 34–35; of advocates, 65–66, 67; knowledge and, 69–70; pretense and reality of, 85–86; independence and, 146–47, 167–68; legal code and, 153–54; multilawyer practices, 245–46
EU, see European Union
Europe, 54ff, 63, 71, 97, 109, 141, 201, 276, 282, 291; civil law in, 2, 22; legal system in, 23, 25; law firms in, 57, 59; legal training in, 124–28, 253. *See also various countries*
European Community, 56, 153, 199
European Community Treaty, 277
European Convention on Human Rights, 107
European Court of Justice, 277, 330n1
European Union (EU), 53, 59, 63, 277, 284. *See also* CCBE
Examinations: to practice law, 122, 319n46; European professional, 126–27; English entrance, 129–30

"Fair hearing" procedures, 97
Family law, 18
Fascism, 86, 100–101, 148
Favoritism: judicial, 83, 85
Federal Rules of Civil Procedure, 207
Fees, 156, 168, 337n26; contingent, 197–98, 264–67; regulation of, 258–64; disputes over, 267–68

Finance, 311nn16, 19; transactions, 199–201; money laundering, 201–2
First Amendment (U.S.), 143, 323n85
Florence, 41
Folk ethics, 114
Formulae, 20
Fourteenth Amendment (U.S. Constitution), 106, 286
France, 13, 31ff, 37, 46, 78, 94, 109, 115, 122, 126, 147, 151, 206, 250, 254, 263, 319n48; civil law in, 22, 66–67, 68, 77, 90, 98, 289; legal codes in, 25, 26–27; legal practice in, 34, 40f, 44; lawyer categories in, 45, 104; judiciary training in, 72–73; client loyalty in, 113, 174–75; professional governance in, 127–28
Franco, Francisco, 86
Fraud, 199
Freedom of contract, 13
Freedom of information, 290
Free press, 144
Free speech, 143
Free will, 12
Friendly, Henry, 202
Functionaries, 33

Galanter, Marc, 29
Gandhi, Mohandas, 166
German Democratic Republic (East Germany), 103–4, 105
Germany, 13, 31, 51, 55, 72, 86, 105, 115, 122, 125, 147, 237, 280, 289, 319n46; civil law in, 22, 66–67, 68, 90, 98; apprenticeships in, 46, 126; judge-lawyer ratio in, 78f; professional values, 109–10; fees for services, 261, 263
Globalization, 18, 53, 26
Gordon, Robert, 66, 159
Governance: professional, 127–28, 251–57
Government, 163, 219; central, 6, 48; actions of, 49–50; legalization of, 51f, 56; constitutional, 93–94; legal independence from, 148–49. *See also* State
Government agencies, 22, 71, 237
Government officials: investigation of, 113–14
Greece, classical, 16, 109
Grotius, Hugo, 13
Guide to the Professional Conduct of Solicitors, The, 119–20, 189, 192
Gulf States, 53

Habermas, Jürgen, 10
Hamilton, Andrew, 167
Harvard Law School, 130ff
Hegel, Georg Wilhelm Friedrich, 4

Herder, Johann, 4
Hickman v. Taylor, 207
Hobbes, Thomas, 13, 91
Holmes, Oliver Wendell, Jr., 4; *The Common Law*, 131
Hong Kong, 17, 53
Honneur, 33–34
Honor, 119
Honorable conduct, 119
Hostility: judicial, 83
House counsel, 22; discharge of, 227–28
House of Lords: as corporate entity, 220–21
Human rights, 92, 94, 100, 106–7, 293
Hume, Alexander, 10, 13

Ibero-American countries, 27, 68, 125
Ideals, 29–30
Identity, 4, 22
Impartiality: of judges, 80–81, 82
Impropriety, 188–89
Imputation, 184, 193–95, 245–46, 329n34
Income: lawyers', 106, 156, 168
Incompetence, 120–21, 124, 136
Independence, 81; professional, 116, 146–48, 149–50, 169; political, 148–49; and self-governance, 150–54; from judiciary, 154–55; from clients, 158–59; and advocacy, 164–65; political and social, 166–67
India, 27, 29, 130
Indigents: representation of, 248–50, 251
Individuals, 6, 8–9, 10
Indonesia, 2
Industrialism, 48
Industrial Revolution, 37
Information, 290; confidentiality of, 117–18; obsolescence of, 192–93; transmission of client, 209–11
Informed consent, 190f, 193, 215
Inns of Court, 40, 45, 104, 319n50
Internal Rules of the Paris Bar, 206
International Bar Association, 257
Islamic law, 2, 15, 87, 299–300n2; legal and religious authority in, 16, 18; money issues, 161–62
Isolation: in law firms, 185
Israel, 18, 82
Italian Ethical Code: conflict of interest, 181, 187–88
Italy, 13, 23, 32, 37, 41, 45, 47, 73, 77, 86, 99, 109, 122, 126, 142, 153, 212, 236; upper-level lawyers in, 31, 34; legal regulations in, 61–62; judges role in, 68, 280; judge-lawyer ratio, 78–79; fascism in, 101, 148; code of conduct

in, 119, 254, 292; admission to practice in, 123, 319n48; legal independence in, 146f, 167; conflict of interest, 181, 187–88; professional duty in, 228–29; law firm relationships in, 246–47; fees for services, 260f

Jackson, Robert, 74
James, King, 14
James, William, 4
Japan, 2, 22, 46, 54, 71, 82, 89, 99, 142, 184, 197, 205, 240, 242, 266; legal system in, 43, 97; business legal departments, 55–56; law firms in, 57, 59; code of ethics, 65, 116–17, 119; civil law, 67, 74, 90, 280; legal scholarship in, 125–26; consent to conflict, 190–91; duty of candor in, 235, 237
Jesus, 20
Jews: Nazi legal system and, 100–101
Johnson, Samuel, 30
Judge-lawyer ratio, 78–79
Judges, 15, 37, 51, 63, 68, 145, 280; and common law, 7–8, 73–74; and advocates, 9–10; authority of, 21, 87–88; and lawyers, 32, 64; common law adversary systems and, 68–69; training, 72–73; structured transactions and, 75–76; abilities of, 77–78; and civil law, 78–79; ethics and behavior of, 79–80; recusal of, 81–82; corruption of, 82–87; and clients, 88–89; truth and, 113–14
Judiciary: independence from, 154–55; lawyer misconduct and, 255–56
Jura novit curia, 68
Jurisconsults, 19, 22
Jury trials, 269
Justice, 6f, 43, 89, 288, 293; access to, 106, 248, 251; administration of, 65–66; common law adversary system in, 67–68; ideal, 77–78, social status and, 94–95; in criminal law, 98–99; client-lawyer relationships and, 172–73; economic costs of, 268–74
Justinian Code, 19–20; commentary on, 24–25

Kant, Immanuel, 10ff, 13, 209
Kleptocracies, 149
Knowledge, 23, 46, 68, 115; legal, 27–28; ethics and, 69–70
Kutak Commission, 221

Land use regulations, 71
Latin America, 46, 54, 127; legal practice in, 59–60
Latvia, 83

Law, 24, 163, 242; criminal vs. civil, 34–35; role of, 6–7; as science, 125, 131–32
Law schools, 283. *See also* Education; Training
Law Society (England), 128; Code for Advocacy, 178
Law firms, 37, 53, 106, 121, 220, 275, 281, 309n102; development of, 39, 57–58, 59–60; practitioners in, 40–41; economic organization of, 58–59; knowledge and ethical procedures, 69–74; placement in, 123–24; entrance into English, 129–30; advertising by, 141–42; professional independence and, 156–57; formation and dissolution of, 157–58; conflict of interest, 184–85; imputation in, 194–95; professional relationships within, 244–47, 258–59; fees charged by, 263–64
Law on Lawyers (People's Republic of China), 114, 239
Law on the Advokatura, 113
Law schools: Middle Ages, 24
Law Society (England), 153
Lawsuits: standardized transactions and, 70–71; frivolous, 238f
Lawyers, 15, 86–87, 88, 280, 321n69, 322–23n81; and rule of law, 1–2; roles of, 2–3, 38–39, 44–45, 63; client loyalty, 8–9, 170–76; rights of, 9–10; definition of, 21–22; access to courts, 23–24; professional lore, 28–29; upper- and lower-level, 30–37, 322n73; solo practitioners of, 37–38, 40; competition among, 42–43; education and training of, 43–44, 45–47; in socialist systems, 51, 104; regulating, 60–62; and judges, 64, 75–82; common law adversary systems, 68–69; office law and, 69–74; judicial elections and, 84–85; access to services of, 94–95; *pro bono* service, 98f, 251; professional virtues of, 109–19, 292; competence of, 119–24, 134–39; reputation in, 127–28; malpractice, 138–39; client selection of, 139–40; advertising by, 140–42; solicitation by, 142–43; media contacts and, 143–44; independence of, 146–47, 154–55, 166–67; joint representation in, 182–83; corporate representation, 218–28; responsibility of, 228–32; obligation of candor, 234–41; as good citizens, 241–42; professional relationships, 242–44; career paths, 282, 312n29; criticism of, 283–86
Legal aid, assistance, 94, 98f, 292; access to, 96–97; adequate, 107–8; structure of, 247–51
Legal assistance offices, 250–51
Legal codes, 26–27, 82, 153–54. *See also by country; specific codes*

Legal counsel, 19, 22, 25, 89
Legalism, legalization, 50ff, 56, 166
Legality: boundary of, 229–32
Legal practice, 37, 120, 322n73; solo practices, 38–39; state-run, 39–40; law firms and, 40–41; evolution of, 59–60; office procedures, 69–74; competence of, 115–16; qualifications to, 122–23; reputation and, 127–28; admission to, 130–31, 321n69; professional independence, 156–57
Legal proceedings: media and, 144–45
Legal profession, 1, 24, 48, 93, 127; as self-governing, 150–55
Legal renaissance, 23
Legal rights, 107
Legal services, 276; costs of, 95–96, 268–74; fees for, 260–61
Legal systems, 7; Western, 15–16; China, 16–17, 22–23; Russian, 17–18; Roman, 19–20; Middle Ages, 21, 24–25; and professional ethics, 35–36; wealth and, 96–97; social justice in, 97–98; Nazi, 100–101; socialist, 103–5; independence and, 166–67; responsibility to, 228–32
Legal technique, 54–55
Legal texts, 27–28
Legal tradition: Western, 15–16
Legal treatises, 27
Liberalism, 14
Licensing, 122
Lincoln, Abraham, 106, 320n61
Litigants: self-representation by, 98
Litigation, 32f, 49, 88, 107, 212, 250, 331n15; and conflict of interest, 186, 191; privilege, 207–8; costs of, 268–69
Loans: Islamic laws, 162
Lobbying, 242
Locke, John, 13, 91
Lombardy, 34
London, 41, 61
London Ordinance (1280), 61–62
Louis XIV, 25
Lower class, 95
Loyal opposition, 13
Loyalty, 333n44; to clients, 110, 116–17, 158–59, 170–76; and conflict of interest, 180–81; confidentiality, 204–5
Lying, 334n5; improper, 288–89
Lyon, 41

Machiavelli, Niccolo, 13
Madison, James, 13
Malpractice, 278, 325n19; legal, 137, 138–39; liability for, 255–56

Marbury v. Madison, 27
Marx, Karl, 4, 100
Marxism, 4, 165
MDP, *see* Multidisciplinary practice
Means tests, 99
Media, 106; lawyers and, 143–44; legal proceedings and, 144–45
Mediocraty, 135
Meehan v. Hopps, 220ff
Mercado Commun del Sur (Mercosur), 53
Meta-ethics, 11
Mexico, 51, 59
Middle Ages, 13f, 24–25, 30, 61–62
Middle class, 93, 95
Middle East, 59
Minister of justice, 35
Misconduct, 61, 143, 327n1; dealing with, 239–41; forensic, 255–56
MJP, *see* Multijurisdictional practice
Model Rules of Professional Conduct (ABA), 159, 239, 284, 306n69, 332–33nn37, 38
Model Rules of Professional Responsibility (ABA), 187, 284, 332–33nn37, 38, 335n30
Monarchy, 13
Money laundering, 201–2
Montesquieu, Baron de La Brède et de, 13
Moral autonomy, 12
Morality, 69
Multidisciplinary practice (MDP), 274–76
Multijurisdictional practice (MJP), 276–79
Mussolini, Benito, 86, 147, 167

NAFTA, *see* North American Free Trade Agreement
Naples, 34
Nationalism, 4
Nationalists: Chinese, 17
Nazi Germany, 86, 100–101, 148
Negligence, 137–38
Negotiation, 210
Netherlands, 13
New York (state), 22, 228
New Zealand, 130, 138, 153
NGOs, *see* Nongovernmental organizations
Nigeria, 130
Nixon, Richard, 113, 219
Nongovernmental organizations (NGOs), 6
Nonimputation, 194
North American Free Trade Agreement (NAFTA), 53
Notaire, 22, 90
Notario, 90

Obligations: lawyer's, 233–34; to court, 234–41
Officials: corporate, 218–28
Open Society Institute, 83
Ostracism: professional, 256, 333n44

Padua, 24
Papacy, 13
Parachuting, 142
Paris, 41
Partisanship, 287
Pavia, 24
Peirce, Charles, 4
People's Republic of China, 39, 56, 100, 103, 114, 147, 239, 311nn16, 19
Perjury, 36, 288, 306n69
Peronism, 148
Philosophy: classical, 10–11; ethics and, 11–12; Confucian, 16–17
Plaintiffs: legal procedures and, 63–64
Podpol'nye advokati, 32
Poland, 101
Polis, 16
Politics, 13, 50, 91; judicial selection and, 84–85; in Nazi Germany, 100–101; legal independence and, 148–49, 166–67
Pontius Pilate, 20
Poor, the: legal services to, 99, 285
Portugal, 125
Powell, Lewis, 167
Practitioners, 32f
Pragmatists, 4
Presidency: U.S. elections, 84
Pretrial discovery, 269
PriceWaterhouseCoopers, 274
Principe dispositif, 77
Principio dispositivio, 67, 77
Prisiazhnye poverennye, 32
Private property, 331n23; protection of, 91–92; in socialist countries, 100f
Private rights, 91
Privilege, 207–8
Professional secret, 118
Pro bono publico, 98f, 251, 285, 335n30
Procedural abuses, 237–38, 239–40
Procedures: legal, 63–64
Procuradores, 32, 44
Procuratori, 32, 45
Procureurs, 44
Production enterprises, 101
Professional gossip, 28
Professionalism, 29, 110, 283–85, 322n73; virtues of, 109–19, 292
Professional lore, 27–29

Profumo case, 113
Property rights, 90ff, 100–101, 331n23
Property transactions, 38, 41, 90
Propria persona, in, 98
Prosecution, 256
Prosecutors: ethical responsibilities of, 34–35; criminal justice and, 98–99; media and, 143–44
Protestant churches, 89
Provincial governments, 6
Prussia, 27, 74
Public administration, 53–54, 97
Public defenders, 248
Pupilage, 47

Qualifications, 122–23
Quebec, 130

Ravenna, 24
Rawls, John, 10
Real estate, 38, 90
Reality constraint, 111
Recusal: of judges, 81–82
Regina v. Neil, 188
Regulations, 3, 9, 71, 102, 110, 152–53, 254, 286; government adopted, 48f; on lawyers, 60–62; of fees, 258–64
Regulatory systems: government, 52–53
Religion, 4, 11, 16ff
Religious courts, 67
Religious law, 17f
Renaissance, 13, 33
Representation, 248, 273; standards of, 99–100; successive, 191–93; commencement and termination of, 195–203; corporate, 216–18, 219
Representatives: in Roman law, 18f
Republican Party of Minnesota v. White, 145
Reputation: professional, 127–28, 139–40, 155–56; advertising and, 140–41
Resignation, 174–75
Responsibility, 118; to legal system, 228–32; lawyer's, 233–34
Restatement of the Law Governing Lawyers (U.S.), 121–22, 181, 191, 228, 278, 284
Retainer, 195–96
Revenues, 163
Right of audience, 10
Rights of property, 13
R (Morgan Grenfell Ltd) v. Special Commissioner of Tax, 204
Roman Empire, 18–20, 21, 34
Roman law, 15, 18–19, 20f, 34, 124, 129

Rome, 24, 34, 41
Roosevelt, Franklin D., 106
Rousseau, Jean-Jacques: *Discourse into the Origins of Inequality of Men*, 94
Rule of law, 1–2, 13, 91, 93, 102
Rule of majority vote, 175–76
Rules of Advertising of Practicing Attorneys (Japan), 142
Rules of Professional Conduct (ABA), 167, 177, 184, 233, 244
Rural sector, 41–42
Russia, 22, 32, 59, 113, 148, 192, 206, 249, 294; legal system in, 17–18; professional independence in, 149–50
Russian Orthodox Church, 17

Sarbanes-Oxley Act (SOX), 202, 226, 333n40
Savings and loan (S&L) crisis, 199
Scholarship, 125–26
Science: law as, 131–32
Scotland, 53
Scriveners, 38, 45
Securities and Exchange Commission (U.S.), 202, 226
Segregation, 148, 167
Self-government: professional, 150–55, 252–57, 315n6
Self-incrimination, 289, 317n20
Separation of powers, 5
Sharia, 18
Singapore, 53, 130
Smoking gun documents, 289f
Social criticism, 291, 323n84
Socialism, 100, 103
Socialist countries, 51; legal system in 103–5
Social justice, 97–98, 250, 286
Social services, 216; legal assistance as, 250–51
Socioeconomic status: of clients, 140
Solicitation: prohibition of, 142–43, 271–72
Solicitors, 22, 38, 47, 53, 56, 137; English, 39, 59, 67, 129–30, 139–40
Solicitors Act (1843), 39
Solicitors' offices, 37
South African Republic, 130, 148, 324n12
Soviet Union, 96, 100f, 149; legal practice in, 39, 44; legal system, 17–18
SOX, *see* Sarbanes-Oxley Act
Spain, 32f, 37, 44, 53, 86, 101, 109, 127, 147; civil law in, 22, 90
Spinoza, Baruch, 13
Standard form documents, 70–71
Star Chamber proceeding, 89
Starr, Kenneth, 113–14

State, 254; activities of, 49–50; independence from, 147f; legal representation and, 248–49
Statute of limitation, 175
Stephen, James Fitzjames, 27
Story, Joseph, 27
Strategic alliances, 275
Studia legale, 24
Super legislation: human rights in, 106–7
Supreme Court (Canada), 188
Supreme Court of the European Union: on corporate clients, 216–17
Sweden, 22
Syndikusanwalt, 55

Taxation, 49, 92
Tax farming, 5
Tax law, 160–61
Territorial boundaries, 176
Testimony, 36–37
Thatcher, Margaret, 107
Third-party interests: in corporation law, 223–24
Tocqueville, Alexis de, 13, 52, 281, 294, 300n8
Trade: global, 53
Training, 253, 283; judiciary, 72–73; English legal, 128–29; American legal, 130–31
Transactions, 18, 290–91; standardized, 70–71, 96; lawyers and, 75–76, 283; in common law system, 90–91; contracts and, 105–6; legal advice and, 160–61; business and, 189–90; financial, 199–200; due diligence in, 200–201; reporting suspicious, 201–2; attorney-client privilege and, 208–9
Transcendence, 13
Transparency, 11f, 201
Transportation, 49
Tribunals: Roman Empire, 20
Truth, 6f, 14, 113–14, 327n2

Unauthorized practice of law, 273–74
United Kingdom, 53
United Nations Convention on Human Rights, 106
United States, 2, 27, 31, 52, 54, 68, 73, 97, 110, 137, 145, 199, 207, 211f, 219, 239, 242, 254, 272, 275, 291, 294, 305n55, 322–23n81, 325n25, 329n34, 333n39; professional ethics, 35–36, 286; law firms in, 37, 57, 59, 281; legal practitioners in, 38f; lawyers as profession in, 45, 312n29; apprenticeship in, 46f; education in, 56, 130–34, 283, 320–21nn61, 62, 63; advocate ethics in, 65–66, 113–14; ethical interactions in, 71–72; judicial selection in, 84–85;

professional virtues in, 115, 117, 119; legal incompetence in, 120–21; disciplinary system in, 136, 240; advertising in, 141–42, 271, 323n85; solicitation in, 142–43; media contacts, 143–44; legal independence in, 147–48, 167; bar governance in, 151, 253; judicial authority in, 154–55; client-lawyer relationships in, 178, 183–84, 215–16; conflict of interest in, 181, 184–85; nonconsentable conflict in, 189–90; contingent fees in, 197–98; suspicious financial transactions, 201–2; corporation law, 221–28, 309n98; law firm relationships, 245f; legal aid, 249–50; fees for services in, 262, 264f, 266–67; cost allocation rule in, 268–69; unauthorized practice of law in, 273–74; admission to practice in, 276, 321n69; multijurisdictional practice, 277–79
United States v. Benjamin, 202
U.S. Congress, 202
U.S. Constitution, 27, 106
U.S. Department of Justice, 201
U.S. Department of Treasury, 201
U.S. Supreme Court, 27, 74, 84, 144f, 165, 207, 272, 331n17
Universalism, 12
Universities, 129, 253; European legal education in, 55f, 124–26; American, 130f, 321n63
Utilitarianism, 12

Values: professional, 109
Venice, 34
Verità processuale, 76
Vico, 13
Virtues: professional, 109–19, 292

Wales, 53, 151
Wealth, 96–97
Weber, Max, 50
Witnesses, 36; examination of, 288–89
Workplace norms, 292–93
Work-product rule, 207f